THE

CONSTITUTIONAL

HISTORY OF ENGLAND.

VOLUME I.

THE CONSTITUTIONAL HISTORY OF ENGLAND

SINCE THE ACCESSION OF GEORGE THIRD

1760–1860

By THOMAS ERSKINE MAY, C.B.

IN TWO VOLUMES.

VOLUME I.

BOSTON:
CROSBY AND NICHOLS.
117 Washington Street
1862.

RIVERSIDE, CAMBRIDGE:
STEREOTYPED AND PRINTED BY
H. O HOUGHTON.

PREFACE.

It is the design of this history to trace the progress and development of the British Constitution, during a period of one hundred years; and to illustrate every material change, — whether of legislation, custom, or policy, — by which institutions have been improved, and abuses in the government corrected.

The accession of George III. presents no natural boundary in constitutional history: but former reigns have already been embraced in the able survey of Mr. Hallam; and frequent allusions are here made to events of an earlier period, connected with the inquiries of the present work.

In considering the history of our mixed government, we are led to study each institution separately, to mark its changes, and observe its relations to other powers and influences in the State. With this view, I have found it necessary to deviate from a strictly chronological narrative, and to adopt a natural division of leading subjects. If this arrangement should appear occasionally to involve an incomplete view of particular events, and repeated references to the same period, under different aspects; I trust it will be found, on the whole, the most convenient and instructive. The form of the work is not the less historical. Each inquiry is pursued throughout the entire century; but is separated from contemporary incidents, which more properly fall under other divisions.

The present volume embraces a history of the prerogatives, influence, and revenues of the Crown; and of the constitution, powers, functions, and political relations of both Houses of Parliament. The second volume will comprise, — among other constitutional subjects, — a history of party: of the press, and political agitation: of the Church, and of civil and religious liberty. It will conclude with a general review of our legislation, — its policy and results, — during the same period.

Continually touching upon controverted topics, I have endeavored to avoid, as far as possible, the spirit and tone of controversy. But, impressed with an earnest conviction that the development of popular liberties has been safe and beneficial, I do not affect to disguise the interest with which I have traced it, through all the events of history. Had I viewed it with distrust, and despondency, this work would not have been written.

The policy of our laws, as determined by successive Parliaments, is so far accepted by statesmen of all parties, and by most unprejudiced thinkers, of the present generation, that I am at liberty to discuss it historically, without entering upon the field of party politics. Not dealing with the conduct and motives of public men, I have been under no restraint in adverting to recent measures, in order to complete the annals of a century of legislation.

LONDON: *January 12th*, 1861.

CONTENTS

OF

THE FIRST VOLUME.

CHAPTER I.

INFLUENCE OF THE CROWN DURING THE REIGN OF GEORGE III.

	PAGE
Influence of the Crown since the Revolution	15
Its sources	16
Restrictions on the personal influence of the sovereign	19
Ministerial power and responsibility	*ib.*
Power of ministers regarded with jealousy by George III.	21
His determination to exalt the kingly office	23
His secret counsellors	24
His policy and its dangers	26
He enforces it against his ministers	29
Lord Bute as premier carries out the king's policy	31
Their efforts to coerce the Opposition	32
Lord Bute resigns	34
Mr. Grenville coöperates in the king's unconstitutional policy	36
The king's differences with the Grenville ministry	38
His reluctant admission of the Rockingham ministry	41
Exerts his influence in Parliament against them	43
The king advances his policy with the aid of Lord Chatham	46
They unite in breaking up parties	*ib.*
Development of the king's policy under Lord North	48
The king his own minister	52
Protests against the influence of the Crown	54
Intimidation of peers in opposition to the Court	56
Lord North driven from office by the Commons	58
Result of twenty years of kingcraft	60
Lord Rockingham's second ministry	61
Measures to restrain the king's influence	62
The Coalition force their way into office	63

PAGE
The king's influence employed against them 66
Use of the king's name in Parliament denounced 67
The Coalition dismissed 68
Mr. Pitt becomes the king's minister 69
Is met by violent opposition in the Commons 70
Motions to delay the supplies 72
Opposition continued 73
Triumph of Mr. Pitt 77
Reflections on this struggle 78
General influence of the Crown augmented 82
The king's influence exerted against Mr. Pitt 83
His Majesty's opposition to Catholic emancipation 85
Mr. Pitt resigns on that question 87
Influence of the Crown during the Addington ministry . . . 89
Mr. Pitt reinstated in office 90
The Grenville administration 92
The king's friends active against them 94
Pledge required of ministers on the Catholic question . . . 96
Their removal from office . . . . *ib.*
Pledge discussed in Parliament . . . . *ib.*
The king's appeal to the people on the Catholic question . . . 103
His supremacy during the Perceval ministry . . . . *ib.*

CHAPTER II.

INFLUENCE OF THE CROWN DURING THE REGENCY, THE REIGNS OF GEORGE IV., WILLIAM IV., AND HER MAJESTY QUEEN VICTORIA.

Influence of the Court over the prince regent 105
His estrangement from the Whigs 106
Position of parties a proof of the paramount influence of the Crown 108
Negotiations on the death of Mr. Perceval 109
Ascendency of Tory politics under Lord Liverpool 112
Proceedings against Queen Caroline 113
The bill of pains and penalties withdrawn 115
Mr. Brougham's motion on the influence of the Crown . . . 117
George IV.'s opposition to Catholic emancipation 118
Parliamentary reform favored by William IV. 120
His support of Earl Grey's ministry 122
He prevails upon the Lords to pass the Reform Bill 123

PAGE
Sudden dismissal of the Melbourne ministry 125
Sir R. Peel called to office while abroad 128
Is driven from office 130
Diminution of the influence of the Crown shown by these events . . . . *ib.*
Lord Melbourne in office on her Majesty's accession 131
The "bedchamber question" . . . . *ib.*
Sir R. Peel's second administration 134
Relations of ministers to the sovereign 135
Lord Palmerston's removal from office 136
Increased influence of the Crown now under due control . . 138
Continued influence of great families 139

CHAPTER III.

PREROGATIVES OF THE CROWN DURING THE MINORITY OR INCAPACITY OF THE SOVEREIGN.

Incapacity of a sovereign not recognized by law 141
George III.'s first regency scheme, 1765 142
Doubts concerning the term "royal family" 145
Attempted exclusion of Princess of Wales from the regency . *ib.*
Meeting of Parliament during the king's second illness, 1788–9 148
The rights of a regent debated 149
Regent to be appointed by bill founded on resolutions . . . 151
Great seal to be used under authority of Parliament 152
A new speaker during the king's incapacity 153
The commission to open Parliament 155
The regency bill stayed by the king's recovery 158
These proceedings considered 159
Ministerial embarrassments caused by the king's third illness, 1801 163
The king's fourth illness, 1804 166
Questions raised as to his capacity for business 167
Meeting of Parliament during his last illness, 1810 172
The precedents of 1788 followed 173
The issue of money authorized by Parliament 178
Act authorizing George IV. to sign by a stamp 179
Rights of an infant king considered on the accession of William IV. 182
The Regency Act, 1830–31 183
The rights of a king's posthumous child 184
The Regency Acts of Queen Victoria 185

CHAPTER IV.

REVENUES OF THE CROWN: THE CIVIL LIST: PENSIONS: PREROGATIVES OF THE CROWN IN RELATION TO THE ROYAL FAMILY.

PAGE
Possessions of the Crown in early times 186
Alienations of Crown lands restrained 189
The Civil List from William and Mary to George III. 191
Settlement of the Civil List on the accession of George III. . 193
Charges and debts upon the Civil List 194
Schemes for economic reform 197
The Civil List Act, 1782 199
Civil Lists since the regency 201
Duchies of Lancaster and Cornwall 204
Private property of sovereigns 205
Provision for the royal family . . . . *ib.*
Debts of the Prince of Wales . . . . *ib.*
Management of the land revenues on behalf of the public . . 207
Pensions on the Civil List and other Crown revenues . . . 210
Restrictions on the grant of pensions 212
Final regulation of the Pension List 214
Powers of the sovereign over grandchildren 216
The Royal Marriage Act, 1772 217
Guardianship of Princess Charlotte 222

CHAPTER V.

THE HOUSE OF LORDS, AND THE PEERAGE.

Progressive increase of the peerage prior to reign of George III. 224
Change in the character of the House by increase of numbers . *ib.*
Profuse creations in the reign of George III. 226
The peerage of Ireland 228
Present state of the peerage 229
Representative character of the House of Lords 232
Rights of Scottish peers 233
Gradual fusion of the peerages of the three kingdoms . . . 235
Hereditary descent the characteristic of the peerage 236
Life peerages 237
The lords spiritual 242
Attempts to exclude them from the House of Lords 244
Increased number of the House of Lords, a source of strength . 246
Political parties in the House 247

PAGE
Collisions between the two Houses averted by the influence of the Crown 248
Position of the Lords in reference to the Reform Bills . . . 249
Proposed creation of peers 252
A creation of peers equivalent to a dissolution 254
The independence of the Lords unimpaired by the reform crisis 255
Their vantage ground 257
Circumstances affecting their political weight 258
The peerage in its social relations 259
The baronetage and orders of knighthood 260

CHAPTER VI.

THE HOUSE OF COMMONS.

Anomalies of representation prior to reform 263
Defects in the electoral system 264
Nomination boroughs 265
Various and limited rights of election 266
Bribery at elections 267
Sale of boroughs 270
Attempts to restrain corruption 274
Act to prevent the sale of seats 277
Government boroughs . . . . *ib.*
Revenue officers disfranchised 278
Vexatious contests in populous cities 279
Territorial influence in counties 282
Defective representation of Scotland 283
And of Ireland 287
Nominee members, the majority of the House 288
Injustice in the trial of election petitions 289
The Grenville Act 291
Improved constitution of election committees 293
Bribery of members by places and pensions 294
Measures to restrain it . . . . *ib.*
Places in the reign of George III. 296
Judicial officers disqualified 298
Pecuniary bribes to members 299
During the reign of George III. 301
Members bribed by shares in loans and lotteries 304
By lucrative contracts 308

PAGE
Various sources of corruption condemned by Parliament . . . 309
State of society favorable to these practices 310
How popular principles were kept alive . . . . ib.
The first schemes of parliamentary reform 312
Mr. Pitt's motions for reform 315
Reform advocated by Mr. Grey 319
Discouraged by the French Revolution 320
Reform motions at the beginning of this century 321
Lord J. Russell's efforts for reform 323
Catholic emancipation a plea for reform 326
Gross cases of bribery at elections, 1826–27 327
Reform motions in 1830 329
Duke of Wellington's declaration 331
Reform ministry 333
First reform bill in the Commons 334
The second rejected by the Lords 336
Passing of the third reform bill . . . . ib.
Reform Act considered 338
Reform Acts of Scotland and Ireland 340
Political results of the Reform Act 341
Bribery since the Reform Act . . . . ib.
Disfranchisement and other Acts to restrain bribery 343
Policy of legislation concerning bribery 348
Efforts to shorten the duration of Parliaments . . . . . . ib.
Motions in favor of vote by ballot 352
Qualification Acts repealed 354
Proceedings at elections improved 355
Later measures of reform 356

CHAPTER VII.

RELATIONS OF PARLIAMENT TO THE CROWN, THE LAW, AND THE PEOPLE.

Proceedings of the Commons against Wilkes 365
And of the Lords 368
Wilkes returned for Middlesex 370
His two years' imprisonment . . . . ib.
His expulsion for libel on Lord Weymouth 371
His reëlections, and final exclusion 374
Lord Chatham's efforts to reverse the proceedings against Wilkes 376

PAGE
Similar proceedings in the Commons 377
City address to the king on Wilkes's expulsion 379
Motions in the Lords to reverse the proceedings against Wilkes . 382
Resolutions against him expunged 383
Exclusion of strangers from parliamentary debates 384
Members of the Commons excluded from the Lords 388
Consequent misunderstanding between the two Houses . . . ib.
Publication of parliamentary debates 390
Commencement of the system 391
Misrepresentations of reporters 392
Their personalities 393
Contest between the Commons and the printers 395
Wilkes and the Lord Mayor interpose in their behalf 396
The Commons proceed against the city magistrates 397
Reports of debates permitted 402
Progress of the system . . . . ib.
Political results of reporting 404
Presence of strangers recognized 406
Publication of division lists . . . . ib.
Publication of parliamentary papers 408
Freedom of comments upon Parliament 409
Early petitions, and rights of petitioners 410
Commencement of modern system of petitioning 412
Petitioning at the beginning of the present century 414
Abuses of petitioning 416
Debates on presenting petitions restrained 417
Pledges of members to candidates considered . . . . ib.
Surrender of certain parliamentary privileges 420
Conflict of privilege and law 421
Sir F. Burdett's case 422
The Stockdale cases 424
Right of Parliament to publish papers affecting character . . 426
Moderation of the Commons in forwarding the admission of Jews to Parliament 428
Control of Parliament over the executive government . . . 429
Over questions of peace and war 430
Advice of Parliament concerning a dissolution 431
Popular addresses on the same subject 432
Relations between the Commons and the ministers of the Crown 434
Votes expressing confidence or otherwise . . . . ib.
Impeachments 435
Improved relations of the Crown with the Commons 437
Stability of governments, before and since reform, considered . ib.

PAGE
Control of the Commons over supply and taxes 440
Demands of the Crown agreed to, without exception, since the Revolution 441
Cases of delaying the supplies 442
Exclusive rights of the Commons over taxation 444
Power of the Lords to reject a money bill considered 445
Rejection of the paper duties bill, 1860 447
Sketch of parliamentary oratory 450
Orators of the age of Chatham and Pitt 451
Orators at the commencement of this century 455
Characteristics of modern oratory 459
Coarse personalities of former times 460
General standard of modern debate 463

THE

CONSTITUTIONAL HISTORY

OF

ENGLAND

SINCE

THE ACCESSION OF GEORGE THE THIRD.

CHAPTER I.

Growth of the Influence of the Crown: — Its Sources: — Restrictions on the Personal Influence of the Sovereign: — Ministerial Responsibility: — Accession of George III.: — His Resolution to Exercise a larger Share of Personal Influence in the Government: — His Policy, and its Effects: — His Relations with successive Ministers during his Reign.

Growth of the influence of the Crown.

THE growth of the influence of the Crown, at a period in the history of this country when government by prerogative had recently been subverted, and popular rights and liberties enlarged, attests the vital power of the Monarchy. At the Revolution, the arbitrary rule of the Stuart kings finally gave way to parliamentary government, with ministerial responsibility. Such a change portended the subjection of future kings to the will of Parliament; but it proved no more than a security for the observance of the law. While the exercise of the royal authority was restrained within the proper limits of the constitution, the Crown was shorn of none of its ancient prerogatives; but remained, as it had ever been, the source of all power, civil and ecclesiastical, — "the fountain of honor," — the first and paramount institution of the state. Its powers, indeed, were now exercised by ministers responsible to Parliament; and the House of Commons was no longer held in awe by royal prerogative. Yet so great were the attributes of royalty, and so numerous its sources of influence, that, for more than a century after the Revolution, it prevailed over the more popular elements of the constitution. A Parliament representing the people little more than in name, and free, in great measure, from the restraint of public opinion, — which had not yet the means of being intelligently formed, or adequately expressed, — promoted the views of rival parties, rather than the interests of the people. This popular institution, designed to control the Crown, was won over to its side, and shared, while it supported, its ascendency. The Crown now governed with more difficulty, and was forced to use all its resources, for the maintenance of its authority: but it governed as completely as ever.

Meanwhile every accession to the greatness of the country favored the influence of the Crown. By the increase of establishments and public expenditure, the means of patronage were multiplied. As the people grew more wealthy, considerable classes appeared in society, whose sympathies were with "the powers that be," and who coveted favors which the Crown alone could bestow. And thus, the very causes which ultimately extended the power of the people, for a long time served to enlarge the influence of the Crown.

Its sources.

Vast and various were the sources of this influence. The Crown bestowed everything which its subjects most desired to obtain; honors, dignities, places, and preferments. Such a power reached all classes, and swayed constituents, as well as parliaments. The House of Lords has ever been more closely associated with the Crown and its interests, than the House of Commons. The nobles of every land are the support and ornament of the court; and in England they are recognized as an outwork of the monarchy, — a defence against the democratic elements of our institutions. The entire body is the creation of the Crown.

The temporal peers, or their ancestors, have all been ennobled by royal favor; many have been raised to a higher dignity in the peerage; and others aspire to such an elevation. A peerage of the United Kingdom is an object of ambition to the Scotch and Irish Peers. The Spiritual Lords owe their dignity to the Crown, and look up to the same source of power, for translation to more important sees. Nearly all the highest honors and offices are engrossed by the nobility. The most powerful duke, who has already enjoyed every other honor, still aspires to the Order of the Garter. The lord-lieutenancy of a county, — an office of feudal grandeur, — confers distinction and influence, of which the noblest are justly proud.[1] Other great appointments in the state and royal household are enjoyed exclusively by peers and their families; while a large proportion of the state patronage is dispensed by their hands. Their rank also brings them within the immediate reach of court favor and social courtesies, by which the most eminent peers naturally become the personal friends of the reigning sovereign. Accordingly, with some rare exceptions, the House of Lords has always ranged itself on the side of the Crown. It has supported the king himself against his own ministers: it has yielded up its convictions at his word; and where, by reason of party connections, it has been opposed to a ministry enjoying the confidence of the Crown, its opposition has been feeble or compliant.[2] Nor has its general support of the throne been inconsistent with the theory of the constitution. The Commons, on the other hand, representing the people, are assumed to be independent of the Crown, and jealous of its influence. How far these have been their actual characteristics, will be examined hereafter:[3] but here it may be briefly said, that until the reform in the represen-

[1] Though the office of Lord-Lieutenant does not date earlier than the reign of Queen Elizabeth, it resembles the ancient dignity of "Comes."

[2] See Chap. V., Peers and Peerage.

[3] See Chap. VI. (House of Commons.)

tation of the people in 1832, the counties were mainly under the influence of great and noble families (as they still are, to a considerable extent): a large proportion of the boroughs were either the absolute property of peers and their connections, or entirely under their control; while in many other boroughs the interest of the government was paramount at elections. The cities and large towns alone had any pretensions to independence. Except on rare occasions, when all classes were animated by a strong public opinion, the representation of the people and popular interests was a constitutional theory, rather than an active political force. Had there been no party distinctions, there could scarcely have been an ostensible opposition to any ministers, whom the king might have chosen to appoint. Members of Parliament sought eagerly the patronage of the Crown. Services at elections, and support in Parliament, were rewarded with peerages, baronetcies, offices and pensions. Such rewards were openly given: the consideration was avowed. There were other secret rewards of a grosser character, which need not here be noticed.[1] Nor were constituents beyond the reach of the same influence. The collection and expenditure of an enormous and continually increasing public revenue provided inferior places, — almost without number, — which were dispensed on the recommendation of members supporting the government. Hence to vote with the ministers of the day was the sure road to advancement: to vote against them, was certain neglect and proscription.

Loyalty of the people.

To these sources of influence must be added the loyalty of the British people. He must indeed be a bad king, whom the people do not love. Equally remarkable are their steady obedience to the law, and respect for authority. Their sympathies are generally on the side of the government. In a good cause their active support may be relied upon; and even in a bad cause, their prejudices have more often been enlisted in favor of the gov-

[1] See Chap. VI.

ernment, than against it. How great then, for good or for evil, were the powers of a British sovereign and his ministers. The destinies of a great people depended upon their wisdom, nearly as much as if they had wielded arbitrary power.

Restrictions on the personal influence of the sovereign.

But while these various sources of influence continued to maintain the political ascendency of the Crown, the personal share of the sovereign in the government of the country was considerably restricted. William III., the most able statesman of his day, though representing the principles of the Revolution, was yet his own minister for foreign affairs, conducted negotiations abroad, and commanded armies in the field. But henceforward a succession of sovereigns less capable than William, and of ministers gifted with extraordinary ability and force of character, rapidly reduced to practice the theory of ministerial responsibility.

Ministerial responsibility.

The government of the state was conducted, throughout all its departments, by ministers responsible to Parliament for every act of their administration, — without whose advice no act could be done, — who could be dismissed for incapacity or failure, and impeached for political crimes; and who resigned when their advice was disregarded by the Crown, or their policy disapproved by Parliament. With ministers thus responsible, "the king could do no wrong." The Stuarts had strained prerogative so far, that it had twice snapped asunder in their hands. They had exercised it personally, and were held personally responsible for its exercise. One had paid the penalty with his head: another with his crown; and their family had been proscribed forever. But now, if the prerogative was strained, the ministers were condemned, and not the king. If the people cried out against the government, — instead of a revolution, there was merely a change of ministry. Instead of dangerous conflicts between the Crown and the Parliament, there succeeded struggles between rival parties for parliamentary majorities; and the successful party wielded all the power of the state. Upon ministers, therefore, devolved the entire burden of public affairs: they relieved the Crown of its cares and perils, but, at the same time, they appropriated nearly all its authority. The king reigned, but his ministers governed.

Kings of the House of Hanover.

To an ambitious prince, this natural result of constitutional government could not fail to be distasteful; but the rule of the House of Hanover had hitherto been peculiarly favorable to its development. With George I. and George II., Hanoverian politics had occupied the first place in their thoughts and affections. Of English politics, English society, and even the English language, they knew little. The troublesome energies of Parliament were an enigma to them; and they cheerfully acquiesced in the ascendency of able ministers who had suppressed rebellions, and crushed pretenders to their crown, — who had triumphed over parliamentary opposition, and had borne all the burden of the government. Left to the indulgence of their own personal tastes, — occupied by frequent visits to the land of their birth, — by a German court, favorites and mistresses, — they were not anxious to engage, more than was necessary, in the turbulent contests of a constitutional government. Having lent their name and authority to competent ministers, they acted upon their advice, and aided them by all the means at the disposal of the court.

Ascendency of the Whig party.

This authority had fallen to the lot of ministers connected with the Whig party, to whom the House of Hanover mainly owed its throne. The most eminent of the Tories had been tainted with Jacobite principles and connections; and some of them had even plotted for the restoration of the Stuarts. From their ranks the Pretender had twice drawn the main body of his adherents. The Whigs, indeed, could not lay claim to exclusive loyalty: nor were the Tories generally obnoxious to the charge of disaffection; but the Whigs having acquired a superior title to the favors of the court, and being once admitted to office, contrived, — by union amongst themselves, by borough interests, and by their monopoly of the influence of the Crown, — to secure an ascendency in Parliament which, for nearly fifty years, was almost unassailable. Until the fall of Sir Robert Walpole the Whigs had been compact and united; and their policy had generally been to carry out, in practice, the principles of the Revolution. When no longer under the guidance of that minister, their coherence, as a party, was disturbed; and they became divided into families and cliques. To use the words of Lord John Russell, this "was the age of small factions." [1] The distinctive policy of the party was lost in the personal objects of its leaders; but political power still remained in the same hands; and, by alliances rather than by union, the "great Whig families," and others admitted to a share of their power, continued to engross all the high offices of state, and to distribute among their personal adherents the entire patronage of the Crown.

Accession of George III. His jealousy of his ministers.

The young king, George III., on succeeding to the throne, regarded with settled jealousy the power of his ministers, as an encroachment on his own, and resolved to break it down. His personal popularity was such as to facilitate the execution of this design. Well knowing that the foreign extraction of his predecessors had repressed the affections of their people, he added, with his own hand, to the draft of his first speech to Parliament, the winning phrase, "Born and educated in this country, I glory in the name of Briton." [2] The Stuarts were now the aliens, and not the Hanoverian king. A new reign, also, was favorable to the healing of political differences, and to the fusion of parties. In Scotland, a few fanatical nonjurors may still have grudged their allegiance to an uncovenanted king. But none of the young king's subjects had

[1] Introduction to vol. iii. of Bedford Correspondence.

[2] The king himself bore testimony to this fact upwards of forty years afterwards. — *Rose's Correspondence*, ii. 189 (Diary).

plotted against his throne; and few could be suspected of adherence to the fallen cause of the Stuarts, which had been hopelessly abandoned since the rebellion of 1745. The close phalanx of the Whig party had already been broken; and Mr. Pitt had striven to conciliate the Tories, and put an end to the bitter feuds by which the kingdom had been distracted. No party was now in disgrace at court; but Whigs, Tories, and Jacobites thronged to St. James's, and vied with each other in demonstrations of loyalty and devotion.[1]

The king's education.

The king was naturally ambitious, and fond of the active exercise of power; and his education, if otherwise neglected,[2] had raised his estimate of the personal rights of a king, in the government of his country. So far back as 1752, complaints had been made that the prince was surrounded by Jacobite preceptors, who were training him in arbitrary principles of government.[3] At that time these complaints were discredited as factious calumnies; but the political views of the king, on his accession to the throne, appear to confirm the suspicions entertained concerning his early education.

His mother, the Princess Dowager of Wales, — herself ambitious and fond of power,[4] — had derived her views of the rights and authority of a sovereign from German courts; and encouraged the prince's natural propensities by the significant advice of "George, be king."[5] Lord Waldegrave,

[1] "The Earl of Lichfield, Sir Walter Bagot, and the principal Jacobites, went to Court, which George Selwyn, a celebrated wit, accounted for from the number of Stuarts that were now at St. James's." — *Walpole's Mem.*, i. 14.

[2] Dodington's Diary, 171. The Princess of Wales said: "His book-learning she was no judge of, though she supposed it small or useless." — *Ibid.*, 357; Wraxall's Mem., ii. 39.

[3] See debate in House of Lords, 22d March, 1753; Walpole's Mem., iv. 139; Dodington's Diary, 190, 194, 197, 228.

[4] Walpole says, "The princess, whose ambition yielded to none." — *Mem.*, i. 12. "The princess was ardently fond of power, and all its appanages of observance." — *Adolph. Hist.*, i. 12.

[5] Rockingham Mem., i. 3.

who had been for some time governor to the prince, describes him as "full of princely prejudices contracted in the nursery, and improved by the society of bedchamber-women and pages of the back-stairs."[1]

His groom of the stole, Lord Bute, — afterwards so notorious as his minister, — had also given the young prince instruction in the theory of the British Constitution; and knowing little more than the princess herself, of the English people and government, had taught him that his own honor, and the interests of the country required the extension of his personal influence, and a more active exercise of his prerogatives. The chief obstacle to this new policy of the court was found in the established authority of responsible ministers, upheld by party connections and parliamentary interest. Accordingly, the first object of the king and his advisers was to loosen the ties of party, and break down the confederacy of the great Whig families.[2] The king desired to undertake personally the chief administration of public affairs, to direct the policy of his ministers, and himself to distribute the patronage of the Crown. He was ambitious not only to reign, but to govern. His will was strong and resolute, his courage high, and his talent for intrigue considerable. He came to the throne determined to exalt the kingly office; and throughout his long reign, he never lost sight of that object.

His determination to govern.

Lord Bolingbroke had conceived the idea of a government under "a patriot king,"[3] — who should "govern as soon as he begins to reign," — who should "call into the administration such men as he can assure himself will serve on the same principles on which he intends to govern," — and who should "put himself at the head of his people in order to govern, or, more properly, to subdue all

Lord Bolingbroke's theory.

[1] Lord Waldegrave's Mem., 9.

[2] See letter of Sir J. Phillips to Mr. Grenville, Sept. 8th, 1763; Grenville Papers, ii. 117; Burke's Present Discontents, *Works*, ii. 231.

[3] The Idea of a Patriot King, *Works*, iv. 274.

parties."[1] But it had been no part of Lord Bolingbroke's conception, that the patriot king should suffer his favorites to stand between him and his "most able and faithful councillors."[2]

The ministry whom the king found in possession of power at his accession, had been formed by a coalition between the Duke of Newcastle and Mr. Pitt. The former had long been the acknowledged leader of the great Whig connection, and enjoyed extended parliamentary interest: the latter, by his eloquence and statesmanship, had become the most popular and powerful of the king's subjects. The ministry also comprised the Grenville and Bedford sections of the Whig party. It was so strong in Parliament, that for some years the voice of opposition had been scarcely heard; and so long as it continued united, its position was impregnable.

Ministry at the time of the king's accession.

But, strong as were the ministers, the king was resolved to wrest all power from their hands, and to exercise it himself. For this purpose he called to his aid the Earl of Bute, and other secret counsellors, drawn from all parties. The greater number were of the Tory party, whose views of prerogative were Jacobite. According to Horace Walpole, "they abjured their ancient master; but retained their principles."[3] It was the king's object not merely to supplant one party, and establish another in its place; but to create a new party, faithful to himself, regarding his personal wishes, carrying out his policy, and dependent on his will. This party was soon distinguished as "the king's men," or "the king's friends."[4] Instead of relying upon the advice of his responsible ministers, the king took counsel with this "double" or "interior cabinet." Even his first speech to Parliament was not submitted to the cabinet.

The king's secret counsellors.

1 The Idea of a Patriot King, *Works*, iv. 281, 282.
2 *Ibid.*, 330.
3 Walp. Mem., i. 15.
4 Burke's Present Discontents, *Works*, ii. 240–242.

It had been drawn up by himself and Lord Bute; and when Mr. Pitt took exception to some of its expressions, the king long resisted the advice of his minister. It had been usual for ministers to rely upon the support of the Crown, in all their measures. They now found themselves thwarted and opposed; and the patronage, which they had regarded as their own, they saw divided by the king amongst his new adherents and their connections. This "influence behind the throne" was denounced by all the leading statesmen of that time, — by Mr. Grenville, Lord Chatham, the Marquess of Rockingham, the Duke of Bedford, and Mr. Burke. Occasionally denied, its existence was yet so notorious, and its agency so palpable, that historical writers of all parties, though taking different views of its character, have not failed to acknowledge it. The bitterness with which it was assailed at the time was due, in great measure, to political jealousies, and to the king's selection of his friends from an unpopular party; but, on constitutional grounds, it could not be defended.

Constitutional relations of the king to his ministers.

A constitutional government insures to the king a wide authority, in all the councils of the state. He chooses and dismisses his ministers. Their resolutions upon every important measure of foreign and domestic policy are submitted to his approval; and when that approval is withheld, his ministers must either abandon their policy, or resign their offices. They are responsible to the king on the one hand, and to Parliament on the other; and while they retain the confidence of the king, by administering affairs to his satisfaction, they must act upon principles, and propose measures, which they can justify to Parliament. And here is the proper limit to the king's influence. As he governs by responsible ministers, he must recognize their responsibilities. They are not only his ministers, but also the public servants of a free country. But an influence in the direction of public affairs thus limited, by no means satisfied the ambition of the king. His courtiers represented that the king was inthralled by the dominant party, which had become superior to the throne itself, and that in order to recover his just prerogative, it was necessary to break up the combination. But what was this in effect but to assert that the king should now be his own minister? that ministers should be chosen, not because they had the confidence of Parliament and the country, but because they were agreeable to himself, and willing to carry out his policy? — And this was the true object of the king. It will be seen that when ministers, not of his own choice, were in office, he plotted against them and overthrew them; and when he had succeeded in establishing his friends in office, he enforced upon them the adoption of his own policy.

His attempts to break up parties.

The king's tactics were fraught with danger, as well to the Crown itself, as to the constitutional liberties of the people; but his personal conduct and character have sometimes been judged with too much severity. That he was too fond of power for a constitutional monarch, none will now be found to deny: that he sometimes resorted to crafty expedients, unworthy of a king, even his admirers must admit. With a narrow understanding, and obstinate prejudices, he was yet patriotic in his feelings, and labored, earnestly and honestly, for the good government of his country. If he loved power, he did not shrink from its cares and toil. If he delighted in being the active ruler of his people, he devoted himself to affairs of state, even more laboriously than his ministers. If he was jealous of the authority of the Crown, he was not less jealous of the honor and greatness of his people. A just recognition of the personal merits of the king himself, enables us to judge more freely of the constitutional tendency and results of his policy.

Danger of the king's tactics.

To revert to a polity under which kings had governed, and ministers had executed their orders, was in itself a dangerous retrogression in the principles of constitutional government. If the Crown, and not its ministers, governed, how could the former do no wrong, and the latter be responsible? If ministers were content to accept responsibility without power, the Crown could not escape its share of blame. Hence the chief safeguard of the monarchy was endangered. But the liberties of the people were exposed to greater peril than the Crown. Power proceeding from the king, and exercised by himself in person, is irreconcilable with popular government. It constitutes the main distinction between an absolute, and a constitutional monarchy. The best and most enlightened of kings, governing from above, will press his own policy upon his subjects. Choosing his ministers from considerations personal to himself, — directing their acts, — upholding them as his own servants, — resenting attacks upon them as disrespectful to himself, — committed to their measures, and resolved to enforce them, — viewing men and things from the elevation of a court, instead of sharing the interests and sympathies of the people, — how can he act in harmony with popular influences?

The system of government which George III. found in operation, was indeed imperfect. The influence of the Crown, as exercised by ministers, prevailed over the more popular elements of the constitution. The great nobles were too powerful. A Parliament, without adequate representation of the people, and uncontrolled by public opinion, was generally subservient to the ministers: but with all its defects, it was still a popular institution. If not freely elected by the people, it was yet composed of men belonging to various classes of society, and sharing their interests and feelings. The statesmen, who were able by their talents and influence to command its confidence, became the ministers of the Crown; and power thus proceeded from below, instead of from above. The country was governed by its ablest men, and not by favorites of the court. The proper authority of Parliament was recognized, and nothing was wanting in the theory of constitutional government, but an improved constitution of Parliament itself. This system, however, the king was determined to subvert. He was jealous of ministers who derived their authority from Parliament rather than from himself, and of the parliamentary organization which controlled his power. The policy which he adopted, and its results, are among the most critical events in the history of the Crown.

King's interest strengthened at the general election.

The dissolution of Parliament, shortly after his accession, afforded an opportunity of strengthening the parliamentary connection of the king's friends. Parliament was kept sitting while the king and Lord Bute were making out lists of the court candidates, and using every exertion to secure their return. The king not only wrested government boroughs from the ministers, in order to nominate his own friends, but even encouraged opposition to such ministers as he conceived not to be in his interest.[1]

At the meeting at the cockpit, the night before the assembling of the new Parliament, to hear the king's speech read, and to agree upon the choice of a speaker, not only the Whigs and parliamentary supporters of the government attended; but also the old Tories in a strong body, though without any invitation from the ministers.[2] The speaker selected by Lord Bute was Sir John Cust, a country gentleman and a Tory.

Measures taken to break up the ministry.

Lord Bute, the originator of the new policy, was not personally well qualified for its successful promotion. He was not connected with the great families who had acquired a preponderance of political influ-

1 The Duke of Newcastle thus wrote at this time to Lord Rockingham: — "My Lord Anson has received *orders from the king himself* to declare to the docks (at Portsmouth) that they may vote for whom they please at the Hampshire election, *even though the Chancellor of the Exchequer is a candidate.*" Lord Bute complained to the First Lord of the Admiralty, that he had disposed of the Admiralty boroughs without acquainting the king. — *Dodington's Diary*, 433; *Rockingham Mem.*, i. 61–64.

2 Rockingham Mem., i. 68; Dodington's Diary, 433.

ence; he was no parliamentary debater: his manners were unpopular: he was a courtier rather than a politician: his intimate relations with the Princess of Wales were an object of scandal; and, above all, he was a Scotchman. The jealousy of foreigners, which had shown itself in hatred of the Hanoverians, was now transferred to the Scottish nation, whose connection with the late civil war had exposed them to popular obloquy. The scheme was such as naturally occurred to a favorite; but it required more than the talents of a favorite to accomplish. While only in the king's household, his influence was regarded with jealousy: remarks were already made upon the unlucky circumstance of his being a "Scot;" and popular prejudices were aroused against him, before he was ostensibly concerned in public affairs. Immediately after the king's accession he had been made a privy councillor, and admitted into the cabinet. An arrangement was soon afterwards concerted, by which Lord Holdernesse retired from office with a pension, and Lord Bute succeeded him as Secretary of State.[1]

It was now the object of the court to break up the existing ministry, and to replace it with another, formed from among the king's friends. Had the ministry been united, and had the chiefs reposed confidence in one another, it would have been difficult to overthrow them. But there were already jealousies amongst them, which the court lost no opportunity of fomenting.[2] A breach soon arose between Mr. Pitt, the most powerful and popular of the ministers, and his colleagues. He desired to strike a sudden blow against Spain, which had concluded a secret treaty of alli-

[1] 25th March, 1761.

[2] Lord Hardwicke said, "He (Lord Bute) principally availed himself with great art and finesse of the dissensions between the Duke of Newcastle and Mr. Pitt: he played off one against the other till he got rid of the popular minister, and when that was compassed, he strengthened himself in the cabinet, by bringing in Lord Egremont and Mr. Grenville, and never left intriguing till he had rendered it impracticable for the old duke to continue in office with credit and honor." — *Rockingham Mem.*, i. 6. See the duke's own letters, *ib.*, 102–109.

ance with France, then at war with this country.[1] Though war minister, he was opposed by all his colleagues except Lord Temple. He bore himself haughtily at the council, —declared that he had been called to the ministry by the voice of the people, and that he could not be responsible for measures which he was no longer allowed to guide. Being met with equal loftiness in the cabinet, he was forced to tender his resignation.[2]

Pension to Mr. Pitt.

The king overpowered the retiring minister with kindness and condescension. He offered the barony of Chatham to his wife, and to himself an annuity of 3,000*l.* a year for three lives.[3] The minister had deserved these royal favors, and he accepted them, but at the cost of his popularity. It was an artful stroke of policy, thus at once to conciliate and weaken the popular statesman, whose opposition was to be dreaded, —and it succeeded. The same Gazette which announced his resignation, also trumpeted forth the peerage and the pension, and was the signal for clamors against the public favorite.

Influence of Lord Bute.

On the retirement of Mr. Pitt, Lord Bute became the most influential of the ministers. He undertook the chief management of public affairs in the cabinet, and the sole direction of the House of Lords.[4] He consulted none of his colleagues, except Lord Egremont and Mr. George Grenville.[5] His ascendency provoked the

[1] Grenville Papers, i. 386.

[2] Ann. Reg., 1761 [43]. Grenville Papers, i. 391, 405. Mr. Pitt, in a letter to Mr. Beckford, October 15th, 1761, says, "A difference of opinion with regard to measures to be taken against Spain, of the highest importance to the honor of the Crown, and to the most essential national interests, and this founded on what Spain had already done, not on what that court may further intend to do, was the cause of my resigning the seals." —*Chatham Corresp.*, ii. 159.

[3] Mr. Pitt said, "I confess, Sir, I had but too much reason to expect your Majesty's displeasure. I did not come prepared for this exceeding goodness. Pardon me, Sir, it overpowers, it oppresses me," and burst into tears. —*Ann. Reg.; Grenville Papers*, i. 413.

[4] Rockingham Mem., i. 54, 86, 101 (Letters of the Duke of Newcastle).

[5] *Ibid.*, 104.

jealousy and resentment of the king's veteran minister, the Duke of Newcastle: who had hitherto distributed all the patronage of the Crown, but now was never consulted. The king himself created seven peers, without even acquainting him with their creation.[1] Lord Bute gave away places and pensions to his own friends, and paid no attention to the recommendations of the duke. At length, in May 1762, his grace, after frequent disagreements in the cabinet and numerous affronts, was obliged to resign.[2]

Lord Bute as premier.

And now, the object of the court being at length attained, Lord Bute was immediately placed at the head of affairs, as First Lord of the Treasury. Rapid had been the rise of the king's favorite. In thirteen months he had been groom of the stole, a privy councillor, ranger of Richmond Park, secretary of state, and premier;[3] and these favors were soon followed by his installation as a Knight of the Garter, at the same time as the king's own brother, Prince William. His sudden elevation resembled that of an eastern vizier, rather than the toilsome ascent of a British statesman. But the confidence of his royal master served to aggravate the jealousies by which the new minister was surrounded, to widen the breach between himself and the leaders of the Whig party, and to afford occasion for popular reproaches. It has been insinuated that he was urged forward by secret enemies, in order to insure his speedier fall;[4] and it is certain that had he been contented with a

1 Walpole Mem., i. 156.

2 The personal demeanor of the king towards him evinced the feeling with which he had long been regarded. The duke complained of it in this manner: "The king did not drop one word of concern at my leaving him nor even made me a polite compliment, after near fifty years' service and devotion to the interests of his royal family. I will say nothing more of myself, but that I believe never any man was so dismissed." — *Letter to Lord Rockingham, May 19th, Rockingham Mem.*, i. 111. Yet Lord Bute, in a letter to Mr. Grenville, May 25th, 1762, says, "The king's conduct to the Duke of Newcastle to-day was great and generous." — *Grenville Papers*, i. 448.

3 His countess also received an English barony.

4 Walpole Mem., i. 44.

less prominent place, the consummation of his peculiar policy could have been more securely, and perhaps more successfully, accomplished.

Arbitrary conduct of the king and the new ministry.

The king and his minister were resolved to carry matters with a high hand,[1] and their arbitrary attempts to coerce and intimidate opponents disclosed their imperious views of the prerogative. Preliminaries of a treaty of peace with France having been agreed upon, against which a strong popular feeling was aroused, the king's vengeance was directed against all who ventured to disapprove them.

The Duke of Devonshire having declined to attend the council summoned to decide upon the peace, was insulted by the king, and forced to resign his office of Lord Chamberlain.[2] A few days afterwards the king, with his own hand, struck his grace's name from the list of privy councillors. For so great a severity the only precedents in the late reign were those of Lord Bath and Lord George Sackville; "the first," says Walpole, "in open and virulent opposition; the second on his ignominious sentence after the battle of Minden."[3] No sooner had Lord Rockingham heard of the treatment of the Duke of Devonshire, than he sought an audience of the king; and having stated that those "who had hitherto deservedly had the greatest weight in the country were now driven out of any share in the government, and marked out rather as objects of his Majesty's displeasure than of his favor," resigned his place in the household.[4]

A more general proscription of the Whig nobles soon followed. The Dukes of Newcastle and Grafton, and the Mar quess of Rockingham having presumed, as peers of Parlia-

[1] "The king, it was given out, *would* be king, — would not be dictated to by his ministers, as his grandfather had been. The prerogative was to shine out: great lords must be humbled." — *Walp. Mem.*, i. 200.

[2] Walp. Mem., i. 201; Rockingham Mem., i. 135 (Letter of Duke of Newcastle to Lord Rockingham).

[3] Walp. Mem., i. 203.

[4] Letter to Duke of Cumberland; Rockingham Mem., i. 142.

ment, to express their disapprobation of the peace, were dismissed from the lord-lieutenancies of their counties.[1] The Duke of Devonshire, in order to share the fate of his friends and avoid the affront of dismissal, resigned the lieutenancy of his county.[2]

Nor was the vengeance of the court confined to the heads of the Whig party. All placemen, who had voted against the preliminaries of peace, were dismissed. Their humble friends and clients were also proscribed. Clerks were removed from public offices, and inferior officers from the customs, and excise, and other small appointments, for no other offence than that of having been appointed by their obnoxious patrons.[3] While bribes were being lavished to purchase adhesion to the court policy, this severity was intended to discourage opposition.

Its effect upon parties.

The preliminaries of peace were approved by Parliament; and the Princess of Wales, exulting in the success of the court, exclaimed, "Now my son *is* king of England."[4] But her exultation was premature. As yet there had been little more than a contention for power, between rival parties in the aristocracy; but these stretches of prerogative served to unite the Whigs into an organized opposition. Since the accession of the House of Hanover, this party had supported the Crown as ministers. It now became their office to assert the liberties of the people, and to resist the encroachments of prerogative. Thus the king's attempt to restore the personal influence of the Sovereign, which the Revolution had impaired, so far from strengthening the throne, advanced the popular cause, and gave it powerful leaders, whose interests had hitherto been enlisted on the side of the Crown. Claims of prerogative became the

1 Rockingham Mem., i. 155.
2 Walp. Mem., i. 235; Rockingham Mem., i. 156.
3 Walp. Mem., i. 233; Grenville Papers, i. 453; Rockingham, Mem., i. 152, 158.
4 Walp. Mem., i. 233.

signal for the assertion of new rights and liberties, on the part of the people.

The fall of the king's favored minister was even more sudden than his rise. He shrank from the difficulties of his position, — a disunited cabinet, — a formidable opposition, — doubtful support from his friends, — the bitter hatred of his enemies, — a libellous press, — and notorious unpopularity.[1] Afraid, as he confessed, "not only of falling himself, but of involving his royal master in his ruin," he resigned suddenly, — to the surprise of all parties, and even of the king himself, — before he had held office for eleven months. But his short administration had indulged the king's love of rule, and encouraged him to proceed with his cherished scheme for taking an active part in the direction of public affairs.

Sudden fall of Lord Bute.

Nor did Lord Bute propose to relinquish his own power together with his office. He retreated to the interior cabinet, whence he could direct more securely the measures of the court;[2] having previously negotiated the appointment of Mr. George Grenville as his successor, and arranged with him the nomination of the cabinet.[3] The ministry of Mr. Grenville was constituted in a manner favorable to the king's personal views, and was expected to be under the control of himself and his favorite. And at first there can be little doubt that Mr. Grenville found himself the mere agent of the court. "The voice was Jacob's voice, but the hands were the hands of Esau." "The public looked still at Lord Bute through the curtain," said Lord Chesterfield, "which indeed was a very transparent one." But Mr. Grenville was by no means contented with the appearance of power. He was jealous of Lord Bute's superior influence, and complained to the king

His continued influence with the king.

The Grenville ministry, 1763.

[1] He was hissed and pelted at the opening of Parliament, 25th Nov., 1762, and his family were alarmed for his personal safety.

[2] Mr. Grenville to Lord Egremont; Grenville Papers, ii. 85.

[3] Grenville Papers, ii. 32, 33.

that his Majesty's confidence was withheld from his minister.[1] As fond of power as the king himself, — and with a will as strong and imperious, — tenacious of his rights as a minister, and confident in his own abilities and influence, — he looked to Parliament rather than to the Crown, as the source of his authority.

The king sends Lord Bute to Mr. Pitt.

The king finding his own scheme of government opposed, and disliking the uncongenial views and hard temper of his minister, resolved to dismiss him on the first convenient opportunity.[2] Accordingly, on the death of Lord Egremont, he commissioned Lord Bute to open negotiations with Mr. Pitt, for the formation of a new administration. And now the king tasted the bitter fruits of his recent policy. He had proscribed the Whig leaders. He had determined "never upon any account to suffer those ministers of the late reign, who had attempted to fetter and enslave him, to come into his service, while he lived to hold the sceptre."[3] Yet these were the very ministers whom Mr. Pitt proposed to restore to power; and stranger still, — the premier, in whom the king was asked to repose his confidence, was Earl Temple, who had recently aroused his bitter resentment. His Majesty was not likely so soon to retract his resolution, and refused these hateful terms: "My honor is concerned," he said, "and I must support it."[4] The Grenville ministry, however distasteful, was not so hard to bear as the restoration of the dreaded Whigs; and he was therefore obliged to retain it. Mr. Grenville now remonstrated more strongly than ever against the influence of the favorite who had been employed to supplant him: the king promised his confidence to the ministers, and Lord Bute retired from the court.[5]

[1] Grenville Papers, ii. 84, 85, 89.

[2] *Ibid.*, ii. 83, 85.

[3] Letter of Lord Bute to the Duke of Bedford, 2d April, 1763; Duke of Bedford's Correspondence, iii. 224; see also Grenville Papers, ii. 93, 105, 196.

[4] Grenville Papers, ii. 96, 107.

[5] Grenville Papers, ii. 106, 483, 500; Chatham Corresp., ii. 236; Parl. Hist., xv. 1327.

Active interest of the king in the measures of government.

Though George III. and Mr. Grenville differed as to their relative powers, they were but too well agreed in their policy. Both were arbitrary in their views, impatient of opposition, and resolute in the exercise of authority. The chief claims of the Grenville ministry to distinction were its arbitrary proceedings against Wilkes, which the king encouraged and approved, and the first taxation of America, which he himself suggested.[1] In the policy of proscription, which had disgraced the late administration, the king was even more forward than his ministers. Earl Temple's friendship for Wilkes was punished by the erasure of his name from the list of privy councillors, and by dismissal from the lord-lieutenancy of his county.[2] General Conway, Colonel Barré, and Colonel A'Court were, for their votes in Parliament, deprived of their military commands,[3] and Lord Shelburne of his office of aide-de-camp to his Majesty.

His violation of the privileges of Parliament.

The privileges of Parliament were systematically violated by the king. In order to guard against the arbitrary interference of the Crown in its proceedings, Parliament had established, for centuries, the constitutional doctrine that the king should not hear or give credit to reports of its debates, and that no member should suffer molestation for his speaking or reasoning.[4] Yet, during the proceedings of the Commons against Wilkes, the king obtained from Mr. Grenville the most minute and circumstantial reports. Not only did he watch the progress of every debate, and the result of each division, but he kept a jealous eye upon the opinions and votes of every member; and expressed his personal resentment against all who did not support the government. It was he who first proposed the dismissal of General Conway, "both from his civil and military commissions:" it was he who insisted on the re-

1 Wraxall's Mem., ii. 111.

2 May 7th, 1763; Grenville Papers, ii. 55.

3 Chatham Correspondence, ii. 275; Walp. Mem., ii. 65.

4 Rot. Parl., iii. 456, 611; 4 Hen. VIII. c. 8.

moval of Mr. Fitzherbert from the Board of Trade, and of all placemen who took a different view of parliamentary privilege from that adopted by the court.[1] Mr. Grenville endeavored to moderate the king's severity: he desired to postpone such violent measures till the proceedings against Wilkes should be concluded;[2] and, in the mean time, opened communications with General Conway in the hope of averting his dismissal.[3] But at length the blow was struck, and General Conway was dismissed not only from his office of Groom of the Bedchamber, but from the command of his regiment of dragoons.[4] Mr. Calcraft was also deprived of the office of Deputy Muster-Master.[5] The king himself was, throughout, the chief promoter of this policy of proscription.[6]

To commit General Conway or Colonel Barré to prison, as James I. had committed Sir Edwin Sandys, and as Charles I. had committed Selden and other leading members of the House of Commons, could not now have been attempted. Nor was the ill-omened venture of Charles I. against the five members likely to be repeated; but the king was violating the same principles of constitutional government as his arbitrary predecessors. He punished, as far as he was able, those who had incurred his displeasure, for their conduct in Parliament; and denied them the protection which they

1 Grenville Papers, ii. 162, 165, 166 (letters from the king to Mr. Grenville, 16th, 23d, and 24th Nov., 1763); *ibid.*, 223, 228–9.

2 *Ibid.*, 224, 229, 230, 266, 267, 484 (Diary, 16th, 25th, and 30th Nov.; 2d Dec., 1763; 19th Jan., 1764).

3 *Ibid.*, 231–233.

4 Grenville Papers, ii. 296. "Mr. Grenville never would admit the distinction between civil and military appointments." — *Grenville Papers*, ii. 234, 507. It has been stated that General Conway voted once only against the ministry on General Warrants, having supported them in the contest with Wilkes (*History of a Late Minority*, 291; *Rockingham Mem.*, i. 178); but this was not the case. Mr. Grenville in his Diary, Nov. 15th, 1763, speaks of Mr. Conway's vote *both* times with the minority. — *Grenville Papers*, ii. 223.

5 *Ibid.*, 231.

6 *Ibid.*, 297; Walp. Mem., i. 403; Rockingham Mem., i. 178.

claimed from privilege, and the laws of their country. Yet the Commons submitted to this violation of their freedom, with scarcely a murmur.[1]

Public discontents.

The riots and popular discontents of this period ought to have convinced the king that his statesmanship was not successful. He had already sacrificed his popularity to an ill-regulated love of power. But he continued to direct every measure of the government, whether of legislation, of administration, or of patronage; and by means of the faithful reports of his minister, he constantly assisted, as it were, in the deliberations of Parliament.[2]

King's differences with the Grenville ministry.

In 1765, differences again arose between the king and the Grenville ministry. They had justly offended him by their mismanagement of the Regency Bill,[3] — they had disputed with him on questions of patronage and expenditure, — they had wearied him with long arguments in the closet;[4] and, in the month of May, having completely lost his Majesty's confidence, he intimated to them his intention of dispensing with their services. But the king, after vain negotiations with Mr. Pitt through the Duke of Cumberland, finding himself unable to form another administration, was again compelled to retain them in office. They had suspected the secret influence of Lord Bute in thwarting their counsels; and to him they attributed their dismissal.[5] The first condition, therefore, on which they

[1] Parl. Hist., xvi. 1765.

[2] Grenville Papers, iii. 4–15, 21–37. The king's communications were sometimes sufficiently peremptory. Writing May 21st, 1765, he says: "Mr. Grenville, I am surprised that you are not yet come, when you know it was my orders to be attended this evening. I expect you, therefore, to come the moment you receive this." — *Grenville Papers*, iii. 40.

[3] See *infra*, p. 144.

[4] Walp. Mem., ii. 161.

[5] So great was the jealousy of Mr. Grenville and the Duke of Bedford of the influence of Lord Bute in 1764, that they were anxious to insist upon his remaining in the country, though he said he was tired of it, and had daughters to marry, and other business. — *Mr. Grenville's Diary*, 16th and 28th Jan., 1764; *Grenville Papers*, ii. 483, 488.

consented to remain in office, was that Lord Bute should not be suffered to interfere in his Majesty's councils "in any manner or shape whatever." [1] To this the king pledged himself,[2] and though suspicions of a secret correspondence with Lord Bute were still entertained, there is every reason for believing that he adhered to his promise.[3] Indeed, he had already acquired so much confidence in his own aptitude for business, that he no longer relied upon the counsels of his favorite.[4] He was able to rule alone; and wanted instruments, rather than advisers. The second condition was the dismissal of Mr. Stuart Mackenzie, Lord Bute's brother, from the office of Privy Seal in Scotland, and from the management of the affairs of that country. In this, too, the king yielded, though solely against his will, as he had promised the office for life.[5] Meanwhile the breach between the king and his ministers became still wider. They had been forced

[1] Minute of Cabinet, 22d May, 1765; Grenville Papers, iii. 41; *ib.*, 184; Adolphus, i. 170.

[2] "At eleven o'clock at night the king sent for Mr. Grenville, and told him he had considered upon the proposals made to him: he did promise and declare to them that Lord Bute should never, directly nor indirectly, have anything to do with his business, nor give advice upon anything whatever." — *Diary; Grenville Papers*, iii. 185.

[3] Mem. of C. J. Fox, i. 65–68, 111; Mr. Mackintosh to Earl Temple, Aug. 30th, 1765, *Grenville Papers*, iii. 81. *Wraxall's Mem.*, ii. 73, &c. Mr. Grenville was still so suspicious of Lord Bute's influence, that being told in November, 1765, by Mr. Jenkinson, that Lord Bute had only seen the king twice during his illness in the spring, he says in his diary: "Which fact Mr. Grenville could not be brought to believe. He owned, however, to Mr. Grenville that the intercourse in writing between his Majesty and Lord Bute always continued, telling him that he knew the king wrote to him a journal every day of what passed, and as minute a one as if, said he, 'your boy at school was directed by you to write his journal to you.'" — *Grenville Papers*, iii. 220.

It was not until Dec. 1768, that Mr. Grenville seems to have been persuaded that Lord Bute's influence was lost. He then concurred in the prevailing opinion of "the king being grown indifferent to him, but the princess being in the same sentiments towards him as before." — *Diary; Grenville Papers*, iv. 408.

[4] Bedford Corresp., iii. 264.

[5] Walp. Geo. III., ii. 175; Grenville Papers, iii. 185. He was afterwards restored in 1766 by the Earl of Chatham. — *Ib.*, 362.

upon him by necessity; they knew that he was plotting their speedy overthrow, and protested against the intrigues by which their influence was counteracted. The Duke of Bedford besought the king "to permit his authority and his favor to go together;"[1] and these remonstrances were represented by the king's friends as insolent and overbearing.[2] An outcry was raised against the ministers that they "desired to enslave the king," who was now determined to make any sacrifices to get rid of them.

Negotiations with the Whigs.

The negotiations for a new ministry were again conducted on behalf of the king, by his uncle the Duke of Cumberland. Such was the popular hatred of Lord Bute and his countrymen, that the Duke's former severities against the Scotch, which had gained for him the name of "the Butcher," were now a claim to popular favor. The rebellious Scots had been treated as they deserved; and he who had already chastised them, was not the man to favor their pretensions at court.

July, 1765.

These negotiations were protracted for seven weeks, while the country was virtually without a government.[3] Mr. Pitt was again impracticable: the further continuance of the Grenville ministry could not be endured; and, at length, the king was reduced to the necessity of surrendering himself once more to the very men whom he most dreaded.

Rockingham ministry.

The Marquess of Rockingham, the leader of the obnoxious Whig aristocracy, — the statesman whom he had recently removed from his lieutenancy, — the king was now obliged to accept as Premier; and General Conway, whom he had deprived of his regiment, became a Secretary of State, and leader of the House of Commons. The policy of proscription was, for a time at least, reversed

1 12th June, 1765; Bedford Correspondence, iii. Introd., pp. xliii. xlv. 286; Grenville Papers, iii. 194.

2 Junius, Letter xxiii.; Burke's Works, ii. 156; Walp. Geo. III., ii. 182; Bedford Corresp., iii. 286.

3 Walp. Mem., ii. 192.

and condemned. Mr. Pitt, when solicited by the Duke of Cumberland to take office, had named as one of his conditions, the restoration of officers dismissed on political grounds. This the king had anticipated, and was prepared to grant.[1] The Rockingham administration insisted on the same terms; and according to Mr. Burke "discountenanced, and it is hoped forever abolished, the dangerous and unconstitutional practice of removing military officers, for their votes in Parliament."[2]

Dismissal of officers condemned.

The Whig leaders were not less jealous of the influence of Lord Bute, than the ministry whom they displaced; and before they would accept office, they insisted "that the thought of replacing Mr. Mackenzie should be laid aside; and also that some of the particular friends of the Earl of Bute should be removed, as a proof to the world that the Earl of Bute should not either publicly or privately, directly or indirectly, have any concern or influence in public affairs, or in the management or disposition of public employments."[3] These conditions being agreed to, a ministry so constituted was likely to be independent of court influence: yet it was soon reproached with submission to the "interior cabinet." Mr. Pitt said, "Methinks I plainly discover the traces of an overruling influence;" and while he disavowed any prejudice against the country of Lord Bute, he declared that "the man of that country wanted wisdom, and held principles incompatible with freedom." This supposed influence was disclaimed on the part of the government by General Conway: "I see nothing of it," said he, "I feel nothing of it: I disclaim it for myself, and as far as my discernment can reach, for the rest of his Majesty's ministers."[4]

Conditions of the Rockingham ministry.

The king's friends.

Whether Lord Bute had, at this time, any influence at

1 Walp. Mem., ii. 165; Duke of Cumberland's Narrative; Rockingham Mem., i. 193–196.

2 Short Account of a Late Short Administration.

3 Paper drawn up by Duke of Newcastle, *Rockingham Mem.*, i. 218.

4 Debate on the Address, 1766, *Parl. Hist.*, xvi. 97, 101.

court, was long a subject of court and controversy. It was confidently believed by the public, and by many of the best informed of his contemporaries; but Lord Bute, several years afterwards, so explicitly denied it, that his denial may be accepted as conclusive.[1] The king's friends, however, had become more numerous, and acted under better discipline. Some of them held offices in the government or household, yet looked to the king for instructions, instead of to the ministers. These generally had obscure but lucrative offices, in the gift of the king himself and other members of the royal family.[2] But the greater part of the king's friends were independent members of Parliament, whom various motives had attracted to the personal support of the king. Many were influenced by high notions of prerogative, — by loyalty, by confidence in the judgment and honesty of the king, and by personal attachment to his Majesty, — and many by hopes of favor and advancement. They formed a distinct party, and their coherence was secured by the same causes which generally contribute to the formation of party ties. But their principles and position were inconsistent with constitutional government. Their services to the king were no longer confined to counsel, or political intrigue; but were organized so as to influence the deliberations of Parliament. And their organization for such a purpose, marked a further advance in the unconstitutional policy of the court.

The king continued personally to direct the measures of

[1] His son, Lord Mountstuart, writing Oct. 23, 1773, said: "Lord Bute authorizes me to say that he declares upon his solemn word of honor, he has not had the honor of waiting on his Majesty, but at his levée or drawing-room; nor has he presumed to offer any advice or opinion concerning the disposition of offices, or the conduct of measures, either directly or indirectly, by himself or any other, from the time when the late Duke of Cumberland was consulted in the arrangement of a ministry in 1765, to the present hour." — *Tomline's Life of Pitt*, i. 452, *n.* See also Rockingham Mem., i. 358–360; Lord Brougham's Sketches of Statesmen, *Works*, iii. 49; Edinb. Rev. cxli. 94; Quart. Rev., cxxxi. 236. Lord John Russell's Introduction to vol. iii. of Bedford Correspondence, xxxiii.

[2] Burke's Present Discontents, *Works*, ii. 254.

the ministers, more particularly in the disputes with the American colonies, which, in his opinion, involved the rights and honor of his crown.[1] He was resolutely opposed to the repeal of the Stamp Act, which the ministers had thought necessary for the conciliation of the colonies. He resisted this measure in council; but finding the ministers resolved to carry it, he opposed them in Parliament by the authority of his name, and by his personal influence over a considerable body of his parliamentary adherents.[2] The king affected, indeed, to support the ministers, and to decline the use of his name in opposing them. "Lord Harcourt suggested, at a distance, that his Majesty might make his sentiments known, which might prevent the repeal of the act, if his ministers should push that measure. The king seemed averse to that, said he would never influence people in their parliamentary opinions, and that he had promised to support his ministers."[3] But, however the king may have affected to deprecate the use of his name, it was unquestionably used by his friends;[4] and while he himself admitted the unconstitutional character of such a proceeding, it found a defender in Lord Mansfield. In discussing this matter with the king, his lordship argued "that, though it would be unconstitutional to endeavor by his Majesty's name to carry questions in Parliament, yet where the lawful rights of the king and Parliament were to be asserted and maintained, he thought the making his Majesty's opinion in support of those rights to be known, was fit and becoming."[5] In order to counteract this secret influence, Lord Rockingham obtained the king's written consent to the passing of the bill.[6]

The king's influence in Parliament.

[1] The king said his ministers "would undo his people, in giving up the rights of his crown; that to this he would never consent." — *Grenville Papers*, iii. 370, 371.

[2] Walp. Mem., ii. 259, 331, *n.* Rockingham Mem., ii. 250, 294.

[3] Mr. Grenville's Diary, Jan. 31, 1766; Grenville Papers, iii. 353.

[4] Grenville Papers, iii. 374; Walp. Mem., ii. 288; Rockingham Mem., i. 277, 292.

[5] Grenville Papers, iii. 374.

[6] Rockingham Mem., i. 300.

The ministers had to contend against another difficulty, which the tactics of the court had created. Not only were they opposed by independent members of the court party; but members holding office, upon whose support ministers were justified in relying, — were encouraged to oppose them; and retained their offices, while voting in the ranks of the Opposition. The king, who had punished with so much severity any opposition to measures which he approved, now upheld and protected those placemen, who opposed the ministerial measures to which he himself objected. In vain the ministers remonstrated against their conduct: the king was ready with excuses and promises; but his chosen band were safe from the indignation of the Government. Nor was their opposition confined to the repeal of the Stamp Act, — a subject on which they might have affected to entertain conscientious scruples: but it was vexatiously continued against the general measures of the administration.[1] Well might Mr. Burke term this "an opposition of a new and singular character, — an opposition of placemen and pensioners."[2] Lord Rockingham protested against such a system while in office;[3] and after his dismissal, took occasion to observe to his Majesty, that "when he had the honor of being in his Majesty's service, the measures of administration were thwarted and obstructed by men in office, acting like a corps; that he flattered himself it was not entirely with his Majesty's inclination, and would assure him it was very detrimental to his service."[4] This system, to use the words of Mr. Burke, tended "to produce neither the security of a free Government, nor the energy of a monarchy that is absolute."[5]

The king, meanwhile, had resolved to overthrow the Rockingham ministry, which was on every account distaste-

[1] Walp. Mem., ii. 259, 331, *n.;* Rockingham Mem., i. 250, 294, 321.
[2] A Short Account of a Late Short Administration.
[3] Walp. Mem., ii. 322.
[4] Rockingham Mem., ii. 53.
[5] Present Discontents, *Works*, ii. 721.

ful to him. He disapproved their liberal policy: he was jealous of their powerful party, which he desired to break up; and, above all, he resented their independence. He desired ministers to execute his will; and these men and their party were the obstacles to the cherished object of his ambition.

At length, in July, 1766, they were ungraciously dismissed;[1] and his Majesty now expected from the hands of Mr. Pitt, an administration better suited to his own views and policy. Mr. Pitt's greatness had naturally pointed him out as the fittest man for such a task, and there were other circumstances which made him personally acceptable to the king. Haughty as was the demeanor of that distinguished man in the senate, and among his equals, his bearing in the royal presence was humble and obsequious. The truth of Mr. Burke's well-known sarcasm, that "the least peep into that closet intoxicates him, and will to the end of his life,"[2] was recognized by all his contemporaries.[3]

Duke of Grafton's ministry, 1766.

A statesman with at least the outward qualities of a courtier, was likely to give the king some repose after his collisions with the two last ministries. He now undertook to form an administration under the Duke of Grafton, with the office of Privy Seal, and a seat in the Upper House, as Earl of Chatham.

For another reason also Lord Chatham was acceptable

[1] Walp. Mem., ii. 337.

[2] Letter to Lord Rockingham, Rockingham Mem., ii. 260.

[3] Chase Price said, "that at the levée, he (*i. e.* Lord Chatham) used to bow so low, you could see the tip of his hooked nose between his legs."— *Rockingham Mem.*, ii. 83. He had been in the habit of kneeling at the bed-side of George II., while transacting business. — *Wraxall's Mem.*, ii. 53. That he was ever true to his character, is illustrated by the abject terms of his letter to the king on resigning the office of Privy Seal, two years afterwards. "Under this load of unhappiness, I will not despair of your Majesty's pardon, while I supplicate again on my knees your Majesty's mercy, and most humbly implore your Majesty's royal permission to resign that high office." 14th October, 1768; Chatham Corresp., iii. 314.

to the king. They agreed, though for different reasons, in the policy of breaking up party connections. This was now the settled object of the king, which he pursued with unceasing earnestness. In writing to Lord Chatham, July 29th, 1766,[1] he said: "I know the Earl of Chatham will zealously give his aid towards destroying all party distinctions, and restoring that subordination to government which can alone preserve that inestimable blessing, liberty, from degenerating into licentiousness." [2] Again, December 2d, 1766, he wrote to the Earl of Chatham: "To rout out the present method of parties banding together, can only be obtained by withstanding their unjust demands, as well as the engaging able men, be their private connections where they will." [3] And again, on the 25th June, 1767: "I am thoroughly resolved to encounter any difficulties rather than yield to faction." [4]

The king's efforts to dissolve parties.

By this policy the king hoped to further his cherished scheme of increasing his own personal influence. To overcome the Whig connection, was to bring into office the friends of Lord Bute, and the court party who were subservient to his views. Lord Chatham adopted the king's policy for a very different purpose. Though in outward observances a courtier, he was a constitutional statesman, opposed to government by prerogative, and court influence. His career had been due to his own genius: independent of party, and superior to it, he had trusted to his eloquence, his statesmanship, and popularity. And now, by breaking up parties, he hoped to rule over them all. His project, however, completely failed. Having offended and exasperated the Whigs, he found himself at the head of an administration composed of the king's friends, who thwarted him, and of discordant elements over which he had no control.

Personal influence of the king.

1 Introduction to vol. iii. of Bedford Corresp., xxvii.
2 Chatham Corresp., iii. 21.
3 *Ibid.*, iii. 137.
4 *Ibid.*, 276.

He discovered, when it was too late, that the king had been more sagacious than himself, — and that while his own power and connections had crumbled away, the court party had obtained a dangerous ascendency. Parties had been broken up, and prerogative triumphed. The leaders of parties had been reduced to insignificance, while the king directed public affairs according to his own will, and upon principles dangerous to public liberty. According to Burke, "when he had accomplished his scheme of administration, he was no longer minister." [1] To repair the mischief which had been done, he afterwards sought an alliance with the party which, when in power, he had alienated from him. "Former little differences must be forgotten," he said, "when the contest is *pro aris et focis*." [2]

Meanwhile, other circumstances contributed to increase the influence of the king. Much of Lord Chatham's popularity had been sacrificed by the acceptance of a peerage; and his personal influence was diminished by his removal from the House of Commons, where he had been paramount. His holding so obscure a place as that of Privy Seal, also took much from his weight as a minister. His melancholy prostration soon afterwards increased the feebleness and disunion of the administration. Though his was its leading mind, for months he was incapacitated from attending to any business. He even refused an interview to the Duke of Grafton, the premier,[3] and to General Conway, though commissioned by the king to confer with him.[4] It is not surprising that the Duke of Grafton should complain of the languor under which "every branch of the administration labored from his absence." [5] Yet the king, writing to Lord Chatham, January 23d, 1768, to dissuade him from resigning the Privy Seal, said: "Though confined to your

[1] Speech on American Taxation.
[2] Rockingham Mem., ii. 143.
[3] Chatham Corresp., iii. 218.
[4] Walp. Mem., ii. 433.
[5] Letter to Lord Chatham, 8th February, 1767; Chatham Corresp., iii. 194.

house, your name has been sufficient to enable my administration to proceed."[1] At length, however, in October, 1768, completely broken down, he resigned his office, and withdrew from the administration.[2]

The absence of Lord Chatham, and the utter disorganization of the ministry, left the king free to exercise his own influence, and to direct the policy of the country, without control. Had Lord Chatham been there, the ministry would have had a policy of its own: now it had none, and the Duke of Grafton and Lord North — partly from indolence, and partly from facility, — consented to follow the stronger will of their sovereign.[3]

On his side, the king took advantage of the disruption of party ties, which he had taken pains to promote. In the absence of distinctive principles, and party leaders, members of Parliament were exposed to the direct influence of the Crown. According to Horace Walpole, "everybody ran to court, and voted for whatever the court desired."[4] The main object of the king in breaking up parties, had thus been secured.

Lord North's ministry, 1770.

On the resignation of the Duke of Grafton, the king's ascendency in the councils of his ministers was further increased by the accession of Lord North to the chief direction of public affairs. That minister, by principle a Tory, and favorable to prerogative, — in character indolent and good tempered, — and personally attached to the king, — yielded up his own opinions and judgment; and for years consented to be the passive instru-

[1] Chatham Corresp., iii. 318.

[2] In his letter to the king, October 14th, he said, "All chance of recovery will be precluded by my continuing longer to hold the Privy Seal." — *Chatham Corresp.*, iii. 314.

So little had Lord Chatham's illness been assumed for political purposes, as it was frequently represented, that in August, 1777, he gave Lady Chatham a general letter of attorney, empowering her to transact all business for him. — *Chatham Corresp.*, iii. 282.

[3] Walp. Mem., iii. 62, 67, *n.*

[4] *Ibid.*, ii. 381, *n.* See also *ibid.*, iii. 92.

ment of the royal will.[1] The persecution of Wilkes, the straining of parliamentary privilege, and the coercion of America, were the disastrous fruits of the court policy. Throughout this administration, the king staked his personal credit upon the success of his measures; and regarded opposition to his ministers as an act of disloyalty, and their defeat as an affront to himself.[2]

In 1770, Lord Chatham stated in Parliament, that since the king's accession there had been no original (*i. e.* independent) minister;[3] and examples abound of the king's personal participation in every political event of this period.

Public affairs directed by the King.

While the Opposition were struggling to reverse the proceedings of the House of Commons against Wilkes, and Lord Chatham was about to move an address for dissolving Parliament, the king's resentment knew no bounds. In conversations with General Conway, at this time, he declared he would abdicate his crown rather than comply with this address. "Yes," said the king, laying his hand on his sword, "I will have recourse to this, sooner than yield to a dissolution of Parliament."[4] And opinions have not been wanting, that the king was actually prepared to resist what he deemed an invasion of his prerogative, by military force.[5]

On the 26th February, 1772, while the Royal Marriage Bill was pending in the House of Lords, the king thus wrote to Lord North: "I expect every nerve to be strained to carry the bill. It is not a question relating to administration, but personally to myself, therefore I have a right to

[1] Walp. Mem., ii. 95, *n.; ib.*, iii. 106, *n.;* Wraxall's Mem., i. 123.

Mr. Massey says, Lord North was "the only man of parliamentary reputation who would not have insisted" on the expulsion of the king's friends. — *Hist.*, i. 424. Always in favor of power and authority, "he supported the king against the aristocracy, the Parliament against the people, and the nation against the colonies." — *Ibid.*, 425.

[2] Walp. Mem., iii. 200 and *n.;* iv. 75.

[3] *Ibid.*, iv. 94; Hansard's Parl. Hist., xvi. 842 (March 2d, 1770).

[4] 14th May, 1770. Rockingham Mem., ii. 179.

[5] Massey, Hist., i. p. 489.

expect a hearty support from every one in my service, *and I shall remember defaulters*."[1] Again, on the 14th March, 1772, he wrote: "I wish a list could be prepared of those that went away, and of those that deserted to the minority (on division in the committee). That would be a rule for my conduct in the drawing-room to-morrow."[2] Again, in another letter, he said: "I am greatly incensed at the presumption of Charles Fox, in forcing you to vote with him last night."[3] . . . . "I hope you will let him know that you are not insensible of his conduct towards you."[4] And the king's confidence in his own influence over the deliberations of Parliament, appears from another letter, on the 26th June, 1774, where he said: "I hope the Crown will always be able, in either House of Parliament, to throw out a bill; but I shall never consent to use any expression which tends to establish, that at no time the right of the Crown to dissent is to be used."[5]

The king not only watched how members spoke and voted,[6] or whether they abstained from voting;[7] but even if they were silent, when he had expected them to speak.[8] No "whipper-in" from the Treasury could have been more keen or full of expedients, in influencing the votes of members in critical divisions.[9] He was ready, also, to take ad-

[1] Fox Mem., i. 76; Lord Brougham's Works, iii. 79.

[2] Lord Brougham's Works, iii. 80.

[3] 15th February, 1774. In proceedings against printers of a libel on the speaker, Sir F. Norton.

[4] Fox Mem., i. 99; Lord Brougham's Works, iii. 84.

[5] Lord Brougham's Works, iii. 85.

[6] King to Lord North, 5th April, 1770; Lord Brougham's Works, iii. 71, 88, 106, 108.

[7] King to Lord North, 12th March, 1772; 6th April, 25th Oct., 1778; 28th Feb., 4th and 9th March, 1779.

[8] King to Lord North, 7th Jan., 1770. "Surprised that T. Townsend was silent." — King to Lord North, 19th Dec., 1772. *Ibid.*, 81. "I should think Lord G. Germaine might with great propriety have said a few words to put the defence in motion." — King to Lord North, 2d Feb., 1778. Lord Brougham's Works, iii. 105. He was incensed against Dundas for the same reason, 24th Feb., 1778. — *Ibid.*, 106.

[9] King to Lord North, 9th Feb., 1775; 5th and 9th March, 1779.

vantage of the absence of opponents. Hearing that Mr. Fox was going to Paris, he wrote to Lord North, 15th November, 1776: "Bring as much forward as you can before the recess, as real business is never so well considered as when the attention of the House is not taken up with noisy declamation."[1]

Military officers were still exposed to marks of the king's displeasure. In 1773, Lieutenant-Colonel Barré and Sir Hugh Williams, both refractory members of Parliament, were passed over in a brevet, or promotion; and Colonel Barré, in order to mark his sense of the injustice of this act of power, resigned his commission in the army.[2] The king, however, appears to have modified his opinions as to his right of depriving members of military commands, on account of their conduct in Parliament. Writing to Lord North, 5th March, 1779, he says: "I am strongly of opinion that the general officers, who through Parliament have got governments, should, on opposing, lose them. This is very different from removing them from their military commands."[3]

Dismissal of officers.

Not without many affronts, and much unpopularity, the king and his minister long triumphed over all opposition in Parliament;[4] but in 1778, the signal failure of their policy, the crisis in American affairs, and the impending war with France, obliged them to enter into negotiations with Lord Chatham, for the admission of that statesman and some of the leaders of Opposition into the ministry. The king needed their assistance, but was resolved not to adopt their policy. He would accept them as instruments of his own will, but not as responsible ministers. If their counsels should prevail, he would himself be humiliated and disgraced.

The king identifies himself with Lord North's ministry.

In a letter to Lord North, 15th March, 1778, the king says: "Honestly, I would rather lose the crown I now wear, than bear the ignominy of possessing it under their

[1] Lord Brougham's Works, iii. 97.
[2] Chatham Corresp., iv. 243, 251.
[3] Lord Brougham's Works, iii. 130.
[4] Fox Mem., i. 115, 119.

shackles."[1] And, again, on the 17th of March, he writes: "I am still ready to accept any part of them that will come to the assistance of my present efficient ministers: but, whilst any ten men in the kingdom will stand by me, I will not give myself up to bondage. My dear Lord, I will rather risk my crown than do what I think personally disgraceful. It is impossible this nation should not stand by me. If they will not, they shall have another king, for I never will put my hand to what will make me miserable to the last hour of my life."[2] Again, on the 18th, he writes: "Rather than be shackled by those desperate men (if the nation will not stand by me), I will rather see any form of government introduced into this island, and lose my crown, rather than wear it as a disgrace."[3] The failure of these negotiations, followed by the death of Lord Chatham, left unchanged the unfortunate administration of Lord North.

The king enforces his own policy.

Overtures, indeed, were made to the Whig leaders, to join a new ministry under Lord Weymouth, which were, perhaps unwisely, declined;[4] and henceforth the king was resolved to admit none to his councils without exacting a pledge of compliance with his wishes. Thus, on the 4th February, 1779, writing to Lord North, he says: "You may now sound Lord Howe; but, before I name him to preside at the Admiralty Board, I must expect an explicit declaration that he will zealously concur in prosecuting the war in all the quarters of the globe."[5] Again, on the 22d June, 1779, he writes: "Before I will hear of any man's readiness to come into office, I will expect to see it signed under his own hand, that he is resolved to keep the empire entire, and that no troops shall consequently be withdrawn from thence (*i. e.* America), nor independence ever allowed."[6]

[1] Lord Brougham's Works, iii. 108; Fox Mem., i. 189.
[2] Lord Brougham's Works, iii. 110; Fox Mem., i. 191.
[3] Lord Brougham's Works, iii. 111; Fox Mem., i. 193.
[4] Fox Mem., i. 207; Lord J. Russell's Life of Fox, i. 193.
[5] Lord Brougham's Works, iii. 127; Fox Mem., i. 211, 212.
[6] *Ibid.*, 236.

At this time it was openly avowed in the House of Commons by Lord George Germaine, that the king was his own minister, and Mr. Fox lamented "that his Majesty was his own unadvised minister."[1] Nor was it unnatural that the king should expect such submission from other statesmen, when his first minister was carrying out a policy of which he disapproved, but wanted resolution to resist,[2] — and when Parliament had hitherto supported his ill-omened measures. In October, 1779, Lord North, writing to the king concerning the resignation of Lord Gower, who was averse to the continuance of the American war, which, in his opinion, "must end in ruin to his Majesty and the country," says: "In the argument Lord North had certainly one disadvantage, which is that he held in his heart, and has held for three years past, the same opinion as Lord Gower."[3]

Is forced to treat with the Opposition.

Again, however, the king was reduced to treat with the Opposition; but was not less resolute in his determination that no change of ministers should affect the policy of his measures. On December 3d, 1779, he was prevailed upon to give Lord Thurlow authority to open a negotiation with the leaders of the Opposition, and expressed his willingness "to admit into his confidence and service any men of public spirit and talents, who will join with part of the present ministry in forming one on a more enlarged scale, provided it be understood that every means are to be employed to keep the empire entire, to prosecute the present just and unprovoked war in all its branches, with the utmost vigor, and that his Majesty's past measures be treated with proper respect."[4] Finding the compliance of independent statesmen less ready than he desired, he writes to Lord Thurlow, 18th December, 1779: "From the cold disdain with which I am treated, it is evident to me what

[1] Dec. 4th, 1778, on Mr. Coke's motion upon Clinton's proclamation; Fox Mem., i. 203.

[2] Fox Mem., i. 211, 212.

[3] King's Letters to Lord North; Lord Brougham's Works, iii. 151.

[4] Lord Brougham's Works, iii. 139; Fox Mem., i. 237.

treatment I am to expect from Opposition, if I was to call them into my service. To obtain their support, I must deliver up my person, my principles, and my dominions into their hands."[1] In other words, the king dreaded the admission of any ministers to his councils, who claimed an independent judgment upon the policy for which they would become responsible.

Protests against the influence of the Crown, 1779-80.

In the mean time, the increasing influence of the Crown, and the active personal exercise of its prerogatives, were attracting the attention of the people and of Parliament. In the debate on the address at the opening of Parliament, 25th November, 1779, Mr. Fox said: "He saw very early indeed, in the present reign, the plan of government which had been laid down, and had since been invariably pursued in every department. It was not the mere rumor of the streets that the king was his own minister; the fatal truth was evident, and had made itself evident in every circumstance of the war carried on against America and the West Indies."[2] This was denied by ministers;[3] but evidence, not accessible to contemporaries, has since made his statement indisputable.

Early in the following year, numerous public meetings were held, associations formed, and petitions presented in favor of economic reforms; and complaining of the undue influence of the Crown, and of the patronage and corruption by which it was maintained.[4] It was for the redress of these grievances that Mr. Burke offered his celebrated scheme of economical reform. He confessed that the main object of this scheme was "the reduction of that corrupt influence, which is itself the perennial spring of all prodigality and of all disorder; — which loads us more than millions of debt; which takes away vigor from our arms, wisdom from our

[1] Lord Brougham's Works, iii. 140; Fox Mem., i. 238.

[2] Parl. Hist., xx. 1120.

[3] See the speeches of the Lord Advocate, the Secretary-at-War, and Attorney-General, *ibid.*, 1130, 1138, 1140.

[4] Parl. Hist., xx. 1370; Ann. Reg., xxiii. 85.

councils, and every shadow of authority and credit from the most venerable parts of our constitution." [1]

Mr. Dunning's resolutions, 1780.

On the 6th April, Mr. Dunning moved resolutions, in a committee of the whole House, founded upon these petitions. The first, which is memorable in political history, affirmed "that the influence of the Crown has increased, is increasing, and ought to be diminished." [2] The Lord Advocate (Mr. Dundas) endeavored to diminish the force of this resolution by the prefatory words, "that it is necessary to declare;" but Mr. Fox, on behalf of the Opposition, at once assented to this amendment, and the resolution was carried by a majority of eighteen. A second resolution was agreed to without a division, affirming the right of the House to correct abuses in the civil list expenditure, and every other branch of the public revenue; and also a third, affirming "that it is the duty of this House to provide, as far as may be, an immediate and effectual redress of the abuses complained of in the petitions presented to this House." The Opposition, finding themselves in a majority, pushed forward their success. They would consent to no delay; and these resolutions were immediately reported and agreed to by the House. This debate was signalized by the opposition speech of Sir Fletcher Norton, the Speaker, who bore his personal testimony to the increased and increasing influence of the Crown.[3] The king, writing to Lord North on the 11th April concerning these obnoxious resolutions, said: "I wish I did not feel at whom they were personally levelled." [4]

Lord Shelburne's motion on public expenditure.

The same matters were also debated, in this session, in the House of Lords. The debate on the Earl of Shelburne's motion, February 8th, for an inquiry into the public expenditure, brought out further

[1] Feb. 11th, 1780; Parl. Hist., xxi. 2 (published speech).

[2] Parl. Hist., xxi. 339.

[3] See also Chapter IV. (Civil List), and Chapter VI. (House of Commons).

[4] King's Letters to Lord North; Lord Brougham's Works, iii. 144.

testimonies to the influence of the Crown. Of these the most remarkable was given by the Marquess of Rockingham; who asserted that since the accession of the king, there had been "a fixed determination to govern this country under the forms of law, through the influence of the Crown." "Everything within and without, whether in cabinet, Parliament, or elsewhere, carried about it the most unequivocal marks of such a system: the whole economy of executive government, in all its branches, proclaimed it, whether professional, deliberative, or official. The supporters of it in books, pamphlets, and newspapers, avowed it and defended it without reserve. It was early in the present reign promulged as a court axiom, 'that the power and influence of the Crown alone was sufficient to support any set of men his Majesty might think proper to call to his councils.' The fact bore evidence of its truth; for through the influence of the Crown, majorities had been procured to support any men or any measures, which an administration, thus constituted, thought proper to dictate."[1]

Intimidation of peers.

This very motion afforded an occasion for the exercise of the prerogative in an arbitrary and offensive manner, in order to influence the votes of peers, and to intimidate opponents. The Marquess of Caremarthen and the Earl of Pembroke had resigned their offices in the household, in order to give an independent vote. Before the former had voted, he received notice that he was dismissed from the lord lieutenancy of the East Riding of the county of York;[2] and soon after the latter had recorded his vote, he was dismissed from the lord lieutenancy of Wiltshire, — an office which had been held by his family, at different times, for centuries.[3] This flagrant exercise of prerogative could not escape the notice of Parliament, and

[1] Parl. Hist., xx. 1346.

[2] *Ibid.*, 1340.

[3] His dismissal was by the personal orders of the king, who wrote to Lord North, 10th Feb., 1780: "I cannot choose the lieutenancy of Wiltshire should be in the hands of Opposition."

on the 6th March, Lord Shelburne moved an address praying the king to acquaint the House whether he had been advised, and by whom, to dismiss these peers "from their employments, for their conduct in Parliament." The motion was negatived by a large majority; but the unconstitutional acts of the king were strongly condemned in debate; and again animadversions were made upon the influence of the Crown, more especially in the administration of the army and militia.[1]

Complaints of the influence of the Crown, 1781.

On the meeting of Parliament, on the 27th November, 1781, amendments were moved in both Houses, in answer to the king's speech, which gave occasion to the expression of strong opinions regarding the influence of the Crown, and the irregular and irresponsible system under which the government of the country was conducted. The Duke of Richmond said, "that the country was governed by clerks, — each minister confining himself to his own office, — and consequently, instead of responsibility, union of opinion, and concerted measures, nothing was displayed but dissension, weakness, and corruption." The "interior cabinet," he declared, had been the ruin of this country.[2] The Marquess of Rockingham described the system of government pursued since the commencement of the reign as "a proscriptive system, — a system of favoritism and secret influence."[3] Mr. Fox imputed all the defeats and disasters of the American War to the influence of the Crown.[4]

Final overthrow of Lord North's ministry.

The king was never diverted by defeat and disaster from his resolution to maintain the war with America: but the House of Commons was now determined upon peace; and a struggle ensued which was to decide the fate of the minister, and to overcome, by the power of Parliament, the stubborn will of the king. On the 22d February, 1782, General Conway moved an address

[1] Parl. Hist., xxi. 218
[2] *Ibid.*, xxii. 651.
[3] *Ibid.*, 655.
[4] *Ibid.*, 706.

deprecating the continuance of the war, but was defeated by a majority of one.[1] On the 27th, he proposed another address with the same object. Lord North begged for a short respite: but an adjournment being refused by a majority of nineteen, the motion was agreed to without a division.[2]

On the receipt of the king's answer, General Conway moved a resolution that "the House will consider as enemies to the king and country all who shall advise, or by any means attempt, the further prosecution of offensive war, for the purpose of reducing the revolted colonies to obedience by force."[3] In reply to this proposal, Lord North astonished the House by announcing, — not that he proposed to resign on the reversal of the policy, to which he was pledged, — but that he was prepared to give effect to the instructions of the House! Mr. Fox repudiated the principle of a minister remaining in office, to carry out the policy of his opponents, against his own judgment; and General Conway's resolution was agreed to. Lord North, however, persevered with his propositions for peace, and declared his determination to retain office until the king should command him to resign, or the House should point out to him, in the clearest manner, the propriety of withdrawing.[4] No time was lost in pressing him with the latter alternative. On the 8th March, a motion of Lord John Cavendish, charging all the misfortunes of the war upon the incompetency of the ministers, was lost by a majority of ten.[5] On the 15th, Sir J. Rous moved that "the House could no longer repose confidence in the present ministers," and his motion was negatived by a majority of nine.[6] On the 20th the assault was about to be repeated, when Lord North announced his resignation.[7]

[1] Parl. Hist., xxii. 1028.
[2] *Ibid.*, 1064.
[3] 4th March. *Ibid.*, 1067.
[4] *Ibid.*, 1107.
[5] Parl. Hist., xxii. 1114.
[6] *Ibid.*, 1170.
[7] *Ibid.*, 1214.

The king had watched this struggle with great anxiety, as one personal to himself. Writing to Lord North on the 17th March, after the motion of Sir J. Rous, he said: "I am resolved not to throw myself into the hands of the Opposition at all events; and shall certainly, if things go as they seem to tend, know what my conscience as well as honor dictates, as the only way left for me."[1] He even desired the royal yacht to be prepared, and talked as if nothing were now left for him but to retire to Hanover.[2] But it had become impossible to retain any longer in his service that "confidential minister," whom he had "always treated more as his friend than minister."[3] By the earnest solicitations of the king,[4] Lord North had been induced to retain office against his own wishes: he had persisted in a policy of which he disapproved; and when forced to abandon it, he still held his ground, in order to protect the king from the intrusion of those whom his Majesty regarded as personal enemies.[5] He was now fairly driven from his post, and the king appreciating the personal devotion of his minister, rewarded his zeal and fidelity with a munificent present from the privy purse.[6]

The king's concern at the fate of his ministers.

The king's correspondence with Lord North[7] gives us a remarkable insight into the relations of his Majesty with that minister, and with the government of the country. Not only did he direct the minister in all important matters of

1 Fox Mem., i. 288; King's Letters to Lord North.

2 Fox Mem., i. 287 (Lord Holland's text).

3 King to Lord North, 2d June, 1778.

4 King's Letters to Lord North, 31st Jan., 17th, 22d, 23d, 29th and 30th March, 8th April, May 6th, 29th, &c., 1778; 30th Nov., 1779; 19th May, 1780; 19th March, 1782.

5 On the 19th March, 1782, the very day before he announced his intention to resign, the king wrote: "If you resign before I have decided what to do, you will certainly forever forfeit my regard."

6 The king, in his letter to Lord North, says: "Allow me to assist you with 10,000*l.*, 15,000*l.*, or even 20,000*l.*, if that will be sufficient." — *Lord Brougham's Life of George III.; Works*, iii. 18. Mr. Adolphus states, from private information, that the present amounted to 30,000*l.*

7 Appendix to Lord Brougham's Life of Lord North; Works, iii. 67.

foreign and domestic policy; but he instructed him as to the management of debates in Parliament, suggested what motions should be made or opposed, and how measures should be carried. He reserved to himself all the patronage,—he arranged the entire cast of the administration, — settled the relative places and pretensions of ministers of state, of law officers, and members of his household,—nominated and promoted the English and Scotch judges, — appointed and translated bishops, nominated deans, and dispensed other preferments in the Church.[1] He disposed of military governments, regiments, and commissions; and himself ordered the marching of troops.[2] He gave or refused titles, honors, and pensions.[3] All his directions were peremptory: Louis the Great himself could not have been more royal: — he enjoyed the consciousness of power, and felt himself "every inch a king."

The king's influence during Lord North's ministry.

But what had been the result of twenty years of kingcraft? Whenever the king's personal influence had been the greatest, there had been the fiercest turbulence and discontent amongst the people, the most signal failures in the measures of the Government, and the heaviest disasters to the State. Of all the evil days of England during this king's long reign, the worst are recollected in the ministries of Lord Bute, Mr. Grenville, the Duke of Grafton, and Lord North. Nor had the royal will, — however potential with ministers, — prevailed in the government of the country. He had been thwarted and humbled by his parliaments, and insulted by demagogues: parliamentary privilege, which he had sought to uphold as boldly as his own prerogative, had been defied and overcome by Wilkes and the printers: the liberty of the press, which he would

Results of the king's policy.

[1] Much to his credit, he secured the appointment of the poet Gray to the professorship of Modern History at Cambridge, 8th March, 1771.

[2] 25th October, 1775: "On the receipt of your letter, *I have ordered* Elliott's dragoons to march from Henley to Hounslow."

[3] "We must husband honors," wrote the king to Lord North on the 18th July, 1777, on refusing to make Sir W. Hamilton a privy-councillor.

have restrained, had been provoked into licentiousness; and his kingdom had been shorn of some of its fairest provinces.

Rockingham ministry, 1782.

On the retirement of Lord North, the king submitted, with a bad grace, to the Rockingham administration. He found places, indeed, for his own friends: but the policy of the cabinet was as distasteful to him as were the persons of some of the statesmen of whom it was composed. Its first principle was the concession of independence to America, which he had so long resisted; the second was the reduction of the influence of the Crown, by the abolition of offices, the exclusion of contractors from Parliament, and the disfranchisement of revenue officers.[1] Shortly after its formation, Mr. Fox, writing to Mr. Fitzpatrick (28th April, 1782), said: "Provided we can stay in long enough to give a good stout blow to the influence of the Crown, I do not think it much signifies how soon we go out after."[2] This ministry was constituted of materials not likely to unite, — of men who had supported the late ministry, and of the leaders of the parliamentary opposition, — or, as Mr. Fox expressed it, "it consisted of two parts, one belonging to the king, the other to the public."[3] Such men could not be expected to act cordially together; but they aimed their blow at the influence of the Crown by passing the Contractors' Bill, the Revenue Officers' Bill, and a bill for the reduction of offices.[4] They also suffered the former policy of the court to be stigmatized, by expunging from the journals of the House of Commons, the obnoxious resolutions which had affirmed the disability of Wilkes. A ministry promoting such measures as these, was naturally viewed with distrust and ill-will by the court. So hard was the struggle between them, that the surly Chancellor, Lord Thurlow, — who had retained his office by the express desire of the king, and voted against all the measures of the government, — af-

[1] Rockingham Mem., i. 452.

[2] Fox Mem., i. 317.

[3] Fox Mem., i. 292.

[4] See Chapter VI.

firmed that Lord Rockingham was "bringing things to a pass where either his head or the king's must go, in order to settle which of them is to govern the country."[1] The king was described by his Tory friends as a prisoner in the hands of his ministers, and represented in the caricatures of the day, as being put in fetters by his jailers.[2] In the same spirit the ministers were termed the "Regency," as if they had assumed to exercise the royal authority. In a few months, however, this ministry was on the point of breaking up, in consequence of differences of opinion and personal jealousies, when the death of Lord Rockingham dissolved it.

Lord Shelburne's ministry. 1st July, 1782.

Mr. Fox and his friends retired, and Lord Shelburne, who had represented the king in the late cabinet, was placed at the head of the new administration; while Mr. William Pitt now first entered office, though little more than twenty-three years of age, as Chancellor of the Exchequer.[3] The secession of the popular party restored the king's confidence in his ministers, who now attempted to govern by his influence, and to maintain their position against a formidable combination of parties. Horace Walpole represents Lord Shelburne as "trusting to maintain himself entirely by the king;"[4] and such was the state of parties that, in truth, he had little else to rely upon. In avowing this influence, he artfully defended it, in the spirit of the king's friends, by retorting upon the great Whig families. He would never consent, he said, "that the King of England should be a King of the Mahrattas; for among the Mahrattas the custom is, it seems, for a certain number of great lords to elect a Peishwah, who is thus the creature of the aristocracy, and is vested with the plenitude of power, while their king is, in fact, nothing more than a royal pageant."[5]

[1] Fox Mem., i. 294.
[2] Rockingham Mem., ii. 466.
[3] Tomline's Life of Pitt, i. 86.
[4] Fox Mem., ii. 11.
[5] Parl. Hist., xxii. 1003.

By breaking up parties, the king had hoped to secure his independence and to enlarge his influence; but now he was startled by a result which he had not anticipated. "*Divide et impera*" had been his maxim, and to a certain extent it had succeeded. Separation of parties had enfeebled their opposition to his government; but now their sudden combination overthrew it. When the preliminary articles of peace with America were laid before Parliament, the parties of Lord North and Mr. Fox, — so long opposed to each other, and whose political hostility had been imbittered by the most acrimonious disputes, — formed a "Coalition," and outvoted the Government in the House of Commons.[1] Overborne by numbers, the minister resigned; and the king alone confronted this powerful Coalition. The struggle which ensued was one of the most critical in our modern constitutional history. The prerogatives of the Crown on the one side, and the powers of Parliament on the other, were more strained than at any time since the Revolution. But the strong will of the king, and the courage and address of his youthful councillor, Mr. Pitt, prevailed. They carried the people with them; and the ascendency of the Crown was established for many years, to an extent which even the king himself could scarcely have ventured to hope.

Combination of parties against the king.

"The Coalition."

17th and 21st Feb., 1783.

The leaders of the Coalition naturally expected to succeed to power; but the king was resolved to resist their pretensions. He sought Mr. Pitt's assistance to form a government, and with such a minister would have braved the united forces of the Opposition. But that sagacious statesman, though not yet twenty-four years of age,[2] had taken an accurate survey of the state of parties, and of public opinion; and seeing that it was not yet the time for putting himself in the front of the battle, he resisted the solicitations of his Majesty, and the advice of his friends,

[1] Lord Auckland's Cor., i. 9, 41.

[2] Mr. Pitt was born 28th May, 1759.

in order to await a more fitting opportunity of serving the king.[1] In vain did the king endeavor once more to disunite the Coalition, by making separate proposals to Lord North and the Duke of Portland. The new confederacy was not to be shaken,—and the king found himself at its mercy. It was long, however, before he would submit. He wrote to Lord Weymouth "to desire his support against his new tyrants;"[2] and "told the Lord Advocate that sooner than yield he would go to Hanover, and had even prevailed upon the Queen to consent." From this resolution he was probably dissuaded by the rough counsels of Lord Thurlow. "Your Majesty may go," said he; "nothing is more easy; but you may not find it so easy to return, when your Majesty becomes tired of staying there." It was not until the country had been for seventeen days without a government, that the king agreed to Lord North's scheme of a Coalition ministry. But further difficulties were raised; and at length the House of Commons interposed. After several debates, in one of which Mr. Fox accused the king's secret friends of breaking off the negotiation, the House addressed his Majesty to form "an administration entitled to the confidence of his people." The address was graciously answered; but still no ministry was formed. Again the king pressed Mr. Pitt to become his premier, who again firmly and finally refused.[3] At length, after an extraordinary interval of thirty-seven days, from the 24th February to the 2d April, the Coalition Ministry was completed, under the Duke of Portland.

23d March, 1783.

24th March.

Coalition Ministry, 1783.

Such are the vicissitudes of political life, that Lord North, who for years had been the compliant and obsequious minister of the king, was now forcing his way into office, in alliance with Mr. Fox, the king's most dreaded opponent, and lately his own. While the

Efforts of the Coalition to restrain the king's influence.

1 Tomline's Life of Pitt, i. 140.
2 Fox Mem., ii. 42 (Horace Walpole).
3 Tomline's Life of Pitt, i. 150.

king was yet holding them at bay, the new friends were concerting measures for restraining his future influence. As no one had submitted to that influence so readily as Lord North, we cannot intrude into their secret conferences without a smile. Mr. Fox insisted that the king should not be suffered to be his own minister, to which Lord North replied: "If you mean there should not be a government by departments, I agree with you. I think it a very bad system. There should be one man, or a cabinet, to govern the whole, and direct every measure. Government by departments was not brought in by me. I found it so, and had not the vigor and resolution to put an end to it. The king ought to be treated with all sort of respect and attention; but the appearance of power is all that a king of this country can have. Though the government in my time was a government by departments, the whole was done by the ministers, except in a few instances."[1]

The king's opposition to his ministers.

But whatever were the views of ministers regarding the king's future authority, he himself had no intention of submitting to them. He did not attempt to disguise his repugnance to the ministry which had been forced upon him; but gave them to understand that they need expect no support from him, and that he would not create any peers upon their recommendation. He told Lord Temple "that to such a ministry he never would give his confidence, and that he would take the first moment for dismissing them."[2] The Coalition had not found favor in the country; and no pains were spared, by the king's friends, to increase its unpopularity. Meanwhile the king watched all the proceedings of his ministers with jealousy, criticised their policy, and assumed towards them an attitude of opposition. Thus, writing to Mr. Fox, who, as Secretary of State, was negotiating the peace, in August, 1783, he said: "I cannot say that I am so surprised at France not putting the last

1 Fox Mem., ii. 38.
2 Court and Cabinets of George III., i. 302.

strokes to the definitive treaty as soon as we may wish, as our having totally disarmed, in addition to the extreme anxiety shown for peace, during the whole period that has ensued, since the end of February, 1782, certainly makes her feel that she can have no reason to apprehend any evil from so slighting a proceeding."[1]

Mr. Fox's India Bill, 1783.

An opportunity soon arose for more active hostility. Mr. Fox's India Bill had been brought into the House of Commons; and, in spite of the most strenuous opposition, was being rapidly passed by large majorities. It was denounced as unconstitutional, and as an invasion of the prerogatives of the Crown; but no means had been found to stay its progress. The king now concerted with his friends a bold and unscrupulous plan for defeating the bill, and overthrowing his ministers. His name was to be used, and an active canvass undertaken by his authority, against the measure of his own ministers. Though this plan was agreed upon eight days before the bill reached the House of Lords, it was cautiously concealed. To arrest the progress of the bill in the Commons was hopeless; and the interference of the Crown, in that House, would have excited dangerous resentment. The blow was therefore to be struck in the other House, where it would have greater weight, and be attended with less danger.[2] Lord Temple, — who had suggested the plan, in concert with Lord Thurlow, and to whom its execution was intrusted, — after an audience with his Majesty, declared himself authorized to protest against the bill in the king's name. And in order to leave no doubt as to his commission, the following words were written upon a card: —

Use of the king's name against it.

"His Majesty allows Earl Temple to say, that whoever voted for the India Bill, was not only not his friend, but would be considered by him as an enemy; and if these words were not strong enough, Earl Temple might use

[1] Fox Mem., ii. 141.
[2] Court and Cabinets of George III., i. 288, 289.

whatever words he might deem stronger, and more to the purpose."[1]

With these credentials, Lord Temple proceeded to canvass the peers, — with what success was soon apparent. On the first reading, supported by Lord Thurlow and the Duke of Richmond, he gave the signal of attack. The peers assumed a threatening attitude,[2] and on the 15th December, placed the ministers in a minority, on a question of adjournment. Little secrecy or reserve was maintained by the king's friends, who took care to proclaim his Majesty's wishes. The use made of the king's name was noticed by the Duke of Portland, the Duke of Richmond, and Earl Fitzwilliam; and was not denied by Lord Temple.[3]

Mr. Fitzpatrick, writing to Lord Ossory, on the 15th December, said: "The proxies of the king's friends are arrived against the bill. The public is full of alarm and astonishment at the treachery, as well as the imprudence, of this unconstitutional interference. Nobody guesses what will be the consequences of a conduct that is generally compared to that of Charles I., in 1641."[4]

Declaration of the Commons against the use of the king's name. 17th Dec., 1783.

Before the success of the court measures was complete, the Commons endeavored to arrest them. On the 17th December, Mr. Baker, after denouncing secret advice to the Crown, against its responsible ministers, and the use of the king's name, moved a resolution, "that it is now necessary to declare, that to report any opinion, or pretended opinion, of his Majesty, upon any bill, or other proceeding, depending in either House of Parliament, with a view to influence the votes of the members, is a high crime and misdemeanor, derogatory to the honor of the Crown, — a breach of the fundamental

1 Court and Cabinets of George III., i. 288, 289; Fox Mem., ii. 253.

2 Many of them withdrew their proxies from the ministers a few hours before the meeting of the House. — *Parl. Hist.*, xxiv. 211.

3 15th Dec., 1783; Parl. Hist., xxiv. 151–160; Tomline's Life of Pitt, i. 222; Rose Corresp., i. 47; Lord Auckland's Corresp., i. 67.

4 Fox Mem., ii. 220.

privileges of Parliament, and subversive of the constitution."[1]

In vain did Mr. Pitt contend that the House could not deal with rumors, and that the hereditary councillors of the Crown had always a right to give advice to their sovereign. Mr. Fox replied in a masterly speech, full of constitutional arguments, and eloquent with indignant remonstrances.[2] The resolution was voted by a majority of 153 to 80. The House then resolved to go into committee on the state of the nation, on the following Monday. But this was not enough. It was evident that the king had determined upon a change of ministers; and lest he should also attempt to overthrow the obnoxious majority by a sudden dissolution, the House, on the motion of Mr. Erskine, agreed to a resolution affirming the necessity of considering a suitable remedy for abuses in the government of the British dominions in the East Indies; and declaring "that this House will consider as an enemy to his country, any person who shall presume to advise his Majesty to prevent, or in any manner interrupt, the discharge of this important duty."[3]

The India Bill lost, and ministers dismissed.

The strange spectacle was here exhibited, of a king plotting against his own ministers, — of the ministers inveighing against the conduct of their royal master, — of the House of Commons supporting them, and condemning the king, — and of the king defying at once his ministers and the House of Commons, and trusting to his influence with the Peers. The king's tactics prevailed. On the very day on which the Commons agreed to these strong remonstrances against his interference, it was crowned with complete success. The bill was rejected by the House

[1] Com. Journ., xxxix. 842; Parl. Hist., xxiv. 199.

[2] Mr. Fox cited the words reported to have been used by Lord Temple, and challenged a contradiction; upon which Mr. W. Grenville said, he was authorized by his noble relative to say that he had never made use of those words. This denial, as Mr. Fox observed, amounted to nothing more than that these had not been the precise words used. — *Parl. Hist.*, xxiv. 207, 225.

[3] Parl. Hist., xxiv. 226.

of Lords,[1] and the next day the king followed up his advantage, by at once dismissing his ministers.[2] To make this dismissal as contemptuous as possible, he sent a message to Lord North, and Mr. Fox, commanding them to return their seals by their under-secretaries, as an audience would be disagreeable to his Majesty.[3] Earl Temple, who had done the king this service, was intrusted with the seals for the purpose of formally dismissing the other ministers: the man who had been the king's chief agent in defeating them, was chosen to offer them this last insult.

Mr. Pitt as premier, 1783.

But the battle was not yet won. The king had struck down his ministers, though supported by a vast majority of the House of Commons: he had now to support a minister of his own choice against that majority, and to overcome it. Mr. Pitt no longer hesitated to take the post of trust and danger, which the king at once conferred upon him. His time had now come; and he resolved to give battle to an angry majority, — under leaders of great talents and experience, — smarting under defeat, — and full of resentment at the unconstitutional means by which they had been overthrown. He accepted the offices of First Lord of the Treasury and Chancellor of the Exchequer; and the king's sturdy friend, Lord Thurlow, was reinstated as Lord Chancellor. Mr. Pitt had also relied upon the assistance of Earl Temple,[4] whose zeal in the king's service was much needed in such a crisis; but that nobleman resigned the seals a few days after he had received them, assigning as his reason a desire to be free to answer any charges against him, arising out of his recent conduct.[5]

[1] 17th Dec., 1783. By a majority of 19. — *Parl. Hist.*, xxiv. 196.

[2] Mr. Fox, writing immediately afterwards, said: "We are beat in the House of Lords by such treachery on the part of the king, and such meanness on the part of his friends in the House of Lords, as one could not expect either from him or them." — *Fox Mem.*, ii. 221, 253.

[3] Annual Reg., xxvii. [71]; Tomline's Life of Pitt, i. 230.

[4] He was intended to lead the House of Lords. — *Tomline's Life of Pitt*, i. 232.

[5] Parl. Hist., xxiv. 237.

Opposition in the Commons.

The contest which the youthful premier had now to conduct, was the most arduous that had ever devolved upon any minister, since the accession of the House of Hanover. So overpowering was the majority against him, that there seemed scarcely a hope of offering it an effectual resistance. His opponents were so confident of success, that when a new writ was moved for Appleby, on his acceptance of office, the motion was received with shouts of derisive laughter.[1] And while the presumption of the boy-minister was ridiculed,[2] the strongest measures were immediately taken to deprive him of his authority, and to intimidate the court, whose policy he supported. Many of Mr. Pitt's advisers, desparing of his prospects with the present Parliament, counselled an immediate dissolution:[3] but the same consummate judgment and foresight, which, a few months earlier, had induced him to decline office, because the time was not yet ripe for action, now led him to the conviction that he must convert public opinion to his side, before he appealed to the people. Though standing alone, — without the aid of a single cabinet minister, in the House of Commons,[4] — he resolved, under every disadvantage, to meet the assaults of his opponents on their own ground; and his talents, his courage and resources ultimately won a signal victory.

Attempts to prevent a dissolution. 19th Dec., 1783.

Secure of their present majority, the first object of the Opposition was to prevent a dissolution, which they believed to be impending. The day after the dismissal of the late ministers, the Opposition insisted on the postponement of the third reading

[1] Tomline's Life of Pitt, i. 237.

[2] Pitt, to use the happy phrase of Erskine, was "hatched at once into a minister by the heat of his own ambition." — *Parl. Hist.*, xxiv. 277. In the Rolliad, his youth was thus ridiculed: —

"A sight to make surrounding nations stare, —
A kingdom trusted to a schoolboy's care."

[3] Tomline's Life of Pitt, i. 241, 242.

[4] *Ibid.*, i. 236.

of the Land-tax Bill for two days, in order, as Mr. Fox avowed, that it might not "go out of their hands until they should have taken such measures as would guard against the evils which might be expected from a dissolution."[1] On the 22d December, the House went into committee on the state of the nation, when Mr. Erskine moved an address to the Crown, representing "that alarming rumors of an intended dissolution of Parliament have gone forth;" that "inconveniences and dangers" were "likely to follow from a prorogation or dissolution of the Parliament in the present arduous and critical conjunction of affairs;" and beseeching his Majesty "to suffer his faithful Commons to proceed on the business of the session, the furtherance of which is so essentially necessary to the prosperity of the public; and that his Majesty will be graciously pleased to hearken to the advice of his faithful Commons, and not to the secret advices of particular persons, who may have private interests of their own, separate from the true interests of his Majesty and his people."[2] Notwithstanding assurances that Mr. Pitt had no intention of advising a dissolution, and would not consent to it if advised by others, the address was agreed to, and presented to the king by the whole House. In his answer the king assured them that he would "not interrupt their meeting by any exercise of his prerogative, either of prorogation or dissolution."[3] This assurance, it was observed, merely referred to the meeting of Parliament after the Christmas recess, and did not remove the apprehensions of the Opposition. On the 24th December, a resolution was agreed to, that the Treasury ought not to consent to the acceptance of any more bills from India, until it should appear to the House that there were sufficient means to meet them.[4]

[1] Parl. Hist., xxiv. 230.

[2] *Ibid.*, 246. The last paragraph of the address was taken from an address to William III. in 1693.

[3] Parl. Hist., xxiv. 264.

[4] *Ibid.*, 267.

These strong measures had been taken in Mr. Pitt's absence; and on his return to the House, after Christmas, the Opposition resumed their offensive attitude. Mr. Fox went so far as to refuse to allow Mr. Pitt to deliver a message from the king; and being in possession of the House, at once moved the order of the day for the committee on the state of the nation.

12th Jan., 1784.

In the debate which ensued, the Opposition attempted to extort a promise that Parliament should not be dissolved; but Mr. Pitt said he would not "presume to compromise the royal prerogative, or bargain it away in the House of Commons."[1] This debate was signalized by the declaration of General Ross that he had been sent for by a Lord of the Bedchamber, and told that if he voted against the new administration on the 12th January, he would be considered as an enemy to the king.[2] Being unable to obtain any pledge from the minister, the Opposition at once addressed themselves to devise effectual obstacles to an early dissolution. The House resolved itself into the committee on the state of the nation, at half-past two in the morning, — by a majority of forty against the ministers, — when Mr. Fox immediately moved a resolution, which was agreed to without a division, declaring it to be a high crime and misdemeanor to issue, after a dissolution or prorogation, money voted for any service which had not been appropriated to such service by Parliament.[3]

Resolution against issue of money unappropriated by Parliament.

He then moved for "accounts of the several sums of money issued, or ordered to be issued, from the 19th December, 1783, to the 14th January, 1784, inclusive, to any person or persons towards" naval, ordnance, army, or civil

[1] Parl. Hist., xxiv. 294.

[2] *Ibid.*, 205, 299.

[3] Com. Journ., xxxix. 858. These grants were revoted in the next Parliament, — a fact overlooked by Dr. Tomline, who states that the Appropriation Act of 1784 included the supplies of the previous session, without any opposition being offered. — *Life of Pitt*, i. 507; 24 Geo. III., Sess. ii. c. 24; *Com. Journ.*, xxxix. 733; *Ibid.*, xl. 56.

services, "or in any other manner whatever, for and towards services voted in the present session of Parliament, but not appropriated by any act of Parliament to such services." He also proposed to add, "that no moneys should be issued for any public service, till that return was made, nor for three days afterwards;" but withdrew this motion, on being assured that it would be attended with inconvenience. He further obtained the postponement of the Mutiny Bill until the 23d February, which still left time for its passing before the expiration of the Annual Mutiny Act.

These resolutions were followed by another, proposed by the Earl of Surrey, "That in the present situation of his Majesty's dominions, it is peculiarly necessary that there should be an administration which has the confidence of this House and the public." This being carried, he proceeded to another, "That the late changes in his Majesty's councils were immediately preceded by dangerous and universal reports; that his Majesty's sacred name had been unconstitutionally abused to affect the deliberations of Parliament; and that the appointments made were accompanied by circumstances new and extraordinary, and such as do not conciliate or engage the confidence of this House."

Earl of Surrey's resolutions.

All these resolutions were reported immediately and agreed to, and the House did not adjourn until half-past seven in the morning.[1]

Two days afterwards the attack was renewed. A resolution was carried in the committee, "That the continuance of the present ministers in trusts of the highest importance and responsibility, is contrary to constitutional principles, and injurious to the interests of his Majesty and his people."[2] The Opposition accused the minister of reviving the distracted times before the Revolution, when the House of Commons was generally at variance with the Crown; but he listened to

Resolutions declaring want of confidence. 14th Jan., 1784.

Jan. 23d.

[1] Parl. Hist., xxiv. 317.

[2] *Ibid.*, 361.

their remonstrances with indifference. He brought in his India Bill: it was thrown out after the second reading. Again, he was goaded to declare his intentions concerning a dissolution; but to the indignation of his opponents, he maintained silence. At length, on the 26th January, he declared that, in the present situation of affairs, he should not advise a dissolution. At the same time, he said that the appointment and removal of ministers did not rest with the House of Commons, and that as his resignation would be injurious to the public service, he still intended to retain office. The House passed a resolution affirming that they relied upon the king's assurances, that the consideration of the affairs of the East India Company should not be interrupted by a prorogation or dissolution.

Attempts to unite parties.

Meanwhile, several influential members were endeavoring to put an end to this unsettled state of affairs, by effecting an union of the ministerial and opposition parties. With this view, on the 2d February, General Grosvenor moved a resolution: "That the present arduous and critical situation of public affairs requires the exertion of a firm, efficient, extended, united administration, entitled to the confidence of the people, and such as may have a tendency to put an end to the unfortunate divisions and distractions of this country."[1] This being carried, was immediately followed by another, proposed by Mr. Coke of Norfolk: "That the continuance of the present ministers in their offices, is an obstacle to the formation of such an administration as may enjoy the confidence of this House." This, too, was agreed to, on a division.[2] As these resolutions had no more effect than any previous votes, in shaking the firmness of the minister, they were ordered, on the following day, to be laid before his Majesty.

The House of Lords now came to the aid of the king and his minister. On the 4th February, the Earl of Effingham moved two resolutions. The first, having reference to the

[1] Parl. Hist., xxiv. 451.

[2] By 223 against 204.

vote of the House of Commons on the 24th December as to the acceptance of bills from India, affirmed, "That an attempt in any one branch of the legislature to suspend the execution of law by separately assuming to itself the direction of a discretionary power, which, by an act of Parliament, is vested in any body of men, to be exercised as they shall judge expedient, is unconstitutional." The second was that "The undoubted authority of appointing to the great offices of executive government is solely vested in his Majesty; and that this House has every reason to place the firmest reliance on his Majesty's wisdom, in the exercise of this prerogative." The first was carried by a majority of forty-seven; the second was agreed to without a division. They were followed by an address to the king, assuring him of their Lordships' support in the exercise of his undoubted prerogative, and of their reliance upon his wisdom in the choice of his ministers. To this address he returned an answer, "that he had no object in the choice of ministers, but to call into his service men the most deserving of the confidence of his Parliament, and of the public in general."[1]

The House of Lords support the king.

To these proceedings the Commons replied by inspecting the Lords' Journal for their obnoxious resolutions, — by searching for precedents of the usage of Parliament, — and, finally, by declaring that the House had not assumed to suspend the execution of law; — and that they had a right to declare their opinion respecting the exercise of every discretionary power, and particularly with reference to public money. They justified their previous votes, and asserted their determination to maintain their own privileges, while they avoided any encroachment on the rights of either of the other branches of the legislature.

Retort of the Commons.

In the mean time, no answer had been returned to the resolutions which the Commons had laid before the king. When this was noticed, Mr. Pitt was silent;[2] and at length,

[1] Parl. Hist., xxiv. 525. See also Lord Auckland's Corr., i. 74.
[2] Feb. 9th; Parl. Hist., xxiv. 571.

on the 10th February, on the report of the ordnance estimates, Mr. Fox said that the House could not vote supplies, until they knew what answer they were to receive. Mr. Pitt engaged that the House should be informed what line of conduct his Majesty intended to pursue; and the report, instead of being agreed to, was recommitted. On the 18th, Mr. Pitt acquainted the House "that his Majesty had not yet, in compliance with the resolutions of the House, thought proper to dismiss his present ministers; and that his Majesty's ministers had not resigned."[1] This announcement was regarded as a defiance of the House of Commons, and again the supplies were postponed: though the leaders of the Opposition disclaimed all intention of refusing them. On the 20th, another resolution and an address were voted,[2] expressing reliance upon the royal wisdom to remove "any obstacle to the formation of such an administration as the House has declared to be requisite." The address was presented by the whole House. The king replied, that he was anxious for a firm and united administration; but that no charge had been suggested against his present ministers; that numbers of his subjects had expressed satisfaction at the late changes in his councils; and that the Commons could not expect the executive offices to be vacated, until such a plan of union as they had pointed out, could be carried into effect.[3] This answer was appointed to be considered on the 1st March, to which day the House adjourned, without entering upon any other business; and thus again the supplies were postponed. On the motion of Mr. Fox, the House then presented a further address to the king, submitting "that the continuance of an administration which does not possess the confidence of the representatives of the people,

Postponement of the supplies.

Further addresses to the king.

[1] Feb. 9th; Parl. Hist., xxiv. 595.

[2] While in the lobby, on the division on the resolution, Mr. Fox proposed to his supporters to move an address immediately afterwards, which was agreed to at five o'clock in the morning.

[3] Parl. Hist., xxiv. 677.

must be injurious to the public service," and praying for its removal. Mr. Fox maintained it to be without precedent for a ministry to hold office, in defiance of the House of Commons. Mr. Pitt retorted that the history of this country afforded no example of a ministry being called upon to retire untried, and without a cause. The king, in his reply, took up the same ground, and affirming that no charge, complaint, or specific objection had yet been made against any of his ministers, again declined to dismiss them. And thus stood the king and his ministers on one side, and the House of Commons on the other, arrayed in hostile attitude, — each party standing firmly on its constitutional rights: the one active and offensive, — the other patiently waiting to strike a decisive blow.

The Mutiny Bill was now postponed for some days, as its passing was expected to be the signal for an immediate dissolution; and one more effort was made to drive the ministers from office. On the 8th March, "a representation" to the king was moved by Mr. Fox,[1] to testify the surprise and affliction of the House on receiving his Majesty's answer to their last address, — reiterating all their previous statements, — comparing the conduct and principles of his advisers with those which characterized the unfortunate reigns of the Stuarts, — justifying the withholding of their confidence from ministers without preferring any charge, as it was their removal and not their punishment which was sought, — and taking credit to themselves for their forbearance, in not withholding the supplies.[2] This was the last struggle of the Opposition. When their encounters with the ministry began, their majority was nearly two to one. This great disproportion soon diminished, though it was still, for a time, considerable. On

Final triumph of the ministers.

[1] On this occasion strangers were excluded, at the instance of Sir James Lowther, who had failed in gaining admission to the gallery for a friend. The debate is not therefore fully reported.

[2] Parl. Hist., xxiv. 736.

the 12th January their majority was fifty-four; on the 20th February it was reduced to twenty. On the 1st March it fell to twelve: on the 5th it was only nine; and now, on this last occasion, it dwindled to one. The parliamentary contest was at an end. The king and his ministers had triumphed, and were about to appeal from Parliament to the people. The Mutiny Bill was passed, — large supplies were voted rapidly, but not appropriated: on the 24th March, Parliament was prorogued, and on the following day dissolved.

Reflections on this struggle.

While this contest was being carried on in Parliament, the contending parties were not idle out of doors. The king, who rushed into it with so much boldness, had not been prepared for the alarming demonstrations of Parliament. If the minister of his choice had now been driven from power, he would have been prostrate before the Coalition. This danger was at first imminent; and the king awaited it with dismay. Defeat in such a contest would have been humiliating and disgraceful. Believing that he could be "no longer of utility to this country, nor could with honor continue in this island," he repeated his threats of retiring to Hanover, rather than submit to what he deemed the destruction of his kingly power.[1] From such extremities, however, he was relieved by the declining numbers of his opponents, and the increasing influence and popularity of his own cause. The Coalition, though powerful in Parliament, by means of a combination of parties, had never been popular in the country. While in power they had been exposed to continual obloquy, which was redoubled after their dismissal. The new ministers and the court party, taking advantage of this feeling, represented Mr. Fox's India Bill as an audacious attempt to interfere with the prerogatives of the Crown, and its authors as enemies of the king and constitution. The loyalty of the people was aroused, and they soon ranged themselves on the side of the

[1] Tomline's Life of Pitt, i. 271, 341, 396.

king and his ministers. Addresses and other demonstrations of popular sympathy were received from all parts of the country; and the king was thus encouraged to maintain a firm attitude in front of his opponents.[1] The tactics of the two parties in Parliament, and the conduct of their leaders, were also calculated to convert public opinion to the king's side. Too much exasperated to act with caution, the Opposition ruined their cause by factious extravagance and precipitancy. They were resolved to take the king's cabinet by storm, and without pause or parley struck incessantly at the door. Their very dread of a dissolution, which they so loudly condemned, showed little confidence in popular support. Instead of making common cause with the people, they lowered their contention to a party struggle. Constitutionally the king had a right to dismiss his ministers, and to appeal to the people to support his new administration. The Opposition endeavored to restrain him in the exercise of this right, and to coerce him by a majority of the existing House of Commons. They had overstepped the constitutional limits of their power; and the assaults directed against prerogative, recoiled upon themselves.

On the other side, Mr. Pitt as minister relied upon the prerogative of the king to appoint him, — the duty of Parliament to consider his measures, — and his own right to advise the king to dissolve Parliament, if those measures were obstructed. The tact, judgment, courage, and commanding talents of Mr. Pitt inspired his party with confidence, and secured popularity for his cause; while, by maintaining a defensive attitude, he offered no diversion to the factious tactics of his opponents. His accession to office had been immediately marked by the defection of several members

[1] Writing to Mr. Pitt, 22d Feb., in reference to his answer to the address of the 20th, the king said: "I trust that while the answer is drawn up with civility, it will be a clear support of my own rights, which the addresses from all parts of the kingdom show me the people feel essential to their liberties." — *Tomline's Life of Pitt*, i. 457.

from the Opposition, — a circumstance always calculated upon by a minister in those times, — and was soon followed by the forbearance of others, who were not prepared to participate in the violent measures of their leaders. The influence of the court and Government was strenuously exerted in making converts; and the growing popularity of their cause discouraged the less zealous of their opponents.

Mr. Pitt had waited patiently while the majorities against him in Parliament were falling away, and public opinion was declaring itself, more and more, in his favor. The results of the dissolution now revealed the judgment with which he had conducted his cause, and chosen his time for appealing to the people.[1] Every preparation had been made for using the influence of the Crown at the elections, — the king himself took the deepest personal interest in the success of the ministerial candidates;[2] and Mr. Pitt's popularity was at its height, when Parliament was dissolved. His enemies were everywhere put to the rout, at the hustings. To support Mr. Pitt was the sole pledge of the popular candidates. Upwards of one hundred and sixty of his late opponents lost their seats;[3] and on the assembling of the new Parliament, he could scarcely reckon his majorities.[4] The minister was popular in the country, all-powerful in Parliament, and had the entire confidence of the court. If such was the success of the minister, what was the triumph of the king! He had

1 "The precedent of 1784 establishes this rule of conduct: that if the ministers chosen by the Crown do not possess the confidence of the House of Commons, they may advise an appeal to the people, with whom rests the ultimate decision. This course has been followed in 1807, in 1831, in 1834, and in 1841. In 1807 and 1831, the Crown was enabled, as in 1784, to obtain the confidence of the New House of Commons. In 1834 and 1841, the decision was adverse to the existing ministry." — *Lord John Russell's Memorials of Fox*, ii. 246.

2 Rose Corresp., i. 61, 62.

3 Tomline's Life of Pitt, i. 469.

4 His India Bill was carried by a majority of 271 to 60. He was defeated, however, on the Westminster Scrutiny, Parliamentary Reform, and the Scheme of Fortifications on the Coast.

expelled one ministry, and retained another, in defiance of the House of Commons. The people had pressed forward loyally to his support; and by their aid he had overborne all opposition to his will. He now possessed a strong government, and a minister in whom he confided; and he enjoyed once more power, freedom, and popularity. Not only had he overcome and ruined a party which he hated; but he had established the ascendency of the Crown, which henceforth, for nearly fifty years, continued to prevail over every other power in the state.

Its results upon the future policy of the state.

Such results, however, were not without danger. Already the king was too prone to exercise his power; and the encouragement he had received, was likely to exalt his views of prerogative. But he had now a minister who — with higher abilities and larger views of state policy — had a will even stronger than his own. Throughout his reign, it had been the tendency of the king's personal administration to favor men whose chief merit was their subservience to his own views, instead of leaving the country to be governed, — as a free state should be governed, — by its ablest and most popular statesmen.[1] He had only had one other minister of the same lofty pretensions, — Lord Chatham; and now, while trusting that statesman's son, — sharing his councils, and approving his policy, — he yielded to his superior intellect. Yet were the Royal predilections not without influence on the minister. Reared in the Whig school, Mr. Pitt soon deserted the principles, as he had been severed from the connections, of that party. He had been raised to power by royal favor, — maintained in it by prerogative, — and he was now in the ascendant, by having made common cause with the Crown. Hence he naturally leant towards prerogative, and Tory principles of government. His contests with his great antagonist, Mr. Fox, and the Whig party, still further alienated him from the principles of his youth. Until the

Relations of Mr. Pitt to the king.

[1] See Lord J. Russell's Introd. to vol. iii. of the Duke of Bedford's Correspondence, pp. l.–lxii.

French Revolution, however, his policy was wise and liberal: but from that time his rule became arbitrary, and opposed to public liberty. And such were his talents, and such the temper of the times, that he was able to make even arbitrary principles popular. During his long administration the people were converted to Tory principles, and encouraged the king and the minister to repress liberty of thought, and to wage war against opinion. If the king was no longer his own minister, — as in the time of Lord North, — he had the satisfaction of seeing his own principles carried out by hands far abler than his own. In prosecutions of the press,[1] and the repression of democratic movements at home,[2] the minister was, perhaps, as zealous as the king: in carrying on war to crush democracy abroad, the king was more zealous than his minister. They labored strenuously together in support of monarchy all over the world; and respected too little the constitutional liberties of their own people.

The king's continued activity.

Nor did the king relax his accustomed activity in public affairs. From the close of the American War until the breaking out of hostilities with France, his pleasure was taken by the Secretary-at-War upon every commission granted in the army; and throughout Mr. Pitt's administration, — and, indeed, as long as His Majesty was capable of attending to business, — every act and appointment was submitted to him, for his judgment and approval.[3]

The influence of the Crown augmented.

And if, during the administration of Mr. Pitt, the king's independent exercise of influence was somewhat less active, the power of the Crown itself, — as wielded jointly by himself and his minister, — was greater than at any former period. The king and his minister were now absolute. A war is generally favorable to authority, by bringing together the people and the Gov-

[1] See Chapter VIII., Press and Liberty of Opinion.

[2] See Chapter IX., Liberty of the Subject.

[3] Mr. Wynn, 14th April, 1812; Hans. Deb., xxii. 334.

ernment, in a common cause and combined exertions. The French War, notwithstanding its heavy burdens and numerous failures, was popular on account of the principles it was supposed to represent; and the vast expenditure, if it distressed the people, multiplied the patronage of the Crown, — afforded a rich harvest for contractors, — and made the fortunes of farmers and manufacturers, by raising the price of every description of produce. The "moneyed classes" rallied round the war minister, — bought seats in Parliament with their sudden gains, — ranged themselves in a strong phalanx behind their leader, — cheered his speeches, and voted for him on every division. Their zeal was rewarded with peerages, baronetcies, patronage, and all the good things which an inordinate expenditure enabled him to dispense. For years, opposition in Parliament to a minister thus supported, was an idle form; and if beyond its walls, the voice of complaint was raised, the arm of the law was strong and swift to silence it.[1] To oppose the minister, had become high-treason to the state.

The king still prepared to use his influence against his ministers.

Great as was the king's confidence in a minister so powerful as Mr. Pitt, yet whenever their views of policy differed, the king's resolution was as inflexible as ever. Nor were his ministers secure from the exercise of his personal influence against them, when he was pleased to use it. The first measure on which Mr. Pitt was likely to encounter objections from the king, was that for Parliamentary Reform. Having pledged himself to the principles of such a measure, while in opposition, he was determined not to be unfaithful to them now. But before he ventured to bring forward his plan, he prudently submitted it to the king, and deprecated the opposition of the court. Writing, on the 20th March, 1785, the king said, Mr. Pitt's "letter expressed that there is but one issue of the business he could look upon as fatal, that is, the possibility of the measure being rejected by the weight of

[1] See Chapter VIII., Press and Liberty of Opinion.

those who are supposed to be connected with the Government. Mr. Pitt must recollect that though I have ever thought it unfortunate that he had early engaged himself in this measure, he ought to lay his thoughts before the House; that out of personal regard to him I would avoid giving any opinion to any one on the opening of the door to Parliamentary Reform, except to him; therefore I am certain Mr. Pitt cannot suspect my having influenced any one on the occasion. If others choose, for base ends, to impute such a conduct to me, I must bear it as former false suggestions."[1] He proceeded to say that every man ought to vote according to his own opinion; and warned Mr. Pitt that "there are questions men will not, by friendship, be biassed to adopt." This incident is significant. Mr. Pitt apprehended the exertion of the influence of the Crown to defeat his measure. The king was aware of the suspicions attaching to himself; but while promising not to interfere, he could not refrain from intimating that the measure would be defeated, — as indeed it was, — without his interference.

Preponderating influence of the Crown.

The extent to which the preponderating influence of the Crown was recognized during this period, is exemplified by the political relations of parties to his Majesty and to the Prince of Wales, on the occasion of the king's illness in 1788.[2] At that time ministers enjoyed the entire confidence of the king, and commanded an irresistible majority in Parliament; yet was it well understood by both parties, that the first act of the Regent would be to dismiss his father's ministers, and take into his councils the leaders of the Opposition.[3] Thus even the party which protested against the influence of the Crown was quite prepared to use it, and by its aid to brave a hostile majority in Parliament, as Mr. Pitt had successfully done a few years before.

[1] Tomline's Life of Pitt, ii. 40.
[2] See Chapter III.
[3] Tomline's Life of Pitt, ii. 480.

At length Mr. Pitt's fall itself, like his rise, was due to the king's personal will; and was brought about in the same way as many previous political events, by irresponsible councils. There is reason to believe that Mr. Pitt's unbending temper, — increased in stubbornness by his long-continued supremacy in Parliament, and in the cabinet, — had become distasteful to the king.[1] His Majesty loved power at least as much as his minister, and was tenacious of his authority, even over those in whom he had confidence. Mr. Pitt's power had nearly overshadowed his own; and there were not wanting opinions amongst friends of the king, and rivals of the statesman, that the latter had "an overweening ambition, great and opiniative presumption, and perhaps not quite constitutional ideas with regard to the respect and attention due to the Crown."[2]

Mr. Pitt's fall.

While this feeling existed in regard to Mr. Pitt, his Majesty was greatly agitated by events which at once aroused his sensitive jealousy of councils to which he had not been admitted, and his conscientious scruples. Mr. Pitt and his colleagues thought it necessary to inaugurate the Union of Ireland, by concessions to the Roman Catholics;[3] and had been, for some time, deliberating upon a measure to effect that object. Upon this question, the king had long entertained a very decided opinion. So far back as 1795, he had consulted Lord Kenyon as to the obligations of his coronation oath; and though his lordship's opinions were not quite decisive upon this point,[4] his Majesty was persuaded that he was morally restrained, by that oath, from assenting

Catholic Question, 1801.

The king's determined opposition to it.

[1] 27th Feb., 1801. "I was told this evening, by Pelham, that his Majesty had for a long time since been dissatisfied with Pitt's, and particularly with Lord Grenville's 'authoritative manners' towards him, and that an alteration in his ministry had long been in his mind." — *Lord Malmesbury's Correspondence*, iv. 24.

[2] Lord Malmesbury's Correspondence, iv. 35.

[3] See Chapter XII., on Civil and Religious Liberty.

[4] They were published by Dr. Phillpotts (afterwards Bishop of Exeter) in 1827.

to any further measures for the relief of the Roman Catholics. Long before the ministers had so far matured their proposal as to be prepared to submit it for his Majesty's approval, he had been made acquainted with their intentions. In September, 1800, Lord Loughborough had shown him a letter from Mr. Pitt upon the subject; and the Archbishop of Canterbury, at the suggestion of Lord Auckland, had also informed the king that a scheme was in contemplation, which was represented as dangerous to the Church.[1] In December, the Lord Chancellor communicated to his Majesty an elaborate paper against the Roman Catholic claims;[2] and Dr. Stuart, Archbishop of Armagh, — a son of the king's old favorite, Lord Bute, — increased his Majesty's repugnance to the measure which the ministers were preparing.[3] The king immediately took counsel with some of the opponents of the Catholic claims; and without waiting for any communication from Mr. Pitt, lost no time in declaring his own opinion upon the measure. At his levée on the 28th January, 1801, he told Mr. Windham, the Secretary-at-War, "that he should consider any person who voted for it, as personally indisposed towards him."[4] On the same occasion he said to Mr. Dundas, "I shall reckon any man my personal enemy, who proposes any such measure. The most Jacobinical thing I ever heard of!"[5] On the 29th, he wrote to Mr. Addington, the Speaker, desiring him to "open Mr. Pitt's eyes on the danger arising from the agitat-

[1] Lord Sidmouth's Life, i. 315; Lord Malmesbury's Corresp., iv. 16, 17, 22.

[2] Lord Campbell's Lives of the Chancellors, vi. 306, 322, *et seq.*; Rose's Corresp., i. 299.

[3] Castlereagh's Corresp., iv. 83.

[4] Lord Malmesbury's Corresp., iv. 2. His Lordship in relating this circumstance, states that Pitt had communicated the measure on the previous day; but it appears from Lord Sidmouth's Life, that this communication was not received by the king until Sunday the 1st Feb., though Lord Grenville and Mr. Dundas had already spoken to his Majesty upon the subject. — *Life*, i. 285, 287.

[5] Wilberforce's Diary; Life, iii. 7; Court and Cabinets of Geo. III., iii. 126; Life of Lord Sidmouth, i. 280; Rose's Corresp., i. 303.

ing this improper question."[1] Mr. Addington undertook this commission, and thought he had dissuaded Mr. Pitt from proceeding with a measure, to which the king entertained insuperable objections.[2] But if at first inclined to yield, Mr. Pitt, after consulting the cabinet and other political friends, determined to take his stand, as a responsible minister, upon the advice he was about to tender to the king.

Mr. Canning is said to have advised Mr. Pitt not to give way on this occasion. It was his opinion, "that for several years so many concessions had been made, and so many important measures overruled, from the king's opposition to them, that Government had been weakened exceedingly; and if on this particular occasion a stand was not made, Pitt would retain only a nominal power, while the real one would pass into the hands of those who influenced the king's mind and opinion, out of sight."[3]

Mr. Pitt refuses to abandon it, and resigns.

Whether sharing this opinion or not, Mr. Pitt himself was too deeply impressed with the necessity of the measure, and perhaps too much committed to the Catholics, to withdraw it. It appears, however, that he might have been induced to give way, if he could have obtained an assurance from his Majesty, that ministers should not be opposed by the king's friends in Parliament.[4] On the 1st February, he made the formal communication to the king, which his Majesty had, for several days, been expecting. The king had been aware of Mr. Pitt's determination before he received this letter, and had wished Mr. Addington, even then, to form a new administration. By Mr. Addington's advice a kind but most unbending answer was returned to Mr. Pitt, in which his Majesty declared that a "principle of duty must prevent him from *discussing* any proposition tending to destroy the

1 The king to Mr. Addington; Life of Lord Sidmouth, i. 286, 287.
2 Life of Lord Sidmouth, i. 287.
3 Malmesbury's Corresp., iv. 5.
4 Rose's Corresp., i. 394, 399.

groundwork of our happy constitution."[1] The intensity of the king's feeling on the subject was displayed by what he said, about this time, to the Duke of Portland: "Were he to agree to it, he should betray his trust, and forfeit his crown; that it might bring the framers of it to the gibbet." His trusty counsellor replied: "he was sure the king had rather suffer martyrdom, than submit to this measure."[2] In vain did Mr. Addington endeavor to accommodate these differences. Mr. Pitt, being as inflexible as the king, resigned; and Mr. Addington was intrusted with the task of forming an anti-Catholic administration; while an active canvass was undertaken by the courtiers against the Catholic cause, as a matter personal to the king himself.[3]

Mr. Pitt's mismanagement of the Catholic question.

Mr. Pitt has been justly blamed for having so long concealed his intentions from the king. His Majesty himself complained to Lord Grenville, that the question had been under consideration since the month of August, though never communicated to him till Sunday, the 1st February; and stated his own belief, that if the unfortunate cause of disunion had been openly mentioned to him "in the beginning, he should have been able to avert it entirely."[4] Whether this delay arose, as Lord Malmesbury has suggested, "either from indolence," or from want of a "sufficient and due attention to the king's pleasure,"[5] it was assuredly a serious error of judgment. It cannot, indeed, be maintained that it was Mr. Pitt's duty to take his Majesty's pleasure, before any bill had been agreed upon by the cabinet; but his reticence,

[1] The king to Mr. Pitt, 1st Feb., 1801; Lord Sidmouth's Life, i. 291. All the correspondence between the king and Mr. Pitt is published in Dr. Phillpotts's Pamphlet, 1827, and in the Quarterly Review, xxxvi. 290, and part of it in Lord Sidmouth's Life; Rose's Corresp., ii. 286, *et seq.*, 303, 309.

[2] Lord Malmesbury's Corresp., iv. 46.

[3] *Ibid.*, iv. 6; Castlereagh's Corresp., iv. 34; Court and Cabinets of Geo. III., iii. 128; Mem. of Fox, iii. 252; Life of Lord Sidmouth, i. 85, &c.

[4] King to Lord Sidmouth, Feb. 7th; Lord Sidmouth's Life, i. 298.

[5] Lord Malmesbury's Corresp., iv. 2.

upon the general question, aroused the suspicions of the king, and gave those who differed from the minister an opportunity of concerting an opposition at court.[1]

His subsequent pledge not to revive.

Resolute as was Mr. Pitt on this occasion, yet being deeply affected, a few weeks afterwards, by hearing that the king had imputed his illness to the recent conduct of his minister, he conveyed an assurance to his Majesty, that he would not revive the Catholic question.[2]

The king's confidence in Mr. Addington.

Mr. Addington enjoyed the confidence, and even the affection of the king, whose correspondence at this period resembles, — both in its minute attention to every department of business, foreign or domestic,[3] and in its terms of attachment — his letters to his former favorite, Lord North.[4]

The king was rejoiced to find himself free from the restraints which the character and position of Mr. Pitt had imposed upon him; and delighted to honor the minister of his own choice, — who shared his feelings and opinions, — who consulted him on all occasions, — whose amiable character and respectful devotion touched his heart, — and whose in-

1 Lord Malmesbury's Corresp., iv. 2; Rose's Corresp., i. 308.

2 Lord Malmesbury's Corresp., iv. 34; Gifford's Life of Pitt, vi. 599; Rose's Correspondence, i. 394.

3 Lord Sidmouth's Life, i. 365, 387, 395, 410, 411.

4 Lord Sidmouth's Life, i. 301, 303. On the 13th Feb., 1801, the king writes: "I mean to have his affection as well as his zeal." — *Ibid.*, 305. On the 5th March, he writes: "The king cannot find words sufficiently expressive of his Majesty's cordial approbation of the whole arrangements which *his own Chancellor of the Exchequer* has wisely, and his Majesty chooses to add, most correctly recommended." — *Ibid.*, 353. Again, on the 19th May, and on other occasions, he terms Mr. Addington "*his* Chancellor of the Exchequer." — *Ibid.*, 394. Sometimes he addresses him as "My dear Chancellor of the Exchequer." — *Ibid.*, 395. On the 14th June, he writes: "The king is highly gratified at the repeated marks of the sensibility of Mr. Addington's heart, which must greatly add to the comfort of having placed him with so much propriety at the head of the Treasury. He trusts their mutual affection can only cease with their lives." — *Ibid.*, 408. On the 8th July, he writes: "The messenger who returned from Cuffnals, agreeable to order, called at Winchester that Mr. Addington might hear of his son." — *Ibid.*, 428.

tellect was not so commanding as to overpower and subdue his own.

Mr. Pitt restored to power, 1804.

But this administration, — formed under circumstances unfavorable to its stability, and beset, from its very commencement, with jealousies and intrigues,[1] — after concluding a peace with France, prepared the way, in less than three years, for Mr. Pitt's restoration to power. It was not without reluctance that the king found himself obliged to part with his favorite minister, and to submit himself again to the loftier temper of Mr. Pitt: but he was convinced of the impracticability of upholding any longer the administration of Mr. Addington.[2]

The king's refusal to admit Mr. Fox.

Mr. Pitt urged upon the king the necessity of forming a strong government, by a union with Lord Grenville and Mr. Fox; but such was his Majesty's repugnance to the latter, that he absolutely refused to admit him into the cabinet.[3] So inveterate was his aversion to this statesman, — aggravated, at this period, by mental disorder, — that he afterwards declared "that he had taken a positive determination not to admit Mr. Fox into his councils, *even at the hazard of a civil war*."[4] Mr. Fox being proscribed, the Opposition would listen to no propositions for an arrangement;[5] and Mr. Pitt was obliged to place himself at the head of an administration, weak in talents as well as in parliamentary support.

Lord Sidmouth's relations to the king and the ministers.

Meanwhile, Mr. Addington took up a position in the House of Commons, as leader of the "king's friends," — a party numbering sixty or seventy members.[6] He was still supposed to be in communication with the king;[7] and his supporters were some-

1 Lord Sidmouth's Life, i. 335–340; ii. 107, 117, &c. &c.; Lord Malmesbury's Corresp., iv. 36, 40, 42, 49, 91, 97, 102, 167, 297, &c. &c.; Rose's Corresp., i. 292, 317, 329, 449; ii. 52.

2 Twiss's Life of Eldon, i. 437–450. See also infra, p. 170.

3 Twiss's Life of Eldon, i. 446–450; Rose's Corresp., ii. 118, 122.

4 Rose's Corresp., ii. 156, 182.

5 *Ibid.*, 124–126; Court and Cabinets of Geo. III., iii. 352; Mem. of Fox, iv. 53.

6 Rose's Corr., 119.

7 *Ibid.*, 141.

times ranged against the Government.[1] He professed personal adherence to the king to be the rule of his political conduct. Writing soon after his retirement from office, he says: "I shall keep aloof from all parties, *adhere to the king*, and take a course that I can conscientiously justify to myself." [2] His attitude was so formidable, that Mr. Pitt was soon obliged to admit him and his followers to a share of the government.[3] The king earnestly desired his union with Mr. Pitt,[4] which the renewal of friendly intercourse between them easily brought about. He accordingly joined the administration, as Viscount Sidmouth, and President of the Council; and induced his friends, who had been lately voting against the Government, to lend it their parliamentary support. But being dissatisfied with the share of influence conceded to himself and his allies in the cabinet, he shortly afterwards threatened to resign.[5] And when, on the impeachment of Lord Melville, Mr. Hiley Addington, and Mr. Bond, who had been promised places, spoke and voted against the Government, differences arose between himself and Mr. Pitt, which led to his resignation.[6]

Evasion of the Catholic Question by Mr. Pitt.

Meanwhile, the only matter on which Mr. Pitt and the king were at variance, was not suffered again to disturb their friendly relations. Mr. Pitt had renewed the assurance which he had given the king in 1801, that he would not revive the question of Catholic emancipation, during his Majesty's life.[7] Not satisfied with this assurance, the king required "an explicit declaration that he would *never*, at any time, agitate or support the question of Catholic emancipation, or the repeal of the Test Act." [8] This latter pledge Mr. Pitt, it would seem, contrived to

[1] Rose's Corr., 153.

[2] Lord Sidmouth's Life, ii. 315.

[3] Court and Cabinets of Geo. III., iii. 388; Lord Sidmouth's Life, ii. 325, 348.

[4] Lord Sidmouth's Life, ii.

[5] Rose's Corresp., ii. 358, 360–364.

[6] *Ibid.*, 368–375.

[7] *Ibid.*, 114, 157–174.

[8] *Ibid.*, 117.

evade;[1] but he was careful to avoid the forbidden ground, and was even obliged to oppose others who ventured to trespass upon it.[2] Though Mr. Pitt recovered the king's confidence, his Majesty continued to form his own independent opinions, and to exercise a large influence in the government and patronage of the State.[3]

Grenville ministry, 1806.

The death of Mr. Pitt, in the midst of defeats, and disasters to the European cause in which he was engaged, once more forced upon the king an administration, formed from a party in whom he had no confidence. It was necessary to accept the ministry of "all the talents," under Lord Grenville and Mr. Fox;[4] and personal intercourse soon overcame the king's antipathy to the latter.[5] Lord Sidmouth having a strong body of parliamentary friends, who, to use the words of his biographer, "constituted a species of armed neutrality, far too powerful to be safely overlooked," and being "understood to enjoy the favor and confidence of the king, and to be faithfully devoted to his Majesty's interests,"[6] was induced to join a party with whom he had neither connection, nor political sympathies. The king's friends were not to be neglected, and were amply provided for.[7] Lord Sidmouth himself, "not wishing to excite jealousy by very frequent intercourse with the king," declined the Presidency of the Council, and accepted the less prominent office of Privy Seal.[8]

1 Lord Sidmouth's Life, ii. 464.

2 Hans. Parl. Deb., v. 1013; see also Chap. XII., on Civil and Religious Liberty.

3 Rose's Corresp., ii. 122, 124, 141, 158, 160. Mr. Pitt was anxious that his friend and biographer, Dr. Tomline, Bishop of Lincoln, should be promoted to the See of Canterbury; but the king insisted upon appointing Dr. Manners Sutton, Bishop of Norwich, notwithstanding all the solicitations of his minister. — *Rose's Corresp.*, ii. 82–91, &c.

4 Rose's Corresp., ii. 236.

5 Twiss's Life of Eldon, i. 510.

6 Lord Sidmouth's Life, ii. 412.

7 *Ibid.*, 424.

8 *Ibid.*, 416; Mr. Abbot's Diary, 424. On the death of Mr. Fox he became President of the Council.

Admission of Lord Ellenborough to the cabinet.

As there was a difficulty in admitting any of Lord Sidmouth's political friends to the cabinet, Lord Ellenborough, the Lord Chief Justice of the Court of King's Bench, was associated with him, in order to give weight to his counsels.[1] This arrangement was open to grave constitutional objections. It had been the policy of our laws to render the judges independent of the Crown;[2] and now the first criminal judge became one of its confidential advisers. Though the appointment was successfully defended in Parliament, where the precedent of Lord Mansfield was much relied on, it was generally condemned by public opinion, and no similar appointment has since been made.[3]

Difference with the king on the administration of the army.

Before the new ministry was completed, the king was alarmed at a supposed invasion of his prerogative. On the 1st February, Lord Grenville proposed to his Majesty some changes in the administration of the army, by which the question was raised whether the army should be under the immediate control of the Crown, through the Commander-in-Chief, or be subject to the supervision of ministers. The king at once said that the management of the army rested with the Crown alone; and that he could not permit his ministers to interfere with it, beyond the levying of the troops, their pay and clothing. Lord Grenville was startled at such a doctrine, which he conceived to be entirely unconstitutional, and to which he would have refused to submit. For some time it was believed that the pending ministerial arrangements would be broken off; but on the following day Lord Grenville presented a minute to his Majesty, stating that no changes in

1 Wilberforce's Life, iii. 256. Lord Rous said: "Lord Sidmouth, with Lord Ellenborough by his side, put him in mind of a faithful old steward with his mastiff, watching new servants, lest they should have some evil designs against the old family mansion." — *Lord Sidmouth's Life*, ii. 417.

2 13 Will. III. c. 32; 1 Geo. III. c. 23.

3 Hans. Deb., vi. 308; Lord Campbell's Lives of Chief Justices, ii. 451; Lives of the Chancellors, vi. 584; Lord Sidmouth's Life, ii. 417; Chapter on Administration of Justice.

the management of the army should be effected without his Majesty's approbation.[1] To the doctrine thus amended, there could be no reasonable objection, and the king assented to it.

Differences with the king on the Army and Navy Service Bill.

The Grenville ministry fell, like that of Mr. Pitt in 1801, by proposing a measure affecting the king's religious scruples. As all the circumstances regarding this measure will be described elsewhere,[2] it is sufficient here to say that on proposing the Army and Navy Service Bill, — by which some of the disqualifications of officers in the army and navy, being Roman Catholics and Dissenters, were removed, — the ministers either neglected to explain its provisions with sufficient distinctness to the king, or failed to make themselves understood. After the bill had been introduced, as they believed, with his "reluctant assent," his Majesty's distaste for it became inflamed into violent disapprobation. To propose such a measure at all, was a strange indiscretion. Knowing the king's repugnance to every concession to the Catholics, they might have profited by the experience of Mr. Pitt. The Chancellor foresaw the danger they were incurring, and with Lord Ellenborough and Lord Sidmouth, protested against the measure. The friends of the Government called it an act of suicide.[3]

Activity of the king's friends.

The king's friends, and the opponents of the ministry, did not neglect this favorable opportunity of turning his Majesty's well-known religious scruples to account; but soon directed his personal influence against his ministers. On the 4th March, Lord Sidmouth "apprised his Majesty of the nature and details of the measure;"[4] said he should himself oppose it; and soon afterwards tendered his resignation to Lord Gren-

[1] Ann. Reg., 1806, 26; Lord Sidmouth's Life, ii. 416.
[2] Chapter XII., on Civil and Religious Liberty.
[3] Lord Malmesbury's Corresp., iv. 381–384.
[4] Lord Sidmouth's Life, ii. 459–462.

ville. On the 12th, the Duke of Portland wrote to the king, expressing his belief that the measure had not received his Majesty's consent, and that it could be defeated in the House of Lords. "But for this purpose," said his grace, "I must fairly state to your Majesty, that your wishes must be distinctly known, and that your present ministers should not have any pretext for equivocating upon the subject, or any ground whatever to pretend ignorance of your Majesty's sentiments and determination, not only to withhold your sanction from the present measure, but to use all your influence in resisting it."[1] Writing on the same day, his grace said: "His Majesty has signified his orders to my nephews, Lords George and James Thynne, to vote against it."[2] On the following day a person came to Lord Malmesbury from the Queen's house, authorized to say, "that his Majesty's wishes, sentiments, and intentions, respecting every measure which may lead to alter the legal restrictions the Catholics are liable to, are invariably the same as they always have been, and always will be so."[3] The king himself also intimated to Lord Grenville, that "he should certainly think it right to make it known that his sentiments were against the measure."[4]

Hence it appears that courtiers and intriguing statesmen were still as ready as they had been twenty-five years before, to influence the king against his ministers, and to use his name for the purpose of defeating measures in Parliament; while the king himself was not more scrupulous in committing himself to irregular interference with the freedom of parliamentary deliberations. On this occasion, however, opposition to the ministry in Parliament by the king's friends, was averted by the withdrawal of the measure. On announcing its abandonment

Withdrawal of the obnoxious bill.

1 Lord Malmesbury's Corresp., v. 369.

2 *Ibid.*, 371.

3 *Ibid.*, 373.

4 Letter to Mr. T. Grenville, 14th March, 1807 (Court and Cabinets of Geo. III., iv. 135).

to the king, the ministers committed a second indiscretion. They reserved to themselves, by a minute of the cabinet, the right of openly avowing their sentiments, should the Catholic Petition be presented, and of submitting to his Majesty, from time to time, such measures as they might deem it advisable to propose.[1] The king not only desired them to withdraw this part of the minute, but demanded from them a written declaration that they would never, under any circumstances, propose to him further concessions to the Catholics, or even offer him advice upon the subject.[2] To such a pledge it was impossible for constitutional ministers to submit. They were responsible for all public measures, and for the good government of the country; and yet, having abandoned a measure which they had already proposed, they were now called upon to fetter their future discretion, and to bind themselves irrevocably to a policy which they thought dangerous to the peace of Ireland. The king could scarcely have expected such submission. The ministers refused the pledge, and the king proceeded to form a new administration under Mr. Perceval. He had regarded this contest with his ministers as "a struggle for his throne;" saying, "he must be the Protestant king of a Protestant country, or no king."[3]

Pledge proposed by the king, and removal of the ministers.

In the Commons, the dismissal of the Government on these grounds, and the constitutional dangers involved in such an exercise of the prerogative, did not pass without animadversion. On the 9th April, Mr. Brand moved a resolution, "That it is contrary to the first duties of the confidential servants of th Crown to restrain themselves by any pledge, expressed or implied, from offering to the king any advice which the course of circumstances may render necessary for the welfare

Proceedings in the Commons on the change of ministry, 1807.

1 Hans. Deb., ix. 231–247; Life of Lord Sidmouth, ii. 463; Lord Malmesbury's Corresp., iv. 380; Rose's Corresp., ii. 321–327.

2 Hans. Deb., ix. 243; Lord Sidmouth's Life, ii. 464; Rose's Correspondence, ii. 328–331.

3 Twiss's Life of Lord Eldon, ii. 34.

and security of the empire." In the debate it was argued, that as the king was not responsible by law, if the ministers should also claim to be absolved from responsibility, by reason of pledges given to the king, there would be no security for the people against the evils of bad government. Had the ministers agreed to such a pledge, they would have violated their oaths as privy-councillors, and the king would have become absolute. To what dangers would the country be exposed if ministers might bind themselves to give such advice only as should be agreeable to the sovereign?[1] Nor did the conduct of secret advisers escape notice, who had counteracted the measures of the public and responsible advisers of the Crown.[2] On the other side it was contended that the stipulation proposed by the ministers, of being at liberty to support in debate a measure which they had withdrawn, — and of which the king disapproved, — was unconstitutional, as tending to place the king in direct opposition to the Parliament, — an evil which was ordinarily avoided by the ministers refraining from supporting any measure to which the king might hereafter have to give his *veto*. The late ministers were even charged with having, in the explanation of the causes of their retirement, arraigned their sovereign at the bar of Parliament.[3] Mr. Perceval denied that the king had conferred with any secret advisers until after the ministers were dismissed; and said that, in requiring the pledge, he had acted without any advice whatever. The ministers, he declared, had brought upon themselves the pledge proposed by the king, which would never have been suggested, had they not desired to impose conditions upon his Majesty.

Sir Samuel Romilly went so far as to maintain that if ministers had subscribed such a pledge, they would have

[1] See also Chapter XII., on Civil and Religious Liberty.
[2] Mr. Plunkett, Hans. Deb., ix. 312.
[3] General Craufurd, Hans. Deb., ix. 299; Mr. Perceval, *ib.*, 316; Mr. Bathurst, *ib.*, 331; Mr. Canning, *ib.*, 342.

been guilty of a high crime and misdemeanor.[1] With regard to Mr. Perceval's statement, that the king had acted without advice, Sir Samuel said, that there could be no exercise of prerogative in which the king was without some adviser. He might seek the counsels of any man, however objectionable; but that man would be responsible for the advice given, and for the acts of the Crown. There was no constitutional doctrine more important than this, for the protection of the Crown. "History had unfolded the evils of a contrary principle having prevailed." It was also well observed by Mr. Whitbread, that the avowal of ministers that the king had acted without advice, amounted to a declaration on their part, that they disowned the responsibility of the act complained of, and left his Majesty to bear the blame of it himself, without that protection which the constitution had provided: but that from this responsibility they could not escape; for by accepting office, they had assumed the responsibility which they had shown so much anxiety to avoid.

But Lord Howick denied that the king had acted without advice, and asserted that there had been secret advisers, who had taken pains to poison the royal mind.[2] On the Saturday before the pledge had been required, Lord Eldon had an audience; and both Lord Eldon and Lord Hawkesbury were consulted by the king, before measures were taken for forming a new administration. They were, therefore, the king's responsible advisers. In answer to these allegations, Mr. Canning stated that Lord Eldon's visit to Windsor had taken place on Saturday se'nnight, preceding the change of ministry; that it had reference to a matter of extreme delicacy, unconnected with these events, and that before he went, Lord Eldon had explained to Lord Grenville the object of his visit, and promised to mention no other subject to his Majesty.[3] He added, that the Duke of Portland, Mr. Per-

[1] Hans. Deb., ix. 327.

[2] *Ibid.*, 339.

[3] Lord Eldon himself expressly denied having had any communication with the king on the Catholic Question, or the ministers. — *Twiss's Life*, ii. 36–38.

ceval, and himself, had endeavored to prevent the separation between the late ministers and the king, by amicable explanations. Mr. Canning concluded by saying, that the ministers were "determined to stand by their sovereign, even though circumstances should occur in which they may find it their duty to appeal to the country."[1] In answer to this threat, Lord Henry Petty said that a great constitutional wrong had been done, and that no such intimidation would induce the House to refrain from expressing their sense of it. This motion had been met by one for reading the other orders of the day, and the latter was carried by a majority of thirty-two.[2] The Opposition were so little prepared for this result, that, during the division, Lord Howick addressed the members in the lobby, and said that being nearly certain of a majority,[3] they must follow up their success with "an address to the throne, to meet the threat which had been thrown out that evening, — a threat unexampled in the annals of Parliament."[4] The House adjourned at half-past six in the morning.

Proceedings in the Lords.

On the 13th April, a discussion was raised in the House of Lords upon a motion to the same effect, proposed by the Marquess of Stafford.[5] The most remarkable speech was that of Lord Erskine, who had already expressed his opinions on the subject, to the king himself.[6] Not being himself, on account of religious scruples,

[1] Hans. Deb., ix. 346. According to Sir S. Romilly, Mr. Canning said, "he had made up his mind, when the Catholic Bill was first mentioned, to vote for it if the king was for it, and against it if the king was against it. Every art was used to interest persons for the king; his age was repeatedly mentioned, his pious scruples, his regard for his coronation oath, which some members did not scruple to say would have been violated if the bill had passed." — *Romilly's Life*, ii. 194.

[2] Ayes, 258; Noes, 226.

[3] A majority of twenty was expected. — *Romilly's Life*, ii. 195.

[4] Hans. Deb., ix. 348. It was intended to follow up this motion, if carried, by resolutions expressing want of confidence in the ministers. — *Romilly's Life*, ii. 194.

[5] It embraced all the words of Mr. Brand's motion, but prefixed a preamble.

[6] Romilly's Life, ii. 188.

favorable to the Catholic claims, he yet ridiculed the argument that the king had been restrained by his coronation oath, from assenting to the late measure. He had assented to the Act of 1793, which admitted Catholic majors and colonels to the army, without perjury; — how then could his oath be violated by the admission of staff-officers? On the question of the pledge he asked, "Is it consistent with the laws and customs of the realm that the king shall make a rule for his own conduct, which his councillors shall not break in upon, to disturb with their advice?" If it were, "the king, instead of submitting to be advised by his councillors, might give the rule himself as to what he will be advised in, until those who are solemnly sworn to give full and impartial counsel, and who are responsible to the public for their conduct as his advisers, might be penned up in a corner of their duties and jurisdiction, and the state might go to ruin."

Again, as to the personal responsibility of the king, he laid it down that "the king can perform no act of government himself, and no man ought to be received within the walls of this House, to declare that any act of Government has proceeded from the private will and determination, or conscience of the king. The king, as chief magistrate, can have no conscience which is not in the trust of responsible subjects. When he delivers the seals of office to his officers of state, his conscience, as it regards the state, accompanies them." "No act of state or government can, therefore, be the king's: he cannot act but by advice; and he who holds office sanctions what is done, from whatever source it may proceed." [1]

By Lord Harrowby the motion was represented as placing the House in the situation "of sitting in judgment upon the personal conduct of their sovereign." But perhaps the best position for the Crown was that assumed by the Earl of Selkirk. The king, he said, could not be accountable to

[1] Hans. Deb., ix. 355–365.

Parliament for his conduct in changing his advisers, and the proposed pledge was merely a motive for such a change, beyond the reach of parliamentary investigation.

Another view was that of Lord Sidmouth. Admitting that for every act of the executive government there must be a responsible adviser, he "contended that there were many functions of the sovereign which, though strictly legitimate, not only might, but must be performed without any such responsibility being attached to them, and which must, therefore, be considered as the personal acts of the king. Of these the constitution does not take cognizance."[1] It was the object of this ingenious argument to absolve from responsibility both the king, who could do no wrong, and his present advisers, who, by accepting office, had become responsible for the measures by which their predecessors had been removed. This unconstitutional position was well exposed by the Earl of Lauderdale.

The example of Lord Danby was felicitously cited both by the Earl of Lauderdale and Lord Holland in support of the constitutional principle that the king can have no separate responsibility. Lord Danby, having been impeached for offences committed as a minister, had produced a written authority from the king in his defence, but was yet held responsible for the execution of the king's commands: nay, the House of Commons voted his plea an aggravation of his offences, as exposing the king to public odium.[2]

This doctrine, in truth, — that for every act of the Crown some adviser must be responsible, — could not be denied; but the artifice of putting forth the king personally, and representing him as being on his trial at the bar, — this repeated use of the king's name, was a tower of strength to the ministerial party.[3]

Lord Stafford's motion had been met by the previous

1 Hans. Deb., ix. 399.
2 *Ibid.*, 405, 414.
3 Romilly's Life, ii. 197.

question; but eventually the division was taken upon the adjournment of the House, which was carried by a majority of eighty-one; and thus the motion was superseded.[1] The House did not adjourn until seven o'clock in the morning.

But even now the question was not set at rest. On the 15th April, Mr. W. H. Lyttleton renewed the discussion, in proposing a resolution expressing regret at the late changes in his Majesty's councils. The debate added little to the arguments on either side, and was brought to a close, at half-past six in the morning, by the House resolving to pass to the orders of the day.[2]

Mr. Lyttleton's motion, 15th April, 1807.

As a question of policy, it had obviously been a false step, on the part of the ministers, to give expression to their reservations in the minute of the Cabinet. They had agreed to abandon the bill which had caused the difference between themselves and his Majesty; and, by virtue of their office, as the king's ministers, were free, on any future occasion, to offer such advice as they might think proper. By their ill-advised minute, they invited the retaliation of this obnoxious pledge. But no constitutional writer would now be found to defend the pledge itself, or to maintain that the ministers who accepted office in consequence of the refusal of that pledge, had not taken upon themselves the same responsibility as if they had advised it.

Impolicy of the cabinet minute.

Meanwhile, though this was the first session of a new Parliament, a speedy dissolution was determined upon. Advantage was taken of the prevalent anti-Catholic feeling which it was feared might subside; but the main issue raised by this appeal to the country was the propriety of the recent exercise of prerogative. In the Lords Commissioners' speech, on the 27th

The dissolution, April 1807.

1 Contents, 171; Non-contents, 90. Hansard's Debates, ix. 422.

2 Ayes, 244; Noes, 198. Hansard's Debates, ix. 432–475.

April, the king said he was "anxious to recur to the sense of his people, while the events which have recently taken place are yet fresh in their recollection." And he distinctly invited their opinion upon them, by declaring that "he at once demonstrates, in the most unequivocal manner, his own conscientious persuasion of the rectitude of those motives upon which he has acted, and affords to his people the best opportunity of testifying their determination to support him in every exercise of the prerogatives of his crown, which is conformable to the sacred obligations, under which they are held, and conducive to the welfare of his kingdom, and to the security of the constitution." The recent exercise of prerogative is thus associated with the obligations of his coronation oath, so as to unite, in favor of the new ministers, the loyalty of the people, their personal attachment to the sovereign, and their zeal for the Protestant establishment. Without such appeals to the loyalty and religious feelings of the people, the influence of the Crown was alone sufficient, at that time, to command a majority for ministers; and their success was complete.

Meeting of Parliament. Amendments to address, 26th June, 1807.

On the meeting of the new Parliament, amendments to the address were proposed in both Houses, condemning the dissolution, as founded upon "groundless and injurious pretences," but were rejected by large majorities.[1]

The three years prior to the regency.

The king's will had prevailed, and was not again to be called in question. His own power, confided to the Tory ministers who were henceforth admitted to his councils, was supreme. Though there was still a party of the king's friends,[2] his Majesty agreed too well with his ministers, in principles and policy, to require the aid of irresponsible advisers. But his rule, once more absolute, — after the struggles of fifty years, — was

[1] In the Lords by a majority of 93, and in the Commons by a majority of 195. — *Hansard's Debates*, ix. 557–658.

[2] Lord Sidmouth's Life, ii. 469; Romilly's Life, ii. 220.

drawing to a close. The will, that had been so strong and unbending, succumbed to disease; and a reign in which the king had been so resolute to govern, ended in a royal "phantom," and a regency.[1]

[1] See Chapter III.

CHAPTER II.

Influence of the Crown during the Regency, the Reigns of George IV., William IV., and Her Majesty, Queen Victoria.

Character of the Prince Regent.

THE Prince Regent differed too much, in character and habits, from his royal father, to be inclined to exercise the influence of the Crown, with the same activity. George III., eager for power, had also delighted in business, to which he had trained himself from early youth.[1] With greater abilities, and superior education, the prince was fond of ease and pleasure, and averse to business. His was not the temperament to seek the labor and anxieties of public affairs: nor had power devolved upon him, until the ambitious spirit of youth had ceased to prompt him to exertion. He loved the "pomp and circumstance" of royalty, without its cares. But though disinclined to the daily toils which his father had undergone for fifty years, — and disposed, by indolence and indifference, to leave more discretion to his ministers, in the ordinary affairs of state; yet whenever his own feelings or interests were concerned, his father himself had scarcely been more imperative.

Influence of his court.

The very qualities, however, which disinclined the prince to laborious activity, exposed him the more readily to the influence of his court. His father's will was strong, and full of energy: his own, inconstant and capricious. The father had judged for himself, with rude vigor and decision: the son, — impulsive, indolent, and without

[1] See debate, 14th April, 1812, on Col. M'Mahon's appointment as Private Secretary to the Prince Regent. — *Hansard's Deb.*, 1st Ser., xxii. 332.

strength of principle or conviction, — was swayed by the advice of those nearest to his person.

The early events of the regency displayed at once the preponderating influence of the Crown, over all other powers of the state, and the subjection of the regent to the counsels of the court.

His separation from his political friends.

To politics, apart from their relations to himself, the prince was indifferent; and his indifference led to the same results, as the king's strong predilections. He readily gave up the opinions, as well as the political friends of his youth. As to his friends, indeed, he had been separated from them for many years, by the French Revolution:[1] the death of Mr. Fox had more recently loosened the tie which had bound them together: the part taken by them against the Duke of York, had further relaxed it; and the proud bearing of the great Whig leaders, — little congenial to the lighter manners of the court, — had nearly broken it asunder. But lately they had exerted themselves strenuously against the restrictions upon the powers of the regent, which the Government, following the precedent of 1788, had proposed; and their general views of policy were supposed to coincide with his own.

Mr. Perceval's administration.

Other circumstances pointed strongly to their being now called to office. The Perceval administration, which had owed its origin to the king's dread of the Roman Catholic claims, was weak and disunited; and while the leading statesmen of all other parties were favorable to the Roman Catholic cause, the sole merit of this ministry lay in their opposition to it. Mr. Perceval himself had been personally obnoxious to the prince, as the friend and adviser of his detested princess, Caroline of Brunswick: nor had the chancellor, Lord Eldon, been free

[1] Mr. Erskine, writing to Mr. Lee, 8th Feb. 1793, said: "We are now plunging, for nothing, or rather for mischief, into a calamitous war, in combination (*not avowed*) with the despots of the North, to restore monarchy in France. And as it is the cause of kings, our prince is drawn into it, and has taken his leave of all of us." — *Rockingham Memoirs*, ii. 127.

from the same offence. The regent had also suspected the latter of keeping him at a distance from his father, and told his lordship afterwards "that there was no person in the whole world that he hated so much, as for years he had hated him."[1]

The prince had further raised the expectations of the Opposition, by confiding to Lord Grenville and Lord Grey the drawing up of his answer to the joint resolutions of the two Houses on the conditions of the regency; and he, as suddenly, repressed these expectations by rejecting their draft for another, — the composition of himself and Mr. Sheridan. This proceeding, so contrary to the views of these noblemen as responsible advisers, drew from them a remonstrance, which, however constitutional in doctrine, was too lofty in its tone, and partook too much of the character of a lecture, to be altogether acceptable to the prince.[2]

The prince neglects the advice of Lords Grenville and Grey.

While the Regency Bill was passing through Parliament, the prince had frequent communications with the Opposition. The plan of a new administration was concerted, and several of the principal places were allotted to the Whig leaders. So assured were they of their speedy accession to power, that, jealous of the influence of Lord Moira and Mr. Sheridan, they were already insisting that the prince should engage to consult none but his future ministers.[3] Nor were ministers less persuaded of the impending change.[4] The king himself, in his lucid intervals, was informed of it by his chancellor; and was prepared to restore his old servants when he recovered.[5] But before the Regency Bill had received the royal assent, the queen addressed a letter to the prince, suggesting the seri-

Hopes of the Opposition.

Their disappointment.

[1] Twiss's Life of Eldon, ii. 197, 198.

[2] Moore's Life of Sheridan, ii. 383, *et seq.;* Duke of Buckingham's Memoirs of the Regency, i. 21, *et seq.*

[3] Rose Corresp., ii. 471–475.

[4] Twiss's Life of Lord Eldon, ii. 197.

[5] *Ibid.*, 477.

ous consequences which a change of ministry might have upon the king's recovery. The prince accordingly acquainted Lord Grenville that the state of his Majesty's health prevented the removal of ministers; but that his confidence was entirely with his lordship, Lord Grey, and his other friends.[1]

His proposal that they should join Mr. Perceval.

When the restrictions upon the prince's powers, as regent, were about to expire, and the king's recovery had become more improbable, it was still believed that he would, at length, form a new administration consisting of the Opposition leaders. He contented himself, however, with proposing, through the Duke of York, that "some of those persons with whom the early habits of his public life were formed," should agree to strengthen Mr. Perceval's administration, — a proposal which they could scarcely have been expected to accept.[2] In suggesting this arrangement, he truly avowed that he had "no predilections to indulge;" having now become as indifferent to the principles, as to the persons, of the Whig leaders.

His estrangement from the Whig leaders.

Restrained for a time, by the possibility of the king's recovery,[3] from making any changes, he had easily become satisfied with existing arrangements, — his contentment being increased by a liberal civil list. This result was imputed to secret counsels, — to the persuasion of the queen, the Hertford family, and the court. Parliament and the press resounded with denunciations of these covert influences.[4] But the events of this period had a deeper import than the intrigues of a court, and the disappointments of a party. They

Paramount influence of the Crown.

[1] Rose Corresp., ii. 478, 479.

[2] Hansard's Debates, xxii. 39, *n.* Duke of Buckingham's Memoirs of the Regency, i. 222. Lord Grenville, writing to the Marquess of Buckingham, Feb. 13th, 1812, said: "The whole will end, I doubt not, in the continuance of Perceval, with Castlereagh and Sidmouth to help him. And this, I believe, is what Lord Yarmouth means, whose intentions are those which are alone of any consequence." — *Ibid.*, 225. Mr. T. Grenville, to same, 14th Feb. — *Ibid.*, 228; Life of Sir J. Romilly, iii. 11.

[3] Rose Corresp., ii. 478, 479.

[4] Debate on Lord Boringdon's motion, 19th March, 1812. Lord Darn-

marked the paramount influence of the Crown in the government of the country. Here were the two great parties in the state looking to royal favor alone, as the source of their power. It was never doubted by the ministers, that, if they retained the confidence of the prince regent, they would be able to command the support of Parliament. It was never doubted by the Opposition, that, if invited to accept office, they would be able to maintain their position as firmly as the ministers, whom they were seeking to displace. Both parties were assured, that the support of Parliament would follow the confidence of the Crown. The Whigs had relied upon the personal friendship of the prince regent: but the ministers, having supplanted their rivals by court favor, continued to govern the country, with the acquiescence of an obsequious Parliament. There was no appeal, on either side, to political principles or policy, or to public service; but all alike looked upwards to the court. The Tory party happened to prevail; and the government of the state was, therefore, conducted on Tory principles. If the Whig party had been placed in power, without any change in public opinion, Whig principles would have been in the ascendant.

Negotiations on the death of Mr. Perceval, 1812.

The assassination of Mr. Perceval made an unexpected opening for a new ministry; but the court appears to have been resolved that no considerable change should follow. Overtures were made to Lord Wellesley and Mr. Canning, to strengthen a government to whose policy they were opposed; but, — as had doubtless been expected, — they refused such conditions.[1]

ley, Earl Grey, &c. — *Hansard's Debates*, xxii. 62, 80. Lord Donoughmore, April 21st, 1812. — *Ibid.*, 525. Mr. Lyttleton, May 4th, 1812, said: "It was notorious that the regent was surrounded with favorites, and, as it were, hemmed in with minions." — *Ibid.*, 1163. Moore's Life of Sheridan, ii. 394, 407; Life of Sir S. Romilly, ii. 366; Wilberforce's Life, iii. 494; Duke of Buckingham's Memoirs of the Regency, i. 25, *et seq.*, 71, 163, 177, 241, 246; Twiss's Life of Lord Eldon, ii. 193.

[1] Twiss's Life of Eldon, ii. 209–213; Court and Cabinets of the Regency, i. 305.

The old government would have been at once revived, had not the Commons addressed the regent, on the motion of Mr. Stuart Wortley, to take measures "to form a strong and efficient administration."[1] Lord Wellesley was now commissioned to form a ministry: but none of the existing ministers would listen to his overtures; and the Opposition declined to accept such a share of the cabinet as was offered to them; and thus his lordship's mission failed, as the court had, probably, intended.

Lord Moira's mission.

At length Lord Moira,—the intimate friend of the prince, and the unconscious tool of the court,—was charged to consult with Lord Grey and Lord Grenville, on the formation of an administration. He stated that he had received this commission without any restrictions upon the consideration of such points as they judged useful for his service. Nothing could exceed the apparent fairness of this proposal; but, as Lords Grey and Grenville had received information that no changes would be permitted in the royal household,[2] they inquired whether they should be at liberty to consider appointments to those great offices in the household, which were usually included in political arrangements, on a change of ministry. Lord Moira, having obtained the prince's consent to part with the officers of the household, if he should advise it, had assured his royal highness, before he undertook this mission, "that he should not part with one of them." In execution of his promise, he now said that it would be impossible for him to concur in the necessity of changing the household on the formation of a new ministry; and upon this issue the negotiations were broken off. As the views of Lord Moira on the one side, and of the Whigs on the other, had been well known before Lord Moira received his commission,[3]

The royal household.

[1] Hansard's Debates, 1st Ser., xxiii. 231, 286.

[2] Mr. T. Grenville to Marquess of Buckingham, 30th April, 1812.—*Duke of Buckingham's Memoirs of Regency*, i. 335. From same to same, June 1st.—*Ibid.*, 336.

[3] Mr. T. Grenville to the Marquess of Buckingham.—*Ibid.*, i. 357.

this proposal would seem to have been as illusory as those which had preceded it. But there was yet another artifice practised upon the Opposition leaders. Though Lord Moira had determined not to agree to any alteration in the household, Lord Hertford, Lord Yarmouth, and the other officers had resolved to resign their offices at court, should the Opposition undertake to form a government. But this important information was prevented, by court intrigues, from reaching the noble lords who were conducting the negotiations.[1] They insisted upon the change in order to give "to a new government that character of efficiency and stability, and those marks of the constitutional support of the Crown, which were required to enable it to act usefully for the public service." Lord Moira rested his resistance to a claim,— which, according to custom, could hardly have been opposed in any *bonâ fide* consultations, — on the ground that changes in the household would give countenance to the imputations which had been thrown upon the court. It need hardly be said that his conduct produced the very result which he had professed his anxiety to avert.

The regent's animosity against the Whigs.

The leaders of the Opposition were persuaded of the hollowness of all the proposals which had been made to them; and, knowing the hostility of the court, were as unwilling as their opponents, that these overtures should lead to any result.[2] Had they been less lofty and unbending, they might perhaps have overcome the obstacles which they dreaded. The regent had not the stubborn will of his royal father, and might have been won over o their side again, if they had once established themselves

[1] Debates in Lords and Commons, 8th and 11th June, 1812; Hansard's Debates, 1st Ser., xxiii. 356, 397, 594, 606, and Appendix of Papers; Moore's Life of Sheridan, ii. 425; Twiss's Life of Eldon, ii. 214–220.

[2] Debates in House of Lords, 3d, 5th, and 8th June, 1812; Hansard's Debates, 1st Ser., xxiii. 332–356, and App. xli.; Twiss's Life of Eldon, ii. 216, 217; Life of Romilly, iii. 42; Horner's Memoirs, ii. 111, 311; Lord Grenville to the Marquess of Buckingham, June 6th and 9th, 1812; Duke of Buckingham's Memoirs of Regency, i. 353, 377; Mr. T. Grenville.— *Ibid.*, 354.

at court. So thought many of their disappointed followers: but the great lords judged otherwise, and proudly shrank from the ungracious task of combating the disfavor of the prince, and the intrigues of his courtiers. The prince, indeed, had now become so violent against the Opposition, that we are reminded of George III. in the days of the Coalition. "He told Lord Wellesley that he had no objection to one or two of them individually, but as a body he would rather abdicate the regency than ever come into contact with them."[1] And again, after the failure of Lord Moira's mission, — "three times that day, before dinner and after dinner, he declared that if Lord Grey had been forced upon him, he should have abdicated."[2]

Reconstitution of the ministry under Lord Liverpool.

These negotiations, meanwhile, had served their purpose. The old administration was immediately reconstituted, under the Earl of Liverpool; and when complaints were made, in the House of Commons, that a strong administration had not been formed in compliance with their address, the blame was thrown upon the impracticable leaders of the Opposition. The ministers were now safe, and gained an easy triumph over Mr. Stuart Wortley and Lord Milton, who endeavored to unsettle the government, by further representations to the regent.[3]

Ascendency of Tory politics.

Henceforth the ascendency of Tory politics, which George III. had established, and which the regent had been expected to overthrow, was maintained more firmly than ever. By the influence of the Crown it had been created; and by the same influence it was upheld during the regency, and throughout the reign of George IV. All opposition being thus defeated, and the ministers and the court party being agreed, the prince regent had no further need of personal interposition in the government of the country.

[1] Duke of Buckingham's Memoirs of the Regency, i. 323.
[2] Moore's Memoirs, by Lord John Russell, i. 360.
[3] June 11th, Hansard's Debates, 1st Ser., xxiii. 397.

On his accession to the throne, he was dissatisfied with ministers for resisting his demands for a larger civil list; but submitted to their judgment, and even, in his speech to Parliament, disclaimed any wish for an increased revenue.[1] Soon afterwards his painful relations with the queen led to proceedings of which his ministers could not approve: but in which, — with the honorable exception of Mr. Canning,[2] — they were induced to support him. The king's personal feelings and honor were concerned; and the embarrassing conduct of the queen herself, led them to accept the responsibility of measures to which the king already stood committed. No sooner had he succeeded to the throne than he desired to obtain a divorce; but his ministers, at that time, resisted his wishes, and explained their objections, in some able minutes of the cabinet.[3] He obtained from them, however, an assurance that, if her Majesty should return to England, they would no longer oppose him in his cherished object.[4] They were little prepared for so embarrassing an event; but it was soon to be brought about by the offensive measures which the king had taken, and his ministers had sanctioned, against her.

Proceedings against the queen, 1820.

The queen had already been irritated by two great insults. Our ambassadors, acting upon their instructions from home, had prevented her recognition as Queen of England at foreign courts; and her name had been omitted, by command of the king, from the liturgy of the Church. Even the legality of this latter act was much doubted.[5] It was at

1 Twiss's Life of Eldon, ii. 363; Com. Journ., lxxv. 110.

2 See Stapleton's Life of Canning, 290–295, 315–323.

3 10th and 14th February, 1820; Stapleton's Life of Canning, 266, 279, 299.

4 Twiss's Life of Eldon, ii. 368.

5 Debates in Lords and Commons, 1820, on the papers relating to the conduct of the queen. Dr. Phillimore, writing to the Marquess of Buckingham, 16th Jan. 1821, said: "The general opinion of lawyers is, I think, unfavorable to the claim." —*Duke of Buckingham's Memoirs of George IV.*, i. 109.

least so disputable as to be an unwise exercise of the prerogative.[1] Such insults as these, naturally provoked the queen to insist upon her proper recognition. At the same time they aroused popular sympathy in her cause, which encouraged her to proceed to extremities. The ministers vainly attempted a compromise: but it was too late. The queen was already on her way to England, loudly asserting her rights. They endeavored to prevent her approach, by submitting a proposal that she should receive an annuity of 50,000*l.* a year, on renouncing her title, and continuing to reside abroad; and threatening proceedings against her in Parliament, if she refused these conditions. She refused them, and hastened to England, — when preliminary proceedings were at once commenced. Even now there was still hope of a compromise, sought by the queen herself. The king was willing to drop all further proceedings against her, and to recognize her title, on condition of her residing abroad; but the queen demanded the restoration of her name in the liturgy, and her recognition in at least one foreign court, — which the king refused to concede.[2]

Conduct of the ministers.

And now the threat was carried out to the fullest extent, by the introduction of a bill into the House of Lords, to deprive her Majesty of her title, prerogatives, and rights, and to dissolve her marriage with the king. The ministers were fully sensible of the difficulties, and even of the danger, of yielding to the king's desire to prosecute this formidable measure. Lord Eldon, writing in June, 1820, said, "I think no administration, who have any regard for him, will go the length he wishes, as an administration, — and if they will, they cannot take Parliament along with them: that body is afraid of disclosures, — not on one side only, — which may affect the monarchy itself."[3]

[1] Mr. C. Wynn to the Marquess of Buckingham. — *Ibid.*, 116.

[2] Debates, 19th June, 1820, when the failure of these negotiations was announced.

[3] Twiss's Life of Eldon, ii. 372.

But on the failure of all their attempts to effect an accommodation of the royal differences, they yielded, — against their better judgment, — to the revengeful spirit of the king.

The disgraceful incidents of the "queen's trial" are too well known to need repetition, even if they ought otherwise to find a place in this history. But what were the constitutional aspects of the case? The king had resolved to execute an act of vengeance rather than of justice against the queen, — whose wrongs had aroused for her protection, the strongest popular feelings, — sympathy with a woman, and resentment of oppression. All the power of the Crown was arrayed on one side, and the excited passions of the people on the other. The impending conflict was viewed with alarm by statesmen of all parties. Many sagacious observers dreaded a civil war. The ministers foresaw the dangers to which the country was exposed: they disapproved of proceedings which, without their acquiescence, could not have been attempted; — yet they lent themselves to gratify the anger and hatred of the king. They were saved from the consummation of their worst fears by the withdrawal of the Bill of Pains and Penalties, at its last stage in the House of Lords: but in proceeding so far, in opposition to their own judgment, they had sinned against their constitutional obligations, as responsible ministers. By consenting to act as instruments of the king's pleasure, they brought him into dangerous collision with his people. Had they refused to permit, what they could not justify to Parliament or the country, they would have spared the king his humiliation, and the state its perils.

Not to have supported the king in a cause affecting his deepest feelings and his honor, might have exposed them to the reproach of deserting their royal master in his utmost need, and even of siding with his hated consort:[1] but a

[1] Lord Brougham has attributed their conduct solely to an unworthy desire to retain their places (*Works*, iv. 33 ;) but perhaps the suggestion in the text is nearer the truth.

higher sense of their responsibilities, and greater firmness in asserting them, would have made them mediators between the king, on the one side, and the queen, the Parliament, and the people, on the other.[1]

The king's animosity against the Opposition.

The Opposition had espoused the queen's cause, — some to protect her from oppression, — some to lead a popular cause against the ministers, — and others, like Cobbett, to gratify their bitter hatred of the government. The king's resentment against those who had opposed him in Parliament, equalled that of his father against Mr. Fox. Mr. Fremantle, writing Dec. 29, 1820, to the Marquess of Buckingham, said: "His invective against Lord Grey was stronger and more violent than I can possibly repeat;" and again: "What I am most anxious to observe to you, was his increased hostility and indignation against the Opposition, and more personally against Lord Grey."[2] Yet the same acute observer, who knew the king well, writing again Jan. 24, 1821, said: "Lord Grenville fancies a Whig government could not last six months, reasoning from the conduct of George III; but in this I am persuaded he would find himself deceived, for the same decision and steadiness of mind does not belong to his successor. And should the change once take place, new attachments and habits would prevail, and obliterate all former anger."[3]

Meanwhile, the popularity of the king, which had suffered

[1] Mr. Canning wrote to Mr. Huskisson, Oct. 2, 1820, that the ministers ought to have held this language to the king: "'Sir, — divorce is impossible!' 'What! if she comes, if she braves, if she insults?' 'Yes, sir, in any case, divorce is impossible. Other things may be tried, other expedients may be resorted to; but divorce, we tell you again, is impossible. It can never be;' . . . . . . and see the fruits" (of their conduct), — "a government brought into contempt and detestation; a kingdom thrown into such ferment and convulsion, as no other kingdom or government ever recovered from without a revolution; but I hope *we* shall." — *Stapleton's Life of Canning*, 299.

[2] Duke of Buckingham's Memoirs of George IV., i. 99.

[3] *Ibid.*, 112.

for a time from these proceedings, was speedily recovered. The monarchy had sustained no permanent injury: its influence was not in the least impaired. The personal character of the king was not such as to command the respect or attachment of the people; yet at no previous period had their loyalty been more devoted — never, perhaps, had the adulation of royalty been so extravagant and servile. There were discontent and turbulence among some classes of the people; but the Crown and its ministers ruled supreme over Parliament, the press, the society, and the public opinion of the country.

Popularity of Geo. IV.

Though the influence of the Crown was acknowledged as fully as at any time in the late reign, it had not been brought under parliamentary discussion for many years; when, in 1822, Mr. Brougham introduced a motion on the subject. He proposed to declare that the influence of the Crown was "unnecessary for maintaining its constitutional prerogatives, destructive of the independence of Parliament, and inconsistent with the well-governing of the realm." By comparing the present expenditure with that of 1780, — the number of places and commissions, the cost of collecting the revenue, and the host of persons looking up to government for patronage, — he pronounced the influence of the Crown to have been greatly increased since Mr. Dunning's celebrated resolution. He admitted, however, that the number of placemen in the House had been diminished. In the time of Lord Carteret there had been two hundred, and at an antecedent period even three hundred: in 1780 there had been between eighty and ninety; and in 1822, eighty-seven, — many of whom, however, could not be said to be dependent on the Crown. He drew an entertaining historical sketch of the manner in which every party, in turn, so long as it held office, had enjoyed the confidence of the House of Commons, but had lost that confidence immediately it was in Opposition, — a coincidence, he attributed to the ascendency of the Crown, which

Motion of Mr. Brougham on the influence of the Crown, June 24, 1822.

alone enabled any ministry to command a majority. The Marquess of Londonderry, in a judicious speech, pointed out that the authority of the Crown had been controlled by the increasing freedom of the press, and by other causes; and after a debate of some interest, Mr. Brougham's motion was negatived by a large majority.[1]

The king's views on the Catholic question.

Early in his reign, the king was supposed to be in favor of a measure for the relief of the Roman Catholics; and its friends were even speculating upon his encouragement to carry it through Parliament.[2] But in 1824 he had become "violently anti-Catholic;" and so paramount was his influence supposed to be over the deliberations of Parliament, that the friends of the cause believed it to be hopeless.[3] Until the death of Lord Liverpool, the Catholic claims having small hope of success, it was sufficient to let the king's opinions be known through common report. But when Mr. Canning, the brilliant champion of the Roman Catholics, had become first minister, his Majesty thought it necessary to declare his sentiments, in a more authentic shape. And accordingly he sent for the Archbishop of Canterbury, and the Bishop of London, and "directed them to make known to their clergy that his sentiments on the Coronation Oath, and on the Catholic question were those his revered father, George III., and lamented brother, the Duke of York, had maintained during their lives, and which he himself had professed when Prince of Wales, and which nothing could shake; finally, assuring them that the recent ministerial arrangements were the result of circumstances, to his Majesty equally unforeseen and unpleasant."[4] And when political necessity had wrung from Sir

[1] Ayes 216, Noes 101.—*Hansard's Debates*, 2d Ser., vii. 1266.

[2] "I hear he is for it," said the Duke of Wellington to Mr. Fremantle. "By the by," he added, "I hear Lady Conyngham supports it, which is a great thing."—*Duke of Buckingham's Memoirs of George IV.*, i. 148; *ib.* 218.

[3] *Ibid.*, ii. 103, 169, 211.

[4] Speech of the Bishop of London at a dinner of the clergy of his dio-

Robert Peel and the Duke of Wellington, a conviction that a measure of relief could no longer be withheld, it was with extreme difficulty that they obtained his assent to its introduction.[1] After he had given his consent, he retracted, and again yielded it: — attempted to deny, or explain it away to his anti-Catholic advisers: — complained of his ministers, and claimed the pity of his friends. "If I do give my assent," said he, "I'll go to the baths abroad, and from thence to Hanover: I'll return no more to England . . . . I'll return no more: let them get a Catholic king in Clarence." Such had once been the threat of the stout old king, who, whatever his faults, at least had firmness and strength of will. But the king who now uttered these feeble lamentations, found solace in his trouble, by throwing his arms round the neck of the aged Eldon.[2] And again, in imitation of his father, — having assented to the passing of the Act, which he had deliberately authorized his ministers to carry, — he gratified his animosity against those who had supported it, — particularly the peers and bishops, — by marked incivility at his levée; while he loaded with attentions, those who had distinguished themselves by opposition to the government.[3]

This concession to the Roman Catholics, — which the ablest statesmen of all parties concurred in supporting, — had already been delayed for thirty years, by the influence of the Crown. Happily this influence had now fallen into weaker hands; or it might still have prevailed over wiser counsels, and the grave interests of the state.

Reign of William IV.

Hitherto we have seen the influence of the Crown invariably exercised against a liberal policy; and often against the rights and liberties of the people. But the earlier years of the reign of William IV. presented the

cese, 8th May, 1827; Duke of Buckingham's Memoirs of George IV., ii. 324; Gentleman's Magazine, xcvii. 457.

1 Peel's Mem., i. 274, &c.; and see Chapter XII., on Civil and Religious Liberty.

2 Twiss's Life of Eldon, iii. 82–87. Peel's Mem., i. 343–350.

3 Twiss's Life of Eldon, iii. 88.

novel spectacle of the prerogatives and personal influence of the king being exerted, in a great popular cause, on behalf of the people. At various times, small expedients had been tried with a view to restrain the influence of the Crown; but the Reform Bill, by increasing the real power of the people in the House of Commons, was the first great measure calculated to effect that object; and this measure, it was everywhere proclaimed that the king himself approved. The ministers themselves announced his Majesty's entire confidence in their policy, and his determination to support them;[1] and the advocates of the cause, in every part of the country, declared that the king was on their side.

His support of parliamentary reform.

Yet, in truth, the attitude of the king in regard to this measure, at first resembled that which his royal predecessors had maintained against a progressive policy. When ministers first proposed to introduce it, he regarded it with dislike and apprehension: he dreaded the increasing influence and activity of the Commons, and, — alarmed by the spirit in which they had investigated the expenditure of his civil list, — he feared lest, strengthened by a more popular representation, they should encroach upon his own prerogatives and independence.[2] The royal family and the court were also averse to the measure, and to the ministers. But when his Majesty had given his consent to the scheme submitted by the cabinet, he was gratified by its popularity, — in which he largely shared, — and which its supporters adroitly contrived to associate with his Majesty's personal character, and supposed political sympathies.

He was still distrustful of his ministers and their policy; yet while the tide of popular favor was running high, and no political danger was immediately impending, he gave them his support and countenance. On their side, they were

[1] At the Lord Mayor's Dinner, Easter Monday, 1831. Twiss's Life of Eldon, iii. 126.

[2] Roebuck's Hist. of the Whig Ministry, ii. 27, 28.

not slow to take advantage of the influence of his name: they knew that it would be a tower of strength to their cause; and, sensible of the insecurity of his favor, they took care that it should be widely proclaimed, as long as it lasted.

Politicians like Lord Eldon, who, for forty years, had relied upon the influence of the Crown to resist every popular measure,— even when proposed by its own responsible ministers, — were now scandalized by this "unconstitutional" cry.[1] Yet what did this cry, in truth, import? The state of parties in Parliament, and of popular feeling in the country, had brought into the king's service, a ministry pledged to the cause of Parliamentary reform. To this ministry he had given his confidence. George III., by some bold stroke or cunning manœuvre, would soon have set himself free from such a ministry. George IV., after giving a doubtful assent to their policy, would have reserved his confidence and his sympathies for their opponents; but William IV. at this time, took a part at once manly and constitutional. His responsible ministers had advised the passing of a great measure, and he had accepted their advice. They were now engaged in a fierce parliamentary struggle; and the king gave them, — what they were entitled to expect, — his open confidence. So long as they enjoyed this confidence, he exercised his prerogatives and influence according to their counsels. His powers were used in the spirit of the constitution, — not independently, or secretly, — but on the avowed advice and responsibility of his ministers.

Dissolution of 1831.

The king was called upon, at a critical period, to exercise his prerogative of dissolving Parliament. In 1831, a new Parliament was yet in its first session; but having been assembled under the auspices of the late administration, before the popular feelings in favor of Parliamentary reform had been aroused, it had become evident that a reform ministry, and this Parliament, could not exist together. The ministers, having been twice defeated in

1 Twiss's Life of Eldon, iii. 126.

three days,[1] had no alternative but to resign their offices, or to appeal from the House of Commons to the people; and they urged the necessity of an immediate dissolution. The time was full of peril, and the king hesitated to adopt the bold advice of his ministers; but when at length he yielded his assent, the prerogative was exercised at once, and by the king in person.[2] If there was something unseemly in the haste with which this was done, and unusual in the manner of doing it,—the occasion was one demanding the promptest action. Lord Wharncliffe had given notice of a motion for an address to the king, remonstrating against a dissolution, and his motion was actually under discussion in the House of Lords, when the king arrived to prorogue Parliament.[3] Both houses would probably have joined in such an address, had time been allowed them, and would have interposed embarrassing obstacles to the exercise of the king's prerogative. By this sudden appeal to the people, ministers at once deprived their opponents of the vantage-ground of parliamentary opposition.

Second Reform Bill, 1831.

The dissolution resulted in an overpowering majority of the new House of Commons, in favor of the government Reform Bill. And now the House of Lords, exercising its constitutional right, rejected it. So important a measure was trying all the powers of the state, to their utmost tension. The popular excitement was so great that it was impossible for ministers to yield. The king still upheld them, and the Commons supported them by a vote of confidence. All the political forces of the country were thus combined against the House of Lords.

After a short prorogation, a third Reform Bill was passed

[1] First, on General Gascoigne's amendment, 19th April, and afterwards on a question of adjournment, 21st April.

[2] For an account of the interview between the king and Lords Grey and Brougham, see Roebuck's Hist. of the Whig Ministry, ii. 149, *et seq.*

[3] Hansard's Debates, 3d Ser., iii. 1806; Roebuck's Hist. of the Whig Ministry, ii. 152; Ann. Register, 1831, p. 110.

by the Commons. The position of the Lords was now too perilous not to cause some wavering; and the second reading of the bill was accordingly agreed to, by the small majority of nine. This concession, however, was followed by an adverse vote in committee. A graver question of prerogative had now to be considered. An appeal from the House of Commons to the people had been decisive; but what appeal was there from the House of Lords? None, save to the Crown, to which that body owed its existence. A creation of peers was the *ultima ratio*, which, after serious doubts and misgivings, ministers submitted to the king. His Majesty's resolution had already been shaken by the threatening aspect of affairs, and by the apprehensions of his family and court; and he, not unnaturally, shrank from so startling an exercise of his prerogative.[1] The ministers resigned, and the Commons addressed the king, praying him to call such persons only to his councils, as would promote the passing of the Reform Bill.[2] The Duke of Wellington having failed to form a government, ready to devise a measure of reform at once satisfactory to the people and to the House of Lords, the ministers were recalled.

Third Reform Bill, 1831-32.

Proposed creation of peers. 8th May, 1832.

Another pressure was now brought to bear upon the House of Lords, — irregular and unconstitutional indeed, but necessary to avert revolution on the one hand, and to save the peers from harsh coercion, on the other. The king having at length agreed to create a sufficient number of peers to carry the bill,[3] — yet anxious to avoid so extreme a measure, — averted the dangers of a great political crisis, by a timely interference. Some of the most violent peers were first dissuaded from proceeding to extremities; and on the 17th May, the following circular letter was addressed, without the knowledge of ministers, to the opposition peers: —

Influence of the king over the peers.

1 Roebuck's Hist. of the Whig Ministry, ii. 222–227, 281.
2 See also Chapters V. and VI.
3 Roebuck's Hist. of the Whig Ministry, ii. 331.

"MY DEAR LORD, — I am honored with his Majesty's commands to acquaint your lordship, that all difficulties to the arrangements in progress will be obviated by a declaration in the House to-night from a sufficient number of peers, that in consequence of the present state of affairs, they have come to the resolution of dropping their further opposition to the Reform Bill, so that it may pass without delay, and as nearly as possible in its present shape.

"I have the honor to be, &c.,

"HERBERT TAYLOR."[1]

The peers took this suggestion, and yielded. Had they continued their resistance, a creation of peers could not have been avoided. This interference of the king with the independent deliberations of the House of Lords was, in truth, a more unconstitutional act than a creation of peers, — the one being an irregular interference of the Crown with the freedom of Parliament, — the other merely the unusual exercise of an undoubted prerogative. But it was resorted to, not to extend the influence of the Crown, or to overawe the Parliament, — but to restore harmonious action to those powers of the state, which had been brought into dangerous opposition and conflict. In singular contrast to the history of past times, the greatest extension of the liberties of the people was now obtained, in the last resort, by the influence of the Crown.

The Whigs lose the confidence of the king.

Two years after these great events, the prerogatives of the Crown were again called into activity, in a manner which seemed to revive the political history of 1784. Lord Grey's government had lost the confidence of the king. His Majesty had already become apprehensive of danger to the Church, when his alarm was increased by the retirement of Lord Stanley, Sir J. Graham, and two other members of the cabinet, on the question of the appropriation of the surplus revenues of the Church of Ireland. And without consulting his ministers, he gave public expression to this alarm, in replying to an address

[1] Roebuck's Hist. of the Whig Ministry, ii. 334.

of the prelates and clergy of Ireland.[1] The ministry of Lord Grey, enfeebled by the retirement of their colleagues, by disunion, and other embarrassments, soon afterwards resigned. Though they had already lost their popularity, they had continued to command a large majority in the House of Commons. Lord Melbourne's administration which succeeded, was composed of the same materials, and represented the great liberal party, and its parliamentary majority. Lord Melbourne had concluded the business of the session of 1834, with the full support of this majority. But the king, who had withdrawn his confidence from Lord Grey, reposed it still less in Lord Melbourne, — having, in the mean time, become entirely converted to the political opinions of the Opposition.

Their sudden dismissal in 1834.

In October, the death of Lord Spencer having removed Lord Althorp from the leadership of the House of Commons, and from his office of Chancellor of the Exchequer, the king seized upon this opportunity for suddenly dismissing his ministers; and consulted the Duke of Wellington upon the formation of a government, from the opposite party. Lord Althorp's elevation to the House of Lords rendered necessary a partial reconstruction of the ministry; but assuredly that circumstance alone would not have suggested the propriety of taking counsel with those who constituted but a small minority of the House of Commons. Lord Melbourne proposed to supply the place of Lord Althorp by Lord John Russell, — a far abler man; but the king was determined that the ministry should be dissolved. All the usual grounds for dismissing a ministry were wanting. There was no immediate difference of opinion between them and the king, upon any measure, or question of public policy, — there was no disunion among themselves, nor were there any indications that they had lost the confidence of Parliament. But the accidental removal of a single minister, — not necessarily even from the government, but only from

[1] Annual Register, 1834, p. 43.

one House of Parliament to the other, — was made the occasion for dismissing the entire administration. It is true that the king viewed with apprehension the policy of his ministers in regard to the Irish Church; but his assent was not then required to any specific measure of which he disapproved; — nor was this the ground assigned for their dismissal. The right of the king to dismiss his ministers was unquestionable; but constitutional usage has prescribed certain conditions under which this right should be exercised. It should be exercised solely in the interests of the state, and on grounds which can be justified to Parliament, — to whom, as well as to the king, the ministers are responsible. Even in 1784, when George III. had determined to crush the Coalition Ministry, he did not venture to dismiss them, until they had been defeated in the House of Lords, upon Mr. Fox's India Bill. And again, in 1807, the ministers were at issue with the king upon a grave constitutional question, before he proceeded to form another ministry. But here it was not directly alleged that the ministers had lost the confidence of the king; and so little could it be affirmed that they had lost the confidence of Parliament, that an immediate dissolution was counselled by the new administration. The act of the king bore too much the impress of his personal will, and too little of those reasons of state policy by which it should have been prompted; but its impolicy was so signal as to throw into the shade its unconstitutional character.

Temporary arrangements under the Duke of Wellington.

The Duke of Wellington advised his Majesty that the difficult task of forming a new administration, should be intrusted to Sir Robert Peel. But such had been the suddenness of the king's resolution, that Sir Robert, wholly unprepared for any political changes, was then at Rome. The Duke, however, promptly met this difficulty by accepting the office of First Lord of the Treasury himself, until Sir Robert Peel's arrival, together with the seals of one of his Majesty's

Principal Secretaries of State, which, — as there was no other secretary, — constituted his grace Secretary for the Home, the Foreign and the Colonial Departments. His sole colleague was Lord Lyndhurst, who was intrusted with the Great Seal; but still retained the office of Lord Chief Baron of the Court of Exchequer.

This assumption of the government by a single man, while Parliament was not sitting, — avowedly for the purpose of forming an administration from a party whose following comprised less than a fourth of the House of Commons,[1] — presented an unpromising view of constitutional government, after the Reform Act.

In defence of this concentration of offices, the precedent of the Duke of Shrewsbury was cited, who, in the last days of Queen Anne, had held the several offices of Lord High Treasurer, Lord Chamberlain, and Lord Lieutenant of Ireland.[2] But the critical emergency of that occasion scarcely afforded an example to be followed, except where some public danger is to be averted. The queen was upon her death-bed: the succession was disputed, — a civil war was impending, — and the queen's ministers had been in secret correspondence with the Pretender. At such a time of peril, any means of strengthening the executive authority were justifiable; but to resort to a similar expedient, when no danger threatened the state, and merely for the purpose of concerting ministerial arrangements and party combinations, — if justifiable on other grounds, — could scarcely be defended on the plea of precedent. Its justification, if possible, was rather to be sought in the temporary and provisional nature of the arrangement. The king had dismissed his ministers, and had resolved to intrust to Sir Robert Peel the formation of another ministry. The accident of Sir Robert's absence

[1] Sir Robert Peel himself appears to have admitted that he could not have depended upon more than 130 votes. — *Speech of Lord John Russell, Hansard's Debates*, 3d Ser., xxvi. 293*.

[2] Hansard's Deb., 3d Ser., xxvi. 224.

deferred, for a time, the carrying out of his Majesty's resolution; and the Duke of Wellington, in the interval, administered the executive business of several departments of the Government, in the same manner as outgoing ministers generally undertake its administration, until their successors are appointed. The provisional character of this inter-ministerial government was shown by the circumstances stated by the duke himself, "that during the whole time he held the seals, there was not a single office disposed of, nor an act done, which was not essentially necessary for the service of the king, and of the country."[1] That it was an expedient of doubtful and anomalous character, — which, if drawn into precedent, might be the means of abuses dangerous to the state, — could scarcely be denied; but as the duke had exercised the extraordinary powers intrusted to him, with honor and good faith, his conduct, though exposed to invective, ridicule, and caricature,[2] did not become an object of parliamentary censure. Such was the temper of the House of Commons, that had the duke's "dictatorship," — as it was called, — been more open to animadversion, it had little to expect from their forbearance.

Sir Robert Peel as premier, 1834.

If any man could have accomplished the task which the king had so inconsiderately imposed upon his minister, Sir Robert Peel was unquestionably the man most likely to succeed. He perceived at once the impossibility of meeting the existing House of Commons, at the head of a Tory administration; and the king was therefore advised to dissolve Parliament.

Assumes the responsibility of the king's acts.

So completely had the theory of ministerial responsibility been now established, that, though Sir Robert Peel was out of the realm when the late ministers were dismissed, — though he could have had no cogni-

[1] Duke of Wellington's Explanations, Feb. 24, 1835; Hansard's Deb., 3d Ser., xxvii. 85.

[2] H. B. represented the duke, in multiform characters, occupying every seat at the Council Board.

zance of the causes which induced the king to dismiss them, — though the Duke of Wellington had been invested with the sole government of the country, without his knowledge, — he yet boldly avowed that, by accepting office after these events, he became constitutionally responsible for them all, — as if he had himself advised them.[1] He did not attempt, like the ministers of 1807, to absolve himself from censure for the acts of the Crown, and at the same time to denounce the criticism of Parliament, as an arraignment of the personal conduct of the king: but manfully accepted the full responsibility which had devolved upon him.

The new Parliament, 1835.

The minister could scarcely have expected to obtain a majority in the new Parliament; but he relied upon the reaction in favor of Tory principles, which he knew to have commenced in the country, and which had encouraged the king to dismiss Lord Melbourne. His party was greatly strengthened by the elections; but was still unequal to the force of the Opposition. Yet he hoped for forbearance, and a "fair trial;" and trusted to the eventual success of a policy as liberal, in its general outline, as that of the Whigs. But he had only disappointments and provocations to endure. A hostile and enraged majority confronted him in the House of Commons, — comprising every section of the "liberal party," — and determined to give him no quarter. He was defeated on the election of the Speaker, where at least he had deemed himself secure; and again upon the address, when an amendment was voted condemning the recent dissolution as unnecessary;[2] and, — not to mention minor discomfitures, — he was at length defeated on a resolution, affirming that no measure on the subject of tithes in Ireland would be satisfactory, that did not pro-

[1] Hansard's Deb., 3d Ser., xxvi. 216, 223.

[2] It lamented that the progress of "reforms should have been interrupted and endangered by the unnecessary dissolution of a Parliament earnestly intent upon the vigorous prosecution of measures, to which the wishes of the people were most anxiously and justly directed." — *Com. Journ.*, xc. 8. Hansard's Deb., xxvi., 3d Ser., 26, 151, 410, 425.

vide for the appropriation of the surplus revenues of the Irish Church.[1]

Efforts of Sir Robert Peel

These few weeks formed the most brilliant episode in Sir Robert Peel's distinguished parliamentary career. He combined the temper, tact, and courage of a great political leader, with oratory of a higher order than he had ever previously attained. He displayed all the great qualities by which Mr. Pitt had been distinguished, in face of an adverse majority, with a more conciliating temper, and a bearing less haughty. Under similar circumstances, perhaps, his success might have been equal. But Mr. Pitt had still a dissolution before him, supported by the vast influence of the Crown: Sir Robert Peel had already tried that venture, under every disadvantage,—and no resource was left him, but an honorable retirement from a hopeless struggle.

His resignation. Causes of his failure.

He resigned, and Lord Melbourne's government, with some alterations, was reinstated. The stroke of prerogative had failed; and its failure offers an instructive illustration of the effects of the Reform Act, in diminishing the ascendant influence of the Crown. In George the Third's time, the dismissal of a ministry by the king, and the transfer of his confidence to their opponents,—followed by an appeal to the country,—would certainly have secured a majority for the new ministers. Such had been the effect of a dissolution in 1784, after the dismissal of the Coalition Ministry: such had been the effect of a dissolution in 1807, on the dismissal of "All the Talents." But the failure of this attempt to convert Parliament from one policy to another, by the prerogative and influence of the Crown, proved that the opinion of the people must now be changed, before ministers can reckon upon a conversion of the Parliament. It is true that the whole of these proceedings had been ill advised on the part of the king, even in the interests of the party whom he was anxious to serve; but there had been times within the memory of many statesmen then liv-

[1] Com. Journ., xc. 208.

ing, when equal indiscretion would not have incurred the least risk of defeat.

Lord Melbourne's second ministry.

The second ministry of Lord Melbourne, though rapidly sinking in the estimation of their own supporters, — and especially of the extreme, or "radical" party, — while their opponents were gaining strength and popularity in the country, — continued in office during the two remaining years of the king's reign, without recovering his favor.

Accession of her Majesty.

Her Majesty, on her most auspicious accession to the throne, finding them the ministers of the Crown, immediately honored them with her entire confidence. The occasion was especially favorable for ministers to secure and perpetuate such confidence. The young queen, having no political experience, was without predilections; and the impressions first made upon her mind were likely to be lasting. A royal household was immediately to be organized for her Majesty, comprising not merely the officers of state and ceremony; but, — what was more important to a queen, — all the ladies of her court. The ministers appointed the former, as usual, from among their own parliamentary supporters; and extended the same principle of selection to the latter. Nearly all the ladies of the new court were related to the ministers themselves, or to their political adherents. The entire court thus became identified with the ministers of the day. If such an arrangement was calculated to insure the confidence of the Crown, — and who could doubt that it was? — it necessarily involved the principle of replacing this household with another, on a change of ministry. This was foreseen at the time, and soon afterwards became a question of some constitutional difficulty.

Her household.

The "Bedchamber Question."

The favor of the ministers at court became a subject of jealousy, and even of reproach, amongst their opponents; but the age had passed away, in which court favor alone could uphold a falling ministry against public opinion. They were weaker now, with the court on their side, than they had been during the late reign, with the influence of the king and his court opposed to them; and in May, 1839, were obliged to offer their resignation. Sir Robert Peel, being charged with the formation of a new administration, had to consider the peculiar position of the household. Since Lord Moira's memorable negotiations in 1812, there had been no difficulties regarding those offices in the household, which were included in ministerial changes; but the court of a queen, constituted like the present, raised a new and embarrassing question.[1] To remove from the society of her Majesty, those ladies who were immediately about her person, appeared like an interference with her family circle, rather than with her household. Yet could ministers undertake the government, if the queen continued to be surrounded by the wives, sisters, and near relatives of their political opponents? They decided that they could not; and Sir Robert Peel went to the palace to acquaint her Majesty that the ministerial changes would comprise the higher offices of her court occupied by ladies, including the ladies of her bedchamber. The queen met him by at once declaring that she could not admit any change of the ladies of her household. On appealing to Lord John Russell on this subject, her Majesty was assured that she was justified, by usage, in declining the change proposed; and afterwards, by the advice of Lord Melbourne and his colleagues, she addressed a letter to Sir Robert Peel, stating that she could not "consent to adopt a course which she conceived to be contrary to usage, and which was repugnant to her feelings."[2] Sir Robert Peel, on the receipt of this letter, wrote to her Majesty to resign the trust he had undertaken: stating that it was essential to the success of the commission with which he had been honored "that he should have that public proof of her Majesty's entire support and confidence, which would

[1] Hansard's Debates, 3d Ser., xlvii. 985, *et seq.*, and see *supra*, p. 111.

[2] Hansard's Debates, 3d Series, xlvii. 985.

be afforded by the permission to make some changes in that part of her Majesty's household, which her Majesty resolved on maintaining entirely without change."[1] By a minute of the cabinet, immediately after these events, the ministry of Lord Melbourne recorded their opinion "that for the purpose of giving to the administration that character of efficiency and stability, and those marks of constitutional support of the Crown, which are required to enable it to act usefully to the public service, it is reasonable that the great offices of the court, and situations in the household held by members of Parliament, should be included in the political arrangements made on a change of the administration; but they are not of opinion that a similar principle should be applied, or extended, to the offices held by ladies in her Majesty's household."[2]

In the ministerial explanations which ensued, Sir Robert Peel pointed out forcibly the difficulties which any minister must be prepared to encounter, who should leave about her Majesty's person, the nearest relatives of his political opponents. It had not been his intention to suggest the removal of ladies, — even from the higher offices of the household, — who were free from strong party or political connection; but those who were nearly related to the outgoing ministers, he had deemed it impossible to retain. The ministers, on the other hand, maintained that they were supported by precedents, in the advice which they had tendered to her Majesty. They referred to the examples of Lady Sunderland and Lady Rialton, who had remained in the bedchamber of Queen Anne, for a year and a half after the dismissal of their husbands from office; and to the uniform practice by which the ladies of the household of every queen consort had been retained, on changes of administration, notwithstanding their close relationship to men engaged in political life. The ministers also insisted much upon the respect due to the personal feelings of her Majesty, and to her natural repug-

[1] Hansard's Debates, 3d Series, xlvii. 986. [2] *Ibid.*, 1001.

nance to sacrifice her domestic society to political arrangements.[1]

The "Bedchamber Question" saved Lord Melbourne's government for a further term. Sir Robert Peel had experienced the evil consequences of the late king's premature recall of his party to office; and his prospects in the country were not even yet assured. The immediate result of the Bedchamber Question was, therefore, not less satisfactory to himself than to the ministers. The latter gained no moral strength, by owing their continuance in office to such a cause; while the former was prepared to profit by their increasing weakness. The queen's confidence in her ministers was undiminished; yet they continued to lose ground in Parliament, and in the country. In 1841, the Opposition, being fully assured of their growing strength, obtained, by a majority of one, a resolution of the Commons, affirming that the ministers had not the confidence of the House; and "that their continuance in office, under such circumstances, was at variance with the spirit of the constitution." The country was immediately appealed to upon this issue; and it soon became clear that the country was also adverse to the ministers. Delay had been fatal to them, while it had assured the triumph of their opponents. At the meeting of the new Parliament, amendments to the address were agreed to in both Houses, by large majorities, repeating the verdict of the late House of Commons.[2]

Increased weakness of Lord Melbourne's government.

Sir Robert Peel was now called upon, at a time of his own choosing, to form a government. Supported by Parliament and the country, he had nothing to fear from court influence, even if there had been any disposition to use it against him. No difficulties were again raised on the Bedchamber Question. Her Majesty was now sensible that the position she

Sir Robert Peel's second administration, 1841.

The household.

[1] Hansard's Debates, 3d Ser., xlvii. 979, 1008.

[2] In the Lords by a majority of 72, and in the Commons by a majority of 91.

had once been advised to assert, was constitutionally untenable. The principle which Sir Robert Peel applied to the household, has since been admitted, on all sides, to be constitutional. The offices of mistress of the robes and ladies of the bedchamber, when held by ladies connected with the outgoing ministers, have been considered as included in the ministerial arrangements. But ladies of the bedchamber belonging to families whose political connection has been less pronounced, have been suffered to remain in the household, without objection, on a change of ministry.

Relations of a secretary of state to the Crown.

In 1851, an incident occurred which illustrates the relations of ministers to the Crown, — the discretion vested in them; and the circumstances under which the pleasure of the sovereign is to be signified, concerning acts of the executive government. To all important acts, by which the Crown becomes committed, it had been generally acknowledged that the sanction of the sovereign must be previously signified. And in 1850 her Majesty communicated to Lord Palmerston, the secretary of state for foreign affairs, — through Lord John Russell, her first minister, — a memorandum, giving specific directions as to the transaction of business between the Crown and the secretary of state. It was in these words: — "The queen requires, first, that Lord Palmerston will distinctly state what he proposes in a given case, in order that the queen may know as distinctly to what she is giving her royal sanction. Secondly, having once given her sanction to a measure, that it be not arbitrarily altered or modified by the minister. Such an act she must consider as failing in sincerity towards the Crown, and justly to be visited by the exercise of her constitutional right of dismissing that minister. She expects to be kept informed of what passes between him and the foreign ministers, before important decisions are taken, based upon that intercourse; to receive the foreign despatches in good time; and to have the drafts for her approval, sent to her in suffi-

The queen's memorandum, 1850.

cient time to make herself acquainted with their contents, before they must be sent off."[1]

Such being the relations of the foreign secretary to the Crown, the sovereign is advised upon questions of foreign policy by her first minister, to whom copies of despatches and other information are also communicated, in order to enable him to give such advice effectually.[2] In controlling one minister, the sovereign yet acts upon the counsels and responsibility of another.

Lord Palmerston's removal from office in 1851.

Immediately after the *coup d'état* of the 2d December, 1851, in Paris, the cabinet determined that the Government of this country should abstain from any interference in the internal affairs of France; and a despatch to that effect, approved by the queen, was addressed to Lord Normanby, the British ambassador in Paris. But before this official communication was written, it appeared that M. Walewski, the French ambassador at the Court of St. James's, had assured his own Government, that Lord Palmerston had "expressed to him his entire approbation of the act of the president, and his conviction that he could not have acted otherwise than he had done." This statement having been communicated to Lord Normanby by M. Turgot, was reported by him to Lord Palmerston. On receiving a copy of Lord Normanby's letter, Lord John Russell immediately wrote to Lord Palmerston requiring explanations of the variance between his verbal communications with the French ambassador, and the despatch agreed upon by the cabinet; and a few days afterwards her Majesty also demanded similar explanations. These were delayed for several days; and in the mean time, in reply to another letter from Lord Normanby, Lord Palmerston, on the 16th of December, wrote to his lordship, explaining his own views in favor of the policy of the recent

1 Hansard's Debates, 3d Series, cxix. 90.

2 Sir Robert Peel's evidence before Select Committee on Official Salaries. Statement by Lord J. Russell; Hansard's Debates, 3d Series, cxix. 91.

coup d'état. On receiving a copy of this correspondence, Lord John Russell conceived that the secretary of state was not justified in expressing such opinions, without the sanction of the Crown and the concurrence of the cabinet, — more particularly as these opinions were opposed to the policy of non-intervention upon which the cabinet had determined, and inconsistent with that moral support and sympathy, which England had generally offered to constitutional government in foreign countries. The explanations which ensued were not deemed satisfactory; and Lord Palmerston was accordingly removed from office, on the ground that he had exceeded his authority as secretary of state, and had taken upon himself alone, to be the organ of the queen's government.[1]

In defence of his own conduct, Lord Palmerston, while fully recognizing the principles upon which a secretary of state is required to act in relation to the Crown and his own colleagues, explained that his conversation with Count Walewski on the 3d of December, and his explanatory letter to Lord Normanby on the 16th, were not inconsistent with the policy of non-intervention upon which the cabinet had resolved; that whatever opinions he might have expressed, were merely his own; and that he had given no official instructions or assurances on the part of the Government, except in the despatch of the 5th of December, which her Majesty and the cabinet had approved.

Though the premier and the secretary of state had differed as to the propriety of the particular acts of the latter, they were agreed upon the general principles which regulate the relations of ministers to the Crown. These events exemplify the effective control which the Crown constitutionally exercises in the government of the country. The policy and conduct of its ministers are subject to its active supervision. In minor affairs the ministers have a separate discretion, in their several departments; but in the general acts

[1] Explanations of Lord J. Russell, Feb. 3, 1852.

of the government, the Crown is to be consulted, and has a control over them all.

Wise use of the influence of the Crown, in the present reign.

From this time no question has arisen concerning the exercise of the prerogatives or influence of the Crown, which calls for notice. Both have been exercised wisely, justly, and in the true spirit of the constitution. Ministers, enjoying the confidence of Parliament, have never claimed in vain the confidence of the Crown. Their measures have not been thwarted by secret influence, and irresponsible advice. Their policy has been directed by Parliament and public opinion, and not by the will of the sovereign, or the intrigues of the court. Vast as is the power of the Crown, it has been exercised, throughout the present reign, by the advice of responsible ministers, in a constitutional manner, and for legitimate objects. It has been held in trust, as it were, for the benefit of the people. Hence it has ceased to excite either the jealousy of rival parties, or popular discontents.

This judicious exercise of the royal authority, while it has conduced to the good government of the state, has sustained the moral influence of the Crown; and the devoted loyalty of a free people, which her Majesty's personal virtues have merited, has never been disturbed by the voice of faction.

General increase of the influence of the Crown.

But while the influence of the Crown in the government of the country, has been gradually brought into subordination to Parliament and public opinion, the same causes, which, for more than a century and a half, contributed to its enlargement, have never ceased to add to its greatness. The national expenditure and public establishments have been increased to an extent which alarms financiers; armies and navies have been maintained, such as at no former period had been endured in time of peace. Our colonies have expanded into a vast and populous empire; and her Majesty, invested with the sovereignty of the East Indies, now rules over two hundred millions of Asiatic subjects. Governors, commanders-in-chief, and bishops attest her supremacy in all parts of the world; and the greatness of the British empire, while it has redounded to the glory of England, has widely extended the influence of the Crown. As that influence, constitutionally exercised, has ceased to be regarded with jealousy, its continued enlargement has been watched by Parliament without any of those efforts to restrain it, which marked the parliamentary history of the eighteenth century. On the contrary, Parliament has met the increasing demands of a community rapidly advancing in population and wealth, by constant additions to the power and patronage of the Crown. The judicial establishments of the country have been extended, by the appointment of more judges in the superior courts, — by a large staff of county court judges, with local jurisdiction, — and by numerous stipendiary magistrates. Offices and commissions have been multiplied, for various public purposes; and all these appointments proceed from the same high source of patronage and preferment. Parliament has wisely excluded all these officers, with a few necessary exceptions, from the privilege of sitting in the House of Commons; but otherwise these extensive means of influence have been intrusted to the executive government, without any apprehension that they will be perverted to uses injurious to the freedom, or public interests of the country.

Continued influence of great families.

The history of the influence of the Crown has now been sketched, for a period of one hundred years. We have seen George III. jealous of the great Whig families, and wresting power out of the hands of his ministers: we have seen ministers becoming more accountable to Parliament, and less dependent upon the Crown; but, as in the commencement of this period, a few great families commanded the support of Parliament, and engrossed all the power of the state, — so under a more free representation, and more extended responsibilities, do we see nearly the same families still in the ascendant. Deprived in great measure of their direct influence over Parliament, — their general weight in the country, and in the councils of the state, has suffered little diminution. Notwithstanding the more democratic tendencies of later times, rank and station have still retained the respect and confidence of the people. When the aristocracy have enjoyed too exclusive an influence in the government, they have aroused jealousies and hostility; but when duly sharing power with other classes, and admitting the just claims of talent, they have prevailed over every rival and adverse interest; and, — whatever party has been in power, — have still been the rulers of the state.

In a society comprising so many classes as that of England, the highest are willingly accepted as governors, when their personal qualities are not unequal to their position. They excite less jealousy than abler men of inferior social pretensions, who climb to power. Born and nurtured to influences, they have studied how to maintain it. That they have maintained it so well, against the encroachments of wealth, — an expanding society, — and popular influences, is mainly due to their progressive policy. As they have been ready to advance with their age, the people have been content to acknowledge them as leaders; but had they endeavored to stem the tide of public opinion, they would have been swept aside, while men from other classes advanced to power.

CHAPTER III.

The Prerogatives of the Crown, during the Minority or Incapacity of the Sovereign. — Illnesses and Regency of George the Third. — Later Regency Acts.

Prerogatives of the Crown in abeyance.

WE have seen the prerogatives of the Crown wielded in the plenitude of kingly power. Let us now turn aside for a while, and view them as they lay inert in the powerless hands of a stricken king.

The melancholy illnesses of George III., at different periods of his reign, involved political considerations of the highest importance, — affecting the prerogatives of the Crown, the rights of the royal family, the duties of ministers, and the authority of Parliament.

First illness of Geo. III. in 1765.

The king was seized by the first of these attacks in 1765. Though a young man, in the full vigor of life, he exhibited those symptoms of mental disorder, which were afterwards more seriously developed. But the knowledge of this melancholy circumstance was confined to his own family, and personal attendants.[1] This illness, however, had been in other respects so alarming, that it led the king to consider the necessity of providing for a regency, in case of his death. The laws of England recognize no incapacity in the sovereign, by reason of nonage; and have made no provision for the guardianship of a king, or for the government of his kingdom, during his minority.[2]

[1] Grenville Papers, iii. 122; Adolphus's History, i. 175, *n.*; Quarterly Review, lxvi. 240, by Mr. Croker.

[2] " In judgment of law, the king, as king, cannot be said to be a minor;

Yet the common sense of every age has revolted against the anomaly of suffering the country to be practically governed by an infant king. Hence special provision has been made for each occasion, according to the age and consanguinity of the surviving relatives of the minor; and as such provision involves not only the care of an infant, but the government of the country, the sanction of Parliament has necessarily been required, as well as that of the king.

Regency Act of 1751.

By the Regency Act of 1751, passed after the death of Frederick Prince of Wales, the Princess Dowager of Wales had been appointed regent, in the event of the demise of George II. before the Prince of Wales, or any other of her children succeeding to the throne, had attained the age of eighteen years. This act also nominated the council of regency; but empowered the king to add four other members to the council, by instruments under his sign-manual, to be opened after his death.[1] But this precedent deferred too much to the judgment of Parliament, and left too little to the discretion of the king himself, to be acceptable to George III. He desired to reserve to himself the testamentary disposition of his prerogatives, and to leave nothing to Parliament but the formal recognition of his power.

The king's first scheme of a regency, 1765.

The original scheme of the regency, as proposed by the king, in 1765, was as strange as some of the incidents connected with its further progress. He had formed it without any communication with his ministers, who consequently received it with distrust, as the work of Lord Bute and the king's friends, of whom they were sensitively jealous.[2] The scheme itself was one to invite suspicion. It was obviously proper, that the appoint-

for when the royall bodie politique of the king doth meete with the naturall capacity in one person, the whole bodie shall have the qualitie of the royall politique, which is the greater and more worthy, and wherein is no minoritie." — *Co. Litt.*, 43.

[1] 24 Geo. II., c. 24; Walpole's Mem. Geo. III., ii. c. 102.

[2] Walpole's Mem., ii. 99, 104; Rockingham Mem., i. 183.

ment of a regent should be expressly made by Parliament. If the king had the nomination, there could be no certainty that any regent would be appointed: — he might become incapable and die intestate, as it were; and this contingency was the more probable, as the king's mind had recently been affected. But his Majesty proposed that Parliament should confer upon him the unconditional right of appointing any person as regent, whom he should select.[1] Mr. Grenville pressed him to name the regent in his speech, but was unable to persuade him to adopt that suggestion. There can be little doubt that the king intended that the queen should be regent; but he was believed to be dying of consumption,[2] and was still supposed to be under the influence of his mother. The ministers feared lest the princess might eventually be appointed regent, and Lord Bute admitted to the council of regency. Some even went so far as to conceive the possibility of Lord Bute's nomination to the regency itself.[3] It was ultimately arranged that the king should nominate the regent himself, but that his choice should be restricted "to the queen and any other person of the royal family usually resident in England;" [4] and the scheme of the regency was proposed to Parliament upon that basis.[5]

Modified by the ministers.

On the 24th of April, 1765, the king came down to Parliament and made a speech to both houses, recommending to their consideration the expediency of enabling him to appoint, "from time to time, by instrument

The king's speech.

1 Grenville Papers (Diary), iii. 126, 129.

2 Walpole's Mem., ii. 98.

3 *Ibid.*, ii. 101, 104.

4 Cabinet Minute, 5th April; Grenville Papers, iii. 15, 16.

5 Lord John Russell says that the ministers "unwisely introduced the bill without naming the regent, or placing any limit on the king's nomination." (Introduction to 3d vol. of *Bedford Correspondence*, xxxix.) This was not precisely the fact, as will be seen from the text; but ministers were equally blamable for not insisting that the queen alone should be the regent.

in writing, under his sign-manual, either the queen, or any other person of his royal family, usually residing in Great Britain, to be the guardian of his successor, and the regent of these kingdoms, until such successor shall attain the age of eighteen years," — subject to restrictions similar to those contained in the Regency Act, 24 Geo. II., — and of providing for a council of regency. A joint address was immediately agreed upon by both Houses, — ultra-loyal, according to the fashion of the time, — approaching his "sacred person" with "reverence," "affection," "admiration," and "gratitude;" scarcely venturing to comtemplate the possibility of "an event which, if it shall please God to permit it, must overwhelm his Majesty's loyal subjects with the bitterest distraction of grief;" and promising to give immediate attention to recommendations which were the result of the king's "consummate prudence," "beneficent intention," "salutary designs," "princely wisdom," and "paternal concern for his people." [1]

The Regency Bill, 1765.

A bill, founded upon the royal speech, was immediately brought into the House of Lords. In the first draft of the bill, the king, following the precedent of 1751, had reserved to himself the right of nominating four members of the council of regency; but on the 29th April, he sent a message to the Lords, desiring that his four brothers and his uncle, the Duke of Cumberland, should be specified in the bill; and reserving to himself the nomination of other persons, in the event of any vacancy.[2] The bill was read a second time on the following day. But first it was asked if the queen was naturalized, — and if not, whether she could lawfully be regent. This question was

[1] Parl. Hist., xvi. 53.

[2] Walpole's Mem., ii. 109; Lords' Journ., xxxi. 162. A memorial by Lord Lyttelton says, "While the bill was in the House of Lords, the clause naming the king's brothers was concerted, with the Duke of Cumberland, unknown to the ministry till the king sent to them. They, to return the compliment, framed the clause for omitting the princess dowager, and procured the king's consent to it." — *Rockingham Mem.*, i. 183.

referred to the judges, who were unanimously of opinion, "that an alien married to a king of Great Britain is, by operation of the law of the Crown (which is a part of the common law), to be deemed a natural-born subject from the time of such marriage; so as not to be disabled by the Act of the 12th William III., or by any other Act, from holding and enjoying any office or place of trust, or from having any grant of lands, &c., from the Crown."[1] Then, suddenly a doubt arose whether the king's mother, the Princess of Wales, was comprehended in the "royal family" or not. It was suggested that this term applied only to members of the royal family in the line of succession to the Crown, and would not extend beyond the descendants of the late king.[2] There can be no question that the king, in his speech, had intended to include the princess; and even the doubt which was afterwards raised, was not shared by all the members of the cabinet, — and by the Lord Chancellor was thought unfounded.[3] Whether it had occurred to those by whom the words had been suggested to the king, is doubtful.

Exclusion of the Princess of Wales.

On the 1st May, Lord Lyttelton moved an address, praying the king to name the regent, which was rejected. On the 2d, the Duke of Richmond moved an amendment in committee, defining the persons capable of the regency to be the queen, the princess dowager, and the descendants of the late king. Strange as it may seem, the ministers resisted this amendment, and it was negatived.[4] The doubt which had been thus raised concerning the Princess of Wales had not been removed, when, on the following day, Lord Halifax and Lord Sandwich had an audience of the king, and represented, that if the Lords should insert the princess's name in the bill, the Commons would strike it out again; and that such an insult might best be

[1] Lords' Journ., xxxi. 174.
[2] Grenville Papers (Diary), iii. 125–148; Walpole's Mem., ii. 118.
[3] *Ibid.*, 148.
[4] Parl. Hist., xvi. 55; Rockingham Mem., i. 183.

avoided by not proposing her name at all.[1] The king was taken by surprise, and either misunderstood the proposal, or failed to show his usual firmness and courage in resisting it.[2] Lord Halifax at once proceeded to the House of Lords, and moved the recommitment of the bill, according to the alleged wishes of his Majesty, in order to make an amendment, which limited the regency to the queen, and the descendants of the late king, usually resident in England. Thus, not satisfied with gaining their point, ministers had the cruelty and assurance to make the king himself bear the blame of proposing an affront to his own mother. Well might Horace Walpole exclaim: "And thus she alone is rendered incapable of the regency, and stigmatized by Act of Parliament!"[3]

The king had no sooner given his consent than he recoiled from its consequences, — complained that he had been betrayed, — and endeavored to obtain the insertion of his mother's name. He could gain no satisfaction from his ministers;[4] but in the Commons, the friends of the princess, encouraged by the king himself, took up her cause; and, on the motion of Mr. Morton, Chief Justice of Chester, which was not opposed by the ministers, — her name was inserted in the bill. The king had been assured that the Commons would strike it out: and yet, after the House of Lords had omitted it, on the supposed authority of the king, there were only thirty-seven members found to vote against its insertion, while one hundred and sixty-seven voted in its favor;[5] and in this form the bill passed.

Her name replaced in the bill.

1 Walpole's Mem., ii. 125.

2 Grenville Papers (Diary), iii. 149, and 154, *n.*

3 Letter to Lord Hertford, May 5th.

4 "The king seemed much agitated, and felt the force of what Mr. Grenville said in regard to the different directions given to his servants in the two Houses, but still enforced the argument of this being moved by the gentlemen of the Opposition. The king was in the utmost degree of agitation and emotion, even to tears." — *Mr. Grenville's Diary*, May 5th, 1765; *Grenville Papers*, iii. 154.

5 Mr. Grenville's Report of the Debate to the King; Grenville Papers, iii. 25, *n.;* Walpole's Mem. George III., ii. 129–146.

Could any lover of mischief, — could Wilkes himself, — have devised more embarrassments and cross purposes, than were caused by this unlucky Regency Bill? Faction and intrigue had done their worst.

Provisions of the Regency Act.

The Regency Act[1] provided for the nomination by the king, under his sign-manual, of the queen, the Princess of Wales, or a member of the royal family descended from the late king, to be the guardian of his successor while under eighteen years of age, and "Regent of the Kingdom," and to exercise the royal power and prerogatives. His nomination was to be signified by three instruments, separately signed, and sealed up, and deposited with the Archbishop of Canterbury, the Lord Chancellor, and the President of the Council. It attached the penalties of præmunire to any one who should open these instruments during the king's life, or afterwards neglect or refuse to produce them before the privy council. It appointed a council of regency, consisting of the king's brothers and his uncle, the Duke of Cumberland, and several great officers of Church and State, for the time being. In case any of the king's brothers or his uncle should die, or be appointed regent, it gave the king the power of nominating another person, being a natural-born subject, to the council of regency, by instruments under his hand in the same form as those appointing the regent. The act also defined the powers of the regent and council. On the demise of his Majesty, the privy council was directed to meet and proclaim his successor.

The king's illness in 1788–9.

The king's next illness was of longer duration, and of a more distressing character. It was the occasion of another Regency Bill, and of proceedings wholly unprecedented. In the summer of 1788, the king showed evident symptoms of derangement. He was able, however, to sign a warrant for the further prorogation of Parliament by commission, from the 25th September to the

[1] 5 George III. c. 27.

20th November. But, in the interval, the king's malady increased: he was wholly deprived of reason, and placed under restraint; and for several days his life was in danger.[1] As no authority could be obtained from him for a further prorogation, both Houses assembled on the 20th November, though they had not been summoned for dispatch of business, and no causes of summons could be communicated to them, in the accustomed manner, by a speech from the throne. These circumstances were explained in both Houses; and, on the suggestion of ministers, they agreed to adjourn for a fortnight, and to summon all their members, by circular letters, to attend at their next meeting.[2] According to long established law, Parliament, without being opened by the Crown, had no authority to proceed to any business whatever: but the necessity of an occasion, for which the law had made no provision, was now superior to the law; and Parliament accordingly proceeded to deliberate upon the momentous questions to which the king's illness had given rise.

Examination of the king's physicians.

In order to afford Parliament authentic evidence of the king's condition, his five physicians were examined by the privy council on the 3d December. They agreed that the king was then incapable of meeting Parliament, or of attending to any business; but believed in the probability of his ultimate recovery, although they could not limit the time. On the following day this evidence was laid before both Houses: but as doubts were suggested whether Parliament should rest satisfied without receiving the personal testimony of the physicians, it was

[1] Tomline's Life of Pitt, ii. 363; Lord Auckland's Corr. ii. 240-298. At such times as these, political events pressed heavily on the king's mind. He said to Lord Thurlow and the Duke of Leeds, "Whatever you and Mr. Pitt may think or feel, I, that am born a gentleman, shall never lay my head on my last pillow in peace and quiet as long as I remember the loss of my American colonies." Lord Malm. Corr., iv. 21. On a later occasion, in 1801, the king's mind showed equally strong feelings as to the supposed dangers of the Church.

[2] Parl. Hist., xxvii. 653, 685. The House of Commons was also ordered to be called over on that day.

afterwards agreed that a committee should be appointed, in each House, for that purpose. In the Lords the committee was nominated by ballot, each peer giving in a list of twenty-one names.[1] Meanwhile, all other business was suspended. In the Commons, the speaker even entertained doubts whether any new writs could be issued for supplying the places of members deceased; but Mr. Pitt expressed a decided opinion, "that though no act could take place which required the joint concurrence of the different branches of the Legislature, yet each of them in its separate capacity was fully competent to the exercise of those powers which concerned its own orders and jurisdiction."[2] And in this rational view the House acquiesced.

Committees appointed.

The reports of these committees merely confirmed the evidence previously given before the privy council; and the facts being thus established, a committee was moved for, in either House, to search for precedents "of such proceedings as may have been had in case of the personal exercise of the royal authority being prevented or interrupted by infancy, sickness, infirmity, or otherwise, with a view to provide for the same." When this motion was made in the Commons, Mr. Fox advanced the startling opinion that the Prince of Wales had as clear a right to exercise the power of sovereignty during the king's incapacity, as if the king were actually dead; and that it was merely for the two Houses of Parliament to pronounce at what time he should commence the exercise of his right.[3] To assert an absolute right of inheritance during his father's life, in defiance of the well-known rule of law, "*nemo est hæres viventis*," was to argue that the heir-at-law is entitled to enter into possession of the estate of a lunatic. Mr. Pitt, on the other hand, maintained that as no legal provision had been made for carrying on the government, it belonged to the Houses of Parliament to make such provision. He even went so far

Committees to search for precedents.

Doctrines of Mr. Fox and Mr. Pitt.

[1] Parl. Hist., xxvii. 658. [2] *Ibid.*, 688. [3] *Ibid.*, 707.

as to affirm, that "unless by their decision, the Prince of Wales had no more right — speaking of strict right — to assume the government, than any other individual subject of the country," [1] — a position as objectionable in one direction, as that of Mr. Fox in the other,[2] — and which gave great umbrage to the prince and his friends. And here the two parties joined issue.

Issue taken as to the rights of the Prince.

When next this matter was discussed, Mr. Fox, being sensible that he had pressed his doctrine of right beyond its constitutional limits, somewhat receded from his first ground. He now spoke of the prince having a legal claim rather than a right to the regency, and contended that it was for Parliament to adjudicate upon that claim, which, when allowed, would become an absolute title to the exercise of all the rights of sovereignty, without any limitation. He stated, also, that he spoke merely his own opinion, without any authority; but that if he had been consulted, he should have advised a message from the prince, stating his claim, to be answered by a joint address of both Houses, calling upon him to exercise the prerogatives of the Crown. It was now his main position that no restrictions should be imposed upon the powers of the regent. But here, again, Mr. Pitt joined issue with him; and while he agreed that, as a matter of discretion, the Prince of Wales ought to be the regent, with all necessary authority, — unrestrained by any permanent council, and with a free choice of his political servants; — he yet contended that any power which was not essential, and which might be employed to embarrass the exercise of the king's authority, in the event of his recovery, ought to be withheld.[3] And as the ques-

[1] Parl. Hist., xxvii. 709.

[2] Lord John Russell says, "The doctrine of Mr. Fox, the popular leader, went far to set aside the constitutional authority of Parliament, while that of Mr. Pitt, the organ of the Crown, tended to shake the stability of the monarchy, and to peril the great rule of hereditary succession." — *Memorials of Fox*, ii. 263.

[3] Dec. 12th. Parl. Hist., xxvii. 727.

tion of right had been raised, he insisted that it ought first to be determined, — since if the right should be held to exist, Parliament having adjudicated upon such right, need not deliberate upon any further measures.

The same questions were debated in the House of Lords, where the Duke of York said that no claim of right had been made on the part of the prince, who "understood too well the sacred principles which seated the House of Brunswick on the throne, ever to assume or exercise any power, be his claim what it might, not derived from the will of the people, expressed by their representatives, and their lordships in Parliament assembled." His Royal Highness, therefore, deprecated pressing for any decision on that point, — in which the Duke of Gloucester concurred.[1]

The Prince of Wales disclaims his right.

Meanwhile, the prince was greatly offended by Mr. Pitt's conduct, and wrote to the chancellor complaining that the premier had publicly announced so much of his scheme of regency, and was prepared, as he conceived, to lay it still more fully before Parliament, without having previously submitted it to his consideration. He desired that Mr. Pitt would send him, in writing, an outline of what he proposed. Mr. Pitt immediately wrote to the prince, explaining his own conduct, and stating that it was not his intention to propose any specific plan until the right of Parliament to consider such a plan had been determined; and that he would then submit to his Royal Highness the best opinions which his Majesty's servants had been able to give.[2]

The Prince offended by Mr. Pitt's conduct.

On the 16th December the House resolved itself into a committee on the state of the nation, when Mr. Pitt again enforced the right of Parliament to appoint a regent, — fortifying his position by reference to the report of precedents,[3] which had then been re-

Mr. Pitt's preliminary resolutions.

1 Parl. Hist., xxvii. 678, 684.

2 Tomline's Life of Pitt, ii. 388; where the letter is printed at length.

3 Commons' Journ., xliv. 11; Lords' Journ., xxxviii. 276.

ceived, — and arguing ably and elaborately that neither law, precedent, nor analogy could be found to support the claim which had been urged on behalf of the Prince of Wales. He concluded by moving three resolutions; affirming, first, that the personal exercise of royal authority was interrupted; second, the right of the two Houses to supply the defect of the personal exercise of the royal authority, in such manner as the exigency of the case may seem to require; and, third, the necessity of "determining the means by which the royal assent may be given to bills passed by the two Houses respecting the exercise of the powers of the Crown, during the continuance of the king's indisposition."

Mr. Fox argued, ingeniously, that the principles maintained by Mr. Pitt tended to make the monarchy elective instead of hereditary; and that if Parliament might elect any one to be regent, for whatever time it thought fit, the monarchy would become a republic. Nor did he omit to seek for support, by intimations that he should be Mr. Pitt's successor, under the regency.

On the report of these resolutions to the House,[1] Mr. Pitt explained (in reference to his third resolution, which had not been clearly understood), that he intended, when the resolutions had been agreed to by both Houses, to propose that the Lord Chancellor should be empowered, by a vote of the two Houses, to affix the Great Seal to commissions for opening the Parliament, and for giving the royal assent to a Regency Bill. The propriety of this singular course of proceeding was much questioned; but, after long debates, the resolutions were agreed to, and communicated to the House of Lords at a conference. In that House the same questions were debated, and Lord Rawdon moved as an amendment, an address to the Prince of Wales, praying him "to take upon himself, as sole regent, the administration of the executive government, in the king's name." Lord

[1] Parl. Hist., xxvii. 782. Twiss's Life of Eldon, i. 191.

Chancellor Thurlow, — though faithless to his colleagues, and intriguing, at the very time, with the queen and the Prince of Wales,[1] — supported the ministerial position with great force. In answer to Lord Rawdon's amendment, he "begged to know what the term 'regent' meant? where was he to find it defined? in what law-book, or what statute? He had heard of *custodes regni*, of lieutenants for the king, of guardians and protectors, and of lords-justices; but he knew not where to look for an explanation of the office and functions of regent. To what end, then, would it be to address the prince to take upon himself an office, the boundaries of which were by no means ascertained? . . . . What was meant by the executive government? Did it mean the whole royal authority? Did it mean the power of legislation? Did it mean all the sovereign's functions without restriction or limitation of any kind whatsoever? If it did, it amounted to the actual dethroning of his Majesty, and wresting the sceptre out of his hand."[2] All the resolutions were agreed to; but were followed by a protest signed by forty-eight peers.[3]

Death of Mr. Speaker Cornwall.

The perplexities arising out of the incapacity of the sovereign, — the constitutional source and origin of authority — were now increased by the death of Mr. Cornwall, the Speaker of the House of Commons. His Majesty's leave could not be signified that the

[1] Nicholls's Recollections, 71; Tomline's Life of Pitt, iii. c. 14; Wilberforce's Life, i. App.; Moore's Life of Sheridan, ii. 31; Lord Campbell's Lives of Chancellors, v. 583, *et seq.*

[2] Parl. Hist., xxvii. 885. The office of regent, however, does not appear to be wholly without recognition, as contended by the chancellor and others. On the accession of Henry III., a minor, the great council of the nation, assembled at Bristol, appointed the Earl of Pembroke regent, as "*Rector Regis et Regni*" (Matthew Paris, Wats's 2d Ed., p. 245; Carte's History of Eng., ii. 2); and when the Duke of York was appointed protector by the Parliament during the illness of Hen. VI., it is entered in the rolls of Parliament that the title of regent was not given him, because "*it emported auctorite of governaunce of the lande.*" Rot. Parl., v. 242, A. D. 1454; Rymer's Fœdera, v. 55.

[3] Parl. Hist., xxvii. 901.

Commons should proceed to the election of another speaker; nor could the new speaker, when elected, be presented for the king's approval. But the necessity of the occasion suggested an easy expedient; and both these customary formalities were simply dispensed with, without any attempt to assume the appearance of the royal sanction.[1]

Mr. Pitt submits his scheme to the prince.

All these preliminaries being settled, Mr. Pitt now submitted to the Prince of Wales the plan of regency which he intended to propose. The limitations suggested were these: — that the care of the king's person and household, and the appointment of officers and servants, should be reserved to the queen: — that the regent should not be empowered to dispose of the real or personal property of the king, or to grant any office in reversion, or any pension or office, otherwise than during pleasure, except those which were required to be granted for life, or during good behavior; or to bestow any peerage except upon his Majesty's issue, having attained the age of twenty-one.[2] These limitations were suggested, he said, on the supposition that the king's illness would not be of long duration, and might afterwards be revised by Parliament.

The prince's reply.

The prince's reply to this communication was a most skilful composition, written by Burke and revised by Sheridan.[3] He regarded the restrictions as "a project for producing weakness, disorder, and insecurity in every branch of the administration of affairs, — a project for dividing the royal family from each other, for separating the court from the state; — a scheme disconnecting the authority to command service, from the power of animating it by reward; and for allotting to the prince all the invidious duties of government, without the means of softening them to the public, by any act of grace, favor, or benignity." And he repudiated as unnecessary, the restric-

1 Parl. Hist., xxvii. 903, 1160.

2 Tomline's Life of Pitt, ii. 422. Parl. Hist., xxvii. 909.

3 Moore's Life of Sheridan, ii. 50.

tion upon his granting away the king's property, — a power which he had shown no inclination to possess.[1]

But before Mr. Pitt was able to bring his proposals before Parliament, fresh discussions were raised by the Opposition on the state of the king's health, which resulted in another examination of his physicians by a select committee. The inquiry lasted for several days: but, while it disclosed much party spirit, intrigue, and jealousy, it established no new facts concerning the probable recovery of the royal patient.[2] The least hopeful physicians were popular with the Opposition: the more sanguine found favor with the court and the ministers. At length, on the 19th January, Mr. Pitt moved, in committee on the state of the nation, five resolutions on which the Regency Bill was to be founded. After animated debates they were all agreed to, and communicated at a conference to the Lords, by whom they were also adopted; but not without a protest signed by fifty-seven peers, headed by the Dukes of York and Cumberland.

Further inquiries concerning the king's health.

Further resolutions on the regency.

The next step was to lay these resolutions before the prince; and to ascertain whether he would accept the regency, with the conditions attached to it by Parliament. The resolutions were accordingly presented by both Houses; and the prince, out of respect for his father, the interests of the people, and the united desires of the two Houses, consented to undertake the trust, though he felt the difficulties which must attend its execution. The resolutions were also presented to the queen, and received a gracious answer.[3]

Laid before the prince.

Another technical difficulty was still to be overcome before the Regency Bill could, at last, be introduced. Parliament had not yet been opened, nor the causes of summons declared, in a speech from the

Commission for opening Parliament.

1 Tomline's Life of Pitt, ii. 425; Parl. Hist., xxvii. 910.
2 Commons' Journ., xliv. 47.
3 Parl. Hist., xxvii. 1122.

throne, — formalities always held to be essential to enable Parliament to proceed with its legislative business. It was
Jan. 31, 1789. now proposed, by a vote of both Houses, to authorize the passing of letters-patent under the great seal, for the opening of Parliament by commission. The necessity of adopting this expedient had been already intimated, and had been described as a "phantom" of royalty, a "fiction," and a "forgery." It was now formally proposed by ministers, on the ground that the opening of Parliament, by royal authority, was essential to the validity of its proceedings; that during the king's incapacity such authority could only be signified by a commission under the great seal; that without the direction of both Houses, the Lord Chancellor could not venture to affix the seal; but that the commission being once issued, with the great seal annexed to it, — the instrument by which the will of the king is declared — no one could question its legality.[1] It was also stated that the royal assent would hereafter be signified to the Regency Bill by commission, executed in the same way. A precedent in 1754 was further relied on, in which Lord Hardwicke had affixed the great seal to two commissions, — the one for opening Parliament, and the other for passing a bill, during a dangerous illness of George II.[2]

It was contended on the other side, with much force, that if this legal fiction were necessary at all, it ought to have been used for the opening of Parliament two months ago: that hitherto the time of Parliament had been wasted, — its deliberations unauthorized, irregular, and fruitless. But this fiction was also an assumption of royal authority. The Houses had already agreed to allot one portion of the prerogatives to the queen, and another to the regent, and now they were about to take another portion themselves: but, after all, the fictitious use of the king's name would be illegal. By the 33d Henry VIII., it was declared that a commission

[1] Lord Camden's Speech. Parl. Hist. xxvii. 1124.

[2] Speeches of Mr. Pitt and Lord Camden. In the latter this precedent is erroneously assigned to 1739.

for giving the royal assent to a bill must be by letters-patent under the great seal, and signed by the king's own hand. The great seal alone would not, therefore, make the commission legal; and the Act for the Duke of Norfolk's attainder had been declared void by Parliament,[1] because the commission for giving the royal assent to it had wanted the king's sign-manual, his name having been affixed by means of a stamp. The course proposed by ministers, however, was approved by both Houses.

The royal dukes decline to be in the commission.

According to invariable custom, the names of all the royal dukes, having seats in the House of Lords, had been inserted in the proposed commission; but the Duke of York desired that his own name and that of the Prince of Wales might be omitted, as he "deemed the measure proposed, as well as every other which had been taken respecting the same subject, as unconstitutional and illegal." The Duke of Cumberland also desired the omission of his name, and that of the Duke of Gloucester.

Opening of Parliament.

On the 3d February, Parliament was at length opened by commission.[2] Earl Bathurst, one of the commissioners who sat as speaker, in the absence of the Chancellor, stated that the illness of his Majesty had made it necessary that a commission *in his name should pass the Great Seal;* and when the commission had been read, he delivered a speech to both Houses, in pursuance of the authority given by that commission, declaring the causes of summons, and calling attention to the necessity of making provision for the care of the king's person, and the administration of the royal authority.

Commission for holding the assizes.

Meanwhile, it became necessary that the usual commission should issue for holding the assizes. Although the sign-manual could not then be obtained, the urgency of the occasion was so great that Lord Thurlow, the chancellor, affixed the great seal to a commission for

[1] 1 Mary, Sess. 2, c. 13 (Private).

[2] See Form of Commission, Lords Journ., xxxviii. 344.

that purpose, by virtue of which the judges went their circuits.[1]

After all these delays, Mr. Pitt now brought the Regency Bill into the House of Commons.[2] The provisions which attracted most observation were the nomination of the queen's council, the restriction upon the creation of peers, the power of the privy council to pronounce his Majesty's restoration to health and capacity, and a clause by which the regent's authority would cease if he married a Roman Catholic. But, as the measure was not destined to pass, the lengthened debates to which it gave rise, need not be pursued any further. The bill had been sent to the Lords, — its clauses were being discussed in committee, — and politicians, in expectation of its early passing, were busily filling up the places in the prince regent's first administration, — when on the 19th February, the Lord Chancellor announced that his Majesty was convalescent; and further proceedings were arrested. The king's recovery was now rapid: on the 25th, he was pronounced free from complaint, and on the 27th, further bulletins were discontinued by his Majesty's own command. On the 10th March another commission was issued, authorizing "the commissioners, who were appointed *by former letters-patent to hold this Parliament*, to open and declare certain further causes for holding the same,"[3] thus recognizing the validity of the previous commission, to which the great seal had been affixed in his name.[4] He thanked Parliament for its attachment to his person, and its concern for the honor of the Crown, and the security of his dominions. Loyal addresses were agreed to

Regency Bill brought in.

The king's sudden recovery.

1 Speech of Lord Liverpool, Jan. 5th, 1811. Hansard's Deb., 1st Ser., xviii. 789.

2 5th February, 1789; see a copy of the Regency Bill as passed by the Commons, Parl. Hist., xxvii. 1258.

3 Commons' Journ., xliv. 159.

4 While the proceedings upon the Regency Bill were pending, several other bills were introduced into both Houses of Parliament, which received the royal assent after his Majesty's recovery.

by both Houses, *nem. con.*, as well as a message of congratulation to the queen.

The 23d April was appointed as a day of public thanksgiving, when the king and royal family, attended by both Houses of Parliament, the great officers of state, and foreign ambassadors, went in procession to St. Paul's. It was a solemn and affecting spectacle: a national demonstration of loyalty, and pious gratitude.

The king goes to St. Paul's.

Thus ended a most painful episode in the history of this reign. Had no delays been interposed in the progress of the Regency Bill, the king, on his recovery, would have found himself stripped of his royal authority. He was spared this sorrow, partly by the numerous preliminaries which the ministers had deemed necessary; and partly by the conduct of the Opposition, who though most interested in the speedy passing of the bill, had contributed to its protracted consideration. By asserting the prince's right, they had provoked the ministers to maintain the authority of Parliament, as a preliminary to legislation. Twice they had caused the physicians to be examined; and they discussed the bill in all its stages, in full confidence that his Majesty's recovery was hopeless.

Fortunate delay in passing the Regency Bill.

Many of the preliminaries, indeed, would seem to have been superfluous: but the unprecedented circumstances with which ministers had to deal, — the entire want of confidence between them and the Prince of Wales, — the uncertainty of the king's recovery, — the conduct of the Opposition, and their relations to the Prince, — together with several constitutional considerations of the utmost difficulty, contributed to the embarrassment of their position.

Comments upon these proceedings.

If it was necessary to authorize the opening of Parliament by a commission under the great seal, this course ought to have been at first adopted; for the law of Parliament does not recognize the distinction then raised, between legislative and any other proceedings. No business whatever can be commenced until the causes of summons have been declared by the Crown.[1] The king having been unable to exercise this function, Parliament had proceeded with its deliberations for upwards of two months, without the accustomed speech from the throne. And if any doubt existed as to the validity of these proceedings, it is difficult to understand how they could be removed by the commission. As the king's authority could not in fact be exercised, and as the great seal, intended to represent it, was affixed by direction of the two Houses, why was the fiction needed? The only real authority was that of Parliament, which might have been boldly and openly exercised, during the incapacity of the king.

The simplest and most direct course would, undoubtedly, have been for both Houses to agree upon an address to the Prince of Wales, praying him to exercise the royal authority, subject to conditions stated in the address itself; and on his acceptance of the trust, to proceed to give legal effect to these conditions by a bill, — to which the royal assent would be signified by the regent, on behalf of the Crown. Either in earlier or in later times, such a course would probably have been followed; but at that period, above all others, lawyers delighted in fiction, and Westminster Hall was peopled with legal "phantoms" of their creation.[2]

Precedent of the Revolution of 1688.

In proposing to proceed by address, the Opposition relied upon the precedent of the Revolution of 1688. On the other side it was contended, and particularly by Sir John Scott, the Solicitor-General, —

[1] Even the election of a speaker and the swearing of members in a new Parliament, are not commenced until the pleasure of the Crown has been signified.

[2] See Chapter on Law and Administration of Justice. Lord John Russell says, "All reasonable restrictions might have been imposed by Act of Parliament, with the royal assent given by the regent, acting on behalf of the Crown." — *Mem. of Fox*, ii. 265. He ridicules the "absurd phantom of a royal assent given by the Houses of Parliament to their own act, by a fiction of their own creation."

by whose advice the Government were mainly guided,—that after the throne had been declared vacant, Parliament solicited the Prince of Orange to assume the royal powers; but here the rights of the lawful sovereign could not be passed by, and superseded.[1] His name must be used in all the proceedings: his great seal affixed by the chancellor of his appointment, to every commission; and his authority recognized and represented, though his personal directions and capacity were wanting. It is obvious, however, that whatever empty forms were observed, the royal authority was, of necessity, superseded. As the throne was not vacant, no stranger was sought to fill it; but all parties concurred in calling upon the heir apparent to exercise his father's royal authority. The two occasions differed in regard to the persons whom Parliament, in times of nearly equal emergency, proposed to invest with the supreme power: but why a simple and direct course of proceeding was not as appropriate in the one case as in the other, we need the subtilty and formalism of the old school of lawyers to perceive.

Conduct of political parties.

As regards the conduct of political parties, it can hardly be questioned that, on the one hand, Mr. Fox and his party incautiously took up an indefensible position; while, on the other, Mr. Pitt was unduly tenacious in asserting the authority of Parliament,—which the prince had not authorized any one to question,—and which his brother, the Duke of York, had admitted. Yet the conduct of both is easily explained by the circumstances of their respective parties. The Prince had identified himself with Mr. Fox and the Whigs; and it was well known to Mr. Pitt, and offensively announced by his opponents, that the passing of the Regency Act would be the signal for his own dismissal. To assert the prince's rights, and resist all restrictions upon his authority, was the natural course for his friends to adopt; while to maintain the prerogatives of the Crown,—to respect the feelings and dignity of the queen,

[1] Parl. Hist., xxvii. 825; Twiss's Life of Eldon, 192.

and at the same time to vindicate the paramount authority of Parliament, — was the becoming policy of the king's minister. Mr. Pitt's view, being favorable to popular rights, was supported by the people: Mr. Fox, on the other hand, committed himself to the assertion of prerogative, and inveighed against the discretionary powers of Parliament. Well might Mr. Pitt exultingly exclaim, "I'll unwhig the gentleman for the rest of his life."[1] The proceedings on the regency confirmed the confidence of the king in Mr. Pitt, and his distrust of Mr. Fox and his adherents; and the popular minister had a long career of power before him.

Proceedings in the Parliament of Ireland.

While these proceedings were pending, the Parliament of Ireland, adopting the views of Mr. Fox, presented an address to the Prince of Wales, praying him to take upon himself "the government of this realm, during the continuance of his Majesty's present indisposition, and no longer, and under the style and title of Prince Regent of *Ireland*, in the name and on behalf of his Majesty, to exercise and administer, according to the laws and constitution of this kingdom, all regal powers, jurisdictions, and prerogatives to the Crown and Government thereof belonging." The lord-lieutenant, the Marquis of Buckingham, having refused to transmit this address, the Parliament caused it to be conveyed directly to his Royal Highness, by some of their own members.[2]

To this address the prince returned an answer, in which, after thanking the Parliament of Ireland for their loyalty and affection, he stated that he trusted the king would soon be able to resume the personal exercise of the royal author-

1 Adolphus's Hist., iv. 326, *n.*; Moore's Life of Sheridan, ii. 38. Lord Grey, speaking in 1810 of the precedent of 1788, was of opinion, "now that the differences which then subsisted are no more, that all the preliminary steps taken . . . were wise and prudent, and conformable to the dictates of a sound and well-exercised discretion." — *Hansard's Debates*, 1st Ser., xviii. 19.

2 Debates of the Parliament of Ireland; Parl. Register of Ireland, ix. 119; Lords Journ. (Ireland), vol. vi. 240; Com. Journ. (Ireland), vol. xiii. 7.

ity, which would render unnecessary any further answer, except a repetition of his thanks.[1]

Soon after his recovery, the king said to Lord Thurlow, "what has happened may happen again: for God's sake make some permanent and immediate provision for such a regency as may prevent the country from being involved in disputes and difficulties similar to those just over." Lord Thurlow and Mr. Pitt agreed as to the expediency of such a measure; but differed as to the mode in which it should be framed. The former was soon afterwards out of office, and the latter thought no more about the matter.[2] It is indeed singular that the king's wise foresight should have been entirely neglected; and that on three subsequent occasions, embarrassments arising from the same cause, should have been experienced.

Wise foresight of the king.

In February, 1801, the king was again seized with an illness of the same melancholy character, as that by which he had previously been afflicted.[3] If not caused, it was at least aggravated by the excitement of an impending change of ministry,[4] in consequence of his difference of opinion with Mr. Pitt on the Roman Catholic question.[5]

The king's illness in 1801.

This illness, though not involving constitutional difficulties so important as those of 1788, occurred at a moment of no small political embarrassment. Mr.

Ministerial changes.

[1] Hansard's Debates, 1st Ser., xviii. 183.

[2] Lord Malmesbury's Diary, iv. 23.

[3] Lord Malmesbury's Diary, Feb. 17th, 1801: "King got a bad cold; takes James's powder; God forbid he should be ill!" Feb. 19th: "This the first symptom of the king's serious illness." Malm. Cor., iv. 11, 13. Feb. 22d: "King much worse; Dr. J. Willis attended him all last night, and says he was in the height of a frenzy-fever, as bad as the worst period when he saw him in 1788." *Ibid.*, 16: Evid. of Dr. Reynolds, 1810. *Hans. Deb.*, xviii. 134.

[4] He had been chilled by remaining very long in church on the Fast Day, Friday, Feb. 13, and on his return home was seized with cramps. — *Lord Malmes. Diary*, iv. 28.

[5] See supra, p. 85 *et seq.*, and Chapter XII., on Civil and Religious Liberty.

Pitt had tendered his resignation; and was holding office only until the appointment of his successor. Mr. Speaker Addington had received the king's commands to form an administration, and had, consequently, resigned the chair of the House of Commons. The arrangements for a new ministry were in progress, when they were interrupted by the king's indisposition. But, believing it to be nothing more than a severe cold, Mr. Addington did not think fit to wait for his formal appointment; and vacated his seat, on the 19th February, by accepting the Chiltern Hundreds, in order to expedite his return to his place in Parliament. In the mean time Mr. Pitt, who had resigned office, not only continued to discharge the customary official duties of Chancellor of the Exchequer,[1] but on the 18th February, brought forward the annual budget,[2] which included a loan of 25,500,000*l.*, and new taxes to the amount of 1,750,000*l.*[3]

Mr. Addington had fully expected that his formal appointment as First Lord of the Treasury and Chancellor of the Exchequer would have been completed before his reëlection; but this was prevented by the king's illness, and as his election could not legally be postponed, he took his seat again on the 27th, not as a minister of the Crown, but as a private member.

On the 22d the king's condition was as bad as at the worst period of his attack in 1788.[4] Towards the evening of the following day he came to himself, and indicated the causes of disturbance which were pressing on his mind, by exclaiming: "I am better now, but I will remain true to the Church;"[5] and afterwards, "the king's mind, whenever he came to himself, reverted at once to the cause of his disquietude."[6] At the beginning of March his fever increased

1 Lord Malmesb. Diary, xiv. 28.

2 Parl. Hist., xxxv. 972.

3 It seems that he spoke from the third bench, on the right hand of the chair. — *Mr. Abbot's Diary; Life of Lord Sidmouth*, i. 345, *n.*

4 Lord Malmesb. Diary, iv. 16.

5 *Ibid.*, 20.

6 *Ibid.*, 28.

again, and for a time his life was despaired of:[1] but about the 5th, a favorable turn took place; and though not allowed to engage in any business, he was from this time gradually recovering.[2] On the 10th, he wrote a letter approving of a minute of the cabinet; and on the 11th he saw Mr. Addington and the Chancellor when he was pronounced, — somewhat prematurely, — to be quite well.[3]

On the 24th February, the bill for repealing the absurd Brown Bread Act of the previous session was awaiting the royal assent, and it was thought very desirable that no delay should occur. Mr. Addington declined presenting the commission for his Majesty's signature; but the Chancellor, Lord Loughborough, waited upon the king, who signed the commission, saying it was a very good bill.[4]

Meanwhile, who was minister — Mr. Pitt or Mr. Addington? or neither? Both were in communication with the Prince of Wales on the probable necessity of a regency: both were in official communication with the king himself.[5] The embarrassment of such a position was relieved by the forbearance of all parties in both Houses of Parliament; and at length, on the 14th March, the king was sufficiently recovered to receive the seals from Mr. Pitt, and to place them in the hands of Mr. Addington. This acceptance of office, however, again vacated his seat, which he was unable to resume as a minister of the Crown, until the 23d March. The king was still for some time obliged to abstain from unnecessary exertion. On the 15th April, he transferred the great seal from Lord Loughborough to Lord Eldon; but though several other things were required to be done, the ministers were unanimous that he should only perform this single act on that day.[6]

1 Lord Malmesb. Diary, iv. 27.
2 *Ibid.*, 30–33, *et seq.*
3 Lord Malmesbury's Cor., iv. 44; Lord Sidmouth's Life, i. 350.
4 Life of Lord Sidmouth, i. 308; Lord Malmesbury's Diary, iv. 17, 18.
5 Life of Lord Sidmouth, i. 348, 350; Malmesb. Diary, iv. 25, &c.
6 Life of Lord Sidmouth, i. 401.

But even after the king had transacted business, and his recovery had been formally announced, his health continued to cause great anxiety to his family and ministers. Apprehensions were entertained lest "his intellectual faculties should be impaired so much as never to recover their former tone."[1] Writing in August, 1801, Mr. T. Grenville says: "The king has seen the chancellor for two hours, and the ministers give out that the king will hold a council in a day or two at farthest."[2]

On this occasion his Majesty's illness, however alarming, passed over without any serious hindrance to public business. It occurred while Parliament was sitting, and at a time when the personal exercise of the royal authority was not urgently required, except for the purposes already noticed. The constitutional questions, therefore, which had been so fully argued in 1788, — though gravely considered by those more immediately concerned, — did not come again under discussion.[3] It must be admitted that the king's speedy recovery affords some justification of the dilatory proceedings adopted regarding the regency, in 1788. Too prompt a measure for supplying the defect of the royal authority, would, on the king's recovery, have been alike embarrassing to his Majesty himself, the ministers, and Parliament.

The king's illness in 1804.

In 1804 the king was once more stricken with the same grievous malady. In January he was attacked with rheumatic gout, and about the 12th February, his mind became affected.[4] He gradually recovered

[1] Lord Malmesbury's Diary, 20th March; Correspondence, iv. 51.

[2] Court and Cabinets of Geo. III., iii. 167.

[3] It was suggested that both parties, who had opposed each other so violently in 1788 upon the question of a regency, should now make mutual concessions, and, if possible, avoid the discussion of their conflicting opinions. In this view, it seems, Lord Spencer, the Duke of Portland, Mr. T. Grenville, and Mr. T. Pelham concurred; but Mr. Pitt appears not to have entirely acquiesced in it. — *Lord Malmes. Cor.*, iv. 19.

[4] Lord Malmesbury says, although "there was a council held about the 24th January at the queen's house, yet before the end of that month it was no longer to be concealed that the king had a return of his old illness." —

towards the end of the month;[1] yet his malady continued, with more or less severity, so as to make it requisite to spare him all unnecessary exertion of mind, till the 23d April, when he presided at a council. He remained under medical care and control until the 10th June.[2] For a time his life was in danger; but his mind was never so completely alienated as it had been in 1788 and 1801.[3]

On the 26th February the archbishop offered a thanksgiving for the happy prospect of his Majesty's speedy recovery; and on the same day, the physicians issued a bulletin, announcing that any rapid amendment was not to be expected.[4]

Meanwhile, the ordinary business of the session was proceeded with. On the 27th February, the king's illness was adverted to in the House of Commons: but ministers were of opinion that a formal communication to the House upon the subject was not required, and could secure no good object. Mr. Addington stated that there was not, at that time, any necessary suspension of such royal functions as it might be needful for his Majesty to discharge.[5] That very day the cabinet had examined the king's physicians, who were unanimously of opinion that his Majesty was perfectly competent to understand the effect of an instrument to which his sign-manual was required; but that it would be imprudent for him to engage in long argument, or fatiguing discussion.[6] The delicate and responsible position of the ministers, however, was admitted. The king having already

Cor. iv. 292. But it appears from Lord Sidmouth's life, that the king's reason was not affected until about the 12th of February. — *Lord Sidmouth's Life*, ii. 246, *et seq.*

1 Lord Sidmouth's Life, ii. 249, *et seq.*

2 Evidence of Dr. Heberden, 1810. He had otherwise been indisposed for a month previously, with symptoms of his old malady. Lord Malmesbury's Cor., iv. 292; Fox's Mem., iv. 24, 35, 37.

3 Lord Malmesbury's Diary, iv. 293.

4 Lord Sidmouth's Life, ii. 250.

5 Hansard's Deb., 1st Ser., i. 307, 526, 530.

6 Twiss's Life of Eldon, i. 421.

been ill for a fortnight, — how much longer might they exercise all the executive powers of the state, without calling in aid the authority of Parliament? At present they accepted the responsibility of declaring that the interference of Parliament was unnecessary. On the 1st March, similar assurances were given by Lord Hawkesbury in the House of Lords: the Lord Chancellor also declared that, at that moment, there was no suspension of the royal functions.

On the 2d March, the matter was again brought forward by Mr. Grey, but elicited no further explanation.[1] On the 5th, the Lord Chancellor stated that he had had interviews, on that and the previous day, with the king, who gave his consent to the Duke of York's Estate Bill, so far as his own interest was concerned; and on the same day the physicians were of opinion "that his Majesty was fully competent to transact business with his Parliament, by commission and message."[2] On the 9th, Mr. Grey adverted to the fact that fifteen bills had just received the royal assent, — a circumstance which he regarded with "uneasiness and apprehension."[3] Among these bills were the annual Mutiny Acts, the passing of which, in the midst of war, could not have been safely postponed. On this day also, the Lord Chancellor assured the House of Lords, "that not satisfied with the reports and assurances of the medical attendants, he had thought it right to obtain a personal interview with the sovereign, and that at that interview due discussion had taken place as to the bills offered for the royal assent, which had thereupon been fully expressed." In reference to this interview, Lord Eldon states in his Anecdote Book, that the king had noticed that he was stated in the commission to have fully considered the bills to which his assent was to be signified; and that to be correct, he ought to have the bills to peruse and consider. His Majesty added, that in the

[1] Hansard's Deb., 1st Ser., i. 663.
[2] Twiss's Life of Eldon, i. 422.
[3] Hansard's Deb., 1st Ser., i. 823.

early part of his reign he had always had the bills themselves, until Lord Thurlow ceased to bring them, saying: "It was nonsense his giving himself the trouble to read them." If there was somewhat of the perverse acuteness of insanity in these remarks, there was yet sufficient self-possession in the royal mind, to satisfy Lord Eldon that he was justified in taking the sign-manual.[1] On the 23d March, seventeen other bills received the royal assent; and on the 26th March, a message from the king, signed by himself, was brought to the House of Commons by Mr. Addington: but no observation was made concerning his Majesty's health. There is little doubt that his Majesty, though for some months afterwards strange and disordered in his family circle, was not incapacitated from attending to necessary business with his ministers.[2] The Opposition, however, and particularly the Carlton House party, were disposed to make the most of the king's illness, and were confidently expecting a regency.[3]

Change of ministry before the king's recovery.

Before his Majesty had been restored to his accustomed health, the fall of his favorite minister, Mr. Addington, was impending; and the king was engaged in negotiations with the chancellor and Mr. Pitt, for the formation of another administration.[4] To confer with his Majesty upon questions so formal as his assent to the Mutiny Bills, had been a matter of delicacy: but to discuss with him so important a measure as the reconstruction of a ministry, in a time of war and public danger, was indeed embarrassing. Mr. Pitt's correspondence discloses

1 Hansard's Debates, 1st Ser., i. 162; Twiss's Life of Eldon, i. 419.

2 Twiss's Life of Eldon, i. 422; Lord Malmesbury's Cor., iv. 317, 325, 327, 344; Lord Sidmouth's Life, ii. 248, *et seq.*

3 Mr. Pitt, on being told that the Prince of Wales had asserted that the king's illness must last for several months, said: "Thy wish was father, Harry, to that thought." —*Lord Malmesbury's Cor.*, iv. 298, 313, 315.

4 The chancellor's conduct, on this occasion, in negotiating for Mr. Pitt's return to office, unknown to Mr. Addington and his colleagues, has exposed him to the severest animadversions. —*Lord Campbell's Lives of the Chancellors*, vii. 166; Law Review, Nos. ii. and xi.

his misgivings as to the state of the king's mind.[1] But on the 7th May, he was with him for three hours, and was amazed at the cool and collected manner in which his Majesty had carried on the conversation.[2] It was probably from this interview that Lord Eldon relates Mr. Pitt to have come out "not only satisfied, but much surprised with the king's ability. He said he had never so baffled him in any conversation he had had with him in his life."[3] Yet, on the 9th May, after another interview, Mr. Pitt wrote to the chancellor: "I do not think there was anything positively wrong; but there was a hurry of spirits and an excessive love of talking." . . . . "There is certainly nothing in what I have observed that would, in the smallest degree, justify postponing any other steps that are in progress towards arrangement." Nor did these continued misgivings prevent the ministerial arrangements from being completed, some time before the king was entirely relieved from the care of his medical attendants.

Imputations upon the conduct of ministers.

The conduct of the Government, and especially of the Lord Chancellor, in allowing the royal functions to be exercised during this period, were several years afterwards severely impugned. In 1811, Lord Grey had not forgotten the suspicions he had expressed in 1804; and in examining the king's physicians, he elicited, especially from Dr. Heberden, several circumstances, previously unknown, relative to the king's former illnesses. On the 28th January, fortified by this evidence, he arraigned the Lord Chancellor of conduct "little short of high-treason," — of "treason against the constitution and the country." He particularly relied upon the fact, that on the 9th March, 1804, the Chancellor had affixed the great seal to a commission for giving the royal assent to fifteen bills; and accused

[1] Letters to Lord Eldon, April 22, May 8; Lord Campbell's Lives, vii. 169, 173.

[2] Lord Malmesb. Cor., iv. 306.

[3] Twiss's Life, i. 449.

the ministers of that day of "having culpably made use of the king's name without the king's sanction, and criminally exercised the royal functions, when the sovereign was under a moral incapacity to authorize such a proceeding."[1] Lord Sidmouth and Lord Eldon, the ministers whose conduct was mainly impugned, defended themselves from these imputations, and expressed their astonishment at Dr. Heberden's evidence, which, they said, was at variance with the opinions of all the physicians, — including Dr. Heberden himself, — expressed in 1804, while in attendance upon the king. They stated that his new version of his Majesty's former illness had surprised the queen, not less than the ministers. And it is quite clear, from other evidence, that Dr. Heberden's account of the duration and continuous character of the king's malady, was inaccurate.[2] Lord Eldon, oddly enough, affirmed, that on the 9th of March, the king understood the duty which the Chancellor had to perform, better than he did himself. This he believed he could prove. A motion was made by Lord King, for omitting Lord Eldon's name from the Queen's Council of Regency; and its rejection was the cause of a protest, signed by nine peers, — including Lords Grey, Holland, Lauderdale, and Erskine, — in which they affirmed his unfitness for that office, on the ground that he had improperly used the king's name and authority, during his incapacity in 1804.[3] In the House of Commons Mr. Whitbread made a similar charge against his lordship; and the Lord Chancellor complained, — not without reason, — that he had been hardly dealt with by his enemies, and feebly defended by his friends.[4]

In 1804 the propriety of passing a regency bill, to provide for any future illness of the king, was once more the

[1] Hansard's Debates, 1st Ser., xviii. 1054.

[2] Lord Malmesbury's Diaries and Lord Sidmouth's Life; and *supra*, p. 168.

[3] Hansard's Debates, 1st Ser., xviii. 1031–1087.

[4] Hansard's Debates, 1st Ser., xix. 87; Lord Sidmouth's Life, iii. 37; Twiss's Life of Eldon, ii. 151–161.

subject of grave consideration among the statesmen of the period;[1] but, — as in 1789, so now again, — no sooner did the king recover, than all further care appears to have been cast aside. Six years later this want of foresight again led to serious embarrassment.

Necessity of a Regency Act canvassed.

The king's last mental disorder commenced in the autumn of 1810. His kingly career was to close forever. Bereft of reason and nearly blind, the poor old king, — who had ruled for fifty years with so high a hand, and so strong a will, — was now tended by physicians, and controlled by keepers. His constitutional infirmity, aggravated by political anxieties and domestic distresses, had overcome him; and he was too far advanced in years, to rally again. It was a mournful spectacle. Like King Lear, he was

King's illness in 1810.

> "A poor old man,
> As full of grief as age: wretched in both."

But as physicians will dispute at the bedside of the dying patient, — so the hopes and fears of rival parties, and the rude collisions of political strife, were aroused into activity by the sufferings of the king. The contentions of 1788 were revived, though the leaders of that age had passed away.

Parliament stood prorogued to the 1st November, and a proclamation had appeared in the "Gazette," declaring the king's pleasure that it should be further prorogued by commission to the 29th. But before this commission could be signed, his Majesty became so ill that the Lord Chancellor, unable to obtain his signature, did not feel justified in affixing the great seal; and in this view of his duty, statesmen of all parties concurred.[2] Following

Meeting of Parliament.

[1] Lord Malmesbury's Cor., iv. 315.

[2] Lord Campbell, however, says, "It would have been but a small liberty to have passed this commission, for there had been an order made at a council, at which the king presided, to prorogue Parliament from the 1st to the 29th November, and to prepare a commission for this purpose." — *Lives of the Chancellors*, vii. 242.

the precedent of 1788, both Houses met on the 1st November; and on being informed of the circumstances under which they were assembled,[1] adjourned until the 15th, — fourteen days being the shortest period within which Parliament may, by law, be summoned for despatch of business. Circular letters were directed to be sent, summoning the members of both Houses to attend on that day. Strong hopes had been entertained by the physicians, of his Majesty's speedy recovery; and in the interval they were confirmed. Both Houses, therefore, on these representations being made, again adjourned for a fortnight. Before their next meeting the king's physicians were examined by the privy council; and as they were still confident of his Majesty's recovery, a further adjournment for a fortnight was agreed upon, — though not without objections to so long an interruption of business, and a division in both Houses.

Nov. 29.

No longer delay could now be suggested; and at the next meeting, a committee of twenty-one members was appointed in both Houses, for the examination of the king's physicians. They still entertained hopes of his Majesty's ultimate recovery, in spite of his age and blindness; but could not form any opinion as to the probable duration of his illness.

Dec. 13.

Continuing to follow generally the precedent of 1788, ministers proposed, on the 20th December, in a committee on the state of the nation, three resolutions, — affirming the king's incapacity, — the right and duty of the two Houses to provide for this exigency, — and the necessity of determining by what means the royal assent should be signified to a bill for that purpose.

Precedent of 1788 followed.

Again the question of proceeding by bill, or by address was argued. The proceedings of 1788 were exposed to a

[1] In the Commons, the Speaker first took his seat at the table, and explained the circumstances under which the House had met, before he took the chair. —*Hansard's Debates*, 1st Ser., xviii. 3. On taking the chair, he acquainted the House that he had issued a new writ during the recess.

searching criticism, and all the precedents of constitutional history, presenting any analogy to the present circumstances, learnedly investigated. The expedients which had delighted Lord Eldon in his early career, found little favor with the more philosophic lawyers of a later school. Sir S. Romilly regarded them "in no other light but as a fraudulent trick," and asked what would be said of "a set of men joining together, and making a contract for another in a state of insanity, and employing a person as his solicitor, to affix his seal or his signature to such a deed?"

Discussions upon that precedent.

Considering the recency and complete application of the precedent of 1778, it is not surprising that both ministers and Parliament should have agreed to follow it, instead of adopting a more simple course; but to most minds of the present age, the arguments of those who contended for an address, and against the "Phantom," will appear the more conclusive. The royal authority was wanting, and could be supplied by Parliament alone. So far all were agreed; but those who argued for proceeding by means of a bill, accepted a notoriously fictitious use of the king's name, as an equivalent for his real authority; while those who supported a direct address, desired that Parliament, — openly recognizing the king's inability to exercise his royal authority, — should from the necessity of the case, proceed to act without it. Of all the speeches against proceeding by way of bill, the most learned, able, and argumentative, was that of Mr. Francis Horner.[1] Comparing the proceedings of 1788, with those of the Revolution of 1688, he said: "It is impossible not to contrast the virtuous forbearance of all parties at the Revolution, in concurring to provide for the public interests, with the struggle that was made for power in the other instance; and, above all, to contrast the studied delays by which power was then so factiously retained, with the despatch with which our ancestors finished, in one short

[1] Hansard's Debates, 1st Ser., xviii. 299.

month, their task of establishing at once the succession to the Crown, reducing its prerogatives within limitations by law, and founding the whole structure of our civil and religious liberties." [1]

Political causes of delay.

But independently of precedents and legal forms, the ministers expecting, like their predecessors in 1788, to be dismissed by the regent, were not disposed to simplify the preliminary proceedings, and accelerate their own fall; while the Opposition, impatient for office, objected to elaborate preliminaries, — as much, perhaps, for the delays which they occasioned, as for their hollow subtlety and uselessness.

Resolutions agreed to Dec. 22.

The resolutions were agreed to, and communicated to the Lords, at a conference. There an amendment was moved by Lord Holland, to the third resolution, by which an address to the Prince of Wales was proposed to be substituted for the proceeding by bill, inviting the prince to take upon himself the exercise of the powers and authorities of the Crown, but to abstain from the exercise of such powers as the immediate exigencies of the state shall not call into action, until Parliament had passed a bill for the future care of his Majesty's person, and securing the resumption of his authority.[2] The Dukes of York and Sussex spoke in favor of this amendment, and all the seven dukes of the blood royal voted for it: [3] but the resolution was carried by a majority of twenty-six. The royal dukes also signed protests against the rejection of the amendment, and against the third resolution.[4] The chancellor differed widely from the royal dukes, declaring that an address from the two Houses to the Prince of Wales, praying him to exercise the royal prerogatives during the king's life, would be treasonable.[5]

1 Hansard's Debates, 1st Ser., xviii. 306.

2 *Ibid.*, 418.

3 York, Clarence, Kent, Cumberland, Sussex, Cambridge, and Gloucester.

4 Hansard's Debates, 1st Ser., xviii. 471.

5 *Ibid.*, 459, 713.

The next step was to propose, in committee on the state of the nation, resolutions to the effect that the Prince of Wales should be empowered, as regent of the kingdom, to exercise the royal authority, in the name and on behalf of his Majesty, subject to such limitations as shall be provided: that for a limited time the regent should not be able to grant any peerage, except for some singular naval or military achievement:[1] nor grant any office in reversion: nor any office otherwise than during pleasure, except such offices as are required by law to be granted for life or during good behavior: that his Majesty's private property, not already vested in trustees, should be vested in trustees for the benefit of his Majesty: that the care of the king's person should be committed to the queen, who for a limited time, should have power to appoint and remove members of the royal household; and that her Majesty should have a council, with power to examine the king's physicians, upon oath, from time to time. It was explained, at the same time, that twelve months would be the period to which the proposed limitations upon the regent's authority would extend.

Four of these resolutions were agreed to in the Commons by small majorities,[2] and not without strong arguments against any restrictions upon the authority of the regent. The fifth was amended on a motion of Earl Gower, in such a manner as to leave the queen merely "such direction of the household as may be suitable for the care of his Majesty's person and the maintenance of the royal dignity."[3]

The resolutions were communicated to the Lords at a conference. There, on the motion of the Marquis of Lans downe, the first resolution was amended by the omission of the last words, viz., "subject to such limitations and restric-

[1] This exception was subsequently omitted.

[2] The first resolution was carried by a majority of 24, the second by 16, the third by 19.

[3] Voted by a majority of 13 against the Government, and the resolution as amended agreed to by a majority of 3.

tions as shall be provided"[1]—thus appointing the regent generally, without restrictions upon his authority. But as the two next resolutions, imposing limitations upon the grant of peerages, places, and pensions, were immediately afterwards agreed to, the words were restored to the first resolution. And thus the restrictions proposed by the Commons were ultimately agreed to without alteration.

Resolutions laid before the prince.

The next step, as in 1789, was to lay these resolutions before the Prince of Wales, and to beg him to accept the trust, subject to the proposed restrictions; and in reply, he signified his acceptance. The queen was also attended in regard to the direction of the royal household.

Commission for opening Parliament.

Again, it was resolved by both Houses that a commission should issue under the great seal for opening Parliament; but warned by the precedent of 1788, ministers had taken the precaution of consulting the royal dukes, and by their desire omitted their names from the commission. On the 15th January, Parliament was opened by virtue of this commission; and the Regency Bill was brought in by the Chancellor of the Exchequer, on the same day. The bill, though still the subject of much discussion, was rapidly passed through both Houses, with some few amendments. Resolutions were agreed to by both Houses, authorizing the issue of letters-patent under the great seal, for giving the royal assent by commission; and on the 5th February, the bill received the royal assent by virtue of that commission.

The Regency Bill passed.

Form of the commission.

It is worthy of note, that both this commission and that for opening Parliament, deviated materially from the usual form of such commissions, and instead of being issued by the advice of the privy council, it was expressed thus: "by the king himself, by and with the advice of the Lords spiritual and temporal, and Commons in Parliament assembled."

[1] By a majority of 3.

During these proceedings, an unexpected difficulty had arisen. Certain sums of money had already been granted, and appropriated by Parliament, for the service of the army and navy; but in consequence of the king's incapacity, the usual warrants under the privy seal, could not be prepared, directing issues to be made from the Exchequer, for such services. The Lord Keeper of the privy seal was willing to take upon himself the responsibility of affixing the seal to such a warrant,[1] although by the terms of his oath he was restrained from using it "without the king's special command:"[2] but the deputy clerks of the Privy Seal held themselves precluded by their oaths of office, from preparing letters to pass the privy seal, until a warrant had been signed by the king himself, for that purpose. The necessities of the public service were urgent; and the Treasury being unable to obtain the money according to the usual official routine, prepared two warrants addressed to the auditor of the Exchequer, directing him to draw one order on the Bank of England for 500,000*l.*, on account of the army, and another to the same amount, for the navy. The auditor, Lord Grenville, doubting the authority of these warrants, desired that the law officers of the Crown should be consulted. It was their opinion that the Treasury warrants were not a sufficient authority for the auditor, who accordingly refused to issue the money; and although the Treasury expressly assumed the entire responsibility of the issue, he persisted in his refusal.

Issue of public money.

Difficulties raised by Lord Grenville.

It was now necessary to resort to Parliament to supply the defect of authority which had been discovered; and on the 4th January the Chancellor of the Exchequer moved a resolution in committee of the whole House, by which the auditor and offi-

Resolution of both Houses directing the issue of money.

[1] Speech of Mr. Perceval, 4th Jan., and of Lord Westmorland, 5th Jan., 1811. — *Hansard's Debates*, 1st Ser., xviii. 759, 798.

[2] Speech of Earl Spencer, 5th Jan., 1811. — *Hansard's Debates*, 1st Ser., xviii. 797.

cers of the Exchequer were "authorized and commanded" to pay obedience to Treasury warrants for the issue of such sums as had been appropriated for the services of the army and navy, as well as money issuable under a vote of credit for 3,000,000*l.* To this resolution it was objected, that it involved a further assumption of the executive powers of the Crown, and was only rendered necessary by the unreasonable delays which ministers had interposed, in providing for the exercise of the royal authority: but the immediate necessity of the occasion could not be denied; and the resolution was agreed to by both Houses. A protest, however, was entered in the Lords' journal, signed by twenty-one peers, including six royal dukes, which affirmed that the principle of the resolution would justify the assumption of all the executive powers of the Crown, during any suspension of the personal exercise of the royal authority; and that this unconstitutional measure might have been avoided without injury to the public service, by an address to the Prince of Wales.[1]

The Royal Sign-Manual Bill, 1830.

Happily there has been no recurrence of circumstances similar to those of 1788 and 1811: but Parliament has since had occasion to provide for the exercise of the royal authority, under other contingencies. From an early period in the reign of George IV., his Majesty's health had excited apprehensions.[2] In 1826 his life was said not to be worth a month's purchase;[3] but it was not until within a few weeks of his death, that he suffered from any incapacity to exercise his royal functions. In 1830, during the last illness of the king, his Majesty found it inconvenient and painful to subscribe with his own hand, the public instruments which required the sign-man-

1 Hansard's Debates, 1st Ser., xviii. 801.

2 Duke of Buckingham's Court of George IV., i. 313, 336, 447; *Ibid.*, ii. 67, 217. Sir William Knighton's Mem. 88, &c.

3 Mr. Plumer Ward to Duke of Buckingham, April 21, 1826. Court of George IV., ii. 297; *Ibid.*, 300, 301.

ual; and accordingly, on the 24th of May, a message was sent to both Houses, desiring that provision should be made for the temporary discharge of this duty.[1] The message was acknowledged by suitable addresses; and a bill was passed rapidly through both Houses, enabling his Majesty to empower by warrant or commission, under his sign-manual, one or more persons to affix, in his presence, and by his command, signified by word of mouth, the royal signature by means of a stamp. In order to prevent the possibility of any abuse of this power, it was provided that the stamp should not be affixed to any instrument, unless a memorandum describing its object had been indorsed upon it, signed by the Lord Chancellor, the President of the Council, the Lord Privy Seal, the First Lord of the Treasury, and the Secretaries of State, or any three of them. The seal was directed to be kept in the custody of one of these officers, and when used, was required to be attested by one or more of them.

Precedents on which founded.

The course thus adopted was not without precedent. Henry VIII. had issued a patent, authorizing the Archbishop of Canterbury, the Lord Chancellor, and other persons to apply a stamp, bearing the impress of the royal signature, to warrants for the payment of money out of the royal treasury; and had also issued several proclamations and other instruments, on which his sign-manual had been impressed by means of a stamp. His signature to the commission for signifying the royal assent to the bill for the attainder of the Duke of Norfolk had been given by means of a stamp, affixed, — not by his own hand, but by that of a clerk, — and was on that account declared by Parliament to be invalid. Edward VI. had issued two proclamations, to which his signature was affixed by means of a stamp. Queen Mary had issued a proclamation, in the same form, calling for aid to suppress the insurrection of Sir Thomas Wyatt. The same queen

[1] Hansard's Debates, New Ser., xxiv. 986, 1001.

had issued a patent, in the fifth and sixth years of her reign, stating that in consequence of the great labor which she sustained in the government and defence of the kingdom, she was unable, without much danger and inconvenience, to sign the commissions, warrants, and other instruments with her own hand; empowering certain persons to affix a seal in her presence; and declaring that all instruments so sealed should be as valid and effectual in law, as if signed with the hand of the queen. It appears also that King William III., being on the point of death, and no longer able to sign his own name, affixed a stamp to a commission, in presence of the Lord Keeper and the clerks of the Parliament, by which the royal assent was signified to the Bill of Abjuration, and the Malt Duty Bill.

But notwithstanding these precedents, — which proved that in former times the kings of England had been accustomed, by their own authority, to delegate to others the right of affixing their sign-manual, — it was now laid down by ministers, and by all legal authorities, that such a right could not lawfully be conferred, except by the sanction of Parliament. This sanction was readily given in this particular case; but not without warnings that as his Majesty's present indisposition was merely physical, the proceedings then adopted should not hereafter be drawn into a precedent, if the mind of any future king should become affected. In such an event, the power of affixing the royal sign-manual to instruments, would invest the ministers of the day with all the authority of the Crown. On more than one occasion, during the late reign, such a power might have been liable to abuse; and it would not again be conferred upon ministers, if there should be any doubt as to the mental capacity of the sovereign.[1]

When William IV. succeeded to the throne, he was nearly

[1] 11 Geo. IV. and 1 Will. IV. c. 23; Hansard's Debates, New Ser., xxiv. 986, 1062, 1132, 1148, 1193; Rymer's Fœdera, x. 261; Cotton, 564; Burnet's Own Time, iv. 559; Hume's Hist., ii. 328; Smollett's Hist., i. 441.

sixty-five years of age, and his heiress presumptive was a princess of eleven. It was, therefore, necessary to provide for a regency; but the ministers were of opinion that they might safely defer this measure, until after the assembling of a new Parliament. Even this brief delay was represented as hazardous. It was said that if the king should die suddenly, the crown would devolve upon an infant princess, — subject, perhaps, to the claims of a posthumous child of his Majesty. This risk, however, the ministers were prepared to encounter. The law did not recognize the incapacity of an infant king; and, in the event of a sudden demise of the Crown before a regent had been appointed, the infant sovereign would be able to give her assent to an act of Parliament, appointing a guardian for herself, and a regent for the kingdom. Henry III., Richard II., and Henry VI. had succeeded to the throne, without any previous parliamentary provision for a regency; and after their accession, Parliament appointed persons to govern the kingdom during their minority.

Question of a regency on the accession of William IV.

The Lord Chancellor said: "On the accession of an infant to the throne, the same course would be adopted as if the sovereign were of mature years: a declaration, similar to that which many of their lordships had witnessed a few days ago, would be made. The infant would have the power of continuing or changing his ministers, and the same responsibility would exist as at present."[1] And this doctrine of the law was thus explained by Lord Eldon: "If an infant sovereign were to be on the throne, whose head could not be seen over the integument which covered the head of his noble and learned friend on the woolsack, he would, by what the Scotch called a fiction of law, and by what the English called presumption, in favor of a royal infant, be supposed to have as much sense, knowledge, and experience, as if he had reached the years of threescore and ten."[2]

This abstract presumption of the law was not denied; but

[1] Hansard's Debates, 2d Ser., xxv. 738. [2] *Ibid.*, 742.

it was argued that to rely upon it in practice, would bring into contempt the prerogatives of the Crown, and might be fraught with dangers to the state. An infant sovereign might indeed appoint her own guardian, and a regent of the kingdom ; but she would scarcely be more competent to exercise the discriminating judgment of a sovereign, than was George III. when the royal assent was given, in his name, to the Regency Bill, by a phantom commission. That necessary act had struck a blow at royalty : it had shown how Parliament could make laws without a king : it had exhibited the Crown as a name, a form, a mere fiction of authority ; and to allow a princess of eleven to assent to another act of regency, would be a dangerous repetition of that precedent. But there were other dangers which ought to be averted. It was easy, before the demise of the Crown, to appoint a regent who might never be called upon to exercise his power ; but to appoint, — possibly from amongst many claimants, — a regent who would at once assume all the authority of the Crown, might be difficult and embarrassing. Still greater would be the embarrassment, if the right of succession should be rendered doubtful, by the prospective claims of an unborn child. An attempt was made, in the Commons, to represent to the king the importance of making immediate provision for a regency ; but the ministers successfully resisted it ; and the question was reserved for the consideration of the new Parliament.[1]

The Regency Bill, 1830-1831.

Happily, these dreaded evils were not encountered ; and on the meeting of the new Parliament, a well-considered Regency Bill was introduced. By this bill the Duchess of Kent was appointed sole regent, until her Majesty should attain the age of eighteen. Departing from former precedents, it was not proposed that the regent should be controlled by a council. It was said that a regent, for the maintenance of the royal authority, needed the free exercise of the prerogatives of the Crown, even more than a king himself. Cases might, indeed, arise in which it

[1] Hansard's Debates, 2d Ser., xxv. 771-828.

would be necessary to control the ambition and influence of a regent, by such a council : but here the regent could never succeed to the throne: her interests were identified with those of the future sovereign, to whom she was united by the tenderest ties; and she could have no object but to uphold, in good faith, the authority of the infant queen. Her Royal Highness would, therefore, be left to administer the government of the country, by means of the responsible ministers of the Crown, and to act upon their advice alone.

Another question of great constitutional delicacy was also wisely dealt with. No precedent was to be found, since the Norman Conquest, of any provision having been made for the exercise of the royal prerogatives, between the demise of the Crown, and the birth of a posthumous child. The law upon this important question was not settled; but reasoning from the analogy of the law of real property, as well as according to the dictates of common sense, it was clear that an unborn child could not be seized of the Crown. There could be no abeyance or vacancy of the Crown. The king never dies. The crown must, therefore, devolve at once upon the heir presumptive; and be resigned, if a child should be born, entitled to inherit it. If Parliament interposed, and appointed a regent to administer the government until the birth of a posthumous child, such a regent would not be governing in the name and on behalf of the sovereign, but would be a parliamentary sovereign, created for the occasion, under the title of regent. And, in the mean time, if no child should be born, the heir presumptive would have been unlawfully deprived of her right to the throne. Upon these sound principles the regency was now to be established. If the king should die during the minority of the Princess Victoria, she was to be proclaimed queen, subject to the rights of any issue of his Majesty, which might afterwards be born of his consort. The Duchess of Kent would at once assume the regency in the name of the Infant Queen, and on her behalf; and should a posthumous child be born, her Majesty Queen Adelaide would forthwith assume the regency, on behalf of her own child. These principles were accepted by statesmen and lawyers of every party; and the Regency Bill, which had been prepared by the government of the Duke of Wellington, was adopted and passed by the government of Lord Grey.[1] It was a wise provision for contingencies, which fortunately never arose. When King William IV. died, in 1837, after a short but eventful reign, her most gracious Majesty had, less than a month before, completed her eighteenth year; and ascended the throne, surrounded by happy auguries, which have since been fully accomplished.

First Regency Act of Queen Victoria.

On the accession of her Majesty, the King of Hanover became heir presumptive to the throne; and as he would probably be resident abroad, it was thought necessary to provide that, in the event of her Majesty's decease, while her successor was out of the realm, the administration of the government should be carried on in his name by lords justices, until his arrival.[2] But the queen's marriage, in 1840, required provision to be made for another contingency, which, though more probable, has, happily not arisen. Following the precedent of 1831, Parliament now provided, that in the event of any child of her Majesty succeeding to the throne before the age of eighteen, Prince Albert, as the surviving parent, should be regent, without any council of regency, or any limitation upon the exercise of the royal prerogatives,—except an incapacity to assent to any bill for altering the succession to the throne, or affecting the uniformity of worship in the Church of England, or the rights of the Church of Scotland. And, founded upon these principles, the bill was passed with the approval of all parties.[3]

Second Regency Act, 1840.

[1] Act 1 Will. IV. c. 2; Hansard's Debates, 3d Ser., i. 499, 764, 954, &c.

[2] 7 Will. IV. and 1 Vict. c. 72.

[3] 3 & 4 Vict. c. 52; Hansard's Debates, 3d Ser., lv. 754, 850, 1074.

CHAPTER IV.

Ancient Revenues of the Crown. — Settlement of the Civil List of William and Mary : — Civil List of Queen Anne, of George I. and George II. — Civil List, Expenditure, and Debts of George III. : — Civil List of the Regency, and of the Reigns of George IV., William IV., and Her Majesty : — Duchess of Lancaster and Cornwall : — Private Property of the Crown. — Provision for the Royal Family : — Management of the Land Revenues, on behalf of the Public : — Civil List Pensions. — Prerogatives of the Crown, in relation to the Royal Family.

Vast possessions of the Crown in early times.

THE history of the land revenues of the Crown presents as many vicissitudes, and varied fortunes, as are to be found in the domestic annals of any family in the kingdom.

The entire lands of the realm were originally held of the Crown, by various feudal tenures; and the royal revenues were derived from fines, fees, first-fruits, and tenths, and other profits arising from these lands, and from the rents of the ancient demesnes of the Crown. To support the barbarous magnificence of his household, — his numerous retainers, and rude hospitality, — was nearly the sole expense of the king; for, as feudal superior, he commanded the services of his tenants in the field, who fought by his side with an array of men and horses, equipped and maintained at their own expense.

Extensive forfeitures.

By means of escheats and forfeitures, there was even a danger of the Crown becoming the absolute proprietor of all the lands of the realm. But vast as were the king's possessions, they were not vast enough to satisfy the rapacity of his followers; and in every succeeding reign, the grants and alienations of crown lands exceeded the escheats and forfeitures. The estates of the Crown were further diminished by wrongful appropriations and encroachments. Repenting their liberality, kings frequently resumed their former grants; and alienations improvidently made, were unjustly and violently revoked. Yet such had been the waste of the once ample revenues of the Crown, that Henry III. complained that they had become too scanty to furnish his royal table; and the needy monarch was reduced to the necessity of giving tallies for the supply of beeves and grain for his household. An extensive resumption of grants, however, and the forfeiture of the estates of rebel barons, retrieved his fallen fortunes. Such was the liberality of Edward II. that an ordinance was passed by Parliament prohibiting the alienation of crown lands, — which was repealed, however, by a Parliament at York, in the 15th year of his reign. But the profusion of this king was supplied by prodigious forfeitures.

Grants and alienations.

Richard II. again, was not less profuse in his grants, nor less prodigal in his confiscations. The Wars of the Roses were so fruitful of forfeitures, that a large proportion of the land of the realm became the property of the Crown. Had it been retained, there would have been no monarchy in Europe so absolute as that of England: but the spoils of one faction were eagerly grasped by the other; and the Crown gained little by the lands which it won upon the field of battle, or wrested from their owners on the scaffold. In the reign of Henry V. the estates of the Crown were considerably augmented by the appropriation of the Alien Priories, one hundred and ten in number. Yet the income of Henry VI. was reduced so low as 5,000*l.* a year; and in his reign, several general resumptions of grants were authorized by Parliament, in order to supply his necessities.

The rapacity of Henry VII. was needed to retrieve the revenues of the Crown; and his exactions and thrift repaired the waste of former reigns. His acquisitions, however, were as nothing compared with the wholesale plunder of the monasteries, and other religious and charitable foundations, by Henry VIII., which has been valued at upwards of 30,000,000*l.* sterling.[1] Yet such were the magnificence and prodigality of this king, that at his death, his treasury was found to be entirely empty. The Crown was as poor as ever: but the great nobles, who were enriched by grants of the Church lands — more provident than their royal master — held them fast for their descendants. In the seventh year of the reign of James I. the entire land revenues of the Crown and Duchy of Lancaster amounted to no more than 66,870*l.* a year, while the king's debts exceeded a million.[2] During his reign he sold lands to the extent of 775,000*l.*, and left debts of about an equal amount.

Increase of land revenues by Henry VII. and VIII.

But more evil days were at hand for the land revenues. Charles I., unable to obtain supplies from Parliament, and gaining little from his illegal exactions, — was forced to sell and mortgage the property of the Crown. The Parliament, after his death, completed the spoliation, of which he had set them the example; and sold nearly all the royal estates, in order to pay the arrears due to the Parliamentary forces, and discharge the debts of the new Government.[3] At the Restoration, these sales were declared void; and many of the estates of the Crown were then recovered. But they were recovered, — to be again squandered and dispersed. In three years, Charles II. had reduced the income of the crown lands from 217,900*l.* to 100,000*l.* a year. In the first year of his reign he surrendered the Court of Wards and Liveries, and the military tenures, in exchange for a settlement of certain duties of excise;[4] being the first instance of a surrender by the Crown, of its interest

Destruction of land revenues during the Commonwealth.

Their recovery and subsequent waste.

[1] St. John on the Land Revenues of the Crown, 68.
[2] *Ib.* 79.
[3] Scobell, part ii. 51, 106, 227, &c.
[4] 12 Car. II. c. 24.

in any part of the hereditary revenues. During this reign, a large proportion of the fee-farm rents belonging to the Crown, was sold by Act of Parliament;[1] and further grants of these rents were made during the reigns of William III. and Queen Anne. The liberality of William III. to his followers, provoked remonstrances from Parliament. He was even obliged to recall an enormous grant to the Earl of Portland, which conveyed to that nobleman four fifths of the county of Denbigh, with a reserved rent of 6*s.* 8*d.*, payable to the Crown:[2] but he compensated the Earl with other lands and manors.[3]

So jealous were the Commons, at this period, of the continual diminution of the hereditary revenues of the Crown, that several bills were brought in to resume all grants made by Charles II. and James II.,[4] and to prevent further alienations of crown lands.[5] At the end of William's reign, Parliament having obtained accounts of the state of the land revenues, found that they had been reduced by grants, alienations, incumbrances, reversions, and pensions, until they scarcely exceeded the rent-roll of a squire.[6]

Alienations of Crown lands restrained.

Such an abuse of the rights of the Crown could no longer be tolerated; and on the settlement of the civil list of Queen Anne, Parliament at length interposed to restrain it. It was now nearly too late. The sad confession was made, "that the necessary expenses of supporting the Crown, or the greater part of them, were formerly defrayed by a land revenue, which had, from time to time, been impaired by the grants of former kings and queens, so that Her Majesty's land revenues could then afford very little towards the support of her Government."[7]

1 22 Car. II. c. 6; 22 and 23 Car. II. c. 24.

2 1695 Parl. Hist. v. 978; Com. Journ., xi. 391, 395, 409.

3 Com. Journ. xi. 608.

4 In 1697, 1699, 1700, 1702, and 1703: Com. Journ. xii. 90; *Ib.* xiii. 208, 350; *Ib.* xiv. 95, 269, 305, &c.

5 In 1697 and 1699, Com. Journ. xii. 90; *Ib.* xiii. 62.

6 Com. Journ. xiii. 478, 498; St. John on the Land Revenues, 99.

7 1 Anne, c. 7, s. 5.

Yet to preserve what was still left, it was now provided that no future lease (except a building lease) should be granted for more than thirty-one years, or three lives; and that a reasonable rent should be reserved. If such a law as this had been passed immediately after the Restoration, the land revenues would probably have provided for the entire charge of the civil list of Queen Anne. But at least the small remnant of crown lands was saved; and in that and the next two reigns, some additions were made to the royal estates, by escheats and forfeitures.[1]

Constitutional results of the improvidence of kings.

While this waste of the crown property had been injurious to the public revenues, it favored the development of the liberties of the people. Kings with vast hereditary revenues, — husbanded and improved, — would have been comparatively independent of Parliament. But their improvidence gradually constrained them to rely upon the liberality of their subjects; and their own necessities, and the increasing expenditure of the state, at length placed them entirely under the control of Parliament.

Importance of a settlement of the revenues of the Crown.

No constitutional change has been more important in securing popular control over the executive Government, than the voting of supplies by the House of Commons: nor has any expedient been better calculated to restrain the undue influence of the Crown, than a strict settlement of its revenues by Parliament. In the reign of Charles II., the principle of appropriating supplies to specific services by statute, — which had not been without previous recognition, — was formally established as one of the conditions, under which Parliament granted money for the ser-

Revenues of the Crown prior to the Revolution.

[1] Much curious learning is to be found concerning the land revenues of the Crown in Wright's Tenures; Hargrave's Notes to Coke on Littleton; Coke's 1st Inst.; Spelman's Works (of Feuds); Lord Hale's History of the Common Law; Gilbert's Hist. of the Exchequer; Maddox's Hist. of the Exchequer; Davenant on Resumptions; Dugdale's Monasticon; Rymer's Fœdera; Rapin's Hist.; and an interesting summary in St. John's Observations on the Land Revenues of the Crown, 4to, 1787.

vice of the state. But until the Revolution, no limitation had been imposed upon the personal expenditure of the sovereign. It had been customary for Parliament to grant to the king, at the commencement of each reign, the ordinary revenues of the Crown, which were estimated to provide, in time of peace, for the support of His Majesty's dignity and civil government, and for the public defence. To these were added, from time to time, special grants for extraordinary occasions. The ordinary revenues were derived, first, from the hereditary revenues of the Crown itself, and, secondly, from the produce of taxes voted to the king for life. The hereditary revenues consisted of the rents of crown lands, of feudal rights, the proceeds of the post-office, and wine-licenses; and, after the surrender of feudal tenures by Charles II., in 1660, of part of the excise duties.

In the reign of James II. the hereditary revenues, together with the taxes voted for the king's life, amounted on an average to 1,500,964*l.* a year.[1] Whatever remained of this annual income, after the payment of the necessary expenses of the Government, was at the king's absolute disposal, — whether for the support of his dignity and influence, or for his pleasures and profusion. Not satisfied with these resources for his personal expenditure, there is no doubt that Charles II. applied to his own privy purse, large sums of money which had been specially appropriated by Parliament, for carrying on the war.[2]

Settlement of the "Civil List" of William and Mary.

To prevent such abuses in future on the accession of William and Mary, Parliament made a separate provision for the king's "Civil List," — which embraced the support of the royal household, and the personal expenses of the king, as well as the payment of civil offices and pensions. The revenue voted for

[1] Parl. Hist. v. 151; Hallam, Const. Hist. ii. 279.

[2] Lord Clarendon's Life, iii. 131; Pepys's Diary, Sept. 23d, and Dec. 12th, 1666, whence it appears that above 400,000*l.* had gone into the Privy Purse since the War. — *Memoirs*, iii. 47, 105.

the support of the Crown in time of peace, was 1,200,000*l.*; of which the Civil List amounted to about 700,000*l.*, being derived from the hereditary revenues of the Crown, estimated at 400,000*l.* a year and upwards, — and from a part of the excise duties, producing about 300,000*l.*[1]

The Civil List comprised items of national expenditure.

The system thus introduced was continued in succeeding reigns; and the Civil List still comprised not only the expenses of the sovereign, but a portion of the civil expenditure of the state.

Civil List of Queen Anne.

The Civil List of Queen Anne was settled by Parliament in the same form, and computed at the same amount as that of William III.[2] Her Majesty, while she feared the revenue granted to her would fall short of that enjoyed by the late king, promised that 100,000*l.* a year should be applied to the public service.[3] So far, however, from fulfilling this promise, — during the twelve years of her reign, she incurred debts amounting to 1,200,000*l.*, which were paid off by Parliament, by way of loans charged upon the Civil List itself.

Of George the First.

The Civil List of George I. was computed at 700,000*l.* a year; and, during his reign, debts were incurred to the extent of 1,000,000*l.*, which were discharged by Parliament, in the same manner.[4]

Of George the Second.

The hereditary revenues were continued to George II., with a proviso that if they should produce less than 800,000*l.* a year, Parliament would make up the deficiency. The king, however, was entitled to any surplus above that sum.[5] This was an approximation to a definite Civil List, as the *minimum* at least was fixed. For the last five years of his reign these revenues had risen, on an average, to 829,155*l.* a year: but during the whole of his

1 Parl. Hist. v. 193; Com. Journ. x. 54, 438; Smollett and Hallam state the Civil List at 600,000*l.*

2 1 Anne, c. 7.

3 Parl. Hist. vi. 11.

4 1 Geo. I. c. 1; Burke's Works, ii. 309.

5 1 Geo. II. c. 1.

reign, they amounted to less than 800,000*l.*[1] In 1746 a debt of 456,000*l.* on the Civil List was discharged by Parliament. This debt was stated by the king to have been incurred in consequence of the hereditary revenues having fallen short of 800,000*l.* a year; and parliament was, therefore, bound by the terms of its original contract, to make up the deficiency.

Civil List of George III.

On the accession of George III., the king consented to make such a disposition of his interest in the hereditary revenues of the Crown in England, as Parliament might think fit. Hitherto the Crown had enjoyed certain revenues which were calculated by Parliament to produce a sufficient income; but now the king agreed to accept a fixed amount as his Civil List, "for the support of his household, and the honor and dignity of the Crown."[2] This was the first time that the direct control of Parliament over the personal expenditure of the king had been acknowledged; and it is not a little curious that so important a change in the relations of the sovereign to Parliament, should have been introduced at the very period when he was seeking to extend his prerogatives, and render himself independent of other influences in the state. It soon appeared, however, from the debts incurred, that his Majesty was not inclined to permit this concession to diminish the influence of the Crown.

The money arising out of the hereditary revenues, secured by various Acts of Parliament to the king's predecessors, was now carried to the "aggregate fund," out of which the annual sum of 723,000*l.* was granted to his Majesty, during the continuance of the existing annuities to the Princess Dowager of Wales, the Duke of Cumberland, and the Princess Amelie; and as these charges ceased, the amount of the Civil List was to be increased until it reached 800,000*l.* a year. He thus accepted the *minimum* Civil List of his

1 Report on Civil List, 1815, p. 4; Burke's Works, ii. 310.

2 Com. Journ. xxviii. 28.

predecessor; and relinquished all claim to the surplus, which for the first eight years of his reign amounted, upon an average, to 100,000*l.* a year.[1]

Other sources of revenue.

But the king enjoyed other sources of income, independent of Parliamentary control. He derived a considerable amount from the Droits of the Crown and Admiralty, the 4½ per cent. duties, and other casual sources of revenue in England. He was in possession of the hereditary revenues of Scotland; and of a separate Civil List for Ireland. He retained the rich Duchies of Cornwall and Lancaster. Mr. Burke estimated the total annual income of the Crown, from these various sources, at little less than a million; exclusive of the revenues of Hanover, and the Bishopric of Osnaburgh.[2] During this long reign, the Droits of the Crown and Admiralty, and the casual revenues, which were wholly withdrawn from the cognizance of Parliament, amounted to the large sum of 12,705,461*l.*: out of which, however, he voluntarily contributed 2,600,000*l.* to the public service; while 5,372,834*l.* were appropriated as the expenses of captors, and payments to persons concerned in taking prizes. The surplus actually enjoyed by the Crown, after making these deductions amounted, therefore, to 4,732,627*l.*[3] George III. also succeeded to 172,605*l.* which the late king, — more frugal than any prince since Henry VII., — had saved out of his Civil List.[4]

Charges on the Civil List.

But great as were these revenues, the burdens on them were still greater. Places and pensions were multiplied, until the royal income was inadequate to provide for them. On the accession of George III., the greater part of the late king's household was retained; and, at the same time, numerous personal adherents of his Majesty were added to the establishment.[5] But while

[1] 1 Geo. III. c. 1; Rep. on Civil List, 1815.
[2] Present Discontents, Burke's Works, ii. 281.
[3] Report on the Civil List, 1815; Hans. Deb. 3d Ser., 143.
[4] Grenville Papers, iii. 144; Wraxall's Mem. ii. 55.
[5] Walp. Mem. i. 25.

the expenditure of the Civil List was increased, the king and his family were living, not only with economy, but even with unkingly parsimony. In 1762 he purchased Buckingham House, and settled it on the queen; "St. James's" according to Horace Walpole, "not being a prison strait enough."[1] Here he lived in privacy, attended only by menial servants, and keeping up none of the splendor of a Court.[2] "In all this," said Burke, "the people see nothing but the operations of parsimony, attended with all the consequences of profusion. Nothing expended — nothing saved. . . . They do not believe it to be hoarded, nor perceive it to be spent."[3]

Parliamentary influence secured by the Civil List expenditure.

While practising this apparent economy, the king was engaged in that struggle to increase the influence, and establish the ascendency of the Crown, which has been described elsewhere.[4] The large expenditure of the Civil List could not fail, therefore, to be associated with the fidelity and subserviency of the court party in Parliament. The Crown was either plundered by its servants; or Parliamentary support was purchased by places, pensions, and pecuniary corruption.[5]

Debt upon the Civil List, 1769.

In February, 1769, before the king had yet been nine years upon the throne, the arrears of the Civil List amounted to 513,511*l.*; and his Majesty was obliged to apply to Parliament to discharge them. This demand was made at an untimely moment, when the people were exasperated by the persecution of Wilkes, — when the policy of the court was odious, and the king him-

1 Walp. Mem. i. 159.

2 The king continued this plain style of living throughout his reign. — *Wraxall's Mem.*, i. 8–10. Mr. Addington, writing to his brother, 29th Dec., 1804, said he had just partaken of the king's dinner, "which consisted of mutton chops and pudding." — *Life of Sidmouth*, ii. 342. Similar examples are to be found in Twiss's Life of Lord Eldon, and in Madame D'Arblay's Memoirs.

3 Present Discontents, Works, ii. 280.

4 See Chapter I.

5 See Chapter VI.

self unpopular. But if the country was discontented, Parliament was held in safe subjection. Inquiry was demanded into the causes of the debt, and explanatory accounts were sought; but all investigation being resisted by ministers, the amount was granted without information. In the following year, motions for inquiry into the expenditure of the Civil List were renewed, with no better success.[1] Lord Chatham avowed his conviction that the Civil List revenues were expended in corrupting members of Parliament;[2] and the Civil List expenditure, — and the withholding from Parliament such an explanation of its causes, as had been customary in former reigns, — formed a prominent topic in Mr. Burke's celebrated pamphlet on "The Causes of the Present Discontents."

Further debt in 1777.

But the same causes of excessive expenditure, — whatever they may have been,— continued without a check; and after the lapse of eight years, the king was again obliged to have recourse to Parliament, not only to discharge a debt of 618,340*l.*, but to increase his annual Civil List to 900,000*l.* a year. On this occasion, accounts explanatory of the arrears were laid before Parliament. Ministers no longer ventured to withhold them: but they were not deemed satisfactory by the Opposition. Again the causes of increased expenditure were freely animadverted upon in Parliament. The income of the king was compared with that of his predecessors, — the large amount of secret-service money, and the increased Pension List were noticed, — and insinuations made of covert influence and corruption.[3] But Parliament acceded to the demands of the king. When the speaker, Sir Fletcher Norton, addressed

[1] Parl. Hist. xvi. 843, 926; Walp. Mem. iii. 343; Rockingham's Mem. ii. 90, 167. The Duke of Richmond, writing to Lord Rockingham as to a division in the Lords, says: "The division of twenty-six on so courtly a point as paying his Majesty's debts, and enabling him to bribe higher, is, I think, a very strong one." — *Rock. Mem.* ii. 92.

[2] Parl. Hist. xvi. 849.

[3] *Ibid.*, xix. 103, 160, 187; Walp. Mem. iv. 92.

the throne, on presenting the bill for the royal assent, he said, the Commons "have not only granted to your Majesty a large present supply, but also a very great additional revenue; great beyond example; great beyond your Majesty's highest expense." The speaker's uncourtly address became the subject of remark and censure in the House of Commons; but his friend Mr. Fox, having come to the rescue, he was thanked for expressing with "just and proper energy, the zeal of this House for the support of the honor and dignity of the Crown, in circumstances of great public charge." [1] His conduct, however, was not forgiven by the court; and in the next Parliament, he was punished by the loss of the speaker's chair.[2]

Debates upon the Civil List, 1779.

Promptly as these demands of the Crown were met, they yet excited lasting dissatisfaction. The public expenditure and the national debt had been prodigiously increased by the American War, when the abuses of the Civil List were again brought under the notice of Parliament. In 1779 the Duke of Richmond moved an address to the Crown praying for the reduction of the Civil List, which was rejected by a majority of more than two to one.[3] But a few days afterwards Mr. Burke gave notice of his motion on Economic Reform, with which his name has since been honorably associated. On the 11th of February, 1780, being fortified by numerous petitions, he propounded his elaborate scheme. This embraced a considerable reduction of offices, a diminution of expenditure, and improved administration and accounts in the various departments of the State; and in his masterly review, the expenditure of the Civil List attracted a large share of his scrutiny. Describing the royal household, he pointed out the social changes which had taken place, and the obsolete character of many of the offices which

Mr. Burke's scheme of Economic Reform, 1780.

[1] Parl. Hist. xix. 227.
[2] Wraxall's Mem. i. 372.
[3] Dec. 7th, 1779; Parl. Hist. xx. 1255.

were still retained. "The royal household," he said, "has lost all that was stately and venerable in the antique manners, without retrenching anything of the cumbrous charge, of a gothic establishment."[1] Examples of profusion and abuse were given, — useless offices, and offices performed by deputy, — the king's turnspit being a member of Parliament,[2] — jobbing, waste, and peculation in every department, without restraint. He proposed the reduction and consolidation of offices, the diminution of the Pension List to 60,000*l.* a year, and the payment of all pensions at the Exchequer.

Mr. Burke obtained leave to bring in five bills to carry out these various objects: but his Establishment Bill[3] was the only one which was discussed in that session. It was read a second time, and several of its provisions were discussed in committee; but it was ultimately defeated by the Government.[4] The discussions, however, led to a proposition from Lord North, for a Commission of Public Accounts.

Mr. Burke's Establishment Bill, 1781.

In the following year Mr. Burke resumed his efforts, and again obtained leave to bring in his Establishment Bill. In advocating this measure he was boldly supported by young William Pitt, who then first offered himself to the notice of Parliament. The Bill was lost on the second reading.[5]

Measures of the Rockingham Ministry, 1782.

But a sudden change soon took place in the prospects of this question. Lord Rockingham's administration acceded to office, pledged to economic reform, and resolved to carry it into effect. Lord Rockingham, in laying his plan before the king, explained "that not a single article of the expense to be retrenched touches anything whatsoever which is personal to your Majesty, or to

[1] Parl. Hist. xxi. 30.

[2] *Ibid.* 33, and Lord Talbot's Speech in 1777; *Ibid.* xix. 176.

[3] See Parl. Hist. xxi. 111, where it is printed at length.

[4] *Ibid.* xxi. 714.

[5] Parl. Hist. xxi. 1292. Wraxall's Mem. ii. 333.

your Majesty's royal family, or which in the least contributes to the splendor of your court;" and that in fact he only intended to reduce the patronage and influence of the ministers.[1] On the 15th April, 1782, a message from the king was sent to both Houses, recommending economy in all branches of the public expenditure, and stating that he had already considered the reform and regulation of his civil establishment. Well might Mr. Burke congratulate the House of Commons and the country on so favorable a change in the policy of the Government, and on the attitude of the king towards his people. In both Houses this communication was cordially received and acknowledged.[2] It was soon followed by another, which though not so satisfactory, at least afforded convincing proof of the necessity of that economy which had been already recommended.

Civil List Debt, 1782.

The king was now obliged to announce to Parliament another debt upon his Civil List; but instead of proposing that it should be discharged, as on previous occasions, out of the general revenues of the state, he intimated that its liquidation was to be secured by intended reductions of the Civil List establishment. Notwithstanding the recent additions to the Civil List, the arrears now amounted to 295,877*l.*; and the proposed savings, instead of being available either to the king or to the country, would thus become immediately mortgaged for the payment of a debt, by annual instalments.

Civil List Act of 1782.

The Civil List Act of Lord Rockingham, though falling short of Mr. Burke's original proposal, was nevertheless a considerable measure. Many useless offices were abolished, restraints were imposed upon the issue of secret-service money, the Pension List was diminished, and securities were provided for a more effectual supervision of the royal expenditure. And now, for the first time, the Civil List expenditure was divided into

[1] Lord Rockingham's Letter to the King. — *Rock. Mem.* ii. 477.

[2] Parl. Hist. xxii. 1269. Wraxall's Mem. 43-47, 54.

classes, eight in number, which led to more important changes hereafter.[1]

Subsequent debts in this reign.

But debt continued to be the normal condition of the Civil List throughout the reign of George III. Again and again applications were renewed to Parliament; and the debts discharged at different periods after 1782, exceeded 2,300,000*l.* From the beginning to the end of this reign, the several arrears paid off by Parliament, exclusive of the debt of 300,000*l.* charged on the Civil List in 1782, amounted to 3,398,000*l.*[2]

Surplus of hereditary revenues.

In defence of these continued excesses it was urged, that they were more than defrayed by the surplus of the hereditary revenues, which the king had surrendered; and which, in 1815, exceeded by upwards of 6,000,000*l.* the entire expenditure of the Civil List since the accession of the king, — including all the debts which had been paid off by Parliament, and the charges from which the Civil List had been relieved.[3]

Charges removed from the Civil List.

Meanwhile the Civil List continued to comprise charges wholly unconnected with the personal comfort and dignity of the sovereign, — the salaries of judges, ambassadors, and other officers of state, — annuities to members of the royal family, and pensions

[1] 22 Geo. III. c. 82; Parl. Hist. xxii. 1395; *Ibid.* xxiii. 121.

[2]

In 1769	£513,511	
1777	618,340	
1784	60,000	
1786	210,000	
1802	990,053	
1804	591,842	
1805	10,458	
1814	118,857	
1814	100,000	(extra expenses.)
1816	185,000	
	£3,398,061	

Report on Civil List, 1815, p. 4; Speech of Mr. Spring Rice, Nov. 23d, 1837. — *Hansard's Debates*, 3d Ser., xxxix. 144.

[3] Report on Civil List, 1815, p. 4.

granted for public services, — all of which were more fairly chargeable to the state revenues, than to the Civil List of the Crown. From many of these charges the Civil List was, from time to time, relieved, — amounting, between the accession of George III. and 1815, to 9,561,396*l.*[1]

Regulation of the Civil List of the Regency.

On the expiration of the first year of the Regency, in 1812, the Civil List was increased by 70,000*l.* a year, and a special grant of 100,000*l.* was voted to the Prince Regent.[2] In 1816 the Civil List was settled at 1,083,727*l.*, including the establishment of the king; and its expenditure was, at the same time, subjected to further regulation. It was relieved from some of the annuities to the royal family: the payments on account of the several classes of expenditure were defined and controlled; and the expenses of the royal household were subjected to the supervision and audit of a treasury officer, the auditor of the Civil List.[3]

Civil List on accession of George IV.

King George IV., on his accession, expected a larger Civil List than he had enjoyed as Prince Regent; but yielding to the persuasion and remonstrances of his ministers, he stated in his speech from the throne, that so far from desiring any arrangement which would lead to the imposition of new burdens upon his people, he had no wish to alter the settlement adopted by Parliament in 1816.[4]

Other revenues of the Crown.

The Civil List being now free from the expenses of the late king, was fixed by Parliament at 845,727*l.* But during the whole of this reign the king enjoyed, in addition to this income, the hereditary revenues of Scotland, amounting on an average to 109,000*l.*,

[1] Report on Civil List, 1815, p. 5.

[2] 52 Geo. III. c. 6, 7; Hans. Deb. 1st Ser. xxi. 151, &c.

[3] 56 Geo. III. c. 46.

[4] Twiss's Life of Eldon, ii. 363; Hansard's Debates, 2d Ser., i. 11.

This concession, "if report be true, was obtained by nothing but the most determined refusal of the Ministers to do more." — *Mr. T. Grenville to the Marquis of Buckingham*, May 4th, 1820.

and the Civil List for Ireland of 250,000*l.* He also received the Droits of the Crown and Admiralty, the 4½ per cent. duties, the West India duties, and other casual revenues, which were still vested in the Crown, and independent of Parliament.[1]

Civil List of William IV.

King William IV., on his accession, for the first time surrendered the interest of the Crown in all these sources of revenue, and accepted a Civil List of 510,000*l.* The future expenditure of this amount was divided into five different classes, to each of which a specific annual sum was appropriated, including a Pension List of 75,000*l.* At the same time, the Civil List was still further relieved from charges, which more properly belonged to the civil government of the State. These charges included judicial salaries, — which had been paid partly out of the Civil List, partly out of the Consolidated Fund, and partly out of the fees of the Courts, — the salaries and pensions of the diplomatic service, — and numerous miscellaneous expenses.[2]

These arrangements were not concluded until the accounts of the Civil List expenditure had been referred to a select committee of the House of Commons, and freely investigated. The Wellington ministry resisted this investigation, and fell: when the settlement of the Civil List was left to the Whig ministry of Lord Grey.[3] The committee, in their inquiries, not thinking it consistent with the respect due to his Majesty to scrutinize the details of his domestic household, nevertheless recommended several reductions in the salaries of the officers of state, amounting in the aggregate to 11,529*l.*[4] The king, however, remonstrated with his ministers against the proposed reduction, saying: — "If the people, according to the new (reform) bill, are really to gov-

[1] Report on Civil Government Charges, 1831; 1 Geo. IV. c. 1.

[2] Report on Civil Government Charges, 1831; Report on Civil List Charges, 1833.

[3] Hans. Deb., 3d Ser., i. 429, 526.

[4] Report on the Civil List Accounts, March 21st, 1831.

ern the House of Commons, and the House of Commons is to decide upon the amount of salary I am to give to my servants, then the prerogatives of the Crown will in reality pass to the people, and the monarchy cannot exist." The ministers yielded to this remonstrance, and induced the House of Commons to restore the Civil List to the amount originally proposed.[1]

Civil List of Her Majesty.

The Civil List of Queen Victoria was settled on the same principles as that of William IV., and amounted to 385,000*l.*: the only material variation being that in lieu of the Pension List of 75,000*l.*, her Majesty was empowered to grant pensions annually to the extent of 1,200*l.* The Crown was thus finally restricted to a definite annuity for the support of its dignity, and for the personal comfort of the sovereign.[2]

No debts upon the Civil List during three reigns.

It may be added, as at once a proof of the wisdom of these arrangements, and of the improved administration of our later sovereigns, that neither in the reign of Her Most Gracious Majesty, nor in the reigns of George IV. and William IV., has any application been made to Parliament for the discharge of debts upon the Civil List.[3]

Importance of relieving Civil List from extraneous charges.

While the Civil List has been diminished in amount, its relief from charges with which it had formerly been encumbered has placed it beyond the reach of misconstruction. The Crown repudiates the indirect influences exercised in former reigns, and is free from imputations of corruption. And the continual increase of the civil charges of the Government, which was formerly a reproach to the Crown, is now a matter for which the House of Commons is alone responsible. In this, as in other examples of constitutional progress, apparent

1 Roebuck's Hist. of the Whig Ministry, ii. 159; Hansard's Debates, 3d Ser., iii. 959.

2 Hansard's Debates, xxxix. 137, *et seq.*

3 Rep. 1837–8, on the Civil List.

encroachments upon the Crown have but added to its true dignity, and conciliated, more than ever, the confidence and affections of the people.

Revenues of Hanover.

Until the accession of her Majesty, every previous sovereign of her royal house had also enjoyed the revenue of the Kingdom of Hanover, which was now detached from the Crown of England. Former sovereigns had also inherited considerable personal property from their predecessors: but her Majesty succeeded to none whatever.

Duchies of Lancaster and Cornwall.

The Crown, however, still retains the revenues of the Duchies of Lancaster and Cornwall. The former are the property of the reigning sovereign; the latter the independent inheritance of the Prince of Wales, as Duke of Cornwall. The estates of both these duchies have been largely augmented by judicious management, and by vigilant attention to the interests of the Crown.

Revenue of the Duchy of Lancaster.

At the commencement of her Majesty's reign, the gross revenue of the Duchy of Lancaster amounted to 23,038*l.*, and the charges to 14,126*l.*, leaving a net revenue of no more than 8,912*l.* In 1859 the gross revenue had increased to 45,349*l.*, and the net revenue to 31,349*l.*, of which 25,000*l.* were paid to her Majesty's Privy Purse.[1]

Revenue of the Duchy of Cornwall.

When George, Prince of Wales, came of age in 1783, the income of the Duchy of Cornwall was less than 13,000*l.* a year. On the accession of her Majesty the gross income was 28,456*l.*, and the payments were 12,670*l.*, leaving a net income of 15,786*l.* In 1859, the gross income had increased to 63,704*l.*, and the net revenue to 50,777*l.*; of which no less than 40,785*l.* were paid over to the trustees and treasurer of his Royal Highness the Prince of Wales.[2] And out of this ample revenue, accumulations exceeding half a million, are said to have been invested for the future benefit of his Royal Highness.

1 Parl. Papers, 1837-8, (665); 1860, (98).

2 Parl. Papers, 1837-8, (665); 1860, (13).

In addition to these public revenues, the rights of the Crown to its own private property have been secured. The alienation of the land revenues of the Crown having been restrained by the 1st Anne, a doubt subsequently arose, whether the restrictions of that Act extended to the private property of the sovereign, acquired by purchase, gift, or devise, or by descent, from persons not being kings or queens of the realm. But such restrictions being without any color of justice, an Act was passed, in 1800, declaring that property so acquired, could be disposed of like the property of subjects.[1] On the accession of George IV., however, doubts were suggested whether this Act applied to property acquired, by the reigning sovereign, before he had succeeded to the throne, which were set at rest by statute in 1823.[2]

Private property of the sovereigns.

While the Civil List has been ample for the support of the personal dignity of the Crown, Parliament has also provided liberally for the maintenance of the various members of the royal family. A separate annuity to the Queen Consort, with a large dowry in case of the death of the king, — annuities to the brothers, sisters, and other relatives of his Majesty, — establishments for each of his children on coming of age, and even allowances for their education and maintenance, — marriage portions for princesses of the royal house, — such are the claims which have been made upon the liberality of Parliament, in addition to the Civil List. To these must be added, in the reign of George III., the debts of the Prince of Wales.

Provision for the royal family.

The prince came of age in 1783, — a time ill-suited for heavy demands upon the public purse. The people were still suffering under the accumulated burdens of the American War; and the abuses of the Civil List had recently undergone a rude exposure. But the prince's Whig friends in the Coalition Ministry, overlook-

Debts of the Prince of Wales.

1 39 & 40 Geo. III. c. 88.

2 4 Geo. IV. c. 18 ; Hansard's Debates, 2d Ser., viii. 509, 651.

ing these considerations, proposed a settlement of 100,000*l.* a year. They were glad to have this opportunity of strengthening their political connection with the heir-apparent. But the king was more sensible than they, of the objections to such a proposal at that time; and being tenacious of his own power, — loving his son but little, and hating his ministers very much, — he declined an arrangement which would have secured the independence of the prince, and drawn him still more closely to the party most obnoxious to himself. He agreed, therefore, to make the prince an allowance of 50,000*l.* a year out of his Civil List, which had already proved unequal to his own expenditure, and limited his demand upon Parliament to an outfit of 60,000*l.*[1] To a prudent prince such an allowance would have been ample; to the spendthrift and the gamester it was a pittance. The prince was soon in difficulties; and his "debts of honor" to the blacklegs of Newmarket, and the sharpers of St. James's, left little for the payment of the royal tradesmen. On the revision of the Civil List in 1786, another effort was made by the prince's friends to obtain for him a more liberal settlement; but Mr. Pitt was cold, and the king inexorable. The prince broke up his establishment, yet failed to pay his debts.

In 1787 his affairs had become desperate, when the heir-apparent was saved from ruin by the friendly intervention of a London alderman. Mr. Alderman Newnham having given notice, in the House of Commons, of an address to the king on the subject of the prince's debts, and being supported by the friends of his Royal Highness, the king thought it better to arrange a compromise. This resulted in the addition of 10,000*l.* a year to the income of the prince out of the Civil List; and the voting of 161,000*l.* for the payment of his debts, and 20,000*l.* for the buildings at Carlton House.[2] No

[1] 25th June, 1783; Parl. Hist. xxiii. 1030; Lord J. Russell's Life and Times of Fox, ii. 8; Lord Auckland's Cor. i. 54.

[2] Parl. Hist. xxvi. 1010, 1048, 1064, 1207; Tomline's Life of Pitt, ii. 260; Lord Auckland's Cor. i. 415, 417.

less than 63,700*l.* were afterwards granted by Parliament, at different times, for the completion of this costly palace,[1] which, after being the scene of tinsel splendor and bad taste for little more than twenty-five years, was razed to the ground to make room for metropolitan improvements.

The king assured the House of Commons that the prince had promised to confine his future expenses within his income; yet so little were these good intentions carried out, that in 1792 his Royal Highness confessed to Lord Malmesbury that his debts then amounted to 370,000*l.*[2] In 1795 they had increased to the extraordinary sum of 650,000*l.*; when he was extricated from these embarrassments, by his ill-fated marriage with Caroline of Brunswick. To propose a grant for the payment of these debts, was out of the question; but an additional annuity of 65,000*l.* was settled upon him, of which nearly the whole was appropriated, for many years, to the gradual discharge of his incumbrances.[3] These were ultimately paid off; and the spendthrift prince, — though still fond of building and enlarging palaces at the public expense, — learned, in his old age, to husband his own resources, with the caution of a miser.

Parliament has since cheerfully granted every suitable provision for members of the royal family: but its liberality has not been discredited by any further application for the payment of their debts.

Mismanagement of the land revenues on behalf of the public.

We have seen that the income arising from the land revenues of the Crown was surrendered to the state, by George III. in exchange for a Civil List; but for a long time the state was deprived, by mismanagement, of the greater part of the benefit to which it was entitled. Leases were improvidently, if not corruptly, granted, — often without any survey of the prop-

1 Viz., 35,000*l.* in 1789, 3,500*l.* in 1791, and 27,500*l.* in 1795.

2 Lord Malmesbury's Cor. ii. 415, 418.

3 King's Message, April 27th, 1795; Parl. Hist. xxxi. 1464, 1496; *Ibid.* xxxii. 90, 135; 35 Geo. III. c. 129.

erty, and even without a copy or counterpart of the lease being retained by the Surveyor-General, on behalf of the Crown: renewals were conceded at the pleasure of the tenants; while extravagant fees, payable at public offices, instead of being charged to the tenants, were deducted from the fines, and became a grievous burden upon the revenues of the Crown. At least seven eighths of the value of the land were received in the shape of fines, and one eighth only in rent; and these fines, again, were computed at high rates of interest, by which the payments to the Crown were further diminished.

Encroachments and waste were permitted upon the royal demesnes, with scarcely a check. Such mismanagement, however, was not due to any want of officers, appointed to guard the public interests. On the contrary, their very number served to facilitate frauds and evasions. Instead of being a check upon one another, these officers acted independently; and their ignorance, incapacity, and neglect went far to ruin the property under their charge. As an illustration of the system it may be stated, that the land-tax was frequently allowed twice over to lessees; from which error alone, a loss was sustained of upwards of fifteen hundred pounds a year. Even without mismanagement, the wide dispersion of the estates of the Crown multiplied the charges of superintendence and administration.

From these various causes the noble estates of the Crown, for the first twenty-five years of the reign of George III. produced an average net revenue little exceeding six thousand pounds a year.[1] Some of these abuses were exposed by Mr. Burke in 1780, who suggested as a remedy, a general sale of the Crown lands.[2] In 1786 the king sent message to Parliament, by the advice of Mr. Pitt, recommending an inquiry into the condition of the woods, forests, and land revenues of the Crown; and a commission was ac-

1 Reports of Commissioners of Inquiry into the Woods, Forests, and Land Revenues, under Act 26 Geo. III. c. 87.

2 Parl. Hist. xxi. 26.

cordingly appointed by Act, to make that inquiry, and to suggest improvements in the system of management.[1] The recommendations of this commission led to the passing of an Act in 1794, by which an improved administration of the land revenues was introduced;[2] and means were taken for making them more productive. This commission had reported that, in their opinion, the estates which had hitherto yielded so insignificant a revenue might, under improved management, eventually produce no less than 400,000*l.* a year. Existing interests postponed for a time the realization of so sanguine an estimate: but in 1798 the Crown lands were valued at 201,250*l.* a year:[3] in 1812 they were valued at 283,160*l.*:[4] in 1820 they actually yielded 114,852*l.*; in 1830, they produced 373,770*l.*; and in the year ending 31st March, 1860, they returned an income of 416,530*l.*[5]

Appropriation of the proceeds of the land revenues.

But when the land revenues of the Crown were at length becoming nearly an equivalent for the Civil List, a considerable proportion of the income was still diverted from the Exchequer. The land revenues, and the woods and forests, were originally managed, each by a Surveyor-General; but in 1810 the functions of these two offices were combined in a Commission of Woods, Forests, and Land Revenues.[6] In 1832 the superintendence of public works was added to the duties of this commission;[7] when it soon became evident that what they received with one hand, they were too ready to pay over to the other. The revenue derived from the property of the Crown, was applied with too much facility, to the execution of public works and improvements: the Exchequer was deprived of the funds which were due to it, in exchange for the Civil List; and Parliament was denied its proper con-

1 Parl. Hist. xxvi. 186, 202.
2 34 Geo. III. c. 75.
3 Report of Surveyor-General, Com. Journ. liii. 187.
4 1st Report of Comm. of Woods and Forests, 1812.
5 Finance Accounts, 1860.
6 50 Geo. III. c. 65.
7 2 & 3 Will. IV. c. 1.

trol over an important branch of the public expenditure. To arrest this evil another administrative change was necessary; and in 1851 the departments of Woods and Forests and of Public Works were again entirely separated.[1] Hence, whatever may be the net proceeds of the property of the Crown, they form part of the public revenue; and whatever sums may be needed for public works, are voted by Parliament out of the general income of the state.

Civil List Pensions.

A very important part of the expenditure of the Civil List has been caused, in every reign but the present, by the payment of pensions. The grant of pensions by the Crown has so often been the subject of political discussion, that a brief explanation of the law and usage by which they were granted, and the funds from which they were payable, will not be devoid of constitutional interest.

Restrictions upon grants of pensions charged upon crown lands.

Prior to the reign of Queen Anne, the Crown had exercised the right of charging its hereditary revenues with pensions and annuities; and it had been held that the king had power, in law, to bind his successors.[2] But on the accession of Queen Anne, in 1701, when alienations of crown lands were for the first time restrained by Parliament,[3] it was also provided that no portion of the hereditary revenues [4] could be alienated for any term, longer than the life of the reigning king.[5]

Pensions on the hereditary revenues.

This act, however, being passed before the union with Scotland, did not extend to the hereditary revenues of the Scottish crown. Nor was any similar Act passed in the Parliament of Ireland, restraining grants from the hereditary revenues of Ireland: neither

[1] 14 & 15 Vict. c. 41.

[2] Bankers' Case, 1691; State Trials, xiv. 3–43.

[3] Supra, p. 189.

[4] The hereditary revenues specified in the Act were these: the hereditary duties on beer, ale, or other liquors, the post-office, first-fruits and tenths, fines on writs, post fines, wine licenses, sheriffs' processes and compositions, and seizures of uncustomed and prohibited goods.

[5] 1 Anne, st. 1, c. 7.

did the Act of Anne extend to the 4½ per cent. duties. Subsequently to this Act, pensions on the hereditary revenues of the Crown in England could only be granted during the life of the reigning sovereign; but were practically regranted at the commencement of every reign. But pensions charged on the hereditary revenues of Scotland and Ireland, and on the 4½ per cent. duties, continued to be granted for the lives of the grantees.

Pensions on the Civil List of George III.

On the accession of George III., the larger branches of the hereditary revenues of the Crown in England being surrendered in exchange for a fixed Civil List, the pensions which had previously been paid out of the hereditary revenues, were henceforth paid out of the Civil List. There was no limit to the amount of the pensions so long as the Civil List could meet the demand; and no principle by which the grant of them was regulated, but the discretion of the Crown and its advisers.

Jealousy of the Pension List.

No branch of the public expenditure was regarded with so much jealousy, as that arising out of the unrestricted power of granting pensions by the Crown. Not only did it involve a serious public burden, — being one of the principal causes of the Civil List debts, — but it increased the influence of the Crown, and impaired the independence of Parliament. Mr. Burke, in bringing forward his scheme of economical reform in 1780, dwelt much on the excessive amount of the Pension List, and the absence of proper regulations; and particularly adverted to a custom which then prevailed, of granting pensions on a private list, during pleasure, by which dangerous corruption might be practised. Mr. Burke proposed that the English Pension List should be gradually reduced to 60,000*l.*, and that pensions should be restricted to the reward of merit, and "real public charity;" extraordinary cases being in future provided for by an address of either house of Parliament.

By the Civil List Act of the Rockingham administration

in 1782,[1] the power of granting pensions was considerably limited. It was provided that until the Pension List should be reduced to 90,000*l.*, no pension above 300*l.* a year should be granted: that the whole amount of pensions bestowed in any year should not exceed 600*l.*, a list of which was directed to be laid before Parliament: that the entire Pension List should afterwards be restricted to 95,000*l.*; and that no pension to any one person should exceed 1200*l.* This Act fully recognized the principles of Mr. Burke's plan: it affirmed almost in his very words, that by the usage of granting secret pensions during pleasure, "secret and dangerous corruption may hereafter be practised;" and it directed that in future all pensions should be paid at the Exchequer. It further acknowledged the principle that pensions ought to be granted for two causes only: — viz. as a royal bounty for persons in distress, or as a reward for desert.

Restriction upon the grant of pensions in 1782.

So far, therefore, the English Pension List was regulated, and made subject to Parliamentary control. But the Crown still retained ample means, from other sources, of rewarding political or personal services. The hereditary revenues of the Crown, in Ireland, amounting to the net sum of 275,102*l.*, were still at the sole disposal of the Crown, and were even alienable, so as to bind future sovereigns. It is natural that this convenient fund should have been largely charged with pensions. They had been granted in every form, — during the pleasure of the Crown, — for the life of the sovereign, — for terms of years, — for the life of the grantee, — and for several lives in being, or in reversion. As there was no control whatever over such grants, the Pension List was continually increasing. Complaints had long been made of the reckless prodigality of the Crown in bestowing pensions; and so far back as 1757, the Irish House of Commons had unanimously resolved "that the granting of so much of the public revenue in pen-

Irish Pension List.

[1] 22 Geo. III. c. 82.

sions is an improvident disposition of the revenue, an injury to the Crown, and detrimental to the people." Yet the Pension List, which in 1757 had amounted to 40,000*l.*, was trebled in the first thirty years of George III.; and, in 1793, had reached the prodigious sum of 124,000*l.* But the abuse had now worked itself out, and could be tolerated no longer. In that year, therefore, the Government itself proposed a change, which was readily adopted by the Irish Parliament.[1] The hereditary revenues were surrendered in Ireland,—as they had previously been surrendered in England,—in exchange for a fixed Civil List of 145,000*l.*, exclusive of pensions; and a Pension List of 124,000*l.*, to be reduced to 80,000*l.* Meanwhile the Crown was restrained from granting pensions in any one year exceeding 1200*l.*: but still retained and exercised the power of granting pensions for life, and in reversion. It was not until 1813 that the Irish Pension List was reduced to 80,000*l.*, as contemplated by this Act. On the accession of George IV., this list was further reduced to 50,000*l.*: no grants exceeding 1200*l.* in one year, being permitted until that reduction had been effected.[2]

Scotch Pension List.

The hereditary revenues of the Crown, in Scotland, remained exempt from parliamentary control until 1810. At that time, the pensions charged upon them amounted to 39,000*l.* It was then arranged by Parliament that no amount greater than 800*l.* should be granted in any one year, until the pensions had been reduced to 25,000*l.*; and that no pension exceeding 300*l.* a year should be given to any one person.[3]

Pensions on the 4½ per cent. duties.

There was still one fund left beyond the control of Parliament, and of course amply charged with pensions. The 4½ per cent. duties were not surrendered until 1830, when William IV. gave up his own life interest in them: the pensions previously granted being still payable by the state.

[1] 33 Geo. III. c. 34 (Ireland).

[2] 1 Geo. IV. c. 1, s. 10.

[3] 50 Geo. III. c. 111.

At this time, the three pension lists of England, Scotland, and Ireland, were consolidated; and the entire Civil Pension List for the United Kingdom was reduced from 145,750*l.* to 75,000*l.*; the remainder of the pensions being charged upon the Consolidated Fund.

Consolidation of the Pension Lists.

Finally, on the accession of her present Majesty, the right of the Crown to grant pensions was restricted to 1200*l.* a year. Such pensions were now confined, according to the terms of a resolution of the House of Commons of the 18th Feb. 1834, to "such persons as have just claims on the royal beneficence, or who, by their personal services to the Crown, by the performance of duties to the public, or by their useful discoveries in science and attainments in literature and the arts, have merited the gracious consideration of their sovereign, and the gratitude of their country."[1] At the same time an inquiry was directed by the House of Commons to be made into the existing Pension List, which resulted in the voluntary surrender of some pensions, and the suspension or discontinuance of others.[2]

Regulation of pensions in 1837.

The pensions thus reduced in amount, and subjected to proper regulation, have since been beyond the reach of constitutional jealousy. They no longer afford the means of corruption, — they add little to the influence of the Crown, — they impose a trifling burden on the people, — and the names of those who receive the royal bounty, are generally such as to command respect and sympathy.

Such being the pecuniary relations of the Crown and royal family to Parliament, let us take a brief review of the relations of the royal family to the reigning sovereign.

Powers of the king over the royal family.

Among the prerogatives of the Crown is to be reckoned a more than parental authority over the royal family; and,

[1] 1 Vict. c. 2; Report on Civil List, Dec. 5th, 1837.

[2] Report on Pensions, 24th July, 1838.

in 1772, the king sought the aid of Parliament in enlarging his powers. The Duke of Gloucester had been married for several years to the Countess Dowager of Waldegrave: but had not publicly acknowledged her as his consort, nor had she assumed his title.[1] At court she was neither recognized as his wife, nor discountenanced as his mistress: but held an equivocal position between these two characters.

Marriage of the Duke of Gloucester.

But in the autumn of 1771, another of the king's brothers, the Duke of Cumberland, announced to the king his marriage with Mrs. Horton, whom he at once called Duchess of Cumberland. By a singular coincidence, his bride was a daughter of Lord Irnham, and a sister of the famous Colonel Luttrell, whom the court party had put into Wilkes's seat for Middlesex. The mortification of the king, was only to be equalled by the malicious triumph of Wilkes. The family which had been made the instrument of his oppression, had now brought shame upon the king.[2] The Duke and Duchess were not only forbidden to appear at court themselves: but their society was interdicted to all who desired to be admitted to the palace.[3] At first the king was not without hope that the validity of the marriage might be questioned. It had been solemnized without the usual formalities prescribed by the law: but the royal family had been excepted from Lord Hardwicke's Marriage Act, by the express command of George II., who would not allow restraints, intended only for his subjects, to be imposed upon his own family.[4] Such restraints might now have postponed, or even prevented this hateful marriage. The alliance of the Duke of Cumberland with a

Of the Duke of Cumberland.

1 Walpole's Mem. iii. 402, 408.

2 Walpole says, "Could punishment be more severe than to be thus scourged by their own instrument? And how singular the fate of Wilkes, that new revenge always presented itself to him when he was sunk to the lowest ebb!" — *Mem.* iv. 356.

3 *Ibid.* 362.

4 Walpole's Mem. iv. 359.

subject, was followed by the public avowal of his marriage by the Duke of Gloucester, whose wife's position would have been seriously compromised by any longer concealment.

The king was now resolved to impose such restrictions upon future marriages in his own family, as had never been contemplated for his subjects. And, in truth, if alliances with persons not of royal blood were to be prevented, the king and his brothers had given proof enough of the dangers to which princes are exposed. In his youth the king had been himself in love with Lady Sarah Lennox:[1] the Duke of York had been attached to Lady Mary Coke; and now his Majesty was deploring the marriages of his brothers.

King's power over his grandchildren.

The prerogative claimed by the Crown, in matters concerning the royal family, was already considerable. In 1718, King George I., when in open enmity with his son, the Prince of Wales, maintained that he had power, by virtue of his prerogative, to direct the education of his grandchildren, and even to dispose of them in marriage, to the exclusion of the parental authority of the prince. A question was submitted to the judges; and ten out of the twelve, led by Lord Chief Justice Parker, afterwards Lord Macclesfield, decided in favor of the king's claim.[2] Even the two dissentient judges, who were of opinion that the education of the king's grandchildren belonged to their father, yet held, "that the care and approbation of their marriages, when grown up, belong to the king of this realm."[3]

It was now proposed to enlarge this prerogative, and extend the king's powers, by the authority of the law. On

[1] Mr. Grenville relates in his Diary, that the king actually proposed to marry her, and that her engagement with Lord Newbottle was consequently broken off: but she broke her leg while out riding, and during her absence, the match was prevented, by representations that she continued her intercourse with Lord Newbottle. — *Grenv. Papers*, iv. 209.

[2] St. Tr. xv. 1195. Lord Campbell's Lives, iv. p. 521.

[3] St. Tr. xv. 1225.

the 20th February, 1772, a message from the king was delivered to both Houses of Parliament, stating that he was desirous "that the right of approving all marriages in the royal family (which ever has belonged to the kings of this realm, as a matter of public concern) may be made effectual;" and recommending to their consideration the expediency of guarding "the descendants of his late Majesty George II." (other than the issue of princesses married into foreign families), from marrying without the approbation of the king.

Royal Marriage Act, 1772.

On the following day, the Royal Marriage Bill was presented to the House of Lords. The preamble affirmed the prerogative, as claimed in the message, to its fullest extent, and the wisdom and expediency of the king's recommendation. The bill provided that no descendant of George II. (except the issue of princesses married into foreign families) should be capable of contracting matrimony, without the king's previous consent, signified under his sign-manual, and declared in council; and that any marriage contracted without such consent, should be null and void. There was a proviso, however, — which it seems had not been contemplated, when the message was delivered, — enabling members of the royal family above twenty-five years of age, to marry without the king's consent, after having given twelve months' previous notice to the Privy Council, unless in the mean time, both Houses of Parliament should signify their disapprobation of the marriage. This concession, it is said, was caused by the resignation of Mr. Fox, who intended to oppose the measure, and by the disapprobation of some of the advisers of the Crown.[1] It was also provided that any person solemnizing, or assisting, or being present at the celebration of such prohibited marriages, should incur the penalties of præmunire.

Prerogative claimed in regard to royal marriages.

This was unquestionably the king's own measure, and was reluctantly adopted by his ministers. His views of preroga-

[1] Fox's Mem. i. 75 (H. Walpole).

tive were exalted; and in his own family at least, he was resolved that his authority should be supreme. The absolute control which he now sought for, over members of his family of full age, was not a little startling. First, as to his claim of prerogative. Had it ever yet been asserted to the same extent? It had been recognized by the "grand opinion" — as it was called, — of the judges in 1718, so far as regarded the king's grandchildren, but no farther; and it is impossible to read the arguments of the judges in that case, without being impressed with the slender grounds, strained constructions of law and precedent, and far-fetched views of expediency, upon which their conclusion was founded. As a matter of state policy, it may be necessary that the king should be empowered to negotiate alliances for the royal family, and for that purpose should have more than parental authority. But the present claim extended to brothers of whatever age, — to uncles, and to cousins. So comprehensive a claim could not be at once admitted. This question, therefore, was put to the judges: "Is the king intrusted by law with the care and approbation of the marriages of the descendants of his late Majesty George II., other than his present Majesty's own children, during their minorities?" As this question extended to all descendants of George II., whether within this kingdom or not, nine judges unanimously answered it in the negative; and to another question, more restricted, they replied, "that the care and approbation of the marriages of the king's children and grandchildren, and of the presumptive heir to the Crown (other than the issue of princesses married into foreign families) do belong to the kings of this realm; but to what other branches of the royal family such care and approbation extend, we do not find precisely determined."[1] It was plain that the bill declared the prerogative to be much more extensive, than that allowed by the judges. Yet in spite of their opinion, the Lord Chancellor, Lord Apsley, with an

Question to the judges.

[1] Parl. Hist. xvii. 387.

effrontery worthy of Lord Thurlow, said that "he would defend every clause, every sentence, every word, every syllable, and every letter" in the bill; and "would not consent to any amendment whatsoever!" The prerogative, he asserted, was founded in its "importance to the state:" an argument which might be extended to any other power claimed by the Crown, on the same ground.

Arbitrary principles of this Act.

The arbitrary character of the bill was conspicuous. It might be reasonable to prescribe certain rules for the marriage of the royal family: as that they should not marry a subject, — a Roman Catholic, — or the member of any royal house at war with this country, without the consent of the king: but to prescribe no rule at all save the absolute will of the king himself, was a violation of all sound principles of legislation. Again, to extend the minority of princes and princesses to twenty-five, created a harsh exception to the general law, in regard to marriages.[1] The prohibition of a marriage might continue until the age of twenty-six; and required nothing but the vote of a Parliament subservient to the Crown, to render it perpetual; and this not by virtue of any general principle of law, — human or divine, —but by the arbitrary will of a superior power.

But the personal will of the king triumphed over all opposition, whether of argument or numbers; and he was implacable against those who opposed it.[2] The bill was passed

1 A squib appeared in answer to the objection that a prince might ascend the throne at eighteen, yet might not marry till twenty-five:

"Quoth Tom to Dick, — 'Thou art a fool,
And little know'st of life:
Alas! 'tis easier far to rule
A kingdom, than a wife.'" —
Parl. Hist. xvii. 407.

2 Fox's Mem. i. 75. Lord Chatham said of the Bill, "The doctrine of the Royal Marriage Bill is certainly new-fangled and impudent, and the extent of the powers given wanton and tyrannical." — *Letter to Lord Shelburne*, April 3d, 1772, Corr. iv. 203.

Horace Walpole said, "Never was an Act passed against which so much, and for which so little was said." — *Fox's Mem.* i. 81.

rapidly through the House of Lords; though not without one protest, signed by fourteen peers, and another signed by seven, in which the most material objections to the measure were concisely expressed. In the Commons the bill met with a more strenuous and protracted opposition: — the Lords' Journals were searched for the opinion of the judges, — and the most serious arguments against the measure were ably and learnedly discussed. But it was still carried with a high hand. The doors of the House were closed against all strangers, — peers in vain sought admission below the bar, — and the Government even went so far as to refuse the printing of the bill, and supported their refusal by a large majority. No amendment was suffered to be made, except one of pedantic form, suggested by the speaker, that the king's consent to a marriage should be signified under the great seal; and on the 24th March the bill was passed. Attempts have since been made, without success, to repeal this law;[1] and to evade its provisions; but it has been inflexibly maintained.

Secret marriage of the Prince of Wales.

In 1785 the Prince of Wales contracted a clandestine marriage with Mrs. Fitzherbert, a Roman Catholic. His marriage being without the king's consent, and consequently invalid, the princely libertine ventured to satisfy the scruples of his paramour, and to indulge his own passions; while he was released from the sacred obligations of the marriage tie, and saved from the forfeiture of his succession to the Crown, which would have been the legal consequence of a valid marriage with a Roman Catholic. Even his pretended marriage, thóugh void in law, would have raised embarrassing doubts and discussions concerning the penal provisions of the Bill of Rights; and, if confessed, would undoubtedly have exposed him to obloquy and discredit. The prince, therefore, denied the fact of his marriage; and made his best friend the unconscious instrument of this falsehood and deception.[2]

[1] By Lord Holland, in 1820; Hansard's Debates, New Ser., i. 1099.

[2] Parl. Hist. xxvi. 1070. See an excellent letter from Mr. Fox to the

Marriages of the Duke of Sussex.

The Duke of Sussex was twice married without the consent of the Crown; first, in 1793, to Lady Augusta Murray; and, later in life, to Lady Cecilia Underwood. His first marriage having been solemnized abroad, a question was raised whether it was rendered invalid by the Royal Marriage Act. It was again celebrated in England, where it was unquestionably illegal.

The king immediately directed a suit of nullity of marriage to be commenced by his proctor, and it was adjudged by the Court of Arches, that the marriage was absolutely null and void.[1]

In 1831 the law officers of the Crown were consulted by the government as to the validity of this marriage; and their opinions confirmed the judgment of the Court of Arches. On the death of the Duke of Sussex in 1843, Sir Augustus D'Este, the son of his Royal Highness by this marriage, claimed the dukedom and other honors of his father. The marriage had been solemnized at Rome in 1793, according to the rites of the Church of England, by a clergyman of that establishment, and would have been a valid contract between British subjects but for the restrictions of the Royal Marriage Act; and it was contended before the House of Lords, that the operation of that Act could not be extended beyond the British dominions. But it was the unanimous opinion of the judges, — in which the House of Lords concurred, — that the prohibition of the statute was personal, and followed the persons to whom it applied, out of the realm, and beyond the British jurisdiction. It was accord-

Prince, Dec. 10th, 1785, dissuading his Royal Highness from the marriage. — *Fox's Mem.* ii. 278, 284, 287. — The prince confessed his marriage to Lord Grèy; *Ibid.* 289. Lord J. Russell's Life and Times of Fox, ii. 177, *et seq.* Lord Holland's Mem. of the Whig Party, ii. 126, *et seq.* Langdale's Mem. of Mrs. Fitzherbert. The general incidents of this discreditable marriage do not fall within the design of this work; but a most animated and graphic narrative of them will be found in Mr. Massey's History, vol. iii. 315–331.

[1] Heseltine *v.* Lady A. Murray, Addam's Reports, ii. 400; Burn's Eccl. Law, ii. 433; Ann. Reg. 1794, p. 23.

ingly decided that the claimant had not made out his claim.[1]

Education of Princess Charlotte, 1804.

The prerogative of the king to direct the education of his grandchildren, which had been established in 1718, was again asserted in 1804. The king claimed the guardianship of the Princess Charlotte; and the Prince of Wales, her father, being perplexed with divided councils, was long in doubt whether he should concede or contest the right.[2] At length he appears to have agreed that the king should have the direction of the princess's education. The understanding not being very precise, a misapprehension arose as to its conditions; and it was said that the prince had withdrawn from his engagement.[3] But Mr. Pitt ultimately arranged this difference by obtaining the removal of the princess to Windsor, without excluding the prince from a share in the control of her education.[4]

[1] Clark and Finnelly's Reports, xi. 85–154.

[2] Lord Malmesbury says: "The two factions pulled the prince different ways: Ladies Moira, Hutchinson, and Mrs. Fitzherbert, were for his ceding the child to the king; the Duke of Clarence and Devonshire House most violent against it, and the prince ever inclines to the faction he saw last. In the Devonshire House Cabal, Lady Melbourne and Mrs. Fox act conspicuous parts so that the alternative for our future queen seems to be whether Mrs. Fox or Mrs. Fitzherbert shall have the ascendency." — *Malm. Diar.*, iv. 343.

[3] Letters of Mr. T. Grenville to the Marquess of Buckingham, Nov. 26th, Dec. 1st and 11th, 1804; Court and Cab. of Geo. III., iii. 372, 385, 389, 391.

[4] *Ibid.* 395, 398.

CHAPTER V.

The House of Lords: — Constant additions to its Numbers: — Profuse creations in the Reign of George III. and since. — Representative Peers of Scotland and Ireland: — Representative Character of the Peerage: — Life Peerages. — The Bishops. — Political Position of the House of Lords: — Its Enlargement a Source of Power: — Threatened creation of Peers to carry the Reform Bill. — The Aristocracy, and Classes associated with it.

Permanence of British institutions.

NOTHING in the history of our constitution is more remarkable than the permanence of every institution forming part of the Government of the country, while undergoing continual, and often extraordinary changes in its powers, privileges, and influence. The Crown, as we have seen, remains with all its prerogatives undiminished, and with its sources of influence increased; yet in the exercise of its great powers by responsible ministers, it has been gradually controlled by Parliament and public opinion, until the authority of the Crown in government and legislation, bears as little resemblance to the sway of the Tudor and Stuart kings, as to that of Louis XIV.

The House of Peers.

So also the House of Lords continues to hold its high place in the state, next to the Crown, and still enjoys the greater part of its ancient privileges. Yet no institution has undergone greater changes. In its numbers, its composition, and its influence, it is difficult to recognize its identity with the "Great Council" of a former age. But the changes which it has undergone have served to bring this great institution into harmony with other parts of the constitution, and with the social condition of the people, upon which time has worked equal mutations.

Constant additions to its numbers.

The continual additions which have been made to the number of temporal peers, sitting in Parliament, have been so remarkable as to change the very constitution and character of the House of Lords. No more than twenty-nine temporal peers received writs of summons to the first Parliament of Henry VII.; and this number had increased at the death of Queen Elizabeth to fifty-nine. The Stuarts were profuse in their creations,[1] and raised the number of the peerage to about one hundred and fifty;[2] which William III. and Queen Anne further increased to one hundred and sixty-eight. In the latter reign no less than twelve peers were created at once, to turn a majority in favor of the court, which they did on the very day of their introduction.[3] In this same reign were also added, on the Union with Scotland, sixteen representative peers, — a number scarcely adequate to represent an ancient peerage, little less numerous than that of England,[4] in a House of Lords, in which sat twenty-six bishops to make laws for Presbyterian Scotland. But if some injustice was then done to the Scottish peerage, it has since been amply redressed, as will be seen hereafter.

Representative peers of Scotland.

This rapid increase of the peerage had been regarded

[1] James I. created sixty-two; Charles I., fifty-nine; Charles II., sixty-four; and James II., eight; being a total number of one hundred and ninety-three; but during these reigns ninety-nine peerages became extinct, and thus the total addition to the peerage was ninety-four. From returns delivered to the House of Lords in 1719. As many of these peerages were sold by James I. and Charles II., it is surprising that the creations were not even more numerous.

[2] In 1661, one hundred and thirty-nine lords were summoned. In 1696, the total number of temporal peers, exclusive of minors, Roman Catholics, and nonjurors, was about one hundred and forty. — *Macaulay's Hist.*, iv. 753.

[3] 2d January, 1711. Lords' Journ. xix. 353. Somerville's Queen Anne, 460. Smollett's Hist. ii. 224.

[4] There was one hundred and fifty-four Scottish peers at the time of the Union. The roll is printed in Lords' Journ. xviii. 458. Lord Haversham said upwards of one hundred peers would be disfranchised.

with much jealousy by that privileged body, whose individual dignity and power were proportionately diminished. Early in the reign of George I., several new creations further aroused the apprehensions of the peers; and, in 1719, partly to gratify their lordships, — but more, perhaps, to further party objects,[1] — a bill was brought into the House of Lords by the Duke of Somerset, proposing an extraordinary limitation of the royal prerogative, — to which the king himself was induced to signify his consent. The Crown was to be restrained from the creation of more than six beyond the existing number of one hundred and seventy-eight peerages, — the power being still reserved of creating a new peerage whenever a peerage should become extinct; and instead of sixteen representative peers of Scotland, it was proposed that twenty-five hereditary peers should have seats in the House of Lords. This bill soon reached a third reading; but not until it had raised so much dissatisfaction in the House of Commons and the country, that its promoters thought it prudent to abandon it.[2] In the next session, however, another bill was introduced, by the Duke of Buckingham, and sent down to the Commons; where, after an effectual exposure of its unconstitutional character, — especially by Sir Richard Steele, and Sir Robert Walpole, — it was rejected by a majority of two hundred and sixty-nine voices, against one hundred and seventy-seven.[3] It was, in truth, an audacious attempt to limit the prerogative of the Crown, and discourage the granting of just rewards to merit, for the sake of perpetuating a close aristocratic body, —

The Peerage Bill of 1719.

[1] The Prince of Wales was supposed not to be friendly to the Whig party then in power, which was said to be the reason why Lord Sunderland persuaded the king to consent to the bill.

[2] Parl. Hist. vii. 589–594. Coxe's Life of Walpole, i. 116.

[3] Parl. Hist. vii. 606–627. Coxe's Life of Walpole, i. 117–125; ii. 551. Sir Robert Walpole also opposed the measure in a pamphlet entitled, "The Thoughts of a Member of the Lower House in relation to a project for restraining and limiting the power of the Crown in the future creation of Peers." Steele likewise opposed it in "The Plebeian," while Addison warmly supported it in "The Old Whig."

independent of the Crown and irresponsible to the people.

Number of peers sitting in Parliament, 1760.

The first two kings of the House of Hanover continued to make additions to the peerage, which on the accession of George III. amounted to one hundred and seventy-four. Of this number, thirteen minors, and twelve Roman Catholics were incapable of sitting and voting in Parliament.[1]

Profuse creations in the reign of George III.

Great as had been the additions to the peerage since the reign of Queen Elizabeth, they were destined to be far exceeded in this and succeeding reigns. The creation of peers, having become an expedient for increasing the influence of the Crown, and the strength of parties, was freely resorted to by successive ministers. In the first ten years of this reign forty-two peers were created, or raised to a higher order in the peerage.[2]

Creations by Lord North.

Lord North was liberal in the creation of peers, with a view to strengthen his own position, and carry out the policy of the court. In 1776, before the continued arrears of the Civil List were again brought before Parliament, ten new peers were created, one baron was raised to the dignity of a viscount, and three were promoted to earldoms.[3] During his administration, he created or promoted about thirty British peers.[4] In Ireland, he distributed honors still more liberally. In 1777 he created eighteen barons, and raised seven barons and five viscounts to higher dignities in the peerage.

Creations by Mr. Pitt.

Mr. Pitt dispensed honors with greater profusion than any former minister. During the first five years of his administration, he had created nearly fifty peers.[5] The influence he had himself derived from thus

[1] Court and City Register for 1760.

[2] Beatson's Political Index, i. 133.

[3] Lord North's Administration, 257.

[4] Beatson's Political Index, i. 137.

[5] In the debates upon the Regency, Mr. Fox said forty-two, and Mr. Sheridan forty-eight. From Beatson's Political Index (i. 140) the latter statement appears to be strictly accurate. Parl. Hist. xxvii. 967, &c.

gratifying his supporters, suggested to him the precaution of restricting the regent in the exercise of this prerogative. This restriction he proposed to extend to the entire period of the regency, which, however, he trusted would be of short duration. Having created peers to consolidate his own power, he was unwilling to leave the same instrument in the hands of his opponents. Had his proposal taken effect, such a restraint, — extending over the whole regency, — was open to many of the objections which are admitted to apply to the more extensive limitation contemplated in 1719. It was said by Mr. Pitt that the exercise of the prerogative was required to reward merit, to recruit the peerage from the great landowners and other opulent classes, and to render the Crown independent of factious combinations amongst the existing peers.[1] All these grounds were as applicable to the regency as to any other time; while the fact of a powerful minister having recently made so large an addition to the House of Lords from his own party, was the strongest argument against the proposed restriction. To tie up the hands of the regent, was to perpetuate the power of the minister. A similar condition was afterwards imposed upon the regent in 1810; but, being limited to one year, was exposed to less objection.

Restriction proposed upon the Regent, in 1789.

Restriction during the regency of 1811.

In 1792, when Mr. Pitt had been eight years in power, he had created between sixty and seventy peers,[2] the greater part of whom owed their elevation to the parliamentary support which they had themselves given to the minister, or to their interest in returning mem-

Continued creations by Mr. Pitt.

[1] His speech on the 16th Jan., 1789, is so imperfectly reported, that his reasoning can only be gathered from the context of the debate, in which his observations are adverted to.

[2] Mr. Sheridan's speech on Parliamentary Reform, April 30th, 1792. Mr. Courtenay, speaking in 1792, said: "It had been a matter of complaint that twenty-eight peers had been made in the reign of George I., which, it was argued, would destroy the balance of power in the other branches of the constitution." But Pitt "had created three times as many." Parl. Hist. xxix. 1494. The number of creations and promotions appears to have been sixty-four. Beatson's Political Index, i. 144.

bers to the House of Commons. He created and promoted no less than thirty-five peers, within the space of two years, in 1796 and 1797.[1] And, in 1801, he had created or promoted, during the seventeen years of his administration, upwards of one hundred and forty peers, sitting by hereditary right.[2] He also introduced as members of that body, in 1801, the Irish representative peers and bishops.

Representative peers of Ireland.

The peerage of Ireland, on the union of that country, was dealt with, in some measure, upon different principles from that of Scotland. The principle of representation was followed; twenty-eight representative peers being admitted to seats in the Parliament of the United Kingdom. But they were elected, not for the Parliament only, as in Scotland, but for life. Again, no Scottish peers could be created after the Union; but the peerage of Scotland was perpetuated, as an ancient and exclusive aristocracy. It was otherwise with Ireland. It was admitted that the peerage of that country was too numerous, and ought gradually to be diminished; and with this view, the royal prerogative was so far restricted, that one Irish peer only can be created, whenever three Irish peerages, — in existence at the time of the Union, — have become extinct. But the object of this provision being ultimately to reduce the number of Irish peers, — not having hereditary seats in Parliament, — to one hundred, it was also provided that when such reduction had been effected, one new Irish peerage may be created as often as a peerage becomes extinct, or as often as an Irish peer becomes entitled by descent or creation, to a peerage of the United Kingdom.

Permission to Irish peers to sit in the House of Commons.

Another peculiar arrangement, made on the Union of Ireland, was the permission granted to Irish peers of sitting in the House of Commons for any place in Great Britain, — a privilege of which they have extensively availed themselves.[3]

[1] Beatson's Political Index, i. 147.

[2] *Ibid.* 149, *et seq.*

[3] By the Reform Bill of 1860, it was proposed to extend this privilege to

At the same time, an addition of four lords spiritual was made to the House of Lords, to represent the episcopal body of Ireland, and to sit by rotation of sessions; of whom an archbishop of the Church in Ireland is always to be one. At the Union there were twenty bishoprics and archbishoprics of the Church in Ireland; but provision was made in 1833, by the Church Temporalities Act, for the reduction of that number to ten.[1]

Irish representative bishops.

Since the Union, further additions have continually been made to the peerage of the United Kingdom; and an analysis of the existing peerage presents some singular results. In 1860, the House of Lords consisted of four hundred and sixty lords, spiritual and temporal. The number of hereditary peers of the United Kingdom, had risen to three hundred and eighty-five, exclusive of the peers of the blood royal. Of these peerages, one hundred and twenty-eight were created, in the long reign of George III.;[2] forty-two in the reign of George IV.;[3] and one hundred and seventeen since the accession of William IV.[4] Thus two and hundred eighty-seven peerages have been created, or raised to their present rank,

Peerages of the United Kingdom.

Summary of creations.

places in Ireland, as well as Great Britain. In "A Letter to the Earl of Listowel, M. P. for St. Alban's, by a 'Joint of the Tail,'" 1841, the position of his lordship as a peer of Ireland and a member of the House of Commons, was thus adverted to: "A peer, and in your own right — and yet a peer without rights! Possessor of a name, of a dignity having no better reality than in a sound. . . . True, you are at this moment a legislator, but by no right of birth, and only as a commoner; and, again, as representative for an English town, not for one in Ireland. However great your stake in that country, you could not, though fifty places were held open for you, accept one; your marrowless dignity gliding ghost-like in, to forbid the proffered seat."

1 3 & 4 Will. IV. c. 37, Schedule B.

2 Viz., two dukes, thirteen marquesses, thirty-eight earls, eight viscounts, and sixty-seven barons.

3 One duke, two marquesses, seven earls, three viscounts, twenty-nine barons.

4 Two dukes, five marquesses, twenty earls, six viscounts, eighty-four barons.

since the accession of George III.; or very nearly three-fourths of the entire number. But this increase is exhibited by the existing peerage alone, — notwithstanding the extinction or merger of numerous titles, in the interval. The actual number of creations during the reign of George III. amounted to three hundred and eighty-eight; or more than the entire present number of the peerage.[1]

Antiquity of the peerage.

No more than ninety-eight of the existing peerages claim an earlier creation than the reign of George III.; but this fact is an imperfect criterion of the antiquity of the peerage. When the possessor of an ancient dignity is promoted to a higher grade in the peerage, his lesser dignity becomes merged in the greater, but more recent title. An earl of the fifteenth century, is transformed into a marquess of the nineteenth. Many of the families from which existing peers are descended, are of great antiquity; and were noble before their admission to the peerage. Nor must the ancient nobility of the Scottish peerage be forgotten in the persons of those high-born men, who now figure on the roll, as peers of the United Kingdom, of comparatively recent creation.

Great as this increase of peerages has been, it has borne no proportion to the demands made upon the favor of the

[1] The following Table, prepared by the late Mr. Pulman, Clarencieux King of Arms, was placed at my disposal by the kindness of his son:

Statement showing the Number of Peerages created within periods of Twenty Years, from 1700 *to* 1821.

	Dukes.	Marquesses.	Earls.	Viscounts.	Barons.
From 1700 to 1720 inclusive	22	14	33	30	58
" 1721 to 1740 "	2	3	14	8	19
" 1741 to 1760 "	2	1	24	15	34
" 1761 to 1780 "	4	1	14	9	46
" 1781 to 1800 "	4	10	24	23	91
" 1801 to 1821 "	3	8	37	34	80
	37	37	146	119	328

Total number of Peerages created, 667; of which 388 were created between 1761 and 1821.

Crown. We find in Lord Malmesbury's Diary for 1807 this entry: — "Lord Whitworth and Mr. Heathcote (Sir William's son) urged me to apply for peerages. I told them truly, there were no less than fifty-three candidates for peerage, and to none of which the king would listen."[1] And every minister since that time, has probably been obliged to resist the solicitations of not less than ten earnest claimants, for every peerage which he has advised the Crown to bestow. When Lord Grey was contemplating the creation of nearly one hundred peers in 1832, there was no lack of candidates, although the occasion was neither flattering to their self-esteem, nor free from offensive imputations. And, more recently, another minister discovered, in a single year, that upwards of thirty of his supporters were ambitious of the peerage, as an acknowledgment of their friendship towards himself, and devotion to his party.

Numerous claims to peerages.

With this large increase of numbers, the peerage has undergone further changes, no less remarkable, in its character and composition. It is no longer a council of the magnates of the land, — the territorial aristocracy, the descendants or representatives of the barons of the olden time; but in each successive age, it has assumed a more popular and representative character. Men who have attained the first eminence in war and diplomacy, at the bar or in the senate, — men wisest in council, and most eloquent in debate, — have taken their place in its distinguished roll; and their historic names represent the glories of the age from which they sprung. Men who have amassed fortunes in commerce, or whose ancestors have enriched themselves by their own industry, have also been admitted to the privileged circle of the peerage. Men of the highest intellects, achievements, and wealth, the peerage has adopted and appropriated to itself: men of secondary pretensions, it has still left to the people.

Changes in the composition of the Peerage.

[1] Lord Malm. Diary, iv. 397.

Its representative character.

A body so constantly changed, and recruited from all classes of society, loses much of its distinctive hereditary character. Peers sitting in Parliament by virtue of an hereditary right, share their privilege with so many, who by personal pretensions have recently been placed beside them, that the hereditary principle becomes divested of exclusive power, and invidious distinction.

Extension of the representative principle.

At the same time, the principle of representation has been largely introduced into the constitution of the House of Lords. The sixteen representative peers of Scotland, elected only for a Parliament; the twenty-eight representative peers of Ireland, elected for life; and the four Irish representative bishops, — form a body as numerous as the entire peerage in the time of Henry VIII. And when to these are added the twenty-six English bishops, holding their seats for life, — the total number of Lords not sitting by virtue of hereditary right, becomes a considerable element in the constitution of the Upper House.[1]

Disproportion between hereditary and representative peers.

In analyzing these numbers, however, the growing disproportion between the representative lords, and the hereditary peers cannot fail to be apparent. If sixteen Scottish peers were deemed an inadequate representation of the ancient peerage of Scotland in the reign of Anne, — what are they now, when the peerage of the United Kingdom has been trebled in numbers? But this inequality, — apparently excessive, — has been corrected by the admission of Scottish peers to hereditary seats in the British House of Lords. At the present time the total number of Scottish peers amounts to seventy-eight,[2] of whom no less than forty,

Scottish peers created peers of Great Britain.

[1] There are seventy-four lords of Parliament not sitting by hereditary right.

[2] There are also two peeresses, and the Prince of Wales, who is Duke of Rothesay.

—or more than half,—sit in Parliament by virtue of British peerages, created in their favor since the Union.

Great was the jealousy with which the House of Lords at first regarded the admission of Scottish peers to the peerage of Great Britain. In 1711, the Duke of Hamilton was created Duke of Brandon, of the peerage of Great Britain: when the lords declared, by a majority of five, that no patent of honor granted to any peer of Great Britain who was a peer of Scotland at the time of the Union, entitled such peer to sit and vote in Parliament, or to sit upon the trial of peers.[1] The undoubted prerogative of the queen was thus boldly set aside for a time, by an adverse determination of the House of Lords.

Their right to sit denied.

At the time of this decision, the Duke of Queensberry was sitting by virtue of a British peerage, created since the Union. The determination of the Lords prevented, for many years, the direct admission of any other Scottish peers to the peerage of Great Britain; but this restriction was cleverly evaded by frequent creations of their eldest sons, who, having obtained seats in the House of Lords, succeeded, on the death of their fathers, to their Scottish peerages.[2] At length, in 1782, the question of the disability of Scottish peers to receive patents of peerage in Great Britain, was referred to the judges, who were unanimously of opinion that no such disability had ever been created by the Act of Union. The Lords, therefore, reversed the decision of 1711; and henceforth Scottish peers were freely admitted to the ranks of the British peerage.[3]

Rights of Scottish Peers admitted.

In 1787, another important question arose, affecting the rights of the Scottish peerage. It had been the plain intention of the Act of Union, that the peers of Scotland,

[1] Lords' Journ. xix. 346; Peere Williams, i. 582; Burnet's Own Time, 586; Somerville's Queen Anne, 549.

[2] Walpole's Mem. of Geo. III. ii. 412.

[3] 6th June, 1782; Lords' Journ. xxxvi. 517.

who were denied a seat in the Parliament of Great Britain, should be entitled to representation by members of their own body, subject to the same political conditions as themselves. The right of the Crown to admit Scottish peers to the peerage of Great Britain having at length been recognized, the king exercised the right in favor of the Earl of Abercorn and the Duke of Queensberry, — both of whom were sitting, at that time, in the House of Lords, as representative peers of Scotland. That these noblemen, who now sat by hereditary right, should continue to be the representatives of the Scottish peerage, was a constitutional anomaly which could not easily be maintained. As well might it have been contended that a member of the Lower House continued to represent the constituents by whom he had been elected, notwithstanding his elevation to a seat in the House of Peers. In 1736, indeed, the Duke of Athol had inherited the Barony of Strange, and had continued to sit as a representative peer, without any decision of the House of Lords, or any question being raised concerning his legal position. But now Lord Stormont brought the matter before the House of Lords, in a clear and unanswerable argument; and though he was boldly opposed by Lord Thurlow, the House resolved that the Earl of Lauderdale and the Duke of Queensberry had ceased to sit as representatives of the peerage of Scotland.[1]

When British peers, their rights as peers of Scotland cease.

The two peers thus disqualified from sitting as representatives, immediately proceeded to vote as Scottish peers for their successors, in contravention of a resolution of the House of Lords in 1708. An attempt was made to defend their right to vote, and to cast doubts upon the former determination of the House; but the Lords were resolute in maintaining the independent rights of the Scottish peerage, according to the spirit of the Act of Union; and directed a copy of the resolution of the 21st of Jan. 1708–9 to be transmitted to the Lord Registrar of Scotland, with an "in-

[1] Lords' Journ. xxxvii. 594; Parl. Hist. xxvi. 596.

junction to him that he do conform thereto;" and since that time this decision has been invariably respected.[1]

Meanwhile, the admission of Scottish peers to hereditary seats in the House of Lords, is tending to a singular result. At no distant period, the Scottish peerage will probably become absorbed in that of the United Kingdom. One half their number have already been absorbed: more may hereafter be admitted to the House of Lords; and, as no new creations can be made, we may foresee the ultimate extinction of all but sixteen Scottish peers, not embraced in the British peerage. These sixteen peers, instead of continuing a system of self-election, will then probably be created hereditary peers of Parliament. The Act of Union will have worked itself out; and a Parliamentary incorporation of the two countries will be consummated, — more complete than any which the most sanguine promoters of the Union could, in their visions of the future, have foreshadowed.

Present position of the Scottish peerage.

A similar absorption of the Irish peerage into the peerage of the United Kingdom has also been observable, though, by the terms of the Act of Union, the full number of one hundred Irish peers will continue to be maintained. In 1860 there were one hundred and ninety-three Irish peers,[2] of whom seventy-one had seats in Parliament, as peers of the United Kingdom. Thus, the peers of Ireland sitting in Parliament, — including the representative peers, — amounted to ninety-nine.

Present position of the Irish peerage.

By this fusion of the peerages of the three kingdoms, the House of Lords has grown at once more national, and more representative in its character. As different classes of society have become represented there, so different nationalities have also acquired a wider representation. Nor ought it to be overlooked that

Fusion of the peerages of the three kingdoms.

[1] Parl. Hist. xxvi. 1158 (May 18th, 1787); Lords' Journ. xxxvii. 709.

[2] There is also one peeress; and the King of Hanover is Earl of Armagh in the peerage of Ireland.

Scotland and Ireland are further represented in the House of Lords by the numerous commoners, of Scottish and Irish birth, who have been raised to the dignity of the peerage for distinguished services, or other eminent qualifications.

Hereditary character of the peerage.

But all temporal peers, — whether English, Scottish, or Irish, and whether sitting by hereditary right or by election, — have been ennobled in blood, and transmit their dignities to their heirs. Hereditary descent has been the characteristic of the peerage, and — with the exception of the bishops — of the constitution of the House of Lords.

Defects in the appellate jurisdiction of the Lords.

In 1856, however, Her Majesty was advised to introduce among the hereditary peers of the realm, a new class of peers, created for life only. Well-founded complaints had been made of the manner in which the appellate jurisdiction of the House of Lords had been exercised. The highest court of appeal was often without judges, their place being filled by peers unlearned in the law, who sat as members of the court, without affecting to participate in its judgments. This had been an evil of long standing; though it had not, until lately, aroused the vigilance of suitors and the public. For some years after the Revolution, there had not been a single law-lord in the House, — Lord Somers having heard appeals as Lord Keeper. When that distinguished lawyer was at length admitted to a seat in the House of Peers, he was the only law-lord. During the greater part of the reigns of George II. and George III., appeals had been heard by Lord Hardwicke, Lord Mansfield, Lord Thurlow, and Lord Eldon, sitting in judicial solitude, — while two mute, unlearned lords were to be seen in the background, representing the collective wisdom of the court. In later times a more decorous performance of judicial duties had been exacted by public opinion; and frequent changes of administration having multiplied ex-chancellors, the number of law-lords was greater than at former periods. But in an age in which reforms in the administration of justice had become an important department of legislation, and a subject of popular interest, theoretical improvements, at least, were demanded in the constitution of the first court of appeal.

Life-peerages.

As an expedient for adding to the judicial strength of the House, without a permanent increase of its numbers, it was suggested that the most eminent judges might be admitted to the privilege of sitting there, for life only. The practice of granting peerages for life was not a constitutional novelty, but had long fallen into desuetude. Between the reigns of Richard II. and Henry VI., several precedents were to be found of the creation of life-peerages. Some of these, however, had been made, — like many other peerages of that period, — in full Parliament: some had been granted to peers already entitled to sit in Parliament by hereditary right: some peers so created had never sat in the House of Peers: one had been a foreigner, who could not claim a seat by virtue of his title: and, for upwards of four hundred years, there was no instance on record, in which any man had been admitted to a seat in the House of Lords, as a peer for life. But there were many later instances, in which ladies had received life-peerages. Charles II. had created the beautiful Louise de Querouaille, Duchess of Portsmouth for life; James II. had created Catherine Sedley a baroness, by the same tenure; George I. had raised Madame de Schulemberg to the rank of Duchess of Kendal for life, and had conferred a life-peerage upon her niece;[1] and George II. had made Madame Walmoden, Countess of Yarmouth for life. Between the reign of James I. and that of George II., peerages for life had been granted to no less than eighteen ladies. But as the fair sex are unable to sit in Parliament, this class of peerages could not be relied upon, in support of the right of the Crown to introduce life-peers into the House of Lords.

Life-peerages to women.

[1] Or reputed daughter, the Countess of Walsingham.

Peerages with remainders over.

There was, however, another class of peerages, whence a strong argument was derived in favor of the royal prerogative. Though peerages in their general character have been hereditary, — descending like estates to the elder son, — yet peerages have been continually granted to persons, with remainder to collateral relatives, or to the elder son of the peer by a second wife, or to the son of a younger brother, or other relative not in the direct line of succession, as heir at law. All grants of this class — being governed, not by the general law of descent, but by the special limitations in the patent — were exceptions from the principle of hereditary succession. The first grantee was, in effect, created a peer for life, though the second grantee became entitled to the peerage, subject to the ordinary rights of succession. But the grant of a peerage of this class was plainly distinguishable from a peerage for life, as it provided — though in an exceptional manner — for the duration of the dignity beyond the life of the first grantee. It was indeed maintained that such peerages afforded further evidence against the legality of life-peerages, as they had been constantly granted, without objection, while none of the latter had been created for centuries.

Authorities in support of life-peerages.

But if these precedents and analogies were obsolete, or of doubtful application, the legality of life-peerages had been recognized by nearly all constitutional authorities. Lord Coke had repeatedly affirmed the doctrine, that the Crown may create peerages "for life, in tail, or in fee;" the learned Selden had referred to the ancient custom without comment; Chief Baron Comyns and Cruise had accepted the authority of Coke as unquestioned law; the popular Blackstone had repeated and enforced it;[1] and, lastly, Lord Redesdale's committee "On the dignity of a

[1] "For a man or woman may be created noble for their own lives, and the dignity not descend to their heirs at all, or descend only to some particular heirs, as where a peerage is limited to a man and the heirs male of his body, by Elizabeth, his present lady, and not to such heirs by any former or future wife." Steph. Blackstone, ii. 589.

Peer," in 1822, had acknowledged it without reserve.[1] Butler was the only eminent writer who had expressed any doubt upon the subject.[2] The doctrine had also been generally received among statesmen as well as lawyers. Lord Liverpool's administration, impressed with the necessity of improving the appellate jurisdiction of the Lords, had, at one time, unanimously resolved to create life-peers. In 1851, the government of Lord John Russell had offered a life-peerage to Dr. Lushington, the distinguished judge of the Admiralty Court, who, by a late statute, had been denied the privilege of sitting in the House of Commons. In the Devon peerage case, Lord Brougham had stated from the woolsack, as Chancellor, that the Crown had not only the power of creating a peerage for the life of the grantee himself, but for the life of another person; and upon a more recent occasion, Lord Campbell had laid it down in debate, that the "Crown might create, by its prerogative, a peerage for life, but not a peerage during a man's continuance in office: *that would require an enactment of the three branches of the legislature.*"[3]

The Wensleydale peerage.

Relying upon these precedents and authorities, the ministers advised her Majesty, before the meeting of Parliament in 1856, to issue letters-patent to Sir James Parke, lately an eminent baron of the Court of Exchequer, creating him Baron Wensleydale for life. The letters-patent were issued; but the peers loudly protested against the intrusion of a life-peer to sit amongst the hereditary nobles of the realm. An untimely fit of the gout disabled Lord Wensleydale from presenting himself, with his writ of summons, on the first day of the session; and on the 7th of February Lord Lyndhurst proposed, in a masterly speech, to refer his exceptional patent to the Committee of Privileges.

1 3d Rep. 37, 38.

2 Coke's Inst., 19th edit., by Hargrave and Butler.

3 Hansard's Debates, June 27th, 1851, 3d Series, cxvii. 1312.

Arguments for and against it.

Throughout the learned debate which followed, the abstract prerogative of the Crown to create a life-peerage was scarcely questioned; but it was denied that such a peerage conferred any right to sit in Parliament. It was treated as a mere title of honor, giving rank and precedence to its possessor, but not a place in an hereditary legislative chamber. The precedents and authorities in support of life-peerages were exposed to a searching criticism, which failed, however, to shake the position that the Crown had, in former times, introduced life-peers to sit in the House of Lords. But it was admitted on all sides, that no such case had occurred for upwards of four hundred years. Hence arose a most difficult question of constitutional law. Had the ancient prerogative of the Crown been lost by desuetude; or could it be exercised, if the Queen thought fit to revive it? The ministers, relying upon the legal maxim, "*nullum tempus occurrit regi*," argued that there could be no loss of prerogative by lapse of time. But their opponents forcibly contended that the Crown could not alter the settled constitution of the realm. In ancient times, — before the institutions of the country had been established by law and usage, — the Crown had withheld writs of summons from peers who were unquestionably entitled, by inheritance, to sit in Parliament: the Crown had disfranchised ancient boroughs by prerogative; and had enfranchised new boroughs by royal charter. What would now be said of such an exercise of the prerogative? By constitutional usage, having the force of law, the House of Lords had been for centuries a chamber consisting of hereditary councillors of the Crown, while the House of Commons had been elected by the suffrages of legally qualified electors. The Crown could no more change the constitution of the House of Lords by admitting a life-peer to a seat in Parliament, than it could change the representation of the people, by issuing writs to Birkenhead and Staleybridge, or by lowering the franchise of electors.

Passing beyond the legal rights of the Crown, the opponents of life-peerages dilated upon the hazardous consequences of admitting this new class of peers. Was it probable that such peerages would be confined to law-lords? If once recognized, would they not be extended to all persons whom the ministers of the day might think it convenient to obtrude upon the House of Lords? Might not the hereditary peers be suddenly overpowered by creatures of the executive government, — not ennobled on account of their public services, or other claims to the favor of the Crown, but appointed as nominees of ministers, and ready to do their bidding? Nay! might not the Crown be hereafter advised to discontinue the grant of hereditary peerages altogether, and gradually change the constitution of the House of Lords from an hereditary assembly, to a dependent senate nominated for life only? Nor were there wanting eloquent reflections upon the future degradation of distinguished men, whose services would be rewarded by life-peerages instead of by those cherished honors, which other men — not more worthy than themselves — had enjoyed the privilege of transmitting to their children. Sitting as an inferior caste, among those whom they could not call their peers, they would have reason to deplore a needless innovation, which had denied them honors to which they were justly entitled.

Decision of the Lords.

Such were the arguments by which Lord Wensleydale's patent was assailed. They were ably combated by ministers; and it was even contended that without a reference from the Crown, the Lords had no right to adjudicate upon the right of a peer to sit and vote in their House; but, on a division, the patent was referred to the Committee of Privileges by a majority of thirty-three.[1] After an inquiry into the precedents, and more learned and ingenious debates, the committee reported, and the House agreed, "that neither the letters-patent, nor the letters-pat-

[1] Content, 138; not content, 105. Hansard's Debates, 3d Ser., cxl. 263.

ent with the usual writ of summons issued in pursuance thereof, can entitle the grantee to sit and vote in Parliament."[1]

Some hereditary peers, who concurred in this conclusion, may have been animated by the same spirit of jealousy which, in 1711, had led their ancestors to deny the right of the Crown to admit Scottish peers amongst them, and in 1719 had favored a more extensive limitation of the royal prerogative; but with the exception of the Lord Chancellor, — by whose advice the patent had been made out, — all the law-lords of both parties supported the resolution, which has since been generally accepted as a sound exposition of constitutional law. Where institutions are founded upon ancient usage, it is a safe and wholesome doctrine that they shall not be changed, unless by the supreme legislative authority of Parliament. The Crown was forced to submit to the decision of the Lords; and Lord Wensleydale soon afterwards took his seat, under a new patent, as an hereditary peer of the realm.

Further proceedings in relation to life-peerages.

But the question of life-peerages was not immediately set at rest. A committee of the Lords having been appointed to inquire into the appellate jurisdiction of that House, recommended that her Majesty should be empowered, by statute, to confer life-peerages upon two persons who had served for five years as judges, and that they should sit with the Lord Chancellor as judges of appeal and "deputy speakers." A bill, founded upon this recommendation, was passed by the House of Lords; but after much discussion, it miscarried in the House of Commons.[2]

Lords spiritual.

In reviewing the rapid growth of the temporal peers sitting in Parliament, it is impossible not to be struck with the altered proportions which they

[1] Hansard's Debates, 3d Ser., cxl. 1152 *et seq.*; Report of Committee of Privileges; Clark's House of Lords' Cases, v. 958.

[2] Hansard's Debates, 3d Ser., cxlii. 780, 899, 1059; *Ibid.*, cxliii. 428, 583, 613.

bear to the lords spiritual, as compared with former times. Before the suppression of the monasteries by Henry VIII., in 1539, when the abbots and priors sat with the bishops, the lords spiritual actually exceeded the temporal lords in number. First in rank and precedence, — superior in attainments, — and exercising high trusts and extended influence, — they were certainly not inferior, in political weight, to the great nobles with whom they were associated. Even when the abbots and priors had been removed, the bishops alone formed about one third of the House of Lords. But while the temporal lords have been multiplied since that period about eight-fold, the English bishops sitting in Parliament, have only been increased from twenty-one to twenty-six, — to whom have been added the four Irish bishops. The ecclesiastical element in our legislature, has thus become relatively inconsiderable and subordinate. Instead of being a third of the House of Lords, as in former times, it now forms less than a fifteenth part of that assembly: nor is it likely to receive any accession of strength. When the pressing demands of the Church obtained from Parliament the constitution of the new bishopric of Manchester, care was taken that not even one spiritual lord should be added to the existing number. The principle of admitting a new bishop to sit in Parliament was, indeed, conceded; but he was allowed that privilege at the expense of the more ancient sees. Except in the case of the sees of Canterbury, York, London, Durham, and Winchester, the bishop last appointed receives no writ of summons from the Crown to sit in Parliament, until another vacancy arises.[1] The principle of this temporary exclusion of the junior bishop, though at first exposed to objections on the part of the Church, has since been found to be not without its advantages. It enables a bishop recently inducted, to devote himself without interruption to the labors of his diocese, while it relieves

[1] Bishopric of Manchester Act, 10 & 11 Vict. c. 108. See also Debates, 1844, in the House of Lords, on the St. Asaph and Bangor Dioceses' Bill.

him from the expenses of a residence in London, at a time when they can be least conveniently borne.

Attempts to exclude bishops from the House of Lords.

But, however small their numbers, and diminished their influence, the presence of the bishops in Parliament has often provoked opposition and remonstrance. This has probably arisen, more from feelings to which episcopacy has been exposed, than from any dispassionate objections to the participation of bishops in the legislation of the country. Proscribed by Presbyterian Scotland, — ejected from Parliament by the English Puritans,[1] — repudiated in later times, by every sect of dissenters, — not regarded with too much favor, even by all the members of their own Church, — and obnoxious, from their dignity and outward pomp, to vulgar jealousies, — the bishops have had to contend against many popular opinions and prejudices. Nor has their political conduct, generally, been such as to conciliate public favor. Ordinarily supporting the government of the day, — even in its least popular measures, — leaning always to authority, — as churchmen, opposed to change, — and precluded by their position, from courting popularity, — it is not surprising that cries have sometimes been raised against them, and efforts made to pull them down from their high places.

In 1834, the Commons refused leave to bring in a bill "for relieving the bishops of their legislative and judicial duties in the House of Peers," by a majority of more than two to one.[2] By a much greater majority, in 1836, they refused to affirm "that the attendance of the Bishops in Parliament, is prejudicial to the cause of religion."[3] And again in the following year, they denied, with equal emphasis, the proposition that the sitting of the bishops in Parliament "tends to alienate the affections of the people from the Established Church."[4] Since that time, there have been no adverse

[1] 16 Car. I. c. 27.

[2] 13th March, 1834. Ayes, 58; Noes, 125.

[3] 26th April, 1836. Ayes, 53; Noes 180.

[4] 16th February, 1837. Ayes, 92; Noes, 197.

motions in Parliament, and few unfriendly criticisms elsewhere, in relation to the Parliamentary functions of the bishops.

Their place in our venerable constitution has hitherto been upheld by every statesman, and by nearly all political parties. At the same time, the liberal policy of the legislature towards Roman Catholics and Dissenters, has served to protect the bishops from much religious animosity, formerly directed against the Church, of which they are the most prominent representatives. Again, the Church, by the zeal and earnestness with which, during the last thirty years, she has followed out her spiritual mission, has greatly extended her own moral influence among the people, and weakened the assaults of those who dissent from her doctrines. And the increased strength of the Church has fortified the position of the bishops. That they are an exception to the principle of hereditary right — the fixed characteristic of the House of Lords — is, in the opinion of many, not without its theoretical advantages.

Circumstances favorable to the bishops.

The various changes in the constitution of the House of Lords, which have here been briefly sketched, have considerably affected the political position and influence of that branch of the legislature.

Political position of the House of Lords.

It is not surprising that peers of ancient lineage should have regarded with jealousy, the continual enlargement of their own privileged order. The proud distinction which they enjoyed lost some of its lustre, when shared by a larger body. Their social preëminence, and the weight of their individual votes in Parliament, were alike impaired by the increasing number of those whom the favor of their sovereign had made equal to themselves. These effects, however, have been rendered much less extensive than might have been anticipated, by the expansion of society, and by the operation of party in all political affairs.

But however the individual privileges of peers may have been affected by the multiplication of their numbers, it is scarcely to be questioned that the House of Lords has gained importance, as a political institution, by its enlargement. Let us suppose, for a moment, that the jealousy of the peers had led either to such a legal restraint upon the prerogative, as that proposed in the reign of George I., or to so sparing an exercise of it, that the peerage had remained without material increase since the accession of the House of Hanover. Is it conceivable that an order so limited in number, and so exclusive in character, could have maintained its due authority in the legislature? With the instinctive aversion to change, which characterizes every close corporation, it would have opposed itself haughtily to the active and improving spirit of more popular institutions. It might even have attempted to maintain some of its more invidious privileges, which have been suffered to fall into desuetude. Hence it would necessarily have been found in opposition to the House of Commons, the press, and public opinion; while its limited and unpopular constitution would have failed to give it strength to resist the pressure of adverse forces. But the wider and more liberal constitution which it has acquired from increased numbers, and a more representative character, has saved the House of Lords from these political dangers. True to the spirit of an aristocracy, and to its theoretical uses in the state, it has been slower than the House of Commons in receiving popular impressions. It has often checked, for a time, the progressive policy of the age; yet, being accessible to the same sympathies and influences as the other House, its tardier convictions have generally been brought, without violence, into harmony with public opinion. And when measures, demanded by the national welfare, have sometimes been injuriously retarded, the great and composite qualities of the House of Lords, — the eminence of its numerous members, — their talents in debate, and wide local influence, — have made it too powerful to be rudely overborne by popular clamor.

Its enlargement a source of strength.

Thus the expansive growth of the House of Lords, — concurring with the increased authority of the House of Commons, and the enlarged influence of the press, — appears to have been necessary for the safe development of our free institutions, in which the popular element has been continually advancing. The same cause has also tended to render the peers more independent of the influence of the Crown. To that influence they are naturally exposed: but the larger their number, and the more various their interests, the less effectually can it be exercised: while the Crown is no longer able to secure their adherence by grants of land, offices, and pensions.

And suited to more popular institutions.

These changes in the constitution of the House of Peers must further be considered in their relations to party. The general object which successive ministers have had in view in creating peers, — apart from the reward of special public services, — has been to favor their own adherents, and strengthen their Parliamentary interest. It follows that the House of Lords has undergone considerable changes, from time to time, in its political composition. This result has been the more remarkable whenever one party has enjoyed power for a great length of time. In such cases the number of creations has sometimes been sufficient to alter the balance of parties; or, if this cause alone has not sufficed, it has been aided by political conversions, — the not uncommon fruit of ministerial prosperity. The votes of the bishops have also been usually recorded with that party, to whom they owed their elevation. Hence it was that, on the accession of George III., — when the domination of the great Whig families had lasted for nearly half a century, — the House of Lords was mainly Whig. Hence it was that, on the accession of William IV., when the Tory rule — commenced under Lord Bute, strengthened by Lord North, and consolidated by Mr. Pitt — had enjoyed ascendency for even a longer period, the House of Lords was mainly Tory.

The peerage viewed in reference to party.

Entire change of party connections at different periods.

Under such conditions as these, when a ministry, having established a sure majority in the House of Lords, is overthrown by an Opposition commanding a majority of the House of Commons, the two Houses are obviously in danger of being brought into collision. A dissolution may suddenly change the political character of the House of Commons, and transfer power from one party to another; but a change in the political character of the House of Lords, may be the work of half a century. In the case of Whig administrations since the Reform Act, the creation of a majority in the Upper House, has been a matter of peculiar difficulty. The natural sympathies of the peerage are conservative; and are strengthened by age, property, and connections. A stanch Whig, raised to the Upper House, is often found a doubting, critical, fastidious partisan, — sometimes an absentee, and not unfrequently an opponent of his own party. No longer responsible to constituents for his votes, and removed from the liberal associations of a popular assembly, he gradually throws off his political allegiance; and if habit, or an affectation of consistency, still retain him upon the same side of the House, or upon the neutral "cross-benches," his son will probably be found an acknowledged member of the Opposition. Party ties, without patronage, have been slack, and easily broken.

Danger from this cause of collisions between the Houses.

While the influence of the Crown was sufficiently great to direct the policy of the country; and while a large proportion of the members of the Lower House were the nominees of peers, collisions between the two Houses, if not wholly averted, were at least easily accommodated. There had been frequent contests between them, upon matters of privilege. It was not without protracted struggles, that the Commons had established their exclusive right to grant supplies and impose taxes. The two Houses had contended violently in 1675 concerning the appellate jurisdiction of the Lords; they had contended, with

The influence of the Crown formerly able to reconcile them.

not less violence, in 1704, upon the jurisdiction of the Commons, in matters of election; they had quarrelled rudely, in 1770, while insisting upon the exclusion of strangers. But upon general measures of public policy, their differences had been rare and unimportant. George III., by inducing the Lords to reject Mr. Fox's India Bill, in order to overthrow the Coalition ministry, brought them into open collision with the Commons; but harmony was soon restored between them, as the Crown succeeded, by means of a dissolution, in obtaining a large majority in the Lower House. In later times, the Lords opposed themselves to concessions to the Roman Catholics, and to amendments of the Criminal Law, which had been approved by the Commons. For several years, neither the Commons nor the people were sufficiently earnest, to enforce the adoption of those measures: but when public opinion could no longer be resisted, the Lords avoided a collision with the Commons, by acquiescing in measures of which they still disapproved. Since popular opinion has been more independently expressed by the Commons, the hazard of such collisions has been greatly increased. The Commons, deriving their authority directly from the people, have increased in power; and the influences which formerly tended to bring them into harmony with the Lords, have been impaired.

The Reform Bill of 1831 rejected by the Lords.

The memorable events of 1831 and 1832, arising out of the measures for extending the representation of the people, exposed the authority of the House of Lords to a rude shock; and even threatened its constitution with danger. Never since the days of Cromwell, had that noble assembly known such perils. The Whig ministry having, by a dissolution, secured a large majority of the Commons in favor of their second Reform Bill; its rejection by the Lords was still certain, if the Opposition should put forth their strength. For seventy years, the House of Lords had been recruited from the ranks of the Tory party; and was not less hostile to the Whig ministry, than to Parliamentary reform. The people had so recently pronounced their judgment in favor of the Bill, at the late election, that it now became a question, — who should prevail, the Lords or the Commons? The answer could scarcely be doubtful. The excited people, aroused by a great cause, and encouraged by bold and earnest leaders, were not likely to yield. The Lords stood alone. The king's ministers, the House of Commons, and the people were demanding that the Bill should pass. Would the Lords venture to reject it? If they should bend to the rising storm, their will indeed would be subdued, — their independent judgment set aside: but public danger would be averted. Should they brave the storm, and stand up against its fury, they could still be overcome by the royal prerogative.

Already, before the second reading, no less than sixteen new peers had been created, in order to correct, in some measure, the notorious disproportion between the two parties in that house; but a majority was still known to be adverse to the Bill. A further creation of peers, in order to insure the success of the measure, was then in contemplation; but the large number that would be required for that purpose, the extreme harshness of such a course, and the hope — not ill-founded — that many of the peers would yield to the peril of the times, discouraged ministers from yet advising this last resource of power. The result was singular. The peers hesitated, wavered, and paused. Many of them, actuated by fear, by prudence, by policy, or by public spirit, refrained from voting. But the bishops, — either less alarmed, or less sensible of the imminent danger of the occasion, — mustered in unusual force. Twenty-two were present, of whom twenty-one voted against the Bill. Had they supported ministers, the Bill would have been saved: but now they had exactly turned the scale, — as Lord Grey had warned them that they might, — and the Bill was lost by a majority of forty-one.

The House of Commons immediately supported the ministers by a vote of confidence: the people were more excited than ever; and the reformers more determined to prevail over the resistance of the House of Lords.

Ministers supported by the Commons.

Parliament was prorogued merely for the purpose of introducing another Reform Bill. This Bill was welcomed by the Commons, with larger majorities than the last; and now the issue between the two Houses had become still more serious. To "swamp the House of Lords" had, at length, become a popular cry; but at this time, not a single peer was created. Lord Grey, however, on the second reading, while he declared himself averse to such a proceeding, justified its use in case of necessity. The gravity of the crisis had shaken the courage of the majority. A considerable number of "waverers," as they were termed, now showed themselves; and the fate of the Bill was in their hands. Some who had been previously absent, including five bishops, voted for the Bill; others, who had voted against the former Bill, abstained from voting; and seventeen who had voted against the last Bill, actually voted for this! From these various causes, the second reading was carried by a majority of nine.

Reform Bill of 1831-2.

Meanwhile it was well known, both to the ministers and the people, that the further progress of the measure was exposed to imminent danger; and while the former were contemplating, with reluctance and dread, the immediate necessity of a further creation of peers, the popular cry was raised more loudly than ever, that the House of Lords must be "swamped." Such a cry was lightly encouraged by reckless and irresponsible politicians; but the constitutional statesmen who had to conduct the country through this crisis, weighed seriously a step which nothing but the peril of the times could justify. Lord Brougham — perhaps the boldest of all the statesmen concerned in these events — has thus recorded his own sentiments regarding them: — "When I went to Windsor with Lord Grey, I had a list of eighty

The crisis.

creations framed upon the principles of making the least possible permanent addition to our House and to the aristocracy, by calling up peers' eldest sons, — by choosing men without any families, — by taking Scotch and Irish peers. I had a strong feeling of the necessity of the case, in the very peculiar circumstances we were placed in; but such was my deep sense of the dreadful consequences of the act, that I much question whether I should not have preferred running the risk of confusion that attended the loss of the Bill as it then stood, — rather than expose the constitution to so imminent a hazard of subversion."[1]

The ministers advise a creation of peers.

No sooner was the discussion of the Bill commenced in committee, than the ministers suddenly found themselves in a minority of thirty-five.[2] Now, then, was the time, if ever, for exercising the royal prerogative; and accordingly the ministers unanimously resolved to advise the king to create a sufficient number of peers, to turn the scale in favor of the Bill; and in the event of his refusal, to tender their resignation. He refused; and the resignation of the ministers was immediately tendered and accepted. In vain the Duke of Wellington attempted to form an administration on the basis of a more moderate measure of reform: the House of Commons and the people were firm in their support of the ministers; and nothing was left for the peers, but submission or coercion. The king unwillingly gave his consent, in writing, to the necessary creation of peers;[3] but, in the mean time, — averse to an offensive act of authority, — he successfully exerted his personal influence with the peers, to induce them to desist

[1] Lord Brougham's Political Philosophy, iii. 308. The British Constitution, 1861, p. 270.

[2] 151 and 116.

[3] "The king grants permission to Earl Grey, and to his chancellor, Lord Brougham, to create such a number of peers as will be sufficient to insure the passing of the Reform Bill, — first calling up peers' eldest sons. WILLIAM R. Windsor, May 17th, 1832." — *Roebuck's Hist. of the Whig Ministry*, ii. 331–333.

from further opposition.[1] The greater part of the Opposition peers absented themselves; and the memorable Reform Bill was soon passed through all its further stages. The prerogative was not exercised; but its efficacy was not less signal in overcoming a dangerous resistance to the popular will, than if it had been fully exerted; while the House of Lords — humbled, indeed, and its influence shaken for a time — was spared the blow which had been threatened to its dignity and independence.

Opinion of the Duke of Wellington.

At no period of our history, has any question arisen of greater constitutional importance than this proposed creation of peers. The peers and the Tory party viewed it with consternation. "If such projects," said the Duke of Wellington, "can be carried into execution by a minister of the Crown with impunity, there is no doubt that the constitution of this House, and of this country, is at an end. I ask, my lords, is there any one blind enough not to see that if a minister can with impunity advise his sovereign to such an unconstitutional exercise of his prerogative, as to thereby decide all questions in this House, there is absolutely an end put to the power and objects of deliberation in this House, and an end to all just and proper means of decision. . . . ? And, my lords, my opinion is, that the threat of carrying this measure of creating peers into execution, if it should have the effect of inducing noble lords to absent themselves from the House, or to adopt any particular line of conduct, is just as bad as its execution; for, my lords, it does by violence force a decision on this House, and on a subject on which this House is not disposed to give such a decision." [2]

Opinion of Earl Grey.

He was finely answered by Lord Grey: "I ask what would be the consequences if we were to suppose that such a prerogative did not exist, or could not be constitutionally exercised? The Commons have a con-

[1] See his Circular Letter, supra, p. 124; and infra, Chapter VI.

[2] May 17th, 1832. Hansard's Debates, 3d Ser., xii. 995.

trol over the power of the Crown, by the privilege, in extreme cases, of refusing the supplies; and the Crown has, by means of its power to dissolve the House of Commons, a control upon any violent and rash proceedings on the part of the Commons; but if a majority of this House is to have the power, whenever they please, of opposing the declared and decided wishes both of the Crown and the people, without any means of modifying that power, — then this country is placed entirely under the influence of an uncontrollable oligarchy. I say, that if a majority of this House should have the power of acting adversely to the Crown and the Commons, and was determined to exercise that power without being liable to check or control, the constitution is completely altered, and the government of this country is not a limited monarchy: it is no longer, my lords, the Crown, the Lords and the Commons, but a House of Lords, — a separate oligarchy, — governing absolutely the others."[1]

A creation of peers equivalent to a dissolution.

It must not be forgotten that, although Parliament is said to be dissolved, a dissolution extends, in fact, no further than to the Commons. The peers are not affected by it, — no change can take place in the constitution of their body, except as to a small number of Scotch representative peers. So far, therefore, as the House of Lords is concerned, a creation of peers by the Crown, on extraordinary occasions, is the only equivalent which the constitution has provided, for the change and renovation of the House of Commons by a dissolution. In no other way can the opinions of the House of Lords be brought into harmony with those of the people. In ordinary times the House of Lords has been converted gradually to the political opinions of the dominant party in the state, by successive creations; but when a crisis arises, in which the party, of whose sentiments it is the exponent, is opposed to the majority of the House of Commons and the country, it must either yield to the pressure of public opinion, or expose itself to the

1 May 17th, 1832. Hansard's Debates, 3d Ser., xii. 1006.

hazard of a more sudden conversion. Statesmen of all parties would condemn such a measure, except in cases of grave and perilous necessity; but, should the emergency be such as to demand it, it cannot be pronounced unconstitutional.

Position of the Lords since the Reform Act.

It was apprehended that, by this moral coercion, the legitimate influence of the peers would be impaired, and their independence placed at the mercy of any popular minister, supported by a majority of the House of Commons. To record the fiats of the Lower House, — sometimes, perhaps, with unavailing protests, — sometimes with feeble amendments, — would now be their humble office. They were cast down from their high place in the legislature, — their ancient glories were departed. Happily, these forebodings have not since been justified. The peers had been placed, by their natural position, in opposition to a great popular cause; and had yielded, at last, to a force which they could no longer resist. Had they yielded earlier, and with a better grace, they might have shared in the popular triumph. Again and again the Commons had opposed themselves to the influence of the Crown, or to popular opinion, and had been overcome; yet their permanent influence was not impaired. And so was it now with the Lords. The Commons may be overborne by a dissolution, — the Lords by a threatened creation of peers, — the Crown by withholding the supplies; and all alike must bow to the popular will, when constitutionally expressed.

Their independence.

The subsequent history of the Lords attests their undiminished influence since the Reform Act. That measure has unquestionably increased the authority of the House of Commons. But the Lords have not shown themselves less independent in their judgment, or less free in their legislative action. It had previously been their practice, not so much to originate legislation, and to direct the policy of the country, as to control, to amend, and to modify measures received from the Commons; and in that function, they have since labored with as much freedom as ever. In 1835 and 1836, the Commons maintained that the principle of appropriating the surplus revenues of the Church of Ireland, was essential to the settlement of the question of Irish tithes. Yet the Lords, by their determined resistance to this principle, obliged the Commons, and the ministers who had fought their way into office by its assertion, definitively to abandon it. They exercised an unconstrained judgment in their amendments to the English Municipal Reform Bill, which the Commons were obliged reluctantly to accept. They dealt with the bills for the reform of the Irish corporations, with equal freedom. For four sessions their amendments, — wholly inconsistent with the principles of legislation asserted by the Commons, — led to the abandonment of those measures. And at length they forced the Commons to accept amendments, repugnant to the policy for which they had been contending. Again, they resisted, for several years, the removal of the Jewish disabilities, — a measure approved by the settled judgment of the Commons and the people; and obliged the advocates of religious liberty to accept, at last, an unsatisfactory compromise. But these examples of independence are thrown into the shade by their proceedings in 1860, when, — treading upon the forbidden ground of taxation, they rejected a Bill which the Commons had passed, — as part of the financial arrangements of the year, — for repealing the duties upon paper. The controverted question of privilege involved in this vote, will be touched upon hereafter;[1] but here it may be said, that the Commons have ever been most jealous of their exclusive rights, in matters of supply and taxation; and that their jealousy has been wisely respected by the Lords. But, finding a strong support in the Commons, — an indifferent and inert public opinion, — much encouragement from an influential portion of the press, — and a favorable state of parties, — the Lords were able to defy at once the government and the Commons. There had been times, when such defi-

[1] Chapter VII. p. 473.

ance would have been resented and returned; but now the Lords, rightly estimating their own strength, and the causes by which retaliation on the part of the Commons was restrained, overruled the ministers of the Crown and the Commons, on a question of finance, and, by their single vote, continued a considerable tax upon the people. The most zealous champion of the independence of the peers, in 1832, would not then have counselled so hazardous an enterprise. Still less would he have predicted that it would be successfully accomplished, within thirty years after the passing of the Reform Act.

In short, though the Lords were driven, in 1832, from an indefensible position, which they had held with too stubborn a persistence, they have since maintained their independence, and a proper weight in the legislature.

Vantage-ground of the Lords.

As a legislative body, the Lords have great facilities for estimating the direction and strength of public opinion. Nearly every measure has been fully discussed, before they are called upon to consider it. Hence they are enabled to judge, at leisure, of its merits, its defects, and its popularity. If the people are indifferent to its merits, they can safely reject it altogether: if too popular, in principle, to be so dealt with, they may qualify, and perhaps neutralize it by amendments, without any shock to public feeling.

At the same time they are able, by their debates, to exercise an extensive influence upon the convictions of the people. Sitting like a court of review upon measures originating in the Lower House, they can select from the whole armory of debate and public discussion, the best arguments, and the most effective appeals to enlightened minds. Nor have there ever been wanting amongst their number, the first orators of their age and country.

But with these means of influence, the political weight of the House of Peers has been much affected by the passive indifference which it ordinarily displays to the business of legislation. The constitution of that assembly, and the social position of its members, have failed to excite the spirit and activity which mark a representative body. This is constantly made apparent by the small number of peers, who attend its deliberations. Unless great party questions have been under discussion, the House has ordinarily presented the appearance of a select committee. Three peers may wield all the authority of the House. Nay, even less than that number are competent to pass or reject a law, if their unanimity should avert a division, or notice of their imperfect constitution. Many laws have, in fact, been passed by numbers befitting a committee, rather than the whole House.[1] That the judgment of so small a number should be as much respected as that of the large bodies of members who throng the House of Commons, can scarcely be expected.

Small attendance of peers affects their political weight.

A quorum of three, — though well suited for judicial business, and not wholly out of proportion to the entire number of its members, in the earlier periods of its history, — has become palpably inadequate for a numerous assembly. That its members are not accountable to constituents, adds to their moral responsibilities; and should suggest safeguards against the abuse of the great powers which the constitution has intrusted to them.

The indifference of the great body of the peers to public business, and their scant attendance, by discouraging the efforts of the more able and ambitious men amongst them, further impair the influence of the Upper House. Statesmen who had distinguished themselves in the House of Commons, have complained, again and again, of the cold apathy by which their earnest oratory

Their indifference to business.

[1] On April 7th, 1854, the Testamentary Jurisdiction Bill was read a third time by a majority of two in a house of twelve. On the 25th August, 1860, the Tenure and Improvement of Land (Ireland) Bill, which had occupied weeks of discussion in the Commons, was nearly lost by a disagreement between the Two Houses; the numbers, on a division, being seven and six.

has been checked in the more patrician assembly. The encouragement of numbers, of ready sympathy, and of warm applause, are wanting; and the disheartened orator is fain to adapt his tone to the ungenial temperament of his audience. Thus to discourage public spirit, and devotion to the great affairs of state, cannot fail to diminish the political influence of the House of Lords.

Their deference to leaders.

The inertness of the House of Lords has produced another result prejudicial to its due influence in public affairs. It has generally yielded, with an indolent facility, to the domination of one or two of its own members, gifted with the strongest wills. Lord Thurlow, Lord Eldon, the Duke of Wellington, and Lord Lyndhurst, have swayed it, at different times, almost with the power of a dictator. Such men had acquired their activity and resolution in a different school from that of an hereditary chamber; and where peers by hereditary descent, like the Earl of Derby, have exercised an equal sway, they have learned how to lead and govern men, amidst the more stirring scenes of the House of Commons. Every assembly must have its leaders; but the absolute surrender of its own judgment to that of a single man, — perhaps of narrow mind, and unworthy prejudices, — cannot fail to impair its moral influence.

The peerage in its social relations.

Such, then, are the political position of the House of Lords, and the causes of its strength and weakness, as a part of the legislature. The peerage is also to be regarded in another aspect, — as the head of the great community of the upper classes. It represents their interests, feelings, and aspirations. Instead of being separated from other ranks in dignified isolation, it is connected with them by all the ties of social life. It leads them in politics: in the magistracy: in local administration: in works of usefulness, and charity: in the hunting-field, the banquet, and the ballroom.

The increase of the peerage has naturally extended the

social ramifications of the aristocracy. Six hundred families ennobled, — their children bearing titles of nobility, — allied by descent or connection with the first county families, and with the wealthiest commoners of other classes, — have struck their roots far and wide into the soil of English society. In every county their influence is great, — in many, paramount.

The aristocracy.

The untitled landed gentry, — upheld by the conservative law of primogeniture, — are an ancient aristocracy in themselves; and the main source from which the peerage has been recruited. In no other country is there such a class, — at once aristocratic and popular, and a bond of connection between the nobles and the commonalty.

The landed gentry.

Many of these have been distinguished by hereditary titles, — inferior to nobility, and conferring no political privileges; yet highly prized as a social distinction. The baronetage, like the peerage, has been considerably increased during the last century. On the accession of George III., there were about five hundred baronets;[1] in 1860, they had been increased to no less than eight hundred and sixty.[2] During the sixty years of this reign, the extraordinary number of four hundred and ninety-four baronetcies were created.[3] Of these a large number have been conferred for political services; and by far the greater part are enjoyed by men of family and fortune. Still the taste for titles was difficult to satiate.

The baronetage.

The ancient and honorable dignity of knighthood was conferred unsparingly by George III. upon little men for little services, until the title was wellnigh degraded. After the king's escape from assassination at the hands of Margaret Nicholson, so many knighthoods were

Orders of knighthood.

[1] Betham's Baronetage. Gentl. Mag. lix. 398.

[2] Viz., six hundred and seventy-four baronets of Great Britain, one hundred and eleven baronets of Scotland and Nova Scotia, and seventy-five of Ireland.

[3] This number is from 1761 to 1821; from a paper prepared by the late Mr. Pulman, Clarencieux King-at-Arms.

conferred on persons presenting congratulatory addresses to the Crown, that "a knight of Peg Nicholson's order" became a byword. The degradation of knighthood by the indiscriminate liberality of the Crown in granting it, continued until a recent time.

Still there were not knighthoods enough; and in 1783 the king instituted the Order of St. Patrick. Scotland had its most ancient Order of the Thistle: but no order of knighthood had, until that time, been appropriated to Ireland. The Hanoverian Guelphic Order of Knighthood had also been opened to the ambition of Englishmen; and William IV., during his reign, added to its roll, a goodly company of English knights.

The Order of the Bath, originally a military order, was enlarged in 1815; and again in 1847, the queen added a civil division to the order, to comprise such persons as by their personal services to the Crown, or by the performance of public duties, have merited the royal favor.[1]

Other classes siding with the aristocracy.

Besides these several titled orders, may be noticed officers enjoying naval and military rank, whose numbers were extraordinarily augmented by the long war with France, and by the extension of the British possessions abroad. Men holding high offices in the state, the church, the law, the universities, and other great incorporations, have also associated their powers and influence with those of the nobility.

Wealth favorable to the aristocracy.

The continual growth and accumulation of property have been a source of increasing strength to the British nobles. Wealth is, in itself, an aristocracy. It may desire to rival the nobility of a country, and even to detract from its glory. But in this land of old associations, it seeks only to enjoy the smiles and favors of the aristocracy, — craves admission to its society, — aspires to its connection, — and is ambitious of its dignities. The learned professions, commerce, manufactures, and public

[1] Letters-Patent, 24th May, 1847; London Gazette, p. 1951.

employments have created an enormous body of persons of independent income; some connected with the landed gentry, others with the commercial classes. All these form part of the independent "gentry." They are spread over the fairest parts of the country; and noble cities have been built for their accommodation. Bath, Cheltenham, Leamington, and Brighton attest their numbers and their opulence.[1] With much social influence and political weight, they form a strong outwork of the peerage, and uphold its ascendency by moral as well as political support.

The professions.

The professions lean, as a body, on the higher ranks of society. The Church is peculiarly connected with the landed interest. Everywhere the clergy cleave to power; and the vast lay patronage vested in the proprietors of the soil, draws close the bond between them and the Church. The legal and medical professions, again, being mainly supported by wealthy patrons, have the same political and social interests.

How vast a community of rank, wealth, and intelligence do these several classes of society constitute! The House of Lords, in truth, is not only a privileged body, but a great representative institution,—standing out as the embodiment of the aristocratic influence, and sympathies of the country.

[1] Bath has been termed the "City of the Three-per-cent Consols."

CHAPTER VI.

The House of Commons: — Nomination Boroughs: — Various and limited Rights of Election: — Bribery at Elections: — Sale of Seats: — Government influence in large Towns: — Revenue Officers disfranchised: — Vexatious Contests in Cities. — Representation of Scotland and Ireland. — Injustice in the Trial of Election Petitions. — Places and Pensions. — Bribes to Members: — Shares in Loans, Lotteries, and Contracts. — Successive Schemes of Parliamentary Reform prior to 1830: — The Reform Bills of 1830–31, 1831, and 1831–32: — Changes effected in the Representation, by the Reform Acts of 1832. — Bribery since 1832, and measures taken to restrain it. — Duration of Parliaments: — Vote by Ballot: — Property Qualification. — Later measures of Parliamentary Reform.

Unfaithfulness of the House of Commons to its trust.

IN preceding chapters, the various sources of political influence enjoyed by the Crown, and by the House of Lords, have been traced out. Their united powers long maintained an ascendency in the councils and government of the state. But great as were their own inherent powers, the main support of that ascendency was found among the representatives of the people, in the House of Commons. If that body had truly represented the people, and had been faithful to its trust, it would have enjoyed an authority equal at least, if not superior, to that of the Crown and the House of Lords combined.

Its dependence and corruption.

The theory of an equipoise in our legislature, however, had been distorted in practice; and the House of Commons was at once dependent and corrupt. The Crown, and the dominant political families who wielded its power, readily commanded a majority of that assembly. A large proportion of the borough members were the nominees of peers and great landowners; or were mainly returned through the political interest of those magnates. Many were the nominees of the Crown; or owed their seats to government influence. Rich adventurers, — having purchased their seats of the proprietors, or acquired them by bribery, — supported the ministry of the day, for the sake of honors, patronage, or court favor. The county members were generally identified with the territorial aristocracy. The adherence of a further class was secured by places and pensions: by shares in loans, lotteries, and contracts; and even by pecuniary bribes.

The extent to which these various influences prevailed, and their effect upon the constitution of the legislature, are among the most instructive inquiries of the historian.

Defects of the representative system.

The representative system had never aimed at theoretical perfection; but its general design was to assemble representatives from the places best able to contribute aids and subsidies, for the service of the Crown. This design would naturally have allotted members to counties, cities, and boroughs, in proportion to their population, wealth, and prosperity; and though rudely carried into effect, it formed the basis of representation, in early times. But there were few large towns: — the population was widely scattered: — industry was struggling with unequal success in different places; and oppressed burgesses, — so far from pressing their fair claims to representation, — were reluctant to augment their burdens, by returning members to Parliament. Places were capriciously selected for that honor by the Crown, — and sometimes even by the sheriff,[1] — and were, from time to time, omitted from the writs. Some small towns failed to keep pace with the growing prosperity of the country, and some fell into decay; and in the mean time, unrepresented villages grew into places of importance. Hence inequalities in the representation were continually increasing. They might have been redressed by

[1] Glanville's Reports, Pref. v.

a wise exercise of the ancient prerogative of creating and disfranchising boroughs; but the greater part of those created between the reigns of Henry VIII. and Charles II. were inconsiderable places, which afterwards became notorious as nomination boroughs.[1] From the reign of Charles II., — when this prerogative was superseded, — the growing inequalities in the representation were left wholly without correction.

From these causes, an electoral system had become established, — wholly inconsistent with any rational theory of representation. Its defects, — originally great, and aggravated by time and change, — had attained monstrous proportions in the middle of the last century.

Nomination boroughs.

The first and most flagrant anomaly was that of nomination boroughs. Some of these boroughs had been, from their first creation, too inconsiderable to aspire to independence; and being without any importance of their own, looked up for patronage and protection to the Crown, and to their territorial neighbors. The influence of the great nobles over such places as these was acknowledged, and exerted so far back as the fifteenth century.[2] It was freely discussed, in the reign of Elizabeth; when the House of Commons was warned, with a wise foresight, lest "Lords' letters shall from henceforth bear all the sway."[3] As the system of parliamentary government developed itself, such interest became more and more important to the nobles and great landowners, who accordingly spared no pains to extend it; and the insignificance of many of the boroughs, and a limited and capricious franchise, gave them too easy a conquest. Places like Old Sarum, with fewer inhabitants than an ordinary hamlet, avowedly returned the nominees of their

1 One hundred and eighty members were added to the House of Commons, by royal charter, between the reigns of Henry VIII. and Charles II. Glanville's Reports, cii.

2 Paston Letters, ii. 103.

3 Debate on the Bill for the validity of burgesses not resiant, 19th April, 1571; D'Ewes Journ. 168–171.

proprietors.[1] In other boroughs of more pretensions in respect of population and property, the number of inhabitants enjoying the franchise was so limited, as to bring the representation under the patronage of one or more persons of local or municipal influence.

Various and limited rights of election.

Not only were the electors few in number; but partial and uncertain rights of election prevailed in different boroughs. The common-law right of election was in the inhabitant householders resident within the borough;[2] but, in a large proportion of the boroughs, peculiar customs prevailed, by which this liberal franchise was restrained. In some, indeed, popular rights were enjoyed by custom; and all inhabitants paying "scot and lot," — or parish rates, — or all "potwallers," — being persons furnishing their own diet, whether householders or lodgers, — were entitled to vote. In others, none but those holding lands by burgage-tenure had the right of voting; in several, none but those enjoying corporate rights by royal charter. In many, these different rights were combined, or qualified by exceptional conditions.

Rights of election determined by the House of Commons.

Rights of election, so uncertain and confused, were founded upon the last determinations of the House of Commons, which, — however capricious, and devoid of settled principles, — had a general tendency to restrict the ancient franchise, and to vest it in a more limited number of persons.[3]

In some of the corporate towns the inhabitants paying scot and lot, and freemen, were admitted to vote; in some, the freemen only; and in many, none but the governing body of the corporation. At Buckingham, and at Bewdley, the right of election was confined to the bailiff and twelve burgesses:

1 Parl. Return, Sess. 1831–32, No. 92.

2 Com. Dig. iv. 288. Glanville's Reports.

3 Glanville's Reports; Determinations of the House of Commons concerning Elections, 8vo., 1780; Introduction to Merewether and Stephens, History of Boroughs; Male's Election Law, 289, 317; Luders' Election Reports, &c.

at Bath, to the mayor, ten aldermen, and twenty-four common-councilmen: at Salisbury, to the mayor and corporation, consisting of fifty-six persons. And where more popular rights of election were acknowledged, there were often very few inhabitants to exercise them. Gatton enjoyed a liberal franchise. All freeholders and inhabitants paying scot and lot were entitled to vote, but they only amounted to seven. At Tavistock, all freeholders rejoiced in the franchise, but there were only ten. At St. Michael, all inhabitants paying scot and lot were electors, but there were only seven.[1]

Number of small boroughs.

In 1793, the Society of the friends of the people were prepared to prove that in England and Wales seventy members were returned by thirty-five places, in which there were scarcely any electors at all; that ninety members were returned by forty-six places with less than fifty electors; and thirty-seven members by nineteen places, having not more than one hundred electors.[2] Such places were returning members, while Leeds, Birmingham, and Manchester were unrepresented; and the members whom they sent to Parliament, were the nominees of peers and other wealthy patrons. No abuse was more flagrant than the direct control of peers, over the constitution of the Lower House. The Duke of Norfolk was represented by eleven members; Lord Lonsdale by nine; Lord Darlington by seven; the Duke of Rutland, the Marquess of Buckingham, and Lord Carrington, each by six.[3] Seats were held, in both Houses alike, by hereditary right.

Bribery at elections.

Where the number of electors in a borough was sufficient to insure their independence, in the exercise of the franchise, they were soon taught that their votes would command a price; and thus, where nomination ceased, the influence of bribery commenced.

Bribery at elections has long been acknowledged as one

1 Parl. Return, Sess. 1831–32, No. 92.
2 Parl. Hist. xxx. 789.
3 Oldfield's Representative Hist. vi. 286.

of the most shameful evils of our constitutional government. Though not wholly unknown in earlier times, it appears, — like too many other forms of corruption, — to have first become a systematic abuse in the reign of Charles II.[1] The Revolution, by increasing the power of the House of Commons, served to enlarge the field of bribery at elections. As an example of the extent to which this practice prevailed, it was alleged that at the Westminster election, in 1695, Sir Walter Clarges, an unsuccessful candidate, expended 2000*l.* in bribery in the course of a few hours.[2]

The Bribery Act of William III.

These notorious scandals led to the passing of the Act 7 William III. c. 4. Bribery had already been recognized as an offence, by the common law;[3] and had been condemned by resolutions of the House of Commons;[4] but this was the first statute to restrain and punish it. This necessary measure, however, was designed rather to discourage the intrusion of rich strangers into the political preserves of the landowners, than for the general repression of bribery. It seems to have had little effect; for Davenant, writing soon afterwards, spoke of "utter strangers making a progress through England, endeavoring by very large sums of money to get themselves elected. It is said there are known brokers who have tried to stock-job elections upon the Exchange; and that for many boroughs there was a stated price."[5] An act of Parliament was not likely to touch the causes of such corruption. The increasing commerce of the country had brought forward new classes of men, who supplied their want of local connections, by the unscrupulous use of riches. Political morality may be elevated

1 Macaulay's Hist. i. 236.

2 *Ibid.* iv. 615.

3 Burr. iii. 1235, 1388; Dougl. iv. 294; Male's Election Law, 339–345.

4 Com. Journ. ix. 411, 517.

5 Essay on the Balance of Power; Davenant's Works, iii. 326, 328. See also Pamphlets, "Freeholder's Plea against Stock-jobbing Elections of Parliament Men;" "Considerations upon Corrupt Elections of Members to serve in Parliament," 1701.

by extended liberties: but bribery has everywhere been the vice of growing wealth.[1]

The prizes to be secured through seats in Parliament during the corrupt administrations of Walpole and Pelham, further encouraged the system of bribery; and early in the reign of George III. its notoriety became a public scandal.

General election in 1761.

The very first election of this reign, in 1761, was signalized by unusual excesses. Never perhaps had bribery been resorted to with so much profusion.[2] One class of candidates, now rapidly increasing, consisted of men who had amassed fortunes in the East and West Indies, and were commonly distinguished as "Nabobs."

The "Nabobs."

Their ambition led them to aspire to a place in the legislature: — their great wealth gave them the means of bribery; and the scenes in which they had studied politics, made them unscrupulous in corruption. A seat in Parliament was for sale, like an estate; and they bought it, without hesitation or misgiving. Speaking of this class, Lord Chatham said: "Without connections, without any natural interest in the soil, the importers of foreign gold have forced their way into Parliament, by such a torrent of corruption as no private hereditary fortune could resist." [3]

To the landed gentry they had long since been obnoxious. A country squire, whatever his local influence, was overborne by the profusion of wealthy strangers. Even a powerful

[1] "The effect produced by the rapid increase in wealth upon political morality [in Rome] is proved by the frequent laws against bribery at elections, which may be dated from the year 181 B.C. In that year it was enacted that any one found guilty of using bribery to gain votes should be declared incapable of becoming a candidate for the next ten years." — *Dr. Liddell's Hist. of Rome.* These laws are enumerated in Colquhoun's Roman Civil Law, § 2402. In France and America, bribery has been practised upon representatives rather than electors. — *De Tocqueville*, i. 264, &c.

[2] "Both the Court and particulars went greater lengths than in any preceding times. In truth, the corruption of electors met, if not exceeded, that of candidates." — *Walp. Mem.* i. 42.

[3] Jan. 22d, 1770. Parl. Hist. xvi. 752.

noble was no match for men, who brought to the contest the "wealth of the Indies." Nor were they regarded with much favor by the leaders of parties; for men who had bought their seats, — and paid dearly for them, — owed no allegiance to political patrons. Free from party connections, they sought admission into Parliament, not so much with a view to a political career, as to serve mere personal ends, — to forward commercial speculations, to extend their connections, and to gratify their social aspirations. But their independence and ambition well fitted them for the service of the court. The king was struggling to disengage himself from the domination of party leaders; and here were the very men he needed, — without party ties or political prepossessions, — daily increasing in numbers and influence, — and easily attracted to his interests by the hope of those rewards which are most coveted by the wealthy. They soon ranged themselves among the king's friends; and thus the court policy, — which was otherwise subversive of freedom, — became associated with parliamentary corruption.

Bribery Act of 1762.

The scandals of the election of 1761 led to the passing of an act in the following year, by which pecuniary penalties were first imposed for the offence of bribery.[1] But the evil which it sought to correct, still continued without a check.

Sale of boroughs.

Where the return of members was left to a small, but independent body of electors, their individual votes were secured by bribery; and where it rested with proprietors or corporations, the seat was purchased outright. The sale of boroughs, — an abuse of some antiquity,[2] and often practised since the time of Charles II., — became, at the commencement of this reign, a general and notorious system. The right of property in boroughs was acknowledged, and capable

[1] 2 Geo. III. c. 24.

[2] In 1571, the borough of Westbury was fined by the House of Commons for receiving a bribe of 4*l.*; and the mayor was ordered to refund the money. — *Com. Journ.* i. 88.

of sale or transfer, like any other property. In 1766, Lord Hertford prevailed upon Lord Chatham's ministry to transfer to him the borough of Orford, which belonged to the Crown.[1] And Sudbury, infamous for its corruption until its ultimate disfranchisement,[2] publicly advertised itself for sale.[3]

If a seat occupied by any member happened to be required by the government, for some other candidate, he was bought out, at a price agreed upon between them. Thus in 1764, we find Lord Chesterfield advising his son upon the best means of securing 1000*l.* for the surrender of his seat, which had cost him 2000*l.* at the beginning of the Parliament.[4]

General election of 1768.

The general election of 1768 was at least as corrupt as that of 1761, and the sale of seats more open and undisguised. Some of the cases were so flagrant as to shock even the moral sentiments of that time. The corporation of Oxford, being heavily embarrassed, offered again to return their members, Sir Thomas Stapylton and Mr. Lee, on payment of their bond debts, amounting to 5670*l.* These gentlemen refused the offer, saying that as they did not intend to sell the corporation, they could not afford to buy them; and brought the matter before the House of Commons. The mayor and ten of the aldermen were committed to Newgate; but after a short imprisonment, were discharged with a reprimand from the Speaker. Not discouraged, however, by their imprisonment, they completed, in Newgate, a bargain which they had already commenced; and sold the representation of their city to the Duke of Marlborough and the Earl of Abingdon. Meanwhile the town clerk carried off the books of the corporation which contained evidence of the bargain; and the business was laughed at and forgotten.[5]

For the borough of Poole, there were three candidates.

1 Walpole's Mem. ii. 361.
2 7 & 8 Vict. c. 53.
3 Walpole's Mem. i. 42.
4 Oct. 19th, 1764, Letters of Lord Chesterfield to his son, iv. 218.
5 Parl. Hist. xvi. 397; Walpole's Mem. iii. 153.

Mauger, the successful candidate, promised the corporation 1000*l.*, to be applied to public purposes, if he should be elected; Gulston made them a present of 750*l.*, as a mark of gratitude for the election of his father on a former occasion; and Calcraft appears to have vainly tempted them with the more liberal offer of 1500*l.* The election was declared void.[1]

The representation of the borough of Ludgershall was sold for 9000*l.* by its owner, the celebrated George Selwyn; and the general price of boroughs was said to be raised at that time, from 2500*l.* to 4000*l.* or 5000*l.*, by the competition of the East and West Indians.[2] It was notorious at the time, that agents or "borough-brokers" were commissioned by some of the smaller boroughs, to offer them to the highest bidder. Two of these, Reynolds and Hickey, were taken into custody, by order of the House; and some others were sent to Newgate.[3] While some boroughs were thus sold in the gross; the electors were purchased elsewhere by the most lavish bribery. The contest for the borough of Northampton was stated to have cost the candidates "at least 30,000*l.* a side."[4] Nay, Lord Spencer is said to have spent the incredible sum of 70,000*l.* in contesting this borough, and in the proceedings upon an election petition which ensued.[5]

New Shoreham case, 1771.

In 1771, the systematic bribery which had long prevailed at New Shoreham was exposed by an election committee — the first appointed under the Grenville Act.[6] It appeared that a corrupt association, comprising the majority of the electors, and calling itself "The Christian Club," had, under the guise of charity, been in the habit of selling the borough to the highest bidder, and

1 Feb. 10th, 1769; Com. Journ. xxxii. 199.

2 Letters of Lord Chesterfield to his son, Dec. 19th, 1767; April 12th, 1768, iv. 269, 274.

3 Walpole's Mem. iii. 157.

4 Lord Chesterfield to his son, April 12th, 1768, iv. 274.

5 Walpole's Mem. iii. 198, *n.* by Sir D. Le Marchant.

6 Cavendish Deb. i. 191.

dividing the spoil amongst its members. They all fearlessly took the bribery oath; as the bargain had been made by a committee of their club, who abstained from voting; and the money was not distributed till after the election. But the returning officer, having been himself a member of the society, and knowing all the electors who belonged to it, had rejected their votes. This case was too gross to be lightly treated; and an act was passed to disfranchise the members of the club, eighty-one in number, and to admit to the franchise, all the forty shilling freeholders of the Rape of Bramber. An address was also voted to prosecute the five members of the committee, for a corrupt conspiracy.[1]

Hindon and Shaftesbury cases.

In 1775, bribery was proved to have prevailed so widely and shamelessly at Hindon, that an election committee recommended the disfranchisement of the borough;[2] and at Shaftesbury the same abuse was no less notorious.[3]

Cricklade case, 1782.

In 1782, the universal corruption of the electors of Cricklade was exposed before an election committee. It appeared that out of two hundred and forty voters, eighty-three had already been convicted of bribery; and that actions were pending against forty-three others.[4] A bill was accordingly brought in, to extend the franchise to all the freeholders of the adjoining hundreds. Even this moderate measure encountered much opposition, — especially in the Lords, where Lord Mansfield and Lord Chancellor Thurlow fought stoutly for the corrupt electors. Though the bill did not seek to disfranchise a single person, it was termed a bill of pains and penalties, and counsel were heard against it. But the cause of the electors, even with such supporters, was too bad to be defended; and the bill was passed.[5]

1 Com. Journ. xxxiii. 69, 102, 179; 11 Geo. III. c. 55.
2 Com. Journ. xxxv. 118.
3 *Ibid.* 311.
4 Parl. Hist. xxii. 1027, 1167, 1388.
5 22 Geo. III. c. 31.

There can be little doubt that the king himself was cognizant of the bribery which, at this period, was systematically used to secure Parliamentary support. Nay, more, he personally advised and recommended it. Writing to Lord North, 16th October, 1779, he said: "If the Duke of Northumberland requires some gold pills for the election, it would be wrong not to satisfy him."[1]

Bribery encouraged by the King.

When the disgraceful traffic in boroughs was exposed in the House of Commons, before the general election of 1768, Alderman Beckford brought in a bill requiring an oath to be taken by every member, that he had not been concerned in any bribery. According to Horace Walpole, the country gentlemen were favorable to this bill, as a protection against "great lords, Nabobs, commissaries, and West Indians;"[2] but the extreme stringency of the oath proposed, — which, it was urged, would result in perjury, — a jealousy lest, under some of the provisions of the bill, the privileges of the House should be submitted to the courts of law, — but above all, a disinclination to deal hardly with practices, which all had been concerned in, had profited by, or connived at, — ultimately secured its rejection.

Attempts to restrain corruption.

Again, in 1782 and 1783, Lord Mahon proposed bills to prevent bribery and expenses at elections; but on both occasions was unsuccessful. The same evil practices continued, — unchecked by legislation, connived at by statesmen, and tolerated by public opinion.

The system of purchasing seats in the House of Commons, however indefensible in principle, was at least preferable to the general corruption of electors, and in some respects, to the more prevalent practice of nomination. To buy a seat in Parliament was often the only means, by which an independent member could gain

Sale of seats: its uses.

1 King's Letters to Lord North; Lord Brougham's Works, iii. 137, 138.

2 Walpole's Mem. iii. 153, 157, 159.

admission to the House of Commons. If he accepted a seat from a patron, his independence was compromised; but if he acquired a seat by purchase, he was free to vote according to his own opinions and conscience. Thus, we find Sir Samuel Romilly, — the most pure and virtuous of public men, — who had declined one seat from the favor of the Prince of Wales,[1] justifying the purchase of another, for the sake of his own independence, and the public interests. Writing in September, 1805, he says: "As long as burgage-tenure representatives are only of two descriptions, — they who buy their seats, and they who discharge the most sacred of trusts at the pleasure, and almost as the servants of another, — surely there can be no doubt in which class a man would choose to enroll himself; and one who should carry his notions of purity so far, that, thinking he possessed the means of rendering service to his country, he would yet rather seclude himself altogether from Parliament, than get into it by such a violation of the theory of the constitution, must be under the dominion of a species of moral superstition which must wholly disqualify him for the discharge of any public duties."[2]

The extent to which the sale of seats prevailed, and its influence over the composition of the House of Commons, may also be exemplified from the Diary of Sir Samuel Romilly, in 1807: "Tierney, who manages this business for the friends of the late administration, assures me that he can hear of no seats to be disposed of. After a Parliament which had lived little more than four months, one would naturally suppose that those seats which are regularly sold by the proprietors of them, would be very cheap: they are, however, in fact, sold now at a higher price than was ever given for them before. Tierney tells me that he has offered 10,000*l.* for the two seats of Westbury, the property of the late Lord Abingdon, and which are to be made the most of

[1] Romilly's Life, ii. 114–120.
[2] Diary; Life, ii. 122.

by trustees for creditors, and has met with a refusal. 6000*l.* and 5500*l.* have been given for seats, with no stipulation as to time, or against the event of a speedy dissolution by the king's death, or by any change of administration. The truth is, that the new ministers have bought up all the seats that were to be disposed of, and at any prices. Amongst others, Sir C. H——, the great dealer in boroughs, has sold all he had to ministers. With what money all this is done I know not, but it is supposed that the king, who has greatly at heart to preserve this new administration, the favorite objects of his choice, has advanced a very large sum out of his privy purse.

"This buying of seats is detestable; and yet it is almost the only way in which one in my situation, who is resolved to be an independent man, can get into Parliament. To come in by a popular election, in the present state of the representation, is quite impossible; to be placed there by some great lord, and to vote as he shall direct, is to be in a state of complete dependence; and nothing hardly remains but to owe a seat to the sacrifice of a part of one's fortune. It is true, that many men who buy seats do it as a matter of pecuniary speculation, as a profitable way of employing their money: they carry on a political trade; they buy their seats and sell their votes."[1] He afterwards bought his seat for Horsham of the Duke of Norfolk, for 2000*l.*

Annual rents for seats in Parliament.

So regular was the market for seats, that where it was inconvenient to candidates to pay down the purchase-money, they were accommodated by its commutation into an annual rent. It was the sole redeeming quality of this traffic, that boroughs were generally disposed of to persons professing the same political opinions as the proprietors.[2]

The practice of selling and letting seats at last became so notorious, that it could no longer be openly tolerated by Parliament. In 1809, Mr. Curwen brought in a bill to pre-

[1] Life of Sir S. Romilly, ii. 200–201. [2] *Ibid.* 202.

vent the obtaining of seats in Parliament by corrupt practices, which after much discussion in both Houses, he succeeded in passing. It imposed heavy penalties upon corrupt agreements for the return of members, whether for money, office, or other consideration; and in the case of the person returned, added the forfeiture of his seat.[1]

Sale of seats restrained by Act, 1809.

But notwithstanding these penalties, the sale of seats, — if no longer so open and avowed, — continued to be carried on by private arrangement, so long as nomination boroughs were suffered to exist, as one of the anomalies of our representative system. The representation of Hastings, being vested in a close corporation, was regularly sold, until the reform act had enlarged the franchise, for 6000*l.*[2] And until 1832, an extensive sale of similar boroughs continued to be negotiated by the Secretary to the Treasury, by the "whippers-in" of the Opposition, and by proprietors and close corporations. So long as any boroughs remained, which could be bought and sold, the market was well supplied both with buyers and sellers.

This Act inoperative.

Boroughs whose members were nominated, as to an office, and boroughs bought in the open market, or corrupted by lavish bribery, could not pretend to popular election. The members for such places were independent of the people, whom they professed to represent. But there were populous places, thriving ports, and manufacturing towns, whence representatives, freely chosen, might have been expected to find their way into the House of Commons. But these very places were the favorite resort of the government candidates.

Government influence in larger boroughs.

The seven years' war had increased the national debt, and the taxation of the country. The number of officers employed in the collection of the revenue, was consequently augmented. Being the servants of the government, their

[1] 49 Geo. III. c. 118; Hansard's Deb. xiv. 354, 617, 837, 1032, &c.

[2] From private information.

votes were secured for the ministerial candidates. It was quite understood to be a part of their duty, to vote for any candidate who hoisted the colors of the minister of the day. Wherever they were most needed by the government, their number was the greatest. The smaller boroughs were already secured by purchase, or overwhelming local interest; but the cities and ports had some pretensions to independence. Here, however, troops of petty officers of customs and excise were driven to the poll, and, — supported by venal freemen, — overpowered the independent electors.

Revenue officers disfranchised.

In 1768, Mr. Dowdeswell had in vain endeavored to insert a clause in Alderman Beckford's bribery bill, for the disqualification of revenue officers. In 1770 he proposed a bill to disqualify these officers from voting at elections, and was supported by Mr. Grenville. It was urged, however, that they were already prohibited from interfering at elections, though not from voting; and that no further restraint could reasonably be required. But, in truth, the ministry of Lord North were little disposed to surrender so important a source of influence; and the bill was accordingly rejected.[1]

The measure, however, was merely postponed for a time. The dangerous policy of the Court, under Lord North, — and its struggle to rule by prerogative and influence, — convinced all liberal statesmen, of the necessity of protecting public liberty, by more effectual safeguards. Meanwhile the disastrous American war further aggravated the evils of taxes, and tax-collectors.

In 1780, a bill to disqualify revenue officers was proposed by Mr. Crewe, and though rejected on the second reading, it met with much more support than Mr. Dowdeswell's previous measure.[2] It was again brought forward in 1781, with less success than in the previous year.[3] But the time was now

[1] By a majority of 263 to 188; Parl. Hist. xvi. 834; Cavendish Deb. i. 442.
[2] The numbers were 224 to 195; Parl. Hist. xxi. 403.
[3] The numbers being 133 to 86; Parl. Hist. xxi. 1398.

at hand, when a determined assault was contemplated upon the influence of the Crown; and in 1782, the disqualification of revenue officers, — which had hitherto been an opposition measure, — was proposed by the ministry of Lord Rockingham. Its imperative necessity was proved by Lord Rockingham himself, who stated that seventy elections chiefly depended on the votes of these officers; and that eleven thousand five hundred officers of customs and excise were electors.[1] In one borough, he said that one hundred and twenty out of the five hundred voters, had obtained revenue appointments, through the influence of a single person.

This necessary measure was now carried through both Houses, by large majorities, though not without remonstrances against its principle, especially from Lord Mansfield. It is not to be denied that the disqualification of any class of men is, abstractedly, opposed to liberty, and an illiberal principle of legislation; but here was a gross constitutional abuse requiring correction; and though many voters were deprived of the rights of citizenship, — these rights could not be freely exercised, and were sacrificed in order to protect the general liberties of the people. Had there been a franchise so extensive as to leave the general body of electors free to vote, without being overborne by the servants of the Crown, it would have been difficult to justify the policy of disfranchisement. But with a franchise so restricted that the electors were controlled by the Crown, in the choice of their representatives, the measure was necessary in the interests of freedom.

Vexatious contests in populous cities.

Such being the dependence and corruption of the smaller boroughs, — and such the government influence in many of the larger towns, — there were still a few great cities, with popular rights of election, whose inhabitants neither landowners nor government could control, and which were beyond the influence of corruption. Here, at least, there might have been a free expression of

[1] June 3d, 1782; Parl. Hist. xxii. 95.

public opinion. But such were the vices of the laws which formerly regulated elections, — laws not designed for the protection of the franchise, — that a popular candidate, with a majority of votes, might be met by obstacles so vexatious and oppressive, as to debar him from the free suffrage of the electors. If not defeated at the poll, by riots and open violence, — or defrauded of his votes, by the partiality of the returning officer, or the factious manœuvres of his opponents, — he was ruined by the extravagant costs of his victory. The poll was liable to be kept open for forty days, entailing an enormous expense upon the candidates, and prolific of bribery, treating, and riots. During this period, the public-houses were thrown open; and drunkenness and disorder prevailed in the streets, and at the hustings. Bands of hired ruffians, — armed with bludgeons, and inflamed by drink, — paraded the public thoroughfares, intimidating voters, and resisting their access to the polling places. Candidates assailed with offensive, and often dangerous missiles, braved the penalties of the pillory; while their supporters were exposed to the fury of a drunken mob. Even now, a contested election, which lasts but a day, is often a reproach to a civilized people. What then must it have been before any of its worst vices had been controlled, and when it continued for upwards of a month?

Westminster election, 1784.

The most conspicuous example of all the abuses of which the old electoral system was capable, was that of the Westminster election, in 1784. Mr. Fox had incurred the violent resentment of the government, by his recent opposition to Mr. Pitt, and the Court party. It had been determined, that all the members who had supported the Coalition should be opposed, at the general election; and Mr. Fox, their ablest leader, was the foremost man to be assailed. The election, — disgraced throughout by scenes of drunkenness, tumult, and violence,[1] — and by the coarsest

[1] In one of the brawls which arose during its progress, a man was killed, whose death was charged against persons belonging to Mr. Fox's party, but they were all acquitted.

libels and lampoons, — was continued for forty days. When the poll was closed, Mr. Fox was in a majority of two hundred and thirty-six above Sir Cecil Wray, one of the Court candidates. But he was now robbed of the fruits of his victory by the High Bailiff; who withheld his return, and commenced a scrutiny into the votes. By withholding the return, after the day on which the writ was returnable, he denied the successful candidate his right to sit in Parliament; and anticipated the jurisdiction of the House of Commons, by which court alone, the validity of the election could then properly be determined. This unwarrantable proceeding would have excluded Mr. Fox from his rightful place in Parliament; but he had already been returned for Kirkwall, and took his seat, at the commencement of the session.

Apart from the vexation and injustice to which Mr. Fox had been exposed, the expense of the scrutiny was estimated at 18,000*l.* In vain his friends endeavored to induce the House of Commons to order the High Bailiff to make an immediate return. That officer was upheld by Mr. Pitt, who was followed, at first, by a large majority. Mr. Fox, in his bitterness, exclaimed: "I have no reason to expect indulgence: nor do I know that I shall meet with bare justice in this House." As no return had been made, which could be submitted to the adjudication of an election committee, Mr. Fox was at the mercy of a hostile majority of the House. The High Bailiff was, indeed, directed to proceed with the scrutiny with all practicable despatch; but at the commencement of the following session, — when the scrutiny had been proceeding for eight months, — it had only been completed in a single parish; and had but slightly affected the relative position of the candidates. Notwithstanding this exposure of the monstrous injustice of the scrutiny, Mr. Pitt still resisted a motion for directing the High Bailiff to make an immediate return. But, — blindly as he had hitherto been followed, — such was the iniquity of the cause which he persisted in supporting, that all his influence failed in commanding a larger majority than nine; and on the 3d of March, he was defeated by a majority of thirty-eight.[1] The minister was justly punished for his ungenerous conduct to an opponent, and for his contempt of the law, — prompted, to use the words of Mr. Fox, by "the malignant wish of gratifying an inordinate and implacable spirit of resentment."[2] But a system which had thus placed a popular candidate, — in one of the first cities of the kingdom, — at the mercy of factious violence, and ministerial oppression, was a flagrant outrage upon the principles of freedom. Parliament further marked its reprobation of such proceedings, by limiting every poll to fifteen days, and closing a scrutiny six days before the day on which the writ was returnable.[3]

Territorial influence in counties.

In the counties, the franchise was more free and liberal, than in the majority of cities and boroughs. All forty-shilling freeholders were entitled to vote; and in this class were comprised the country gentlemen, and independent yeomanry of England. Hence the county constituencies were at once the most numerous, the most responsible, and the least corrupt. They represented public opinion more faithfully than other electoral bodies; and on many occasions, had great weight in advancing a popular cause. Such were their respectability and public spirit, that most of the earlier schemes of Parliamentary reform contemplated the disfranchisement of boroughs, and the simple addition of members to the counties. But notwithstanding their unquestionable merits, the county electors were peculiarly exposed to the influence of the great nobles, who held nearly a feudal sway. Illustrious ancestry, vast possessions, high offices, distinguished political services and connections, placed them at the head of the society of their

[1] By 162 against 124; Ann. Reg., 1784, xxvii. 180; Adolphus's Hist. iv. 115–118, 168.

[2] Parl. Hist. xxiv. 808, 843, 846; *ibid.* xxv. 3; Tomline's Life of Pitt, i. 542; ii. 7, 24, &c.; Lord J. Russell's Life of Fox, ii. 99.

[3] 25 Geo. III. c. 84.

several counties; and local influence, and the innate respect for aristocracy which animates the English people, combined to make them the political leaders of the gentry and yeomanry. In some counties, powerful commoners were no less dominant. The greater number of the counties in England and Wales were represented by members of these families, or by gentlemen enjoying their confidence and patronage.[1]

A contested election was more often due to the rivalry of great houses, than to the conflict of political principles among the electors; but, as the candidates generally belonged to opposite parties, their contentions produced political discussion and enlightenment. Such contests were conducted with the spirit and vigor which rivalry inspires, and with an extravagance which none but princely fortunes could support. They were like the wars of small states. In 1768, the Duke of Portland is said to have spent 40,000*l.* in contesting Westmoreland and Cumberland with Sir James Lowther; who, on his side, must have spent at least as much.[2] And, within the memory of some men still living, an election for the county of York has been known to cost nearly 150,000*l.*[3]

Representation of Scotland.

Great as were the defects of the representation of England, — those of Scotland were greater, and of more general operation. The county franchise consisted in "superiorities," which were bought and sold in the market, and were enjoyed independently of property or residence. The burgh franchise was vested in self-elected town-councillors. The constituencies, therefore, represented neither population nor property; but the narrowest local interests. It was shown in 1823, that the total number of persons enjoying the franchise was less than three thousand. In no county did the number of electors exceed two hundred and forty: in one it was as low as nine; and of this small number, a considerable propor-

1 Oldfield's Representative Hist. vi. 285.

2 Walpole's Mem. iii. 197.

3 Speech of Lord J. Russell, March 1st, 1831; Hansard's Deb., 3d Ser., ii. 1074.

tion were fictitious voters, — without property, and not even resident in the country.[1]

In 1831, the total number of county voters did not exceed two thousand five hundred; and the constituencies of the sixty-six boroughs, amounted to one thousand four hundred and forty. Thus the entire electoral body of Scotland was not more than four thousand. The county of Argyll, with a population of one hundred thousand, had but one hundred and fifteen electors, of whom eighty-four were out-voters, without any land within the county. Caithness, with thirty thousand inhabitants, contained forty-seven freeholders, of whom thirty-six were out-voters. Inverness-shire, with ninety thousand inhabitants, had but eighty-eight freeholders, of whom fifty were out-voters. Edinburgh and Glasgow, the two first cities of Scotland, had each a constituency of thirty-three persons.[2]

With a franchise so limited and partial as this, all the counties and burghs, without exception, had fallen under the influence of political patrons.[3] A great kingdom, with more than two millions of people, — intelligent, instructed, industrious, and peaceable, — was virtually disfranchised. Meanwhile, the potentates who returned the members to Parliament, — instead of contending among themselves, like their brethren in England, and joining opposite parties, — were generally disposed to make their terms with the ministers; and by skilful management, the entire representation was engrossed by the friends and agents of the government. It was not secured, however, without a profuse distribution of patronage, which, judiciously administered, had long retained the allegiance of members coming from the north of the Tweed.[4]

[1] Hansard's Deb., 2d Ser., ix. 611.

[2] Speech of Lord Advocate, Sept. 23d, 1831; Hansard's Deb., 3d Ser., vii. 529.

[3] Oldfield's Representative Hist. vi. 294; Edinburgh Review, Oct. 1830, Art. X.

[4] It was said of one Scotch county member, "that his invariable rule was never to be present at a debate, or absent at a division; and that he had

Lord Cockburn, a contemporary witness, — has given a spirited account of the mode in which elections in Scotland were conducted. He says: "The return of a single opposition member was never to be expected. . . . The return of three or four was miraculous, and these startling exceptions were always the result of local accidents. . . . Whatever this system may have been originally, it had grown, in reference to the people, into as complete a mockery, as if it had been invented for their degradation. The people had nothing to do with it. It was all managed by town-councils, of never more than thirty-three members; and every town-council was self-elected, and consequently perpetuated its own interests. The election of either the town or the county member, was a matter of such utter indifference to the people, that they often only knew of it by the ringing of a bell, or by seeing it mentioned next day in a newspaper; for the farce was generally performed in an apartment from which, if convenient, the public could be excluded, and never in the open air." [1]

Where there were districts of burghs, each town-council elected a delegate, and the four or five delegates elected the member; "and, instead of bribing the town-councils, the established practice was to bribe only the delegates, or indeed only one of them, if this could secure the majority." [2]

A case of inconceivable grotesqueness was related by the Lord Advocate, in 1831. The county of Bute, with a population of fourteen thousand, had twenty-one electors, of whom *one* only resided in the county. "At an election at Bute, not beyond the memory of man, only one person attended the meeting, except the Sheriff and the returning officer. He, of course, took the chair, constituted the meeting, called over the roll of freeholders, answered to his own

only once, in his long political life, ventured to vote according to his conscience, and that he found on that occasion he had voted wrong." — Hansard's Deb., 3d Ser., vii. 543.

[1] Life of Jeffrey, i. 75.

[2] Cockburn's Mem. i. 88.

name, took the vote as to the Preses, and elected himself. He then moved and seconded his own nomination, put the question as to the vote, and was unanimously returned." [1]

This close system of elections had existed even before the Union; but though sufficiently notorious, the British Parliament had paid little attention to its defects.

Motions by Lord Archibald Hamilton, 1818, 1823.

In 1818, and again in 1823, Lord Archibald Hamilton had shown the state of the Royal Burghs, — the self-election, and irresponsibility of the councillors, — and their uncontrolled authority over the local funds. The questions then raised referred to municipal rather than parliamentary reform; but the latter came incidentally under review, and it was admitted that there was "no popular election, or pretence of popular election." [2] In 1823, Lord Archibald exposed the state of the county representation, and the general electoral system of the country, and found one hundred and seventeen supporters.[3]

Representation of Edinburgh, 1826.

In 1824, the question of Scotch representation was brought forward by Mr. Abercromby. The inhabitants of Edinburgh complained, by petition,[4] that the representation of this capital city, — the metropolis of the North, with upwards of one hundred thousand inhabitants, — was returned by thirty-three electors, of whom nineteen had been chosen by their predecessors in the town-council! Mr. Abercromby moved for leave to bring in a Bill to amend the representation of that city, — as an instalment of Parliamentary reform in Scotland. His motion failed, and being renewed in 1826, was equally unsuccessful. Such proposals were always met in the same manner. When general measures of reform were advocated, the mag-

1 Hansard's Deb., 3d Ser., vii. 529.

2 Sir J. Mackintosh; Hansard's Deb., 1st Ser., xxxvii. 434; *Ibid.*, 2d Ser., viii. 735.

3 Hansard's Deb., 2d Ser., ix. 611.

4 This petition had been presented May 5th, 1823, drawn up by Mr. Jeffrey, and signed by 7000 out of the 10,000 householders of the city. — *Cockburn's Mem.* 404.

nitude of the change was urged as the reason for rejecting them; and when, to obviate such objections, the correction of any particular defect was attempted, its exceptional character was a decisive argument against it.[1]

Representation of Ireland.

Prior to 1801, the British Parliament was not concerned in the state of the representation of the people of Ireland. But on the union of that country, the defects of its representation were added to those of England and Scotland, in the constitution of the united Parliament. The counties and boroughs in Ireland were at least as much under the influence of great patrons, as in England. It is true, that in arranging the terms of the Union, Mr. Pitt took the opportunity of abolishing several of the smaller nomination boroughs; but many were spared, which were scarcely less under the patronage of noblemen and landowners; and places of more consideration were reduced, by restricted rights of election, to a similar dependence. In Belfast, in Carlow, in Wexford, and in Sligo, the right of election was vested in twelve self-elected burgesses: in Limerick and Kilkenny, it was in the corporation and freemen. In the counties, the influence of the territorial families was equally dominant. For the sake of political influence, the landowners had subdivided their estates into a prodigious number of forty-shilling freeholds; and until the freeholders had fallen under the dominion of the priests, they were faithful to their Protestant patrons. According to the law of Ireland, freeholds were created without the possession of property; and the votes of the freeholders were considered as the absolute right of the proprietor of the soil. Hence it was, that after the Union more than two thirds of the Irish members were returned, not by the people of Ireland, but by about fifty or sixty influential patrons.[2]

1 Hansard's Deb., 2d Ser., x. 455; *Ibid.* xiv. 107; *Ibid.* xv. 163.

2 Wakefield's Statistical and Political Account of Ireland, ii. 299, *et seq.*; Oldfield's Representative Hist. vi. 209–280.

Majority of the members nominated.

Such being the state of the representation in the United Kingdom, an actual majority of the members of the House of Commons, were returned by an inconsiderable number of persons. According to a statement made by the Duke of Richmond in 1780, not more than six thousand men returned a clear majority of the House of Commons.[1] It was alleged in the petition of the Society of the Friends of the People, presented by Mr. Grey in 1793, that eighty-four individuals absolutely returned one hundred and fifty-seven members to Parliament; that seventy influential men secured the return of one hundred and fifty members; and that, in this manner, three hundred and seven members, — being the majority of the House, before the union with Ireland, — were returned to Parliament by one hundred and fifty-four patrons; of whom forty were peers.[2] In 1821, Mr. Lambton stated that he was prepared to prove by evidence, at the bar of the House of Commons, "that one hundred and eighty individuals returned, by nomination or otherwise, three hundred and fifty members."[3]

Dr. Oldfield's Representative History furnishes still more elaborate statistics of parliamentary patronage. According to his detailed statements, no less than two hundred and eighteen members were returned for counties and boroughs, in England and Wales, by the nomination or influence of eighty-seven peers; one hundred and thirty-seven were returned by ninety commoners, and sixteen by the Government; making a total number of three hundred and seventy-one nominee members. Of the forty-five members for Scotland, thirty-one were returned by twenty-one peers, and the remainder by fourteen commoners. Of the hundred members for Ire-

1 Parl. Hist. xxi. 686.

2 *Ibid.* xxx. 787.

3 Hansard's Deb., 2d Ser., v. 359. Writing in 1821, Sydney Smith says: "The country belongs to the Duke of Rutland, Lord Lonsdale, the Duke of Newcastle, and about twenty other holders of boroughs. They are our masters." —*Mem.* ii. 215.

land, fifty-one were returned by thirty-six peers, and twenty by nineteen commoners. The general result of these surprising statements is, — that of the six hundred and fifty-eight members of the House of Commons, four hundred and eighty-seven were returned by nomination ; and one hundred and seventy-one only were representatives of independent constituencies.[1] Such matters did not admit of proof, and were beyond the scope of Parliamentary inquiries : but after making allowances for imperfect evidence and exaggeration, we are unable to resist the conclusion, that not more than one third of the House of Commons, were the free choice even of the limited bodies of electors then intrusted with the franchise.

Injustice in the trial of election petitions.

Scandalous as were the electoral abuses which law and custom formerly permitted, the conduct of the House of Commons, in the trial of election petitions, was more scandalous still. Boroughs were bought and sold, — electors were notoriously bribed by wholesale and retail, — returning officers were partial and corrupt. But, in defiance of all justice and decency, the majority of the House of Commons connived at these practices, when committed by their own party ; and only condemned them, when their political opponents were put upon their trial. *Dat veniam corvis, — vexat censura columbas.* The Commons having, for the sake of their own independence, insisted upon an exclusive jurisdiction in matters of election, were not ashamed to prostitute it to party. They were charged with a grave trust, and abused it. They assumed a judicial office, and dishonored it. This discreditable perversion of justice had grown up with those electoral abuses, which an honest judicature would have tended to correct ; and reached its greatest excesses, in the reigns of George II. and George III.

Originally, controverted elections had been tried by select committees specially nominated, and afterwards by the Com-

[1] Oldfield's Representative Hist. 1816, vi. 285–300.

mittee of Privileges and Elections. This latter committee had been nominated by the House itself, being composed of Privy Councillors and eminent lawyers, well qualified by their learning, for the judicial inquiries intrusted to them. In 1603, it comprised the names of Sir Francis Bacon and Sir Thomas Fleming;[1] in 1623, the names of Sir Edward Coke, Sir Heneage Finch, Mr. Pym, Mr. Glanville, Sir Roger North, and Mr. Selden.[2] The committee was then confined to the members nominated by the House itself;[3] but being afterwards enlarged by the introduction of all Privy Councillors and Gentlemen of the Long Robe, it became, after 1672, an open committee, in which all who came were allowed to have voices. This committee was henceforth exposed to all the evils of large and fluctuating numbers, and an irresponsible constitution; and at length, in the time of Mr. Speaker Onslow, a hearing at the bar of the House itself, — which in special cases had already been occasionally resorted to, — was deemed preferable to the less public and responsible judicature of the committee. Here, however, the partiality and injustice of the judges were soon notorious. The merits of the election, on which they affected to adjudicate, were little regarded. To use the words of Mr. Grenville, "The Court was thin to hear, and full to judge."[4] Parties tried their strength, — the friends of rival candidates canvassed and manœuvred, — and seats corruptly gained, were as corruptly protected, or voted away. The right of election was wrested from the voters, and usurped by the elected body, who thus exercised a vicious self-election. The ministers of the day, when they commanded a majority, sustained their own friends; and brought all their forces to bear against the members of the Opposition. This flagitious cus-

[1] Com. Journ. i. 149 (March 23d, 1603). There are earlier appointments in D'Ewes' Journal.

[2] Com. Journ. i. 716; Glanville's Rep., Pref., vii.

[3] Com. Journ. i. 716; Cavendish Deb. i. 508.

[4] This had been previously said of the House of Lords, by the Duke of Argyll.

tom formed part of the parliamentary organization, by which the influence of the Crown and its ministers, was maintained. It was not until a government was falling, that its friends were in danger of losing their seats. The struggle between Sir Robert Walpole and his enemies was determined in 1741, — not upon any question of public policy, — but by the defeat of the minister on the Chippenham Election Petition.

The Grenville Act, 1770

To remedy these evils, and remove the opprobrium of notorious injustice from the House of Commons, Mr. Grenville introduced in 1770, his celebrated measure, — since known as the Grenville Act, and a landmark in Parliamentary history. He proposed to transfer the judicature, in election cases, from the House itself, to a committee of thirteen members, selected by the sitting members and petitioners from a list of forty-nine, chosen by ballot, — to whom each party should add a nominee, to advocate their respective interests. This tribunal, constituted by Act of Parliament, was to decide, without appeal, the merits of every controverted election: being, in fact, a court independent of the House, though composed of its own members.[1] The main objection urged against this measure was that the privileges of the House were compromised, and its discretion limited, by the binding obligations of a statute. It is certain that much might have been done by authority of the House itself, which was henceforth regulated by statute, — the only legal power required, being that of administering an oath. But Mr. Grenville distrusted the House of Commons, and saw no security for the permanence, or honest trial of the new system, except in a law which they could not set aside.

This Act was at first limited to one year; and Horace Walpole insinuates that Mr. Grenville, when in opposition, was willing "to give a sore wound to the influence of the Crown;" but hoping to return to office, took care not to

[1] Parl. Hist. xvi. 904–923; Cavendish Deb. i. 476, 505.

weaken his own future power as a minister.[1] But the suggestion for making the Act temporary proceeded from Lord Clare,[2] and not from Mr. Grenville, who was honestly persuaded that the "system must end in the ruin of public liberty, if not checked."[3] At this time his health and spirits were failing; and he died a few months after the passing of his measure.

Made perpetual.

The Grenville Act was continued from time to time; and in 1774, Sir Edwin Sandys brought in a bill to make it perpetual. It encountered a strong opposition, especially from Mr. Fox, who dreaded the surrender of the privileges of the House; but the successful operation of the Act, in the five cases which had already been tried under its provisions, was so generally acknowledged, that the bill was passed by a large majority.[4] "This happy event," wrote Lord Chatham, "is a dawn of better times: it is the last prop of Parliament: should it be lost in its passage, the legislature will fall into incurable contempt, and detestation of the nation." "The Act does honor to the statute-book, and will endear forever the memory of the framer."[5]

This Act was passed on the eve of another general election, which does not appear — so far as evidence is accessible — to have been marked by so much corruption as that of 1768. But the value of boroughs had certainly not declined in the market, as Gatton was sold for 75,000*l.*[6]

Its imperfect success.

For a time this measure undoubtedly introduced a marked improvement in the judicature of the House of Commons. The disruption of the usual party combinations, at that period, was favorable to its success; and the exposure of former abuses discouraged their immediate renewal, in another form. But too soon it became

1 Walp. Mem. Geo. III. ii. 384, *n.*

2 Cavendish Deb. i. 513.

3 Hatsell's Prec. ii. 21.

4 250 to 122; Parl. Hist. xvii. 1071; Fox Mem. i. 95, 133.

5 Letter to Lord Shelburne, March 6th, 1774; Corresp. iv. 333.

6 Lord Mahon's Hist. vi. 27.

evident, that corruption and party spirit had not been overcome.[1] Crowds now attended the ballot, as they had previously come to the vote, — not to secure justice, but to further political interests. The party which attended in the greatest force, was likely to have the numerical majority of names, drawn for the committee. From this list each side proceeded to strike thirteen of its political opponents; and the strongest thus secured a preponderance on the committee. Nor was this all. The ablest men, being most feared by their opponents, were almost invariably struck off, — a process familiarly known as "knocking the brains out of the committee;" and thus the committee became at once partial and incompetent. The members of the committee were sworn to do justice between the rival candidates; yet the circumstances under which they were notoriously chosen, their own party bias, and a lax conventional morality, — favored by the obscurity and inconsistencies of the election law, and by the conflicting decisions of incapable tribunals, — led to this equivocal result: — that right was generally discovered to be on the side of that candidate, who professed the same political opinions as the majority of the committee.[2] A Whig candidate had scant justice from a Tory committee; a Tory candidate pleaded in vain before a Whig committee.

Improved constitution of election committees.

By these means, the majority of the House continued, — with less directness and certainty, and perhaps with less open scandal, — to nominate their own members, as they had done before the Grenville Act. And for half a century, this system, with slight variations of procedure, was suffered to prevail. In 1839, however, the ballot was at length superseded by Sir Robert Peel's Act:[3] committees were reduced to six members, and nominated by an impartial body, — the general committee

[1] Walpole's Mem. iv. 111 and *n.*

[2] These evils were ably exposed in the Report of the Committee on Controverted Elections (Mr. C. Buller), 1837–38, No. 44.

[3] 2 & 3 Vict. c. 38; Hansard's Deb., 3d Ser., xlv. 379; *ibid.* xlvii. 576, &c.

of elections. The same principle of selection has since been adhered to in later Acts, with additional securities for impartiality; and the committee has been finally reduced to five members.[1] The evil was thus greatly diminished; but still the sinister influence of party was not wholly overcome. In the nomination of election committees, one party or the other has necessarily had a majority of one; and though these tribunals have since been more able and judicial, their constitution and proceedings have too often exposed them to imputations of political bias.

Distribution of places and pensions.

Such being the vices and defects of the electoral system, — what were their results upon the House of Commons? Representatives holding their seats by a general system of corruption, could scarcely fail to be themselves corrupt. What they had bought, they were but too ready to sell. And how glittering the prizes offered as the price of their services! Peerages, baronetcies, and other titles of honor; patronage and court favor for the rich, — places, pensions, and bribes for the needy. All that the government had to bestow, they could command. The rapid increase of honors[2] attests the liberality with which political services were rewarded; while contemporary memoirs and correspondence disclose the arts, by which many a peerage has been won.

Restrained by Parliament.

From the period of the Revolution, places and pensions have been regarded as the price of political dependence; and it has since been the steady policy of Parliament to restrain the number of placemen, entitled to sit in the House of Commons. To William III. fell the task of first working out the difficult problem of a constitutional government; and amongst his expedients for controlling his Parliaments, was that of a multiplication of offices. The country party at once perceived the danger with which

[1] 4 & 5 Vict. c. 58, and 11 & 12 Vict. c. 98; Report on Controverted Elections, 1844, No. 373.

[2] See *supra*, p. 224, 260.

their newly-bought liberties were threatened from this cause, and endeavored to avert it. In 1693, the Commons passed a bill to prohibit all members hereafter chosen from accepting any office under the Crown; but the Lords rejected it. In the following year it was renewed, and agreed to by both Houses; when the king refused his assent to it. Later in his reign, however, this principle of disqualification was commenced, — the Commissioners of Revenue Boards being the first to whom it was applied.[1] And at last, in 1700, it was enacted that after the accession of the House of Hanover, "no person who has an office or place of profit under the king, or receives a pension from the Crown, shall be capable of serving as a member of the House of Commons."[2] This too stringent provision, however, was repealed, — before it came into operation,[3] — early in the reign of Anne. It was, indeed, incompatible with the working of constitutional government; and if practically enforced, would have brought Parliament into hopeless conflict with the executive.

Acts of Anne, George I., and II.

By the Act of Settlement of that reign, other restrictions were introduced, far better adapted to correct the evils of corrupt influence. The holder of every new office created after the 25th of October, 1705, and every one enjoying a pension from the Crown, during pleasure, was incapacitated from sitting in Parliament; and members of the House of Commons accepting any old office from the Crown, were obliged to vacate their seats, though capable of reëlection.[4] It was the object of this latter provision to submit the acceptance of office by a representative, to the approval of his constituents; a principle which, — notwithstanding several attempts to modify it, — has since been resolutely maintained by the legislature. Restrictions were also imposed upon the multiplication of commissioners.[5]

[1] 4 & 8 Will. & Mary, c. 21 (Stamps); 11 & 12 Will. III. c. 2 (Excise).
[2] 12 & 13 Will. III. c. 2, s. 3.
[3] 4 Anne, c. 8, s. 25.
[4] 4 Anne, c. 8.
[5] 6 Anne, c. 7.

At the commencement of the following reign, incapacity was extended to pensioners for terms of years;[1] but as many pensions were then secretly granted, the law could not be put in force. In the reign of George II. several attempts were made to enforce it; but they all miscarried.[2] Lord Halifax, in debating one of these bills, said that secret pensions were the worst form of bribery: "A bribe is given for a particular job; a pension is a constant, continual bribe."[3] Early in the reign of George III. Mr. Rose Fuller — who had been a stanch Whig, — was bought off by a secret pension of 500*l.* which he enjoyed for many years. The cause of his apostasy was not discovered till after his death.[4]

Secret Pensions.

Still the policy of restricting the number of offices capable of being held by members of the House of Commons, was steadily pursued. In 1742 the Place Bill, which had been thrice rejected by the Commons, and twice by the Lords, at length received the Royal assent.[5] It was stated in a Lords' protest, that two hundred appointments were then distributed amongst the members of the House of Commons.[6] This Act added many offices to the list of disqualifications, but chiefly those of clerks and other subordinate officers of the public departments.

The Place Bill of 1742.

By these measures the excessive multiplication of offices had been restrained; but in the reign of George III. their number was still very considerable; and they were used, — almost without disguise, — as the means of obtaining parliamentary support. Horace Walpole has preserved a good example of the unblushing manner, in which bargains were made for the votes of members,

Places in the reign of Geo. III.

1 1 Geo. I. c. 56.

2 No less than six bills were passed by the Commons, and rejected by the Lords; Parl. Hist. viii. 789; *ibid.* ix. 369; *ibid.* xi. 510; *ibid.* xii. 591.

3 Parl. Hist. xi. 522.

4 Almon's Corr. ii. 8; Rockingham Mem. i. 79, *n.*

5 15 Geo. II. c. 22.

6 Lords' Protest, 1741; Parl. Hist. xii. 2.

in exchange for offices. Mr. Grenville wrote him a letter, proposing to appoint his nephew, Lord Orford, to the rangership of St. James's and Hyde Parks. He said, "If he does choose it, I doubt not of his and his friend Boone's hearty assistance, and believe I shall see you, too, much oftener in the House of Commons. This is offering you a bribe, but 'tis such a one as one honest good-natured man may, without offence, offer to another." As Walpole did not receive this communication with much warmth, and declined any participation in the bargain, payments due to him on account of his patent-offices in the Exchequer, were stopped at the Treasury, for several months.[1]

Lord Rockingham's Act 1782.

The Whig statesmen of this period, who were striving to reduce the influence of the Crown, were keenly alive to the means of corruption which a multiplicity of places still afforded. "The great number of offices," said Lord Rockingham, "of more or less emolument, which are now tenable by parties sitting in Parliament, really operate like prizes in a lottery. An interested man purchases a seat, upon the same principle as a person buys a lottery-ticket. The value of the ticket depends upon the quantum of prizes in the wheel." [2] It was to remove this evil, even more than for the sake of pecuniary saving, that Mr. Burke, in 1780, proposed to abolish thirty-nine offices held by members of the House of Commons, and eleven held by peers. And by Lord Rockingham's Act for the regulation of the Civil List expenditure in 1782, several offices connected with the government and royal household were suppressed, which had generally been held by members of Parliament; and secret pensions were discontinued.[3]

Offices in Ireland.

In 1793, the Parliament of Ireland adopted the principles of the English act of Anne, and disqualified the holders of all offices under the Crown or Lord-

[1] Nov. 21st, 1762; Walpole's Mem. i. 213–216.
[2] Rockingham Mem. ii. 399.
[3] 22 Geo. III. c. 82, Wraxall's Mem. iii. 44, 50, 54. See also *supra*, 211.

Lieutenant, created after that time. On the union with Ireland, all the disqualifications for the Irish Parliament, were extended to the Parliament of the United Kingdom; and several new disqualifications were created, in reference to other Irish offices.[1]

Further disqualifications.

The general scheme of official disfranchisement was now complete: but the jealousy of Parliament was still shown by the disqualification of new officers appointed by Acts of Parliament. So constant has been this policy, that upwards of one hundred statutes, still in force, contain clauses of disqualification; and many similar statutes have been passed, which have since expired, or have been repealed.[2]

The result of this vigilant jealousy, has been a great reduction of the number of placemen sitting in the House of Commons. In the first Parliament of George I. there had been two hundred and seventy-one members holding offices, pensions, and sinecures. In the first Parliament of George II. there were two hundred and fifty-seven; in the first Parliament of George IV. there were but eighty-nine, exclusive of officers in the army and navy.[3] The number of placemen sitting in the House of Commons, has been further reduced by the abolition and consolidation of offices; and in 1833 there were only sixty members holding civil offices and pensions, exclusive of eighty-three holding naval and military commissions.[4]

Judicial officers disqualified.

The policy of disqualification has been maintained to the present time. The English judges had been excluded from the House of Commons, by the law of Parliament. In the interests of justice, as well as on grounds of constitutional policy, this exclusion was extended to their brethren of the Scottish bench, in the

[1] 41 Geo. III. c. 52.

[2] Author's Pamphlet on the Consolidation of the Election Laws, 1850.

[3] Report on Returns made by Members, 1822 (542); 1823 (569); Hansard, 3d Ser., ii. 1118, *n.*

[4] Report on Members in Office, 1833, No. 671.

reign of George II.,[1] and to the judges of the courts in Ireland, in the reign of George IV.[2] In 1840, the same principle was applied to the Judge of the Admiralty Court.[3] All the new judges in equity were disqualified by the Acts under which they were constituted. The solitary judge still enjoying the capacity of sitting in the House of Commons, is the Master of the Rolls. In 1853, a Bill was introduced to withdraw this exceptional privilege; but it was defeated by a masterly speech of Mr. Macaulay.[4]

Policy of disqualifications.

These various disqualifications were deemed necessary for securing the independence of Parliament; and the policy is still recognized, when the dangers they were designed to avert, are less to be apprehended. It is true that independence has been purchased at the cost of much intellectual eminence, which the House of Commons could ill afford to spare; but this sacrifice was due to constitutional freedom, and it has been wisely made.

Pecuniary bribes to members.

But the independence of Parliament was formerly corrupted by grosser expedients than places and pensions. Vulgar bribes were given, — directly and indirectly, — for political support. Our Parliamentary history has been tainted with this disgrace, from the reign of Charles II. far into that of George III. That Charles, himself unscrupulous and corrupt, should have resorted to bribery, is natural enough. His was a debased reign, in which all forms of corruption flourished.

Members were then first exposed to the temptation of pecuniary bribes. In the reigns of the Tudors and the first two Stuarts, prerogative had been too strong to need the aid of such persuasion; but after prerogative had been rudely shaken by the overthrow of Charles I., it was sought to sup-

1 7 Geo. II. c. 16.

2 1 & 2 Geo. IV. c. 44.

3 Much to the personal regret of all who were acquainted with that eminent man, Dr. Lushington, who lost the seat in which he had so long distinguished himself.

4 Judges' Exclusion Bill, June 1st, 1853; Hansard's Deb., 3d Ser., cxxvii. 996.

port the influence of the Crown, by the subtle arts of corruption. Votes which were no longer to be controlled by fear, were purchased with gold. James II., again, — secure of a servile Parliament, and bent upon ruling once more by prerogative, — disdained the meaner arts of bribery.[1]

The Revolution, however favorable to constitutional liberty, revived and extended this scandal; and the circumstances of the times unhappily favored its development. The prerogative of the Crown had been still further limited; the power and activity of Parliament being proportionately increased, while no means had yet been taken to insure its responsibility to the people. A majority of the House of Commons, — beyond the reach of public opinion, — not accountable to its constituencies, — and debating and voting with closed doors, — held the political destinies of England at its mercy. The Constitution had not yet provided worthier means of influence and restraint; and William III., though personally averse to the base practices of Charles II., was forced to permit their use. His reign, otherwise conducive to freedom and national greatness, was disgraceful to the character of the statesmen, and to the public virtue of that age.[2]

The practice of direct bribery notoriously continued in the three succeeding reigns; and if not proved by the records of Parliament, was attested by contemporary writers, and by the complaints openly made of its existence. Under the administration of Sir Robert Walpole, it was reduced to an organized system, by which a majority of the House of Commons was long retained in subjection to the minister.[3] It is true, that after his fall, his enemies failed in proving their charges

[1] Burnet's Own Time, i. 626.

[2] Parl. Hist. v. 807, 840; Burnet's Own Time, ii. 144, 145. See Lord Macaulay's instructive sketch of the Rise and Progress of Parliamentary Corruption, Hist. iii. 541, 687; *ibid.* iv. 146, 305, 427, 478, 545, and 551; Com. Journ. xi. 331, May 2d, 1695.

[3] Debates, Lords and Commons, 1741, on motions for the removal of Sir R. Walpole, Parl. Hist. xi. 1027–1303; Coxe's Mem. of Sir R. Walpole, i. 641, 719; Debates on appointment of Committee of Inquiry, Parl. Hist. xii. 448, *et seq.*

against him; but the entire strength of the court, the new ministry, and the House of Lords, was exerted to screen him. The witnesses refused to answer questions; and the Lords declined to pass a bill of indemnity, which would have removed the ground of their refusal.[1] Nor must it be overlooked that, however notorious corruption may be, it is of all things the most difficult of proof.

This system was continued by his successors, throughout the reign of George II.; and is believed to have been brought to perfection, under the administration of Mr. Henry Pelham.

Bribery under Lord Bute.

In approaching the reign of George III., it were well if no traces could be found of the continued existence of this system; but unhappily the early part of this reign presents some of its worst examples. Lord Bute, being resolved to maintain his power by the corrupt arts of Sir Robert Walpole, secured, by the promise of a peerage, the aid of Walpole's experienced agent, Mr. Henry Fox, in carrying them out with success.[2] The office intrusted to him was familiarly known as "the management of the House of Commons."

In October, 1762, Mr. Grenville had impressed upon Lord Bute the difficulties of carrying on the business of the House of Commons, "without being authorized to talk to the members of that House upon their several claims and pretensions."[3] And these difficulties were effectually overcome.

Horace Walpole relates a startling tale of the purchase of votes by Mr. Fox, in December, 1762, in support of Lord Bute's preliminaries of peace. He says, "A shop was publicly opened at the Pay Office, whither the members flocked, and received the wages of their venality in bank-bills, even to so low a sum as 200*l.* for their votes on the treaty. 25,000*l.*,

1 Report of Committee of Inquiry, 1742; Parl. Hist. xii. 626, 788; Coxe's Mem. of Sir R. Walpole, i. 711.

2 Rockingham Mem. i. 127.

3 Grenville Papers, i. 483.

as Martin, Secretary of the Treasury, afterwards owned, were issued in one morning; and in a single fortnight, a vast majority was purchased to approve the peace!"[1] Lord Stanhope, who is inclined wholly to reject this circumstantial story, admits that Mr. Fox was the least scrupulous of Walpole's pupils, and that the majority was otherwise unaccountable.[2] The account is probably exaggerated; but the character of Mr. Fox and his Parliamentary associates is not repugnant to its probability; nor does it stand alone. A suspicious circumstance, in confirmation of Horace Walpole, has been brought to light. Among Mr. Grenville's papers has been preserved a statement of the secret-service money from 1761 to 1769; whence it appears that in the year ending 25th October, 1762, 10,000*l.* had been disbursed to Mr. Martin, Secretary to the Treasury; and in the following year, to which the story refers, no less than 41,000*l.*[3]

The general expenditure for secret service, during Lord Bute's period, also exhibits a remarkable excess, as compared with other years. In the year ending 25th October, 1761, the secret-service money had amounted to 58,000*l.* Lord Bute came into office on the 29th May, 1762; and in this year, ending 25th October, it rose at once to 82,168*l.* In the next year, — Lord Bute having retired in April, — it fell to 61,000*l.* In 1764, it was reduced to 36,837*l.*; and in 1765, to 29,374*l.*[4]

Under the Grenville Ministry.

The Grenville Ministry distributed bribes or gratuities with less profusion than Lord Bute, yet with so little restraint, that a donation to a member of Parliament appears to have been regarded as a customary compliment. It might be offered without offence.

[1] Walp. Mem. Geo. III. i. 199.

[2] Lord Mahon's Hist. v. 15.

[3] Grenville Papers, iii. 144.

[4] There is an obscurity in these accounts; but it seems as if the secret-service money had been derived from different sources, the amount paid from one source, between 1761 and 1769, being 156,000*l.*, and from the other 394,507*l.* The details of the latter sum only are given.

if declined, an apology was felt to be due to the minister. In the Grenville Papers we find a characteristic letter from Lord Say and Sele, which exemplifies the relations of the minister with his Parliamentary supporters.

"London, Nov. 26th, 1763.

"Honored Sir,—I am very much obliged to you for that freedom of converse you this morning indulged me in, which I prize more than the lucrative advantage I then received. To show the sincerity of my words (pardon, Sir, the perhaps over niceness of my disposition), I return inclosed the bill for 300*l.* you favored me with, as good manners would not permit my refusal of it, when tendered by you.

"P. S.—As a free horse wants no spur, so I stand in need of no inducement or *douceur*, to lend my small assistance to the king, or his friends in the present administration."[1]

Mr. Grenville, however, complained,—and apparently with justice,—"that the secret-service money was by a great deal less than under any other minister."[2]

Under Lord North.

Throughout the administration of Lord North, the purchase of votes in Parliament, by direct pecuniary bribes, was still a common practice. The king's complicity,—always suspected,—is now beyond a doubt. Writing to Lord North on the 1st March, 1781, His Majesty said:—"Mr. Robinson sent me the list of the speakers last night, and of the very good majority. I have this morning sent him 6000*l.*, to be placed to the same purpose as the sum transmitted on the 21st August."[3] No other conclusion can be drawn from this letter, than that the king was in the habit of transmitting money, to secure majorities for the minister, who was then fighting his battles in the House of Commons.

1 Grenville Papers, iii. 145.

2 *Ibid.* 144.

3 King's Letters to Lord North; Lord Brougham's Works, iii. 157. Mr. Robinson, as Secretary to the Treasury, had the management of the House of Commons, and was the depository of the *Livre rouge*, supposed to contain the names of members retained by ministers.—*Wraxall Mem.* ii. 225.

Subsequent decline of the system.

The system of bribery did not long survive the ministry of Lord North.[1] It may not have wholly died out; and has probably been since resorted to, on rare and exceptional occasions. But the powerful and popular administration of Mr. Pitt did not need such support. The Crown had triumphed over parties, — its influence was supreme, — and Mr. Pitt himself, however profuse in the distribution of honors to his adherents, was of too lofty a character, to encourage the baseness of his meaner followers.

Shares in loans and lotteries.

Another instrument of corruption was found, at the beginning of this reign, in the raising of money for the public service, by loans and lotteries. This form of bribery, though less direct, was more capable of proof. A bribe could be given in secret; the value of scrip was notorious. In March, 1763, Lord Bute contracted a loan of three millions and a half, for the public service; and having distributed shares among his friends, — the scrip immediately rose to a premium of 11 per cent. in the market! So enormous a miscalculation of the terms upon which a loan could be negotiated, is scarcely to be reconciled with honesty of purpose; and, according to the practice of that time, the minister was entirely free from control in the distribution of the shares. Here the country sustained a loss of 385,000*l.*; and the minister was openly charged with having enriched his political adherents, at the public expense. The bank-bills of Mr. Fox had been found so persuasive, that corruption was applied on a still

Lord Bute's loan, 1763.

[1] Mr. Hallam says that the practice of direct bribery of Members of Parliament "is generally supposed to have ceased about the termination of the American War." — *Const. Hist.* iii. 256.

Mr. William Smith, one of the oldest members of the House of Commons, related the following anecdote of his own time: — A gentleman, being at Sir Benjamin Hammett's Bank, heard a Member, one of Lord North's friends, ask to have a 500*l.* bill "broken," which was done; and upon the applicant leaving the bank, Sir B. Hammett saw a cover lying on the floor, which he picked up and put into his friend's hand, without comment. It was addressed to the member, "with Lord North's compliments."

larger scale, in order to secure the power of the minister. The participation of many members, in the profits of this iniquitous loan, could not be concealed; and little pains were taken to deny it.[1]

Duke of Grafton's loan, 1767.

The success of this expedient was not likely to be soon forgotten. Stock-jobbing became the fashion; and many members of Parliament were notoriously concerned in it. Horace Walpole, the chief chronicler of these scandals, states that, in 1767, sixty members were implicated in such transactions, and even the Chancellor of the Exchequer himself.[2] Another contemporary, Sir George Colebrooke, gives an account quite as circumstantial, of the monstrous corruption of the time. He says, "The Duke of Grafton gave a dinner to several of the principal men in the city, to settle the loan. Mr. Townshend came in his nightgown, and after dinner, when the terms were settled, and every one present wished to introduce some friend on the list of subscribers, he pretended to cast up the sums already subscribed, said the loan was full, huddled up his papers, got into a chair, and returned home, reserving to himself, by this manœuvre, a large share in the loan."[3]

Lotteries.

A few years later, similar practices were exposed in another form. Lotteries were then a favorite source of revenue; and it appeared from the lists of subscribers in 1769 and 1770, that shares had been allotted to several members of Parliament. On the 23d of April, 1771, Mr. Seymour moved for the list of persons who had subscribed to the lotteries of that year, alleging that it appeared from the lists of 1769, that twenty thousand tickets had been disposed of to members of Parliament, which sold at a premium of nearly 2*l.* each. His motion was refused.[4] On the 25th April, Mr. Cornwall moved to prohibit any member from

1 Parl. Hist. xv. 1305; Adolphus, i. 111; History of the late Minority, 107; "The North Briton," No. 42; Lord Mahon's Hist. v. 20.

2 Walpole's Mem. Geo. III. ii. 428.

3 Cited in Walpole's Mem. iii. 100, *n.*

4 Parl. Hist. xvii. 174.

receiving more than twenty tickets. He stated that he was "certainly informed," that fifty members of Parliament had each subscribed for five hundred tickets, which would realize a profit of 1000*l.*, and secure the minister fifty votes. His motion also was rejected.[1]

Lord North's loan, 1781.

Again, in 1781, the very circumstances of Lord Bute's flagitious loan, were repeated under Lord North. A loan of 12,000,000*l.* was then contracted, to defray the cost of the disastrous American war, of which lottery-tickets formed a part. Its terms were so favorable to the subscribers, that suddenly the scrip, or omnium, rose nearly 11 per cent.[2] The minister was assailed with injurious reproaches, and his conduct was repeatedly denounced in Parliament as wilfully corrupt. These charges were not made by obscure men; but by the Marquess of Rockingham, Mr. Fox, Mr. Burke, Mr. Byng, Sir G. Savile, and other eminent members of Opposition. It was computed by Mr. Fox, that a profit of 900,000*l.* would be derived from the loan; and by others, that half the loan was subscribed for by members of the House of Commons. Lord Rockingham said, "the loan was made merely for the purpose of corrupting the Parliament to support a wicked, impolitic, and ruinous war." Mr. Fox declared, again and again, that a large sum had been placed in the "hands of the minister to be granted as *douceurs* to members of that House, . . . as a means of procuring and continuing a majority in the House of Commons, upon every occasion, and to give strength and support to a bad administration."[3]

1 Walp. Mem. iv. 320; Chatham's Corresp. iv. 148, *n.*; Parl. Hist. xvii. 185.

2 Sir P. J. Clerke, on the 8th March, said it had risen from 9 to 11 in the Alley that day. Lord North said it had only risen to 9, and had fallen again to 7½. Lord Rockingham estimated it at 10 per cent.

3 Debates in the Commons, 7th, 8th, 12th, and 14th March, and in the Lords, 21st March, 1781; Parl. History, xxi. 1334–1386; Rockingham Mem. ii. 437; Lord J. Russell's Life of Fox, i. 235–241. Wraxall's Mem. ii. 360–375. Among the subscribers to this loan were seven members for

The worst feature of this form of corruption, was its excessive and extravagant cost to the country. If members of Parliament were to be bribed at all, — bank-notes, judiciously distributed, were far cheaper than improvident loans. Lord Bute had purchased a majority, on the preliminaries of peace, with thirty or forty thousand pounds. Lord North's experiment laid a burden upon the people of nearly a million. It was bad enough that the representatives of the people should be corrupted; and to pay so high a price for their corruption was a cruel aggravation of the wrong.

Lord North's loan, 1782.

In 1782, Lord North, in raising another loan, did not venture to repeat these scandals; but disappointed his friends by a new system of close subscriptions. This arrangement did not escape animadversion; but it was the germ of the modern form of contracts, by sealed tenders.[1] Mr. Pitt had himself condemned the former system of jobbing-loans and lotteries; and when he commenced his series of loans for the French revolutionary war in 1793, he took effectual means to discontinue it. That the evil had not been exaggerated, may be inferred from the views of that sagacious statesman, as expounded by his biographer and friend Dr. Tomline. Mr. Pitt "having, while in opposition, objected to the practice of his predecessors in distributing beneficial shares of loans and lottery-tickets, under the market price, among their private friends, and the Parliamentary supporters of the Government, adopted a new plan of contracting for loans and lotteries by means of sealed proposals from different persons, which were opened in the presence of each other; and while this competition insured to the public, the best terms which could be obtained under existing circumstances,

Discontinuance of the system by Mr. Pitt.

70,000*l.*; others for 50,000*l.*; and one for 100,000*l.*; but the greater number being holders of scrip only, did not appear in the list. — *Wraxall Mem.* ii. 367.

[1] Parl. Hist. xxii. 1056; Wraxall's Mem. 320.

it cut off a very improper source of showing favor to individuals, and increasing ministerial influence."[1]

Contractors.

One other form of Parliamentary corruption yet remains to be noticed. Lucrative contracts for the public service, necessarily increased by the American war, were found a convenient mode of enriching political supporters. A contract to supply rum or beef for the navy, was as great a prize for a member, as a share in a loan or lottery. This species of reward was particularly acceptable to the commercial members of the House. Nor were its attractions confined to the members who enjoyed the contracts. Constituents being allowed to participate in their profits, were zealous in supporting government candidates. Here was another source of influence, for which again the people paid too dearly. Heavy as their burdens were becoming, they were increased by the costly and improvident contracts, which this system of Parliamentary jobbing encouraged. The cost of bribery in this form, was even greater and more indefinite than that of loans and lotteries. In the latter case, there were some limits to the premium on scrip, which was public and patent to all the world; but who could estimate the profits of a contract loosely and ignorantly — not to say corruptly — entered into, and executed without adequate securities for its proper fulfilment? These evils were notorious; and efforts were not wanting to correct them.

In 1779 Sir Philip Jennings Clerke obtained leave to bring in a bill to disqualify contractors from sitting in Parliament, except where they obtained contracts at a public bidding; but on the 11th of March, the commitment of the bill was negatived.[2] Again, in February 1780, Sir Philip renewed his motion, and succeeded in passing his bill through the Commons, without opposition; but it was rejected by the Lords on the second reading.[3] In 1781 it was brought

[1] Life of Pitt, iii. 533.
[2] Parl. Hist. xx. 123–129.
[3] Parl. Hist. xxi. 414.

forward a third time, but was then lost in the House of Commons.[1]

Meanwhile, Lord North's administration was falling; the Opposition were pledged to diminish the influence of the Crown, and to further the cause of economic reform; and in 1782, Sir Philip was able to bring in his bill, and carry the second reading.[2] In committee, Mr. Fox introduced clauses, which omitted the exception in favor of contracts obtained at a public bidding, and extended it to existing as well as future contracts. Immediately afterwards, the Rockingham ministry coming into office, adopted a measure so consonant with their own policy; and, under such auspices, it was at length passed.[3] It was another legislative condemnation of corrupt influences in Parliament.

Abuses condemned by Parliament.

In weighing the evidence of parliamentary corruption, which is accessible to us, allowance must be made for the hostility of many of the witnesses. Charges were made against the government of the day, by its bitterest opponents; and may have been exaggerated by the hard coloring of party. But they were made by men of high character and political eminence; and so generally was their truth acknowledged, that every abuse complained of, was ultimately condemned by Parliament. Were all the measures for restraining corruption and undue influence groundless? Were the evils sought to be corrected imaginary? The historian can desire no better evidence of contemporary evils, than the judgment of successive Parlia-

[1] Parl. Hist. xxi. 1390.

[2] Parl. Hist. xxii. 1214, 1335, 1356. Debates, 19th March; 15th and 17th April; 1st and 27th May, 1782.

[3] The Bill contained an exception in favor of persons subscribing to a public loan. It was said, however, that the loan was a more dangerous engine of influence than contracts, and ultimately the exception was omitted, "it being generally understood that a separate Bill should be brought in for that purpose," which, however, was never done. This matter, as stated in the debates, is exceedingly obscure and inconsistent, and scarcely to be relied upon, though it was frequently adverted to, in discussing the question of Baron Rothschild's disability in 1855.

ments, — pronounced again and again, and ratified by posterity.[1] The wisdom of the legislature averted the ruin of the constitution, which the philosophical Montesquieu had predicted, when he said, "Il périra lorsque la puissance legislative sera plus corrompue que l'exécutrice."[2]

State of society early in the reign of Geo. III.

Such was the state of society in the first years of the reign of George III. that the vices of the government received little correction from public opinion. A corrupt system of government represented but too faithfully, the prevalent corruption of society. Men of the highest rank openly rioted in drunkenness, gambling, and debauchery: the clergy were indifferent to religion: the middle classes were coarse, ignorant, and sensual; and the lower classes brutalized by neglect, poverty, and evil examples. The tastes and habits of the age were low: its moral and intellectual standard was debased. All classes were wanting in refinement, and nearly all in education. Here were abounding materials for venal senators, greedy place-hunters, and corrupt electors.

How popular principles were kept alive.

Having viewed the imperfections of the representative system, and the various forms of corruption by which the constitution was formerly disfigured, we pause to inquire how popular principles, statesmanship, and public virtue were kept alive, amid such adverse influences?[3] The country was great and glorious; and its history, — though stained with many blots, — is such as Englishmen may justly contemplate with pride. The

[1] In painting the public vices of his age, Cowper did not omit to stigmatize, as it deserved, its political corruption.

"But when a country (one that I could name),
In prostitution sinks the sense of shame;
When infamous Venality, grown bold,
Writes on his bosom, '*to be let or sold.*'" — *Table Talk.*

[2] Livre xi. c. 6.

[3] "Of all ingenious instruments of despotism," said Sydney Smith, "I most commend a popular assembly where the majority are paid and hired, and a few bold and able men, by their brave speeches, make the people believe they are free." — *Mem.* ii. 214.

people, if enjoying less freedom than in later times, were yet the freest people in the world. Their laws, if inferior to modern jurisprudence, did not fall short of the enlightenment of the age, in which Parliament designed them. How are these contrasts to be explained and reconciled? How were the people saved from misgovernment? What were the antidotes to the baneful abuses which prevailed? In the first place, parliamentary government attracted the ablest men to the service of the state. Whether they owed their seats to the patronage of a peer, or to the suffrages of their fellow-countrymen, they equally enlightened Parliament by their eloquence, and guided the national councils by their statesmanship. In the next place, the representation, — limited and anomalous as it was, — comprised some popular elements; and the House of Commons, in the worst times, still professed its responsibility to the people. Nor can it be denied that the small class, by whom a majority of the House of Commons was returned, were the most instructed and enlightened in the country; and as Englishmen, were generally true to principles of freedom.

Two other causes, which exercised a wholesome restraint upon Parliament and the governing class, are to be found in the divisions of party, — finely called by Sir Bulwer Lytton "the sinews of freedom," — and the growing influence of the press. However prone the ruling party may sometimes have been to repress liberty, the party in opposition were forced to rely upon popular principles; and pledged to maintain them, at least for a time, when they succeeded to power. Party again supplied, in some degree, the place of intelligent public opinion. As yet the great body of the people had neither knowledge nor influence; but those who enjoyed political power, were encouraged by their rivalries and ambition, not less than by their patriotism, to embrace those principles of good government, which steadily made their way in our laws and institutions. Had all parties combined against popular rights, nothing short of another revolution could have overthrown them. But as they were divided and opposed, the people obtained extended liberties, before they were in a position to wrest them from their rulers, by means of a free representation.

Meanwhile the press was gradually creating a more elevated public opinion, to which all parties were obliged to defer. It was long, however, before that great political agent performed its office worthily. Before the press can be instructive, there must be enlightenment, and public spirit among the people: it takes its color from society, and reflects its prevailing vices. Hence, while flagrant abuses in the government were tolerated by a corrupt society, the press was venal, — teeming with scurrilous libels and factious falsehoods, in the interests of rival parties, — and disfigured by all the faults of a depraved political morality. Let us be thankful that principles of liberty and public virtue were so strong, as constantly to advance in society, in the press, and in the government of the country.

Arguments for Parliamentary Reform.

The glaring defects and vices of the representative system, which have now been exposed, — the restricted and unequal franchise, the bribery of a limited electoral body, and the corruption of the representatives themselves, — formed the strongest arguments for parliamentary reform. Some of them had been partially corrected; and some had been ineffectually exposed and denounced; but the chief evil of all, demanded a bolder and more hazardous remedy. The theory of an equal representation, — at no time very perfect, — had, in the course of ages, been entirely subverted. Decayed boroughs, without inhabitants, — the absolute property of noblemen, — and populous towns without electors, returned members to the House of Commons; but great manufacturing cities, distinguished by their industry, wealth, and intelligence, were without representatives.

Schemes for partially rectifying these inequalities were proposed at various times, by statesmen of very different opinions. Lord Chatham was the first to advocate reform. Speaking, in 1766, of the borough representation, he called it "the rotten part of our constitution;" and said, "It cannot continue a century. If it does not drop, it must be amputated."[1] In 1770, he suggested that a third member should be added to every county, "in order to counterbalance the weight of corrupt and venal boroughs."[2] Such was his opinion of the necessity of a measure of this character, that he said: "Before the end of this century, either the Parliament will reform itself from within, or be reformed with a vengeance from without."[3]

Lord Chatham's scheme of reform, 1770. 14th May.

The next scheme was that of a very notable politician, Mr. Wilkes. More comprehensive than Lord Chatham's, — it was framed to meet, more directly, the evils complained of. In 1776, he moved for a bill to give additional members to the Metropolis, and to Middlesex, Yorkshire, and other large counties; to disfranchise the rotten boroughs, and add the electors to the county constituency; and lastly, to enfranchise Manchester, Leeds, Sheffield, Birmingham, and "other rich populous trading towns."[4] His scheme, indeed, comprised all the leading principles of parliamentary reform, which were advocated for the next fifty years without success, and have been sanctioned within our own time.

Mr. Wilkes's scheme, 1776.

The next measure for reforming the Commons, was brought forward by a peer. On the 3d June, 1780, in the midst of Lord George Gordon's riots, the Duke of Richmond presented a bill for establishing annual

Duke of Richmond's Bill, 1780.

[1] Debates on the Address, January, 1766.

[2] Walpole's Mem. iv. 58; Chatham's Corresp. iv. 157, where he supports his views by the precedent of a Scotch Act at the Revolution. Strangers were excluded during this debate, which is not reported in the Parliamentary History.

[3] Parl. Hist. xvii. 223, *n.*

[4] 21st March, 1776, Parl. Hist. xviii. 1287. The motion was negatived without a division.

parliaments, universal suffrage, and equal electoral districts.[1] It was rejected without a division.

Other schemes of reform, 1780.

Nor was the Duke's extravagant proposal an isolated suggestion of his own. Extreme changes were at this time popular, — embracing annual parliaments, the extinction of rotten boroughs, and universal suffrage. The graver statesmen, who were favorable to improved representation, discountenanced all such proposals, likely to endanger the more practicable schemes of economic reform by which they were then endeavoring, — with every prospect of success, — to purify Parliament, and reduce the influence of the Crown. The petitioners by whom they were supported, prayed also for a more equal representation of the people; but it was deemed prudent to postpone for a time, the agitation of that question.[2]

The disgraceful riots of Lord George Gordon, rendered this time unfavorable for the discussion of any political changes. The Whig party were charged with instigating and abetting these riots, just as, at a later period, they became obnoxious to imputations of Jacobinism. The occasion of the king's speech at the end of the session of 1780, was not lost by the tottering government of Lord North. His Majesty warned the people against "the hazard of innovation;" and artfully connected this warning, with a reference to "rebellious insurrections to *resist* or to *reform* the laws."[3]

Among the more moderate schemes discussed at this period, by the temperate supporters of parliamentary reform, was the addition of one hundred county members to the House of Commons. It was objected to, however, by some of the leading Whigs, "as being prejudicial to the democratical part of the Constitution, by throwing too great a weight into the scale of the aristocracy."[4]

[1] Parl. Hist. xxi. 686.

[2] Ann. Reg. xxiv. 140, 194; Rockingham Mem. ii. 395, 411.

[3] Parl. Hist. xxvi. 767.

[4] Letter of Duke of Portland; Rockingham Mem. ii. 412.

Mr. Pitt was now commencing his great career; and his early youth is memorable for the advocacy of a measure, which his renowned father had approved. His first motion on this subject was made in 1782, during the Rockingham administration. The time was well chosen, as that ministry was honorably distinguished by its exertions for the purification of Parliament. On the 7th May, after a call of the House, he introduced the subject in a speech, as wise and temperate as it was able. In analyzing the state of the representation, he described the Treasury and other nomination boroughs, without property, population, or trade; and the boroughs which had no property or stake in the country but their votes, which they sold to the highest bidder. The Nabob of Arcot, he said, had seven or eight members in that House: and might not a foreign State in enmity with this country, by means of such boroughs, have a party there? He concluded by moving for a committee of inquiry. He seems to have been induced to adopt this course, in consequence of the difficulties he had experienced in obtaining the agreement of the friends of reform, to any specific proposal.[1] This motion was superseded by reading the order of the day, by a majority of twenty only.[2]

Mr. Pitt's motion for inquiry, 1782.

Again, in 1783, while in opposition to the Coalition ministry, Mr. Pitt renewed his exertions in the same cause. His position had, in the mean time, been strengthened by numerous petitions, with 20,000 signatures.[3]

Mr. Pitt's resolutions, May 7th, 1783.

He no longer proposed a committee of inquiry, but came forward with three distinct resolutions: — 1st, That effectual measures ought to be taken for preventing bribery and expense at elections: 2d, That when the majority of voters for any borough should be convicted of corruption, before an

1 Ann. Reg. xxv. 181.

2 161 to 141; Parl. Hist. xxii. 1416; Fox Mem. i. 321–2.

3 All the petitions which had been presented for the last month, had been brought into the House by the Clerk, and laid on the floor near the table.

election committee, the borough should be disfranchised, and the unbribed minority entitled to vote for the county: 3d, That an addition should be made to the knights of the shire, and members for the metropolis. In support of his resolutions, he attributed the disasters of the American war to the corrupt state of the House of Commons, and the secret influence of the Crown, which, he said, "were sapping the very foundation of liberty, by corruption." Universal suffrage he condemned; and the disfranchisement of "rotten boroughs" he as yet shrank from proposing.[1]

Yorkshire petition Jan. 16th, 1784.

Before Mr. Pitt had occasion again to express his sentiments, he had been called to the head of affairs, and was carrying on his memorable contest with the Coalition. On the 16th January, 1784, Mr. Duncombe presented a petition from the freeholders of Yorkshire, praying the House to take into serious consideration the inadequate state of the representation of the people. Mr. Pitt supported it, saying, that he had been confirmed in his opinions in favor of reform, by the recent conduct of the Opposition. "A temperate and moderate reform," he said, "temperately and moderately pursued, he would at all times, and in all situations, be ready to promote to the utmost of his power." At the same time, he avowed that his cabinet were not united in favor of any such measure; and that he despaired of seeing any cabinet unanimous in the cause. In this opinion Mr. Fox signified his concurrence; but added, that Mr. Pitt had scarcely introduced one person into his cabinet, who would support his views in regard to parliamentary reform.[2]

Mr. Pitt's Reform Bill, 1785.

The sincerity of Mr. Pitt's assurances was soon to be tested. In the new Parliament he found himself supported by a powerful majority; and he enjoyed at once the confidence of the king and the favor of the people. Upon one question only, was he powerless.

[1] Parl. Hist. xxiii. 827; Fox Mem. ii. 79; Wrax. Mem. iii. 400.
[2] Parl. Hist. xxiv. 347.

To his measure of parliamentary reform, the king was adverse,[1] — his cabinet were indifferent or unfriendly; and his followers in the House of Commons, could not be brought to vote in its favor. The Tories were generally opposed to it; and even a large portion of the Whigs, including the Duke of Portland and Lord Fitzwilliam, failed to lend it their support.[2] Public feeling had not yet been awakened to the necessity of reform; and the legislature was so constituted, that any effective scheme was hopeless.

In the first session of the new Parliament he was not prepared with any measure of his own; but he spoke and voted in favor of a motion of Mr. Alderman Sawbridge; and promised that, in the next session, he should be ready to bring the question forward himself.[3] He redeemed this pledge, and on the 18th April, 1785, moved for leave to introduce a Bill "to amend the representation of the people of England, in Parliament." Having proved, by numerous references to history, that the representation had frequently been changed, according to the varying circumstances of the country; that many decayed boroughs had ceased to return members to Parliament, while other boroughs had been raised or restored to that privilege; he proposed that seventy-two members then returned by thirty-six decayed boroughs should be distributed among the counties and the Metropolis. But this part of his scheme was accompanied by the startling proposal, that these boroughs should not be disfranchised, except with the consent of their proprietors, who were to receive compensation from the State, amounting to a million sterling! He further proposed to purchase the exclusive rights of ten corporations, for the benefit of their fellow-citizens; and to obtain by the same means, the surrender of the right of returning members from four small boroughs, whose members could be transferred to populous towns. By these sev-

1 See *supra*, p. 76.

2 Lord J. Russell's Life of Fox, ii. 176.

3 Parl. Hist. xxiv. 975.

eral means, a hundred seats were to be redistributed. The enlargement of the county constituency, by the addition of copyholders to the freeholders, formed another part of his plan. It was estimated that by this change, and by the enfranchisement of great towns, a total addition of ninety-nine thousand would be made to the electoral body. The portion of this scheme most open to objection was that of compensating the proprietors of boroughs; and he admitted that it "was a tender part; but at the same time it had become a necessary evil, if any reform was to take place." It seems indeed, that not hoping to convince those interested in the existing state of the representation, of the expediency of reform, he had sought to purchase their support. The boroughs which were always in the market, he proposed to buy, on behalf of the State; and thus to secure purity, through the instruments of corruption. Such a sacrifice of principle to expediency may have been necessary: but it did not save his scheme of reform from utter failure. His motion for leave to bring in the bill, was negatived by a majority of seventy-four.[1]

Mr. Pitt's sincerity.

As this was the last occasion on which Mr. Pitt advocated the cause of parliamentary reform, his sincerity, even at that time, has been called in question. He could scarcely have hoped to carry this measure; but its failure was due to causes beyond his control. To have staked his power as a minister, upon the issue of a measure fifty years in advance of the public opinion of his day, — and which he had no power to force upon Parliament, — would have been the act of an enthusiast, rather than a statesman. The blame of his subsequent inaction in the cause was shared by the Whigs, who, for several years, consented to its entire oblivion.

Mr. Flood's motion, 1790.

In the five ensuing years of Mr. Pitt's prosperous administration, the word "Reform" was scarcely whispered in Parliament. At length, in 1790, Mr.

[1] Ayes 174, Noes 248. Parl. Hist. xxv. 432–475; Tomline's Life of Pitt, ii. 41.

Flood moved for a bill to amend the representation of the people. His plan was to add one hundred members to the House of Commons, to be elected by the resident householders of every county. Mr. Pitt, on this occasion, professed himself to be as firm and zealous a friend as ever to parliamentary reform; but could not assent to Mr. Flood's motion, which was superseded by the adjournment of the House.[1]

"Friends of the People."

Meanwhile, the cause of parliamentary reform had been advocated by several political associations, and more particularly by the "Friends of the People." This society embraced several men eminent in politics and literature; and twenty-eight members of Parliament, of whom Mr. Grey and Mr. Erskine took the lead. It was agreed amongst them, that the subject should again be pressed upon the attention of Parliament.

Mr. Grey's notice, 30th April, 1792.

And, accordingly, on the 30th of April, 1792, Mr. Grey gave notice of a motion, in the ensuing session, for an inquiry into the representative system.[2] A few years earlier, the cause of reform, — honestly supported by moderate men of all parties, — might have prevailed; but the perils of the time had now become too grave to admit of its fair discussion. That ghastly revolution had burst forth in France, which for two generations, was destined to repress the liberties of England. Mr. Pitt avowed that he still retained his opinion of the propriety of parliamentary reform; but was persuaded that it could not then be safely tried. He saw no prospect of success, and great danger of anarchy and confusion in the attempt. "This is not a time," said he, "to make hazardous experiments." He had taken his stand against revolutionary principles, and every question with which they could be associated. Mr. Burke, the honored reformer of an earlier period, and in another cause,[3]

[1] Parl. Hist. xxviii. 452.

[2] Mr. Speaker Addington permitted a debate to arise on this occasion, which, according to the stricter practice of later times, would have been wholly inadmissible. — *Lord Sidmouth's Life*, i. 88.

[3] Mr. Burke had never supported parliamentary reform.

and many respected members of his party, henceforth supported the minister, and ranged themselves with the opponents of reform. A period was commencing, not only hostile to all change, but repressive of freedom of opinion; and the power of Mr. Pitt, as the champion of order against democracy, was absolute.[1]

Mr. Grey's motion, 1793.

On the 6th of May, 1793, Mr. Grey brought forward the motion, of which he had given notice in the previous session. First he presented a long and elaborate petition from the society of the Friends of the People, exposing the abuses of the electoral system, and alleging various grounds for parliamentary reform. This petition having been read, Mr. Grey proceeded to move that it be referred to the consideration of a committee. Like Mr. Pitt, on a former occasion, — and probably for the same reasons, — he made no specific proposal; but contented himself with arguments against the existing system. A more unsuitable time for such a motion could not have been found. The horrors of the French revolution had lately reached their climax, in the execution of the King: many British subjects had avowed their sympathy with revolutionary principles: the country was at war with the French republic: the Whig party had been broken up; and the great body of the people were alarmed for the safety of their institutions. At such a time, the most moderate proposals were discountenanced; and after two nights' debate, Mr. Grey's motion found only forty-one supporters.[2]

Mr. Grey's motion, 1797.

After such discouragement, and under circumstances so adverse, Mr. Grey did not attempt to renew the discussion of Parliamentary reform, until 1797. He now had a definite plan; and on the 26th May, he moved for leave to bring in a Bill for carrying it into effect. He proposed to increase the county members from ninety-two to

[1] Parl. Hist. xxix. 1300; Tomline's Life of Pitt, iii. 322.

[2] Parl. Hist. xxx. 787-925; Ayes 41, Noes 232; Lord J. Russell's Life of Fox, ii. 281-283, 349.

one hundred and thirteen, by giving two members to each of the three ridings of the county of York, instead of two for the whole county, and by similar additions to other large counties; and to admit copyholders and leaseholders for terms of years, as well as freeholders, to the county franchise. As regards the boroughs, he proposed to substitute for the numerous rights of election, one uniform household franchise. And in order to diminish the expense of elections, he suggested that the poll should be taken, throughout the whole kingdom, at one time. His scheme comprised, in fact, an outline of the great measure, which this eminent statesman was ultimately destined to mature, as the consummation of his labors during half a century. His motion was seconded by Mr. Erskine, in a speech which went far to contradict the assertion, — so often made, — that in the House of Commons this great forensic orator was wholly unequal to his reputation. At once eloquent, impassioned, and argumentative, it displayed those rare qualities, which have never been equalled at the British bar, and not often in the senate. The motion was also supported, in an admirable speech, by Mr. Fox. But vain were moderate and well-considered plans, — vain were eloquence and argument. The feelings, fears, and prejudices of the people were adverse to the cause: reform being now confounded with revolution, and reformers with Jacobins. Whatever was proposed, — more was said to be intended; and Paine and the "Rights of Man" were perversely held up, as the true exponents of the reformer's creed. The motion was rejected by a large majority.[1]

Further discouragement of reform.

Again the question slept for many years. The early part of the present century was a period scarcely more favorable for the discussion of parliamentary reform, than the first years of the French revolution. The prodigious efforts of the country in carrying on the war, — victories and disasters, — loans, taxes, and subsidies, — engrossed the attention of Parliament, and the thoughts of

[1] Parl. Hist. xxxiii. 644. Ayes 91, Noes 256.

the people. The restoration of peace was succeeded by other circumstances, almost equally unpropitious. The extreme pressure of the war upon the industrial resources of the country, had occasioned suffering and discontent amongst the working classes. The Government were busy in repressing sedition; and the governing classes, trained under a succession of Tory administrations, had learned to scout every popular principle. Under such discouragements, many of the old supporters of reform, either deserted the cause, or shrank from its assertion; while demagogues of dubious character, and dangerous principles, espoused it. "Hampden Clubs," and other democratic associations, — chiefly composed of working men, — were demanding universal suffrage and annual Parliaments, which found as little favor with the advocates of reform, as with its opponents; and every moderate scheme was received with scorn, by ultra-reformers.[1]

Sir F. Burdett's plan, 1809.

But notwithstanding these adverse conditions, the question of reform was occasionally discussed in Parliament. In 1809, it was revived, after the lapse of thirteen years. Mr. Pitt and Mr. Fox, — who had first fought together in support of the same principles, and afterwards on opposite sides, — were both no more: Mr. Grey and Mr. Erskine had been called to the House of Peers; and the cause was in other hands. Sir Francis Burdett was now its advocate, — less able and influential than his predecessors, and an eccentric politician, — but a thorough-bred English gentleman. His scheme was such as to repel the support of the few remaining reformers. He proposed that every county should be divided into electoral districts; that each district should return one member; and that the franchise should be vested in the taxed male population. So wild a project found no more than fifteen supporters.[2]

Earl Grey, 1810.

On the 13th June, 1810, Earl Grey, in moving an address on the state of the nation, renewed his public connection with the cause of reform, — avowed his

[1] Com. Journ. lxv. 360, &c.

[2] Hansard's Deb., 1st Ser., xiv. 1041. Ayes 15, Noes 74.

adherence to the sentiments he had always expressed, — and promised his future support to any temperate and judicious plan, for the correction of abuses in the representation. He was followed by Lord Erskine, in the same honorable avowal.[1]

Sir F. Burdett, 1818-19.

In 1818, Sir F. Burdett, now the Chairman of the Hampden Club of London, proposed resolutions in favor of universal male suffrage, equal electoral districts, vote by ballot, and annual Parliaments. His motion was seconded by Lord Cochrane; but found not another supporter in the House of Commons. At this time, there were numerous public meetings in favor of universal suffrage; and reform associations, — not only of men but of women, — were engaged in advancing the same cause. And as many of these were advocating female suffrage, Sir F. Burdett, to avoid misconstruction, referred to male suffrage only.[2]

In 1819, Sir F. Burdett again brought forward a motion on the subject. He proposed that the House should, early in the next session, take into its consideration the state of the representation. In the debate, Lord John Russell, who had recently been admitted to Parliament, expressed his opinion in favor of disfranchising such boroughs as were notoriously corrupt. The motion was superseded by reading the orders of the day.[3]

Lord J. Russell, 1820.

At the commencement of the following session, Lord John Russell, — whose name has ever since been honorably associated with the cause of reform, — proposed his first motion on the subject. In the preceding session, he had brought under the notice of the House the scandalous proceedings at Grampound. He now took broader ground, and embraced the general evils of the electoral system.[4] The time was not favorable to moderate counsels.

1 Hansard's Deb., 1st Ser., xvii. 559, 590.

2 See a learned and ingenious article in the Edin. Rev., January, 1819, by Sir J. Mackintosh, on Universal Suffrage, Art. VIII.

3 Hansard's Deb., 1st Ser., xl. 1440.

4 *Ibid.* xli. 302, 1091.

On one side were the intemperate advocates of universal suffrage: on the other the stubborn opponents of all change in the representation.[1] But such was the moderation of Lord John's scheme of reform, that it might have claimed the support of the wiser men of all parties. He showed, in a most promising speech, that in former times decayed boroughs had been discharged from sending members, and populous places summoned by writ to return them; he described the wonderful increase of the great manufacturing towns, which were unrepresented; and the corruption of the smaller boroughs, which sold their franchise. He concluded by moving resolutions: — 1. That boroughs in which notorious bribery and corruption should be proved to prevail, should cease to return members, — the electors not proved guilty, being allowed to vote for the county: 2. That the right thus taken from corrupt boroughs, should be given to great towns with a population of not less than 15,000, or to some of the largest counties: 3. That further means should be taken to detect corruption; and lastly, that the borough of Grampound should cease to send members.

Grampound Disfranchisement Bill.

As the motion was met by the government in a conciliatory manner; and as Lord Castlereagh was ready to concur in the disfranchisement of Grampound; Lord John Russell consented to withdraw his resolutions, and gave notice of a bill for disfranchising Grampound.[2] The progress of this bill was interrupted by the death of the king; but it was renewed in the following session, and reached the House of Lords, where after evidence being taken at the bar, it dropped by reason of the prorogation. Again it was passed by the Commons, in 1821. That House had given the two vacant seats to the great town of

[1] Notwithstanding the small encouragement given at this time to the cause of reform, it was making much progress in public opinion. Sydney Smith, writing in 1809, said: "I think all wise men should begin to turn their minds reformwards. We shall do it better than Mr. Hunt or Mr. Cobbett. Done it *must*, and *will* be." — *Mem.* ii. 191.

[2] Hansard's Deb., 1st Ser., xli. 1091–1122.

Leeds; but the Lords still avoided the recognition of such a principle, by assigning two additional members to the county of York: in which form the bill was at length agreed to.[1]

Mr. Lambton's proposal, 1821.

In 1821, two motions were made relating to Parliamentary reform, the one by Mr. Lambton, and the other by Lord John Russell. On the 17th April, the former explained his scheme. In lieu of the borough representation, he proposed to divide counties into districts containing twenty-five thousand inhabitants, each returning a member, — to extend the franchise for such districts, to all householders paying taxes, — to facilitate polling by means of numerous polling-booths, and by enabling overseers to receive votes, — and to charge the necessary expenses of every election upon the poor-rates. To the county constituencies he proposed to add copyholders, and leaseholders for terms of years. After a debate of two days, his motion was negatived by a majority of twelve.[2] On the 9th of May, Lord John Russell moved resolutions with a view to the discovery of bribery, the disfranchisement of corrupt boroughs, and the transfer of the right of returning members, to places which had increased in wealth and population. His resolutions were superseded by the previous question, which was carried by a majority of thirty-one.[3]

Lord J. Russell's plan, 1821.

And in 1822.

In 1822, Lord John Russell having, as he said, "served an apprenticeship in the cause of reform," again pressed the matter upon the notice of the House. The cry for universal suffrage had now subsided, — tranquillity prevailed throughout the country, — and no circumstance could be urged as unfavorable to its fair consideration. After showing the great increase of the wealth and intelligence of

[1] 1 & 2 Geo. IV. c. 47.

[2] Ayes 43, Noes 55. Hansard's Debates, 2d Series, v. 359–453. Mr. Lambton had prepared a bill, which is printed in the Appendix to that volume of Debates.

[3] Hans. Deb., 2d Ser., v. 603.

the country, he proposed the addition of sixty members to the counties, and forty to the great towns; and, — not to increase the total number of the House of Commons, — he suggested that one hundred of the smallest boroughs should each lose one of their two members. His motion, reduced to a modest resolution, "that the present state of representation required serious consideration," was rejected by a majority of one hundred and five.[1]

In 1823. In 1823, Lord John renewed his motion in the same terms. He was now supported by numerous petitions, — and amongst the number by one from seventeen thousand freeholders of the county of York; but after a short debate, was defeated by a majority of one hundred and eleven.[2]

Lord J. Russell's motion, 1826. Again, in 1826, Lord John proposed the same resolution to the House; and pointed out forcibly, that the increasing wealth and intelligence of the people, were daily aggravating the inequality of the representation. Nomination boroughs continued to return a large proportion of the members of the House of Commons, while places of enormous population and commercial prosperity were without representatives. After an interesting debate, his resolution was negatived by a majority of one hundred and twenty-four.[3]

Lord Blandford's views, 1829–30. In 1829, a proposal for reform proceeded from an unexpected quarter, and was based upon principles entirely novel. The measure of Catholic Emancipation had recently been carried; and many of its opponents, of the old Tory party, — disgusted with their own leaders, by whom it had been forwarded, — were suddenly converted to the cause of parliamentary reform. Representing their opinions, Lord Blandford, on the 2d June, submitted a motion on the subject. He apprehended that the Roman Catholics would now enter the borough-market, and purchase

[1] Hansard's Deb., 2d Ser., vii. 51–139. Ayes 164, Noes 269.
[2] *Ibid.* viii. 1260. Ayes 169, Noes 280.
[3] *Ibid.* xv. 51. Ayes 127, Noes 247.

seats for their representatives, in such numbers as to endanger our Protestant constitution. His resolutions condemning close and corrupt boroughs, found only forty supporters, and were rejected by a majority of seventy-four.[1] At the commencement of the next session, Lord Blandford repeated these views, in moving an amendment to the address, representing the necessity of improving the representation. Being seconded by Mr. O'Connell, his anomalous position as a reformer was manifest.[2]

Soon afterwards he moved for leave to bring in a bill to restore the constitutional influence of the Commons in the Parliament of England, which contained an elaborate machinery of reform, including the restoration of wages to members.[3] His motion served no other purpose, than that of reviving discussions upon the general question of reform.

Northampton and Leicester cases, 1826-27.

But in the mean time, questions of less general application had been discussed, which eventually produced the most important results. The disclosures which followed the general election of 1826, and the conduct of the government, gave a considerable impulse to the cause of reform. The corporations of Northampton and Leicester were alleged to have applied large sums from the corporate funds, for the support of ministerial candidates. In the Northampton case, Sir Robert Peel went so far as to maintain the right of a corporation to apply its funds to election purposes; but the House could not be brought to concur in such a principle; and a committee of inquiry was appointed.[4] In the Leicester case, all inquiry was successfully resisted.[5]

Feb. 21st.
Mar. 15th.

Penryn and East Retford cases, 1826-27.

Next came two cases of gross and notorious bribery, — Penryn and East Retford. They were not worse than those of Shoreham and Grampound, and might have been as easily disposed of; but, —

1 Hansard's Deb., 2d Ser., xxi. 1672. Ayes 40, Noes 114.
2 *Ibid.* xxii. 171.
3 *Ibid.* 678.
4 *Ibid.* xvi. 606.
5 *Ibid.* 1198.

treated without judgment by the ministers, — they precipitated a contest, which ended in the triumph of reform.

Penryn had long been notorious for its corruption, which had been already twice exposed;[1] yet the ministers resolved to deal tenderly with it. Instead of disfranchising so corrupt a borough, they followed the precedent of Shoreham; and proposed to embrace the adjacent hundreds, in the privilege of returning members. But true to the principles he had already carried out in the case of Grampound, Lord John Russell succeeded in introducing an amendment in the bill, by which the borough was to be entirely disfranchised.[2]

In the case of East Retford, a bill was brought in to disfranchise that borough, and to enable the town of Birmingham to return two representatives. And it was intended by the reformers, to transfer the franchise from Penryn to Manchester. The session closed without the accomplishment of either of these objects. The Penryn Disfranchisement bill, having passed the Commons, had dropped in the Lords; and the East Retford bill had not yet passed the Commons.

Penryn and East Retford bills, 1828.

In the next session, two bills were introduced; one by Lord John Russell, for transferring the franchise from Penryn to Manchester; and another by Mr. Tennyson, for disfranchising East Retford, and giving representatives to Birmingham.[3] The government proposed a compromise. If both boroughs were disfranchised, they offered, in one case to give two members to a populous town, and in the other to the adjoining hundreds.[4] When the Penryn bill had already reached the House of Lords, — where its reception was extremely doubtful, — the East Retford bill came on for discussion in the Commons. The government now opposed the transferrence of the franchise to Birmingham. Mr. Huskisson, however, voted for

[1] In 1807 and 1819.
[2] Hansard's Deb., 2d Ser., xvii. 682, 1855.
[3] *Ibid.* xviii. 83.
[4] *Ibid.* 1144, 1282.

it; and his proffered resignation being accepted by the Duke of Wellington,[1] led to the withdrawal of Lord Palmerston, Lord Dudley, Mr. Lamb, and Mr. Grant, — the most liberal members of the government, — the friends and colleagues of the late Mr. Canning. The cabinet was now entirely Tory; and less disposed than ever, to make concessions to the reformers. The Penryn bill was soon afterwards thrown out by the Lords on the second reading; and the East Retford bill, — having been amended so as to retain the franchise in the hundreds, — was abandoned in the Commons.[2]

Proposal to enfranchise Leeds, Birmingham, and Manchester, 1830.

It was the opinion of many attentive observers of these times, that the concession of demands so reasonable would have arrested, or postponed for many years, the progress of reform. They were resisted; and further agitation was encouraged. In 1830, Lord John Russell, — no longer hoping to deal with Penryn and East Retford, — proposed at once to enfranchise Leeds, Birmingham, and Manchester; and to provide that the three next places proved guilty of corruption, should be altogether disfranchised.[3] His motion was opposed, mainly on the ground that if the franchise were given to these towns, the claims of other large towns could not afterwards be resisted. Where, then, were such concessions to stop? It is remarkable that on this occasion, Mr. Huskisson said of Lord Sandon, who had moved an amendment, that he "was young, and would yet live to see the day when the representative franchise must be granted to the great manufacturing districts. He thought such a time fast approaching; and that one day or other, His Majesty's ministers would come down to that House, to propose such a measure, as necessary for the salvation of the country." Within a year, this prediction had been verified; though the unfortu-

[1] Hans. Deb., 2d Ser., xix. 915.
[2] *Ibid.* 1530.
[3] *Ibid.* xxii. 859.

nate statesman did not live to see its fulfilment. The motion was negatived by a majority of forty-eight;[1] and thus another moderate proposal, — free from the objections which had been urged against disfranchisement, and not affecting any existing rights, — was sacrificed to a narrow and obstinate dread of innovation.

Other proposals in 1830.

In this same session, other proposals were made of a widely different character. Mr. O'Connell moved resolutions in favor of universal suffrage, triennial Parliaments, and vote by ballot. Lord John Russell moved to substitute other resolutions, providing for the enfranchisement of large towns, and giving additional members to populous counties; while any increase of the numbers of the House of Commons was avoided, by disfranchising some of the smaller boroughs, and restraining others from sending more than one member.[2] Sir Robert Peel, in the course of the debate, said: "They had to consider whether there was not, on the whole, a general representation of the people in that House; and whether the popular voice was not sufficiently heard. For himself he thought that it was." This opinion was but the prelude to a more memorable declaration, by the Duke of Wellington. Both the motion and the amendment failed; but discussions so frequent served to awaken public sympathy in the cause, which great events were soon to arouse into enthusiasm.

Dissolution in 1830.

At the end of this session, Parliament was dissolved, in consequence of the death of George IV. The government was weak, — parties had been completely disorganized by the passing of the Roman Catholic Relief Act, — much discontent prevailed in the country; and the question of parliamentary reform, — which had been so often discussed in the late session, — became a popular topic at the elections. Meanwhile a startling event abroad, added to the usual excitement of a general election. Scarcely

[1] Ayes 140, Noes 188.

[2] Hansard's Deb., 2d Ser., xxiv 1204.

had the writs been issued, when Charles X. of France, — having attempted a *coup d'état*, — lost his crown, and was an exile on his way to England.[1] As he had fallen, in violating the liberty of the press, and subverting the representative constitution of France, this sudden revolution gained the sympathy of the English people, and gave an impulse to liberal opinions. The excitement was further increased by the revolution in Belgium, which immediately followed. The new Parliament, elected under such circumstances, met in October. Being without the restraint of a strong government, acknowledged leaders, and accustomed party connections, it was open to fresh political impressions; and the first night of the session determined their direction.

Duke of Wellington's declaration.

A few words from the Duke of Wellington raised a storm, which swept away his government, and destroyed his party. In the debate on the address, Earl Grey adverted to reform, and expressed a hope that it would not be deferred, like Catholic Emancipation, until government would be "compelled to yield to expediency, what they refused to concede upon principle." This elicited from the Duke, an ill-timed profession of faith in our representation. "He was fully convinced that the country possessed, at the present moment, a legislature which answered all the good purposes of legislation, — and this to a greater degree than any legislature ever had answered, in any country whatever. He would go further, and say that the legislature and system of representation possessed the full and entire confidence of the country, — deservedly possessed that confidence, — and the discussions in the legislature, had a very great influence over the opinions of the country. He would go still further, and say, that if at the present moment he had imposed upon him the duty of forming a legislature for any country, — and particularly for a country like this, in possession of great property of various

[1] Parliament was dissolved July 24th. The "three days" commenced in France, on the 27th.

descriptions, — he did not mean to assert that he could form such a legislature as they possessed now, for the nature of man was incapable of reaching such excellence at once; but his great endeavor would be to form some description of legislature, which would produce the same results. . . . . Under these circumstances he was not prepared to bring forward any measure of the description alluded to by the noble lord. He was not only not prepared to bring forward any measure of this nature; but he would at once declare that, as far as he was concerned, as long as he held any station in the government of the country, he should always feel it his duty to resist such measures, when proposed by others."[1]

At another time such sentiments as these might have passed unheeded, like other general panegyrics upon the British constitution, with which the public taste had long been familiar. Yet, so general a defence of our representative system had never, perhaps, been hazarded by any statesman. Ministers had usually been cautious in advancing the theoretical merits of the system, — even when its abuses had been less frequently exposed, and public opinion less awakened. They had spoken of the dangers of innovation, — they had asserted that the system, if imperfect in theory, had yet "worked well," — they had said that the people were satisfied and desired no change, —they had appealed to revolutions abroad, and disaffection at home, as reasons for not entertaining any proposal for change; but it was reserved for the Duke of Wellington, — at a time of excitement like the present, — to insult the understanding of the people, by declaring that the system was perfect in itself, and deservedly possessed their confidence.

Fall of the government.

On the same night, Mr. Brougham gave notice of a motion on the subject of parliamentary reform. Within a fortnight, the Duke's administration re-

[1] Hansard's Deb., 3d Ser., i. 52. The Duke, on a subsequent occasion, explained this speech, but did not deny that he had used the expressions attributed to him. — *Ibid.* vii. 1186.

signed, after an adverse division in the Commons, on the appointment of a committee to examine the accounts of the Civil List.[1] Though this defeat was the immediate cause of their resignation, the expected motion of Mr. Brougham was not without its influence, in determining them to withdraw from further embarrassments.

Earl Grey was the new Minister; and Mr. Brougham his Lord Chancellor. The first announcement of the premier was that the government would "take into immediate consideration the state of the representation, with a view to the correction of those defects which have been occasioned in it, by the operation of time; and with a view to the reëstablishment of that confidence upon the part of the people, which he was afraid Parliament did not at present enjoy, to the full extent that is essential for the welfare and safety of the country, and the preservation of the government."[2]

Lord Grey's ministry.

The government were now pledged to a measure of parliamentary reform; and during the Christmas recess, were occupied in preparing it. Meanwhile, the cause was eagerly supported by the people. Public meetings were held, political unions established,[3] and numerous petitions signed, in favor of reform. So great were the difficulties with which the government had to contend, that they needed all the encouragement that the people could give. They had to encounter the reluctance of the king,[4] — the interests of the proprietors of boroughs, which Mr. Pitt, unable to overcome, had sought to purchase, — the opposition of two thirds of the House of Lords, and perhaps of a majority of the House of Commons, — and above all,

Agitation in favor of reform.

[1] Sydney Smith, writing Nov. 1830, says: "Never was any administration so completely and so suddenly destroyed; and, I believe, entirely by the Duke's declaration, made, I suspect, in perfect ignorance of the state of public feeling and opinion." — *Mem.* ii. 313.

[2] Hansard's Deb., 3d Ser., i. 606.

[3] See Chap. VIII. Press and Liberty of Opinion.

[4] *Supra*, p. 120.

the strong Tory spirit of the country. Tory principles had been strengthened by a rule of sixty years. Not confined to the governing classes, but pervading society; they were now confirmed by the fears of impending danger. On the other hand, the too ardent reformers, while they alarmed the opponents of reform, embarrassed the government, and injured the cause, by their extravagance.

First Reform Bill, 1830-31.

On the 3d February, when Parliament reassembled, Lord Grey announced that the government had succeeded in framing "a measure which would be effective, without exceeding the bounds of a just and well-advised moderation," and which "had received the unanimous consent of the whole government."

On the 1st March, this measure was brought forward in the House of Commons by Lord John Russell, to whom, — though not in the cabinet, — this honorable duty had been justly confided. In the House of Commons he had already made the question his own; and now he was the exponent of the policy of the government. The measure was briefly this: — to disfranchise sixty of the smallest boroughs; to withdraw one member from forty-seven other boroughs; to add eight members for the metropolis; thirty-four for large towns; and fifty-five for counties, in England; and to give five additional members to Scotland, three to Ireland, and one to Wales. By this new distribution of the franchise, the House of Commons would be reduced in number from six hundred and fifty-eight, to five hundred and ninety-six, or by sixty-two members.[1]

For the old rights of election in boroughs, a 10*l.* household franchise was substituted; and the corporations were deprived of their exclusive privileges. It was computed that half a million of persons would be enfranchised. Improved arrangements were also proposed, for the registration of votes, and the mode of polling at elections.

This bold measure alarmed the opponents of reform, and

[1] Hansard's Deb., 3d Ser., ii. 1061.

failed to satisfy the radical reformers; but on the whole, it was well received by the reform party, and by the country. One of the most stirring periods in our history was approaching: but its events must be rapidly passed over. After a debate of seven nights, the bill was brought in without a division. Its opponents were collecting their forces, while the excitement of the people in favor of the measure, was continually increasing. On the 22d March, the second reading of the bill was carried by a majority of one only, in a House of six hundred and eight, — probably the greatest number which, up to that time, had ever been assembled at a division. On the 19th of April, on going into committee, ministers found themselves in a minority of eight, on a resolution proposed by General Gascoyne, that the number of members returned for England, ought not to be diminished.[1] On the 21st, ministers announced that it was not their intention to proceed with the bill. On that same night, they were again defeated on a question of adjournment, by a majority of twenty-two.[2]

Dissolution in 1831.

This last vote was decisive. The very next day, Parliament was prorogued by the king in person, "with a view to its immediate dissolution."[3] It was one of the most critical days in the history of our country. At a time of grave political agitation, the people were directly appealed to by the king's government, to support a measure by which their feelings and passions had been aroused, — and which was known to be obnoxious to both Houses of Parliament, and to the governing classes.

The people were now to decide the question; — and they

[1] Hansard's Deb., 3d Ser., iii. 1687.

[2] *Ibid.* 1806. It has often been represented, — and was so stated by Lord Brougham on the following day, — that this vote amounted to "stopping the supplies." It cannot, however, bear such a construction, the question before the House being a motion concerning the Liverpool election. Late down in the list of orders of the day, a report from the Committee of Supply was to be received, which dropped by reason of the adjournment.

[3] Hansard's Deb., 3d Ser., iii. 1810. See *supra*, p. 122.

decided it. A triumphant body of reformers was returned, pledged to carry the reform bill; and on the 6th July, the second reading of the renewed measure was agreed to, by a majority of one hundred and thirty-six.[1] The most tedious and irritating discussions ensued in committee, — night after night; and the bill was not disposed of until the 21st September, when it was passed by a majority of one hundred and nine.[2]

Second Reform Bill, 1831.

That the peers were still adverse to the bill was certain; but whether, at such a crisis, they would venture to oppose the national will, was doubtful.[3] On the 7th October, after a debate of five nights, — one of the most memorable by which that House has ever been distinguished, and itself a great event in history, — the bill was rejected on the second reading, by a majority of forty-one.[4]

Rejected by the Lords.

The battle was to be fought again. Ministers were too far pledged to the people to think of resigning; and on the motion of Lord Ebrington, they were immediately supported by a vote of confidence from the House of Commons.[5]

Third Reform Bill, 1831-32.

On the 20th October, Parliament was prorogued; and after a short interval of excitement, turbulence, and danger, met again on the 6th December. A third reform bill was immediately brought in, — changed in many respects, — and much improved by reason of the recent census, and other statistical investigations. Amongst other changes, the total number of members was no longer proposed to be reduced. This bill was read a second time on Sunday morning, the

1 Hansard's Deb., 3d Ser., iv. 906. Ayes, 367; Noes, 231.

2 *Ibid.* vii. 464. The division was taken on the question, "That this Bill do pass."

3 The position of the Peers at this time has been already noticed, *supra*, p. 249, *et seq.*

4 Hansard's Deb., 3d Ser., viii. 340. This debate I heard myself, being present in the House of Lords until the daylight division on the 7th October. It was the first debate in the Lords, which I had yet had the privilege of attending.

5 Hansard's Deb., 3d Ser., viii. 380.

18th of December, by a majority of one hundred and sixty-two.[1] On the 23d March, it was passed by the House of Commons, and once more was before the House of Lords.

Read second time by the Lords.

Here the peril of again rejecting it could not be concealed, — the courage of some was shaken, — the patriotism of others aroused; and after a debate of four nights, the second reading was affirmed by the narrow majority of nine. But danger still awaited it. The peers who would no longer venture to reject such a bill, were preparing to change its essential character by amendments. Meanwhile the agitation of the people was becoming dangerous. Compulsion and physical force were spoken of; and political unions, and monster meetings assumed an attitude of intimidation. A crisis was approaching, — fatal, perhaps, to the peace of the country: violence, if not revolution, seemed impending.

Disfranchising clauses postponed.

The disfranchisement of boroughs formed the basis of the measure; and the first vote of the peers, in committee on the bill, postponed the consideration of the disfranchising clauses, by a majority of thirty-five.[2] Notwithstanding the assurances of opposition peers, that they would concede a large measure of reform, — it was now evident that amendments would be made, to which ministers were bound in honor to the people and the Commons, not to assent. The time had come, when either the Lords must be coerced, or the ministers must resign.[3] This alternative was submitted to the king. He refused to create peers: the ministers resigned, and their resignation was accepted. Again the Commons came to the rescue of the bill and the reform ministry. On the motion of Lord Ebrington, an address was immediately voted by them, renewing their expressions of unaltered confidence in the late ministers, and imploring his Majesty "to call to his councils such persons only, as will carry into effect, unimpaired in

[1] Hansard's Deb., 3d Ser., ix. 546.

[2] *Ibid.* xii. 677.

[3] See *supra*, p. 251.

all its essential provisions, that bill for reforming the representation of the people, which has recently passed this House."

The king, meanwhile, insisted upon one condition, — that any new ministry, — however constituted, — should pledge themselves to an extensive measure of reform.[1] But, even if the Commons and the people had been willing to give up their own measure, and accept another at the hands of their opponents, — no such ministry could be formed. The public excitement was greater than ever; and the government and the people were in imminent danger of a bloody collision, when Earl Grey was recalled to the councils of his sovereign. The bill was now secure. The peers averted the threatened addition to their numbers, by abstaining from further opposition; and the bill, — the Great Charter of 1832, — at length received the Royal Assent.[2]

Reform Act passed.

It is now time to advert to the provisions of this famous statute; and to inquire how far it corrected the faults of a system, which had been complained of for more than half a century. The main evil had been the number of nomination, or rotten boroughs enjoying the franchise. Fifty-six of these, — having less than two thousand inhabitants, and returning one hundred and eleven members, — were swept away. Thirty boroughs, having less than four thousand inhabitants, lost each a member. Weymouth and Melcombe Regis lost two. This disfranchisement extended to one hundred and forty-three members. The next evil had been, that large populations were unrepresented; and this was now redressed. Twenty-two large towns, including metropolitan districts, received the privilege of returning two members; and twenty more, of returning one. The large county populations were also regarded in the distribution of seats, — the number of county members

The Reform Act, England, 1832.

[1] Hansard's Deb., 3d Ser., xii. 783; *Ibid.* 995, the Duke of Wellington's explanation, May 17th; Roebuck's Whig Ministry, ii. 313.

[2] 2 & 3 Will. IV. c. 45.

being increased from ninety-four to one hundred and fifty-nine. The larger counties were divided; and the number of members adjusted with reference to the importance of the constituencies.

Another evil was the restricted and unequal franchise. This too was corrected. All narrow rights of election were set aside in boroughs; and a 10*l.* household franchise was established. The freemen of corporate towns were the only class of electors whose rights were reserved; but residence within the borough was attached as a condition to their right of voting. Those freemen, however, who had been created since March 1831, were excepted from the electoral privilege. Crowds had received their freedom, in order to vote against the reform candidates at the general election: they had served their purpose, and were now disfranchised. Birth or servitude were henceforth to be the sole claims to the freedom of any city, which should confer a vote.

The county constituency was enlarged by the addition of copyholders and leaseholders, for terms of years, and of tenants-at-will paying a rent of 50*l.* a year. The latter class had been added in the Commons, on the motion of the Marquess of Chandos, in opposition to the government. The object of this addition was to strengthen the interests of the landlords, which it undoubtedly effected; but as it extended the franchise to a considerable class of persons, it was at least consistent with the liberal design of the reform act.

Another evil of the representative system had been the excessive expenses at elections. This too was sought to be mitigated by the registration of electors, the division of counties and boroughs into convenient polling districts, and the reduction of the days of polling.

It was a measure, at once bold, comprehensive, moderate, and constitutional. Popular; but not democratic: — it extended liberty, without hazarding revolution. Two years before, Parliament had refused to enfranchise a single unrepresented town; and now this wide redistribution of the franchise had been accomplished! That it was theoretically complete, and left nothing for future statesmen to effect, — its authors never affirmed; but it was a masterly settlement of a perilous question. Its defects will be noticed hereafter, in recounting the efforts which have since been made to correct them; but whatever they were, — no law since the Bill of Rights, is to be compared with it in importance. Worthy of the struggles it occasioned, — it conferred immortal honor on the statesmen who had the wisdom to conceive it — and the courage to command its success.

The Reform Act, Scotland.

The defects of the Scotch representation, being even more flagrant and indefensible than those of England, were not likely to be omitted from Lord Grey's general scheme of reform. On the 9th March, 1831, a bill was brought in to amend the representation of Scotland; but the discussions on the English bill, and the sudden dissolution of Parliament, interrupted its further progress. The same lot awaited it, in the short session of 1831; but in 1832, its success was assured in the general triumph of the cause.[1] The entire representation was remodelled. Forty-five members had been assigned to Scotland at the Union: this number was now increased to fifty-three, of whom thirty were allotted to counties, and twenty-three to cities and burghs. The county franchise was extended to all owners of property of 10*l.* a year, and to certain classes of leaseholders; and the burgh franchise to all 10*l.* householders.

The Reform Act, Ireland, 1832.

The representation of Ireland had many of the defects of the English system. Several rotten and nomination boroughs, however, had already been disfranchised on the union with England; and disfranchisement, therefore, did not form any part of the Irish Reform Act. But the right of election was taken away from the corporations, and vested in 10*l.* householders; and large additions were made to the county constituency. The number

[1] 2 & 3 Will. IV. c. 65.

of members in Ireland, which the Act of Union had settled at one hundred, was now increased to one hundred and five.[1]

Further extension of the Irish franchise, 1850.

This measure was the least successful of the three great reform acts of 1832. Complaints were immediately made of the restricted franchise which it had created; and the number of electors registered, proved much less than had been anticipated. After repeated discussions, a measure was passed in 1850, by which the borough franchise was extended to householders rated at 8*l.*; and further additions were made to the county franchise.[2]

Political results of the Reform Acts.

The representation of the country had now been reconstructed on a wider basis. Large classes had been admitted to the franchise; and the House of Commons represented more freely the interests and political sentiments of the people. The reformed Parliament, accordingly, has been more liberal and progressive in its policy than the Parliaments of old; more vigorous and active; more susceptible to the influence of public opinion; and more secure in the confidence of the people. But in its constitution, grave defects still remained to be considered.

Bribery since the Reform Act.

Prominent among the evils of the electoral system which have been noticed, was that of bribery at elections. For the correction of this evil, the reform acts made no direct provision. Having increased the number of electors, the legislature trusted to their independence and public spirit in the exercise of the franchise; and to the existing laws against bribery. But bribery is the scandal of free institutions in a rich country; and it was too soon evident, that as more votes had been created, more votes were to be sold. It was not in nomination boroughs, or in boroughs sold in gross, that bribery had flourished: but it had been the vice of places where a small body of electors, — exercising the same privilege as proprietors, — sold the seats

[1] 2 & 3 Will. IV. c. 88. Hansard's Deb., 3d Ser., iii. 862; *Ibid.* ix. 595; *Ibid.* xiii. 119.

[2] 13 & 14 Vict. c. 69.

which by their individual votes they had the power of conferring.

The reform act had suppressed the very boroughs which had been free from bribery: it had preserved boroughs, and classes of voters, familiarized with corrupt practices; and had created new boroughs, exposed to the same temptations. Its tendency, therefore, — unless corrected by moral influences, — was to increase rather than diminish corruption, in the smaller boroughs. And this scandal, — which had first arisen out of the growing wealth of the country, — was now encouraged by accumulations of property, more vast than in any previous period in our history. If the riches of the nabobs had once proved a source of electoral corruption, — what temptations have since been offered to voters, by the giant fortunes of our own age? Cotton, coal, and iron, — the steam-engine, and the railway, — have called into existence thousands of men, more wealthy than the merchant-princes of the olden time. The riches of Australia alone, may now vie with the ancient wealth of the Indies. Men enriched from these sources have generally been active and public spirited, — engaged in enterprises which parliamentary influence could promote; ambitious of distinction, — and entitled to appeal to the interests and sympathies of electors. Such candidates as these, if they have failed to command votes by their public claims, have had the means of buying them; and their notorious wealth has excited the cupidity of electors. This great addition to the opulent classes of society, has multiplied the means of bribery; and the extension of the franchise has enlarged the field over which it has been spread. Nor has the operation of these causes been sufficiently counteracted by such an enlargement of borough constituencies, as would have placed them beyond the reach of undue solicitation.

So far the moral and social evils of bribery may have been encouraged; but its political results have been less material. Formerly a large proportion of the members of the House of Commons owed their seats to corruption, in one form or another: now no more than an insignificant fraction of the entire body are so tainted. Once the counterpoise of free representation was wanting: now it prevails over the baser elements of the constitution. Nor does the political conduct of members chosen by the aid of bribery, appear to be gravely affected by the original vice of their election. Eighty years ago, their votes would have been secured by the king, or his ministers: now they belong indiscriminately to all parties. Too rich to seek office and emolument, — even were such prizes attainable, — and rarely aspiring to honors, — they are not found corruptly supporting the government of the day; but range themselves on either side, according to their political views, and fairly enter upon the duties of public life.

Sudbury and St. Albans disfranchised.

The exposure of corrupt practices since 1832, has been discreditably frequent; but the worst examples have been presented by boroughs of evil reputation, which the reform act had spared. Sudbury had long been foremost in open and unblushing corruption;[1] which being continued after the reform act, was conclusively punished by the disfranchisement of the borough.[2] St. Albans, not less corrupt, was a few years later, wholly disfranchised.[3] Corrupt practices were exposed at Warwick,[4] at Stafford,[5] and at Ipswich.[6] In corporate towns, freemen had been the class of voters most tainted by bribery; and their electoral rights having been respected by the reform act, they continued to abuse them. At Yarmouth their demoralization was so general, that they were disfranchised, as a body, by act of parliament.[7] But bribery was by no means confined to the freemen. The 10*l.* householders created by the reform act, were too often found unworthy of their new franchise. Misled by bad examples, — and gen-

1 See *supra*, p. 271.
2 7 & 8 Vict. c. 53.
3 15 & 16 Vict. c. 9.
4 Rep. of Committee, 1833, No. 295.
5 *Ibid.* No. 537.
6 *Ibid.* 1835, No. 286.
7 11 & 12 Vict. c. 24.

erally encouraged by the smallness of the electoral body, — they yielded to the corrupt influences by which their political virtue has been assailed. In numerous cases these constituencies, — when their offence was not sufficiently grave to justify a permanent disfranchisement, — were punished in a less degree, by the suspension of the writs.[1]

Measures for the prevention of bribery.

Meanwhile, Parliament was devising means for the more general exposure and correction of such disgraceful practices. It was not enough that writs had been suspended, and the worst constituencies disfranchised: it was necessary for the credit of the House of Commons, and of the new electoral system, that gross abuses of the franchise should be more effectually restrained.

Bribery Act, 1841.

The first measure introduced with this object, was that of Lord John Russell in 1841. Many members who had won their seats by bribery, escaped detection, under cover of the rules of evidence, then followed by election committees. These committees had, — not unnaturally, — required a preliminary proof that persons alleged to have committed bribery, were agents of the sitting member or candidate. Until such agency had been established, they declined to investigate general charges of bribery, which unless committed by authorized agents would not affect the election. When this evidence was wanting, — as it often was, — all the charges of bribery at once fell to the ground; the member retained his seat, and the corrupt electors escaped exposure. To obviate this cause of failure, the act of 1841,[2] — inverting the order of proceeding, — required committees to receive evidence generally upon the charges of bribery, without prior investigation of agency; and thus proofs or implications of agency have since been elicited from the general evidence. And even where agency has not been established, every act of bribery, by whomsoever committed, has been disclosed by witnesses, and reported to the House.

[1] Warwick, Carrickfergus, Hertford, Stafford, Ipswich, &c.

[2] 4 & 5 Vict. c. 57.

While this measure has facilitated the exposure of bribery, it has often pressed with undue severity upon the sitting member. Inferences rather than proofs of agency having been accepted, members have forfeited their seats for the acts of unauthorized agents, without any evidence of their own knowledge or consent. In the administration of this law, committees, — so far from desiring to screen delinquents, — have erred rather on the side of severity. The investigation of corrupt practices has also been, incidentally, facilitated by the amendment of the law of evidence, which permits the personal examination of sitting members and candidates.[1]

Bribery Acts, 1842 and 1852.

The act of 1841 was followed by another, in the next year,[2] which provides for the prosecution of investigations into bribery, after an election committee has closed its inquiries, or where charges of bribery have been withdrawn. But this measure not having proved effectual; another act was passed in 1852,[3] providing for the most searching inquiries into corrupt practices, by commissioners appointed by the Crown, on the address of the two Houses of Parliament. In the exposure of bribery, — and the punishment of its own members when concerned in it, — Parliament has shown no want of earnestness; but in the repression of the offence itself, and the punishment of corrupt electors, its measures have been less felicitous. The disclosures of commissions have been barren of results. At Canterbury one hundred and fifty-five electors had been bribed at one election, and seventy-nine at another: at Maldon, seventy-six electors had received bribes: at Barnstaple, two hundred and fifty-five; at Cambridge, one hundred and eleven; and at Kingston-upon-Hull no less than eight hundred and forty-seven. At the latter place, 26,606*l.* had been spent in three elections. In 1854, bills were brought in for the prevention of bribery in those places, and the disfranchise-

[1] Lord Denman's Act; 14 & 15 Vict. c. 99.
[2] 5 & 6 Vict. c. 102.
[3] 15 & 16 Vict. c. 57.

ment of the electors who had been proved to be corrupt.[1] But under the act which authorized these inquiries, voters giving evidence were entitled to claim an indemnity; and it was now successfully contended that they were protected from disfranchisement, as one of the penalties of their offence. These bills were accordingly withdrawn.[2] Again in 1858, a commission having reported that one hundred and eighty-three freemen of Galway had received bribes, a bill was introduced for the disfranchisement of the freemen of that borough; but for the same reasons, it also miscarried.[3]

Gloucester election, 1859.

In 1860 there were strange disclosures affecting the ancient city of Gloucester. This place had been long familiar with corruption. In 1816 a single candidate had spent 27,500*l.* at an election; in 1818 another candidate had spent 16,000*l.*; and now it appeared that at the last election in 1859, two hundred and fifty electors had been bribed, and eighty-one persons had been guilty of corrupting them.[4]

Wakefield election, 1859.

Up to this time, the places which had been distinguished by such mal-practices, had returned members to Parliament prior to 1832; but in 1860 the perplexing discovery was made, that bribery had also extensively prevailed in the populous and thriving borough of Wakefield, — the creation of the reform act. Eighty-six electors had been bribed; and such was the zeal of the canvassers, that no less than ninety-eight persons had been concerned in bribing them.[5]

The writs for Gloucester and Wakefield were suspended, as a modified punishment of these corrupt places; but the House of Commons was as much at fault as ever, in providing any permanent correction of the evils which had been discovered.

In 1854, a more general and comprehensive measure was

[1] Hans. Deb., 3d Ser., cxxxi. 1018.
[2] *Ibid.* cxxxiii. 1064.
[3] *Ibid.* cxlix. 378, &c.
[4] Report of Commissioners, 1860.
[5] *Ibid.*

devised, for the prevention of corrupt practices at elections.[1] It restrained candidates from paying any election expenses, except through their authorized agents, and the election auditor; and provided for the publication of accounts of all such expenses. It was hoped that these securities would encourage, and perhaps enforce, a more legal expenditure; but they have since received little credit for advancing the cause of purity.

Corrupt practices Act, 1854.

This temporary act has since been continued from time to time, and in 1858 was amended. The legality of travelling expenses to voters had long been a matter of doubt, — having received discordant constructions from different committees. The payment of such expenses might be a covert form of bribery; or it might be a reasonable accommodation to voters, in the proper exercise of their franchise. This doubt had not been settled by the act of 1854; but it had been adjudged in a court of law,[2] that the payment of travelling expenses was not bribery, if paid *bonâ fide* to indemnify a voter for the expenses he had incurred in travelling to the poll, — and not as a corrupt inducement to vote. The act of 1858, following the principle of this judgment, — but adding a further security for its observance, — permitted the candidate, or his agent appointed in writing, to provide conveyance for voters to the poll; but prohibited the payment of any money to voters themselves, for that purpose.[3] But it was objected at the time, — and the same objection has since been repeated, — that the legalizing of travelling expenses, even in this guarded manner, tends to increase the expenses of elections; and this debatable question will probably receive further consideration from the legislature.

Bribery Act of 1858. Travelling expenses.

It is the policy of these recent acts to define clearly the expenses which a candidate may lawfully incur, and to in-

1 17 & 18 Vict. c. 102.

2 Cooper *v.* Slade; 6 E. and B. 447; Rogers on Elections, 334.

3 21 & 22 Vict. c. 87.

sure publicity to his accounts. So far their provisions are a security to the candidate who is resolved to resist the payment of illegal expenses; and an embarrassment, at least, to those who are prepared to violate the law. That they have not been effectual in the restraint of bribery, the recent disclosures of election committees, and commissions sufficiently attest. [Though large constituencies have, in some instances, proved themselves accessible to corruption, bribery has prevailed most extensively in the smaller boroughs. Hence some remedy may be sought in the enlargement of electoral bodies, and the extension of the area of voting.] To repress so grave an evil, more effectual measures will doubtless be devised; but they may still be expected to fail, until bribery shall be unmistakably condemned by public opinion. The law had treated duelling as murder, yet the penalty of death was unable to repress it; but when society discountenanced that time-honored custom, it was suddenly abandoned. Voters may always be found to receive bribes, if offered; but candidates belong to a class whom the influence of society may restrain from committing an offence, condemned alike by the law, and by public opinion.

Policy of legislation concerning bribery.

Other questions affecting the constitution of Parliament, and the exercise of the elective franchise, have been discussed at various times, as well before as since the reform act, and here demand a passing notice.

To shorten the duration of Parliaments, has been one of the changes most frequently urged. Prior to 1694, a Parliament once elected, unless dissolved by the Crown, continued in being until the demise of the reigning king. One of the Parliaments of Charles II. had sat for eighteen years. By the Triennial Act[1] every Parliament, unless sooner dissolved, came to a natural end in three years. On the accession of George I. this period was extended to seven years, by the well known

Duration of Parliaments.

The Septennial Act.

[1] 6 Will. and Mary, c. 2.

Septennial Act.[1] This act, though supported on the ground of general expediency, was passed at a time of political danger; — when the country had scarcely recovered from the rebellion of 1715, and the Jacobite adherents of the Pretender were still an object of apprehension to the government.

In the reign of George II. attempts were made to repeal the Septennial Act;[2] and early in the next reign, Alderman Sawbridge submitted motions, year after year, until his death, for shortening the duration of Parliaments. In 1771 Lord Chatham "with the most deliberate and solemn conviction declared himself a convert to triennial Parliaments."[3] The question afterwards became associated with plans of Parliamentary reform. It formed part of the scheme proposed by the "Friends of the People" in 1792. At that period, and again in 1797, it was advocated by Mr. Grey, in connection with an improved representation, as one of the means of increasing the responsibility of Parliament to the people.[4] The advocates of a measure for shortening the duration of Parliaments, were not then agreed as to the proper limit to be substituted: whether one, three, or five years.[5] But annual Parliaments have generally been embraced in schemes of radical reform.

In times more recent, the repeal of the Septennial Act, — as a distinct question of public policy, — has often been fairly and temperately discussed in Parliament. In 1817 Mr. Brougham gave notice of a motion on the subject; but did not bring it forward. In 1818 Sir Robert Heron moved for leave to bring in a bill, and was supported by Sir Samuel Romilly and Mr. Brougham; but the proposal met with little favor or attention.[6] The subject was not revived until after the passing of the reform act. It was then argued with much ability by Mr. Tennyson, in 1833, 1834, and

[1] 1 Geo. I. c. 38.
[2] In 1734 and 1741.
[3] Parl. Hist. xvii. 223.
[4] Parl. Hist. xxxiii. 650.
[5] Rockingham Mem. ii. 395.
[6] Hansard's Deb., 1st Ser., xxxviii. 802.

1837; and on each occasion met with the support of considerable minorities.[1] On the last occasion, the motion was defeated by a majority of nine only.[2] It did not, however, receive the support of any of the leading statesmen, who had recently carried parliamentary reform. That measure had greatly increased the responsibility of the House of Commons to the people; and its authors were satisfied that no further change was then required in the constitution of Parliament. In 1843, Mr. Sharman Crawfurd revived the question; but met with scant encouragement.[3] Lastly, in 1849, Mr. Tennyson D'Eyncourt obtained leave to bring in a bill, by a majority of five.[4] But notwithstanding this unexpected success, the question, if discussed elsewhere as a matter of theoretical speculation, has since ceased to occupy the attention of Parliament.

Arguments against the Septennial Act.

The repeal of the Septennial Act has been repeatedly advocated on the ground that the Parliament of George I. had abused its trust, in prolonging its own existence; and that, even admitting the overruling necessity of the occasion, — the measure should at least have been temporary. To this it has been answered, that if any wrong was done, it was committed against the people of that day, to whom no reparation can now be made. But to contend that there was any breach of trust, is to limit the authority of Parliament, within bounds not recognized by the constitution. Parliament has not a limited authority, — expressly delegated to it; but has absolute power to make or repeal any law; and every one of its acts is again open to revision. Without a prior dissolution of Parliament, the Unions of Scotland and Ireland were effected, at an interval of nearly a century; — measures involving the extinction of the Parliaments of those countries,

[1] Hansard's Deb., 3d Ser., xix. 1107; *Ibid.* xxiii. 1036; *Ibid.* xxxviii. 680.
[2] Ayes 87, Noes 96.
[3] Hansard's Deb., 3d Ser., lxix. 490.
[4] Ayes 46, Noes 41. Hans. Deb., 3d Ser., cv. 848.

and a fundamental change in that of England, much greater than the Septennial Act had made. That act could have been repealed at any time, if Parliament had deemed it advisable; and no other ground than that of expediency, can now be reasonably urged, for shortening the duration of Parliaments.

The main ground, however, on which this change has been rested, is the propriety of rendering the representatives of the people, more frequently accountable to their constituents. The shorter the period for which authority is intrusted to them, — the more guarded would they be in its exercise, and the more amenable to public opinion. It is said that a Parliament cannot be trusted, if independent of the people, and exposed to the influence of ministers, for seven years. And again, the circumstances of the country are likely to be changed during so prolonged a period; and the conduct of members, approved at first, may afterwards be condemned.

Arguments against change.

On the other side it has been argued, that in practice no Parliament is permitted to continue longer than six years; and that frequent dissolutions have reduced Parliaments, at several periods, to an average duration of three or four years.[1] If Parliaments were elected for three years only, they would often be reduced by various contingencies, to annual Parliaments. They are already elected often enough to make them responsible to their constituents; and more frequent elections would unduly foment political excitement, and increase the expenses of elections, which are already a just ground of complaint.

Of late years the popularity of this question has declined, not so much on account of any theoretical preference for sep-

[1] Sir Samuel Romilly stated, in 1818, that out of eleven Parliaments of Geo. III. eight had lasted six years. Hansard's Deb., 1st Ser., xxxviii. 802. But later periods present a different result. Since the accession of Will. IV., in 1830, — a period of thirty years, — there have been no less than ten Parliaments, showing an average duration of three years only.

tennial Parliaments, as from a conviction that the House of Commons has become accountable to the people, and prompt in responding to their reasonable desires.

Vote by ballot.

The "ballot" is another question repeatedly debated in Parliament, and a popular topic at the hustings, at public meetings, and in the newspaper press. No sooner had the reform act passed, than complaints were made that the elective franchise, so recently enlarged, could not be freely exercised. It was said that the landlords in counties, and wealthy customers in towns, coerced the free will of the electors, and forced them to vote against their opinions and consciences. As a protection against such practices, the necessity of secret voting was contended for. To give the franchise, without the means of exercising it, was declared to be a mockery.

It was not for the first time that the influence now complained of, had been exerted over electors. It had formerly been recognized as one of the natural rights of property. It was known that a few landowners could nominate the county members. They conducted the freeholders to the poll, as naturally as a Highland chieftain led forth his clan to the foray. But now a new electoral policy had been commenced. The people at large had been enfranchised; and new classes of electors called into existence. The political ties which had bound the electors to the landlords were loosened; and the latter, being deprived of their absolute ascendency, endeavored to sustain it by other means. The leaseholders enfranchised by the reform act, being the most dependent, were the very class peculiarly needing protection. The ballot had been called by Cicero the silent assertor of freedom, — *tabella, vindex tacita libertatis*; and it was now proposed, in order to insure freedom of election.

The ballot has been sought mainly for the protection of voters from intimidation and undue influence; but it has also been recommended as a safeguard against bribery. It has been resisted by arguments too various to be briefly reviewed.

The strongest, perhaps, is that every political function being publicly and responsibly exercised, and every debate and vote in Parliament published for the information of the people,— electors can scarcely claim an exemption from that law of publicity, to which their rulers and representatives are subject. Why are they alone, to be irresponsible? Apart from theory, its practical efficacy has also been denied. It has been said that if intimidation were intended, means would be taken to discover the votes of electors, in spite of all the machinery of the ballot. Nor would bribery be prevented, as a candidate would secure fulfilment of corrupt promises, by making his payment for votes, contingent upon his success at the poll.

The advocates of the ballot have, perhaps, exaggerated the advantages of their favored scheme, while its opponents have magnified its evils and its dangers. It is a measure upon which sincere reformers have been, and continued to be, divided. At times, it has made progress in the number and influence of its supporters. Yet such have been its vicissitudes, that it is still difficult for a political observer to divine, whether it will be suddenly adopted, — in the crisis of some party struggle, — or be laid aside as a theory for the disputation of pamphleteers, and debating societies.

In 1833, Mr. Grote took possession of the question of the ballot; and from that time until 1839, he continued to advocate the cause, in a series of temperate and philosophical speeches, — as creditable to his political wisdom, as to his learning and ability. He argued in the calm and earnest spirit of the theoretical statesman; not with the fierce temper of the democrat. His honest labors greatly advanced the popularity of the cause, and improved its parliamentary position. In 1833 he found but one hundred and six supporters;[1] in 1839 he had two hundred and sixteen.[2]

[1] Hansard's Deb., 3d Ser., xvii. 608 — Ayes 106, Noes 211; *Ibid.* xxviii. 369; *Ibid.* xxxiv. 781; *Ibid.* xxxvii. 7; *Ibid.* (1838), xl. 113.

[2] *Ibid.* xlviii. 442 — Ayes 216, Noes 333.

Mr. Grote having retired from Parliament, the question was not allowed to be forgotten. In 1842 Mr. Ward adopted it;[1] and since 1848, Mr. Henry Berkeley has made it his own.[2] With ample stores of fact and anecdote, and with varied resources of humor, he has continued to urge on the question, year after year; but without increased support.

In 1848 his motion was carried by a majority of five.[3] In 1849, it was defeated by a majority of fifty-one: in 1852, by a majority of one hundred and two; and in 1860, by a majority of one hundred and seven. Such reaction of opinion, upon a popular measure, is more significant of ultimate failure, than a steady position, without progress indeed, yet without reverses.

Qualification Acts.

Since the reform act, the qualification laws, — which in different forms had existed for one hundred and fifty years, — have passed away. It was ostensibly to correct the evils of bribery at elections, that property in land was first proposed as a qualification for a member of Parliament. The corruption of boroughs being mainly due to the intrusion of rich commercial men, without local connection, the natural jealousy of the landowners suggested this restraint upon their rivals. In 1696, the first measure to establish a qualification in land, was received with so much favor, that it passed both Houses; but the king, leaning rather to the commercial interests, withheld his assent. In the following year, a similar bill was passed by the Commons, but rejected by the Lords; who had now begun to think that a small landed qualification would increase the influence of the squires, but diminished the authority of the great nobles, who filled the smaller boroughs with members of their own family, and dependents.

The policy of excluding all but the proprietors of land,

[1] Hansard's Deb., 3d Ser., lxiv. 348.
[2] *Ibid.* c. 1225.
[3] Ayes 86, Noes 81.

from the right of sitting in the House of Commons, was at length adopted in the reign of Queen Anne,[1] and was maintained until 1838. In that year this exclusive principle was surrendered; and a new qualification substituted, of the same amount, either in real or personal property, or in both combined.[2] In 1858, the law of property qualification was abandoned altogether.[3] In its original form, it had been invidious and unjust; and, from its beginning to its end, it had been systematically evaded. It would probably not have survived so long the jealousies from which it had sprung, had it not been invested with undue importance, by radical reformers. But when the repeal of this insignificant law was proclaimed as one of the five points of the "Charter," it is not surprising that more moderate politicians should have regarded it as one of the safeguards of the constitution.

Proceedings at elections improved.

Since the passing of the reform act, various minor amendments have been made in the electoral laws. The registration of electors has been improved and simplified,[4] the number of polling-places has been increased,[5] and the polling reduced, in counties as well as in boroughs, a single day.[6] Even the Universities, which had retained their fifteen days of polling, were glad to accept five days, in 1853.

Promptitude in election proceedings has further been insured by the change of some ancient customs. The prescriptive period of forty days between the summons of a new Parliament and its meeting — enlarged by custom to fifty days since the Union with Scotland, — having become an anomaly in an age of railways and telegraphs, has been reduced to thirty-five.[7] Another ancient custom has also

1 9 Anne, c. 5; 33 Geo. II. c. 15.
2 1 & 2 Vict. c. 48.
3 21 & 22 Vict. c. 26.
4 6 & 7 Vict. c. 18.
5 6 & 7 Will. IV. c. 102.
6 5 & 6 Will. IV. c. 36; 16 & 17 Vict. c. 15.
7 By Lord Brougham's Act, 1852; 15 Vict. c. 23.

given way to a more simple procedure. By a recent act the writs for an election are addressed direct to the several returning officers, instead of passing through the sheriff of the county.[1]

Later measures of reform.

A more general revision of the representative system, as settled by the reform acts of 1832, has also been the aim of several administrations, and Parliaments. For some years, there had been a natural reluctance to disturb the settlement which those important measures had recently effected. The old Whig party had regarded it as a constitutional charter, and contended for its "finality." But their advanced Liberal supporters, — after many discussions in Parliament, and much agitation and "pressure from without," — at length prevailed over the more cautious policy of their leaders; and a promise was given, in 1851, that the consideration of the representative system should, at a fitting opportunity, be resumed.[2]

Reform Bill of 1852.

In fulfilment of this promise, Lord John Russell, — twenty years after the settlement of 1832, — proposed its further revision. That measure had not proposed to redistribute the franchise, in precise correspondence with the population of different parts of the country. Not founded upon theoretical views of equal representation; it had not assumed to frame a new constitution; but had provided a remedy for the worst evils of a faulty and corrupt electoral system. It had rescued the representation from a small oligarchy of peers and landowners; and had vested it in the hands of the middle classes. But it had spared many boroughs, which were perhaps too small to exercise their suffrage independently; it had overlooked the claims of some considerable places; and had not embraced the working classes within its scheme of enfranchisement. Lord John

[1] 16 & 17 Vict. c. 78.

[2] Speech of Lord John Russell, 20th Feb. 1851; Hansard's Deb., 3d Ser., cxiv. 863. See also Speech 20th June, 1848: *Ibid.* xcix. 929.

Russell now sought to correct these partial defects, which time had disclosed in the original measure.

He proposed that every existing borough, having less than five hundred electors, should be associated with adjacent places, in the right of returning members; and that Birkenhead and Burnley should be enfranchised. In twenty years there had been a vast increase of population, wealth, and industry, throughout the country. The spread of education and political enlightenment had been rapid: a more instructed generation had grown up: and a marked improvement had arisen, in the social condition of the working classes. It was, therefore, thought right and safe to lower the franchise so far as to embrace classes not hitherto included, and particularly the most skilled artificers, — men who had given proof of their intelligence and good conduct, by large earnings, and a high position among their fellow workmen. With this view, it was proposed to extend the borough franchise to the occupiers of houses of *5l.* rated value; and the county franchise to tenants-at-will rated at *20l.*, and copyholders and lease-holders rated at *5l.* It was also intended to create a new franchise, arising out of the annual payment of *40s.* in direct taxes to the state. Lord John Russell's administration soon afterwards resigned; and this measure was withdrawn before the second reading.[1]

Reform Bill of 1854.

In 1854, Lord John Russell, as a member of Lord Aberdeen's government, proposed another measure, more comprehensive than the last. It comprised the disfranchisement of nineteen small boroughs, returning twenty-nine members; the deprivation of thirty-three other boroughs of one of their members; and the redistribution of the vacant seats, sixty-six in number,[2] amongst the counties and larger boroughs, the Inns of Court, and the University of London. It proposed to reduce the franchise in counties to *10l.*; and in boroughs to the municipal rating

1 Hansard's Deb., 3d Ser., cxix. 252, 971; Bill, No. 48, of 1852.

2 Including the vacant seats of Sudbury and St. Albans.

franchise of 6*l.* Several new franchises were also to be added, in order to modify the hard uniformity of the household franchise. A salary of 100*l.* a year: an income of 10*l.* from dividends: the payment of 40*s.* in direct taxes: a degree at any of the universities; and 50*l.* in a savings' bank, were accounted sufficient securities for the proper exercise of the suffrage. In the distribution of seats, a novel principle was to be established, with a view to insure the representation of minorities. Some counties and other large places were to return three members each; but no elector would be entitled to vote for more than two candidates out of three. This theory of representation, — though very ably advocated by some speculative writers,[1] — found little favor in Parliament, with men accustomed to determine every disputed question among themselves, by the votes of the majority. The consideration of this measure was postponed, by the outbreak of the war with Russia.[2]

The Reform Bill of 1859.

The next measure of parliamentary reform was proposed in 1859, by the government of Lord Derby. Lord Derby, — having been one of the most eloquent, spirited, and courageous of Lord Grey's colleagues in 1832, — was now the leader of the great Conservative party, which had opposed the first reform act. But his party, deferring to the judgment of Parliament, had since honorably acquiesced in that settlement. Meanwhile, the revision of that measure had been thrice recommended from the throne; and three successive administrations had been pledged to undertake the task. Some scheme of reform had thus become a political necessity. The measure agreed upon by the ministers, and the principles upon which it was founded, were ably explained by Mr. Disraeli. It was not sought to reconstruct the representation of the country solely

1 Minorities and Majorities; their relative Rights, by James Garth Marshall, 1853; Edinb. Rev., July 1854, Art. vii.; and more lately Hare on the Election of Representatives, 1859.

2 Hansard's Deb., 3d Ser., cxxx. 491; *Ibid.* cxxxi. 277.

on the basis of population and property: but having reference to those material elements, as well as to the representation of various interests, and classes of the community,—this measure comprehended some considerable changes. It was not proposed wholly to disfranchise any borough; but one member was to be taken from fifteen boroughs, having a population under six thousand. Eight of the vacant seats were assigned to the great county populations of Yorkshire, South Lancashire, and Middlesex; and seven to new boroughs; which according to this scheme, would complete the representation of the several interests of the country.

The two previous measures of Lord John Russell had contemplated a reduction of the borough franchise. No such reduction was now proposed; but the franchise in counties, was assimilated to that in boroughs. Hitherto the borough franchise had been founded upon occupation; and the county franchise generally upon property. This distinction it was now proposed to abolish; and to substitute an identity of franchise, between the county and the town. The 40*s.* freeholders resident in towns, would be transferred from the constituency of the county, to that of the town. Several new franchises were also to be created, similar to those proposed in 1854, but more comprehensive. Men possessed of 10*l.* a year arising from dividends: 60*l.* in a savings' bank; or a pension of 20*l.*: lodgers paying 20*l.* a year,—equal to 8*s.* a week: graduates of all universities: ministers of religion of every denomination: members of the legal profession in all its branches: registered medical practitioners; and schoolmasters holding a certificate from the Privy Council, were to be entitled to vote, wherever they were resident. And facilities for exercising the franchise, were to be afforded by means of voting papers.[1]

Objections urged against this measure.

This scheme encountered objections from two different quarters. Two influential members of the government,—Mr. Walpole and Mr. Henley,—alarmed by the proposed identity of franchise,

[1] Hansard's Deb., 3d Ser., clii. 966.

resigned their seats in the cabinet.[1] The Opposition, partly taking up the same ground, were unwilling to deprive the 40*s*. freeholders resident in boroughs, of their county votes; and insisted upon the lowering of the borough suffrage. The government, weakened by these resignations, had now to meet a formidable amendment, moved by Lord John Russell on the second reading of the bill, which expressed the views of the opposition. The identity of franchise was objected to by Mr. Walpole and Mr. Henley, on account of the supposed danger of drawing one broad line between the represented, and the unrepresented classes. Lord John Russell concurred in this objection, believing that such a principle would eventually lead to electoral districts. He also opposed the bill on two other grounds: first, that the 40*s*. freeholders, being the most liberal element in the county constituencies, ought not to be disfranchised; and secondly, that their admission to the borough franchise would encourage the manufacture of fagot votes,— like the old burgage tenure, which had been the means of extending the influence of patrons. He objected to the continuance of the 10*l*. household suffrage in boroughs, on the ground that considerable classes of people, worthy to be intrusted with votes, had sprung up since that franchise had been established. After seven nights' debate, the amendment was carried by a majority of thirty-nine.[2] Upon the issue raised by this decision, the government determined to dissolve Parliament, and appeal to the people.[3] On the assembling of a new Parliament, the ministers, having failed to secure a majority at the elections, were at once driven from office by an amendment to the address, declaring that they had not the confidence of the House of Commons.[4]

Reform Bill of 1860.

And now the question of reform was resumed, once more, by Lord John Russell, on behalf of Lord Palmerston's administration. On the 1st March, 1860, he introduced a bill, in accordance with the spirit of

[1] Hansard's Deb., 3d Ser., clii. 1058.
[2] *Ibid.* cliii. 389–1157.
[3] *Ibid.* 1301.
[4] *Ibid.* cliv. 98–297.

the amendment by which he had destroyed the measure of the previous year; but differing materially from the bills of 1852 and 1854. Like the bill of Lord Derby's government, it spared all the smaller boroughs. None were to be disfranchised; but it deprived twenty-five boroughs, with a population under seven thousand, of one of their members. This disfranchisement fell far short of that proposed in 1854; and it was avowed that if any more places had been condemned, their representatives, combining with the Conservative Opposition, would have succeeded in defeating the bill. If such was now the difficulty of contending with these personal and local interests, what must have been the difficulties of Mr. Pitt in 1784, and of Lord Grey in 1832? One minister vainly attempted to buy off his opponents; the other overcame them by strong popular support. The first expedient was now wholly out of the question: the latter source of strength was wanting.

Fifteen of the vacant seats were distributed amongst the counties; and ten given to the larger cities, and some new boroughs. The 50*l.* occupation franchise in counties, was reduced to a 10*l.* *bonâ fide* holding. The 10*l.* borough franchise was lowered to 6*l.*, avowedly for the purpose of comprehending many of the working classes. It was calculated that the new franchise would add two hundred thousand electors to the cities and boroughs. None of the varied franchises, which had formed part of the bills of 1854 and 1859, were again proposed. Sneered at as "fancy franchises," and distrusted as the means of creating fictitious votes, they were now abandoned; and the more rude, but tangible tests of good citizenship inflexibly maintained.[1]

Bill lost by delays and indifference.

This bill was defeated, neither by adverse majorities, nor by changes in the government; but by delays, and the pressure of other important measures. It was not until the 3d of May, — after six adjourned debates, — that it was read a second time, without

1 Hansard's Deb., 3d Ser., clvi. 2050.

a division. Discussions were renewed on going into committee; and at length, on the 11th of June, the bill was withdrawn.[1] Bills to amend the representation in Scotland and Ireland, which had been hopelessly awaiting discussion, had already been abandoned.[2]

Obstacles to Parliamentary Reform.

Such obstacles as these, — however harassing and inconvenient, — would have been easily overcome if the government had been cordially supported by their own party in the House of Commons, and by popular acclamations. But within the walls of the House, parliamentary reform was received with coldness, — if not with ill-disguised repugnance, — even by its professed supporters; and throughout the country, there prevailed the most profound indifference. The cause which had once aroused enthusiasm, now languished from general neglect. The press was silent or discouraging: petitions were not forthcoming: public meetings were not assembled: the people were unmoved. Whence this indifference? Why so marked a change of popular feeling, in less than thirty years? The settlement of 1832 had secured the great object of representation, — good government. Wise and beneficent measures had been passed: enlightened public opinion had been satisfied. The representation was theoretically incomplete; but Parliament had been brought into harmony with the interests and sympathies of the people. It had nearly approached Mr. Burke's standard, according to whom, "The virtue, spirit, and essence of a House of Commons, consists in its being the express image of the feelings of a nation."[3] The best results of reform had been realized: the country was prosperous and contented. It has ever been the genius of the English people to love freedom: they are roused by injustice: they resent a public or private wrong; but they are rarely moved by theoretical

1 Hansard's Deb., 3d Ser., clix. 226.
2 *Ibid.* 143.
3 Burke's Works, ii. 288 (Present Discontents).

grievances. Living under a settled form of government, they have cared little for model constitutions; and united in the bonds of a highly civilized society, they have never favored democracy. Again, since 1832, political power has been vested mainly in the middle classes; and the employers of labor, being masters of the representation, are unwilling to share their power with the working classes, by whom they are outnumbered. Hence the inertness of existing constituencies. They enjoy exclusive political privileges; and desire to maintain them.

One other cause must not be omitted. While these moderate measures of reform were being proposed by successive governments, other schemes had been discussed elsewhere, — designed to extend largely the influence of numbers, — and conceived and advocated in the spirit of democracy. Such proposals increased the indisposition of moderate reformers, and of the classes already enfranchised, to forward an extension of the suffrage. At the same time, the advocates of more comprehensive schemes of reform, — while they coldly accepted measures falling far short of their own, — were not unwilling that they should be postponed to some period more promising for the adoption of their advanced principles. And thus, with the tacit acquiescence of all parties, the question of parliamentary reform was again suffered to sleep.

CHAPTER VII.

Relations of Parliament to the Crown, the Law, and the People. — Abuses of Privilege in Proceedings against Wilkes. — Exclusion of Strangers: — Publication of Debates restrained: — Contest with the Printers, 1771: — Freedom of Reporting Established: — Its Political Results: — Entire Publicity of Proceedings in Parliament: — Petitions: — Pledges of Members. — Conflict of Privilege and Law. — Increased Power, and Moderation of the Commons. — Control of Parliament over the Executive: — Impeachments: — Control of the Commons over Taxes and Expenditure. — Sketch of Parliamentary Oratory.

We have traced, in the last chapter, the changes which have been successively introduced into the constitution of the House of Commons, — the efforts made to reduce the influence of the Crown, the ministers, and the aristocracy over its members, — to restrain corruption, and encourage an honest and independent discharge of its duties to the public. We have now to regard Parliament, — and mainly the House of Commons, — under another aspect: to observe how it has wielded the great powers intrusted to it, — in what manner it has respected the prerogatives of the Crown, the authority of the law, and other jurisdictions, — and how far it has acknowledged its own responsibilities to the people.

Contests of the Commons on questions of privilege.

Throughout its history, the House of Commons has had struggles with the Crown, the House of Lords, the courts of law, the press, and the people. At one time straining its own powers, at another resisting encroachments upon its just authority: successful in asserting its rights, but failing in its usurpations; it has gradually assumed its proper position in the State, — controlling all other powers, but itself controlled and responsible. The worst period of its dependence and corruption, was also marked by the most flagrant abuses of its power. And the more it has been brought under the control of public opinion, — the greater have been its moderation and forbearance.

The reign of George III. witnessed many remarkable changes in the relations of Parliament to the people, which all contributed to increase its responsibility. Moral causes also extended the control of the people over their rulers, even more than amendments of the law, by which constitutional abuses were corrected. Events occurred early in this reign, which brought to a decisive issue, important questions affecting the privileges of Parliament, and the rights of the subject.

Proceedings of the Commons against Wilkes, 1763.

The liberty of the subject had already been outraged by the imprisonment of Wilkes, under a general warrant, for the publication of the celebrated No. 45 of the "North Briton;" [1] when Parliament thrust itself forward, as if to prove how privilege could still be abused, as well as prerogative. Being a member of the House of Commons, Wilkes had been released from his imprisonment, by the Court of Common Pleas, on a writ of *habeas corpus*, on the ground of his privilege.[2]

Wilkes denied his privilege.

The only exceptions to the privilege of freedom from arrest, which had ever been recognized by Parliament, were "treason, felony, and breach of the peace," "or refusing to give surety of the peace." The Court properly acknowledged the privilege, as defined by Parliament itself; and discharged Wilkes from his imprisonment. He was afterwards served with a subpœna, on an information against him in the Court of King's Bench, to which, on the ground of privilege, he had not entered an appearance. On the meeting of Parliament, however, in November, 1763, he lost no time in stating that if his privilege

1 See Chap. X., on the Liberty of the Subject.

2 Wilson's Reports, ii. 150. St. Tr. xix. 539.

should be affirmed, he was ready to waive it, "and to put himself upon a jury of his countrymen."[1] Parliament, — which had ordinarily been too prone to enlarge its privileges — was now the first to abridge and surrender them. Eager to second the vengeance of the king, the Commons commenced by voting that the "North Briton," No. 45, was "a false, scandalous, and malicious libel," and ordering it to be burned by the hands of the common hangman. Then, in defiance of their own previous resolutions, they resolved "that privilege of Parliament does not extend to the case of writing and publishing seditious libels, nor ought to be allowed to obstruct the ordinary course of law, in the speedy and effectual prosecution of so heinous and dangerous offence."[2]

To the principle of the latter part of this resolution there can be little exception; but here it was applied *ex post facto* to a particular case, and used to justify a judicial decision, contrary to law and usage. Mr. Pitt, while he denounced the libel and the libeller, remonstrated against the abandonment of the privilege. These resolutions being communicated to the Lords, were agreed to; but not without a most able protest, signed by seventeen Peers, against the surrender of the privilege of Parliament "to serve a particular purpose, *ex post facto, et pedente lite*, in the Courts below."[3]

Such a libel as that of Wilkes, a few years later, would have attracted little notice; but at that time it is not surprising that it provoked a legal prosecution. It was, however, a libel upon the king's ministers, rather than upon the king himself. Upon Parliament it contained nothing but an obscure innuendo,[4] which alone brought the matter legitimately within

[1] Parl. Hist. xv. 1361.

[2] Com. Journ. xxix. 689; Parl. Hist. xv. 1362–1378.

[3] Parl. Hist. xv. 1371; Ann. Reg. 1763, 135. Horace Walpole says it was drawn up by Chief Justice Pratt.

[4] The passage reflecting upon Parliament was as follows: "As to the entire approbation of Parliament [of the peace] which is so vainly boasted of, the world knows how that was obtained. The large debt on the Civil

the limits of privilege. There were, doubtless, many precedents, — to be avoided, rather than followed, — for pronouncing writings to be seditious; but sedition is properly an offence cognizable by law. So far as the libel affected the character of either House, it was within the scope of privilege; but its seditious character could only be determined by the courts, where a prosecution had already been commenced. To condemn the libel as seditious was, therefore, to anticipate the decision of the proper tribunal; and to order it to be burned by the hands of the common hangman, — if no great punishment to the libeller, — yet branded him as a criminal before his trial. The mob took part with Wilkes, — assailed the Sheriffs who were executing the orders of Parliament; and having rescued part of the obnoxious "North Briton" from the flames, bore it in triumph to Temple Bar, beyond the limits of the city jurisdiction. Here they made another bonfire, and burned a jack-boot and a petticoat, the favorite emblems of the late unpopular minister Lord Bute, and the Princess.[1] This outrage was resented by both Houses; an address being voted for a prosecution of all persons concerned in it.[2]

Wilkes absconds, and is expelled.

The severities of Parliament were still pursuing Wilkes. He had been ordered by the Commons to attend in his place, with a view to further proceedings; but having been wounded in a duel, — provoked and forced upon him by Mr. Martin, one of their own members,[3] — his attendance was necessarily deferred. Meanwhile, expecting no mercy either from the Crown or from Parliament, — tracked by spies, and beset with petty persecutions,[4] — he prudently withdrew to Paris. Being absent, in contempt of the orders of the House, the proceedings were no longer

List, already above half a year in arrear, shows pretty clearly the transactions of the winter."

1 Walpole's Mem. i. 330.

2 Parl. Hist. xv. 1380.

3 See Corresp. Parl. Hist. xv. 1356, *n*.

4 Grenville Papers, ii. 155.

stayed; and evidence having been taken at the bar, of his being the author and publisher of the "North Briton," No. 45, he was expelled the House. In expelling a member, whom they had adjudged to have committed the offence of writing and publishing a seditious libel, the Commons acted within their powers; but the vote was precipitate and vindictive. He was about to be tried for his offence; and they might at least have waited for his conviction, instead of prejudging his cause, and anticipating his legal punishment.

Proceedings of the Lords.

But the Lords far outstripped the other House, in this race of persecution. On the first day of the session, while the Commons were dealing with the "North Briton," Lord Sandwich complained to the Lords of an "Essay on Woman," with notes, to which the name of Bishop Warburton was affixed; and of another printed paper called "The *Veni Creator* paraphrased." Of the "Essay on Woman," thirteen copies only had been printed, in Wilkes's private printing-press: there was no evidence of publication; and a proof-copy of the work had been obtained through the treachery of one of his printers. If these writings were obscene and blasphemous, their author had exposed himself to the law: but the only pretence for noticing them in Parliament, was the absurd use of the name of a bishop, — a member of their Lordships' House. Hence it became a breach of privilege! This ingenious device was suggested by the Chancellor, Lord Henley; and Mr. Grenville obtained the bishop's consent to complain of the outrage, in his name.[1] But it was beneath the dignity of the House to notice such writings, obtained in such a manner; and it was notorious that the politics of the author were the true ground of offence, and not his blasphemy, or his irreverence to the bishop. The proceeding was the more ridiculous, from the complaint of obscenity having been made by the most profligate of peers, — "Satan rebuking sin."[2] Nevertheless the Lords were not

1 Grenville Papers, ii. 154.

2 "'The Beggar's Opera' being performed at Covent-Garden Theatre

ashamed to examine the printers, from whom the proof-sheets had been obtained, in order to prove that Wilkes was the author. They at once addressed the king to order a prosecution of Wilkes; but as he was, at this time, laid up with his wounds, proceedings against him for the breach of privilege were postponed. On the 24th January, when he had escaped from their jurisdiction, they ordered him into custody.[1] They were at least spared the opprobrium of further oppression; but their proceedings had not escaped the indignation and ridicule which they deserved.

Leaving Wilkes, for a time, as a popular martyr, — and passing over his further contests with the government in the courts of law, — we shall find him, a few years later, again coming into collision with Parliament, and becoming the successful champion of popular rights.

"Droit Le Roi" ordered to be burned.

The discussions on his case were scarcely concluded, when a complaint was made to the Lords, by Lord Lyttelton, of a book with the title of "*Droit Le Roi.*" It was the very opposite of Wilkes's writings, — being a high prerogative treatise, founded upon statutes, precedents, and the dicta of lawyers before the Revolution. It was too monstrous to be defended by any one; and, like the "North Briton," it was ordered by both Houses to be burned by the hands of the common hangman.[2] There was no pretence for dealing with this case as a breach of privilege; but as the popular cause had suffered from the straining of privilege, in the person of Wilkes, no one attempted to save this ultra-loyal treatise from the flames.

At the dissolution of Parliament in 1768, Wilkes, who had,

soon after this event, the whole audience, when Macheath says, 'That Jemmy Twitcher should peach me, I own surprises me,' burst out into an applause of application; and the nick-name of Jemmy Twitcher stuck by the earl so as almost to occasion the disuse of his title." — *Walpole's Mem.* i. 314.

[1] Parl. Hist. xv. 1346.

[2] Parl. Hist. xv. 1418; Lords' Journ. xxx. 477, &c.; Walpole's Mem. i. 383.

in the mean time, resided abroad, — an exile and an outlaw, — offered himself as a candidate for the city of London. He was defeated; but the memory of his wrongs was revived; and with no other claim to popular favor, he found himself the idol of the people. He now became a candidate for Middlesex, and was returned by a large majority. His triumph was celebrated by his partisans; who forced the inhabitants of London to illuminate, and join in their cry of "Wilkes and liberty," — marking every door, as they passed along, with the popular number "45."

Wilkes returned for Middlesex, 1768.

But he was soon to suffer the penalties of his past offences. On the first day of the ensuing session, having appeared before the Court of King's Bench on his outlawry, he was committed on a *capias utlagatum.* Rescued by the mob, he again surrendered himself; and his imprisonment was the unhappy occasion of riots, and of a collision between the military and the people. His outlawry was soon afterwards reversed; but he was sentenced to two years' imprisonment for his libels.

His imprisonment by the Court of King's Bench.

During the first session of this Parliament, therefore, Wilkes was unable to take his seat; and as yet no proceedings were commenced against him in the House of Commons. At the opening of the second session, in November, he brought himself into notice by accusing Lord Mansfield, — in a petition to the House, — of having altered the record on his trial; and Mr. Webb, the Solicitor of the Treasury, of having bribed Curry, the printer, with public money, to appear as a witness against him. His charges were voted to be groundless; but they served the purpose of exciting popular sympathy. He was brought down to Westminster to prove them, attended by a large concourse of people;[1] and for a moment he perplexed the House by submitting whether, being a member, he could stand at the bar, without having taken the oaths,

Wilkes's charges against Lord Mansfield and Mr. Webb, 1768.

[1] Walpole's Mem. iii. 314.

and delivered in his qualification. But he soon received the obvious answer that being in custody at the bar, the acts affecting members sitting in the House, did not apply to his case.[1]

Libel upon Lord Weymouth.

But a graver matter in which Wilkes had involved himself, was now to be considered. He had published a letter from Lord Weymouth to the magistrates of Surrey, advising them to call in the military for the suppression of riots; with a prefatory letter of his own, in which he had applied the strongest language to the Secretary of State; and had designated the late collision between the troops and the populace in St. George's Fields, as a bloody massacre. Here again, a strange and irregular proceeding was resorted to. The letter was a libel upon a Secretary of State, as an officer of the Crown; who, being also a peer, complained of it as a breach of privilege. But instead of proceeding against the author in the House of Lords, the paper was voted an insolent, scandalous, and seditious libel; and a conference was held with the Commons on the conduct of Wilkes, as a member of their House.[2] They immediately took the matter up; and rushing headlong into a quarrel which did not concern them, called upon Wilkes for his defence. He boldly confessed himself the author of the prefatory letter; and gloried in having brought "to light that bloody scroll" of Lord Weymouth. The letter was voted to be an insolent, scandalous, and seditious libel. A motion was then made for the expulsion of Wilkes, founded upon several distinct grounds: first, this last seditious libel, which, if a breach of privilege, was cognizable by the Lords, and not by the Commons; and, if a seditious libel, was punishable by law: secondly, the publication of the "North Briton," five years before, for which Wilkes was already under sentence, and had suffered expul-

Resolutions for his expulsion.

[1] Com. Journ. Nov. 14th, 1768, to Feb. 1st, 1769; Cavendish Deb. i. 46–131.

[2] Lords' Journ. xxxii. 213.

sion from a former Parliament: thirdly, his impious and obscene libels, for which he was already suffering punishment, by the judgment of a criminal court; and, fourthly, that he was under sentence of the court to suffer twenty-two months' imprisonment.

Such were the cumulative charges, upon which it was now proposed to expel him. Nothing can be more undoubted than the right of the House of Commons to expel one of its own members, for any offence which, in its judgment, deserves such punishment, — whether it be a breach of privilege or not. But here the exercise of this right was unjust and oppressive. It was forcibly argued, that for all the offences enumerated, but one, Wilkes had already suffered, and was still suffering. For his remaining offence, — the libel on a Secretary of State, — it was not the province of the House to condemn and punish him by this summary process. It should be left to the courts to try him, — and, if found guilty, to inflict the punishment prescribed by law. For his old offences he could scarcely be expelled. During a whole session he had been a member; and yet they had not been held to justify his expulsion. Then why should they now call for such severity? Clearly on the ground of his libel on Lord Weymouth. The very enumeration of so many grounds of expulsion, implied their separate weakness and insufficiency; while it was designed to attract the support of members, influenced by different reasons for their votes. These arguments were urged by Mr. Burke, Mr. Pitt, Mr. Dowdeswell, Mr. Beckford, Mr. Cornwall, and, above all, by Mr. George Grenville.[1] The mastery speech of the latter does great credit to his judgment and foresight. When a minister, he had been the first to bring the House of Commons into collision with Wilkes; but he now recoiled from the struggle which was impending. Having shown the injustice of the proposed punishment, he proceeded to show its impolicy and danger. He predicted that Wilkes would be rëelected, and

[1] Parl. Hist. xvi. 546; Cavendish Deb. i. 151.

that the House would have but two alternatives — both objectionable; either to expel him again, and suspend the issue of the writ for the entire Parliament; or to declare another candidate, — with a minority of votes, — to be elected, on the ground of Wilkes's legal disqualification. In both cases the law would be violated, and the rights of the electors invaded. And in warning them of the dangerous contest they were about to commence, he predicted that the power and popularity of the demagogue would suddenly be reduced, if he were relieved from his martyrdom, and admitted to the legislature, where his true character would be discovered.

But all these arguments and cautions, were proffered in vain. The House, — making common cause with the court, — had resolved to scourge the insolent libeller who had intruded himself into their councils; and, regardless of future consequences, they voted his expulsion by a large majority. According to Burke, "the point to be gained by the cabal was this: that a precedent should be established, tending to show that the favor of the people was not so sure a road as the favor of the court, even to popular honors and popular trusts." "Popularity was to be rendered, if not directly penal, at least highly dangerous."[1] This view, however, is too deep and philosophical, to have been the true one. The court party, having been defied and insulted by a political opponent, were determined to crush him; and scarcely stopped to consider whether the laws were outraged or not.

Up to this time, whatever may have been the injustice and impolicy of their proceedings, the Commons had not exceeded their legal powers. The grounds on which they had expelled a member may have been insufficient; but of their sufficiency, they alone were competent to judge.

Wilkes re-elected.

They were now, however, about to commit unwarrantable excesses of jurisdiction, and to violate the clearest principles of law. As Mr. Grenville had pre-

[1] Present Discontents; Works, ii. 294.

dicted, Wilkes was immediately reëlected without opposition.[1] The next day, on the motion of Lord Strange, the House resolved that Mr. Wilkes "having been, in this session of Parliament, expelled the House, was and is incapable of being elected a member, to serve in this present Parliament." The election was accordingly declared void, and a new writ issued.[2] There were precedents for this course;[3] for this was not the first time the Commons had exceeded their jurisdiction; but it could not be defended upon sound principles of law. If by a vote of the House, a disability, unknown to the law, could be created, — any man who became obnoxious might, on some ground or other, be declared incapable. Incapacity would then be declared, — not by the law of the land, but by the arbitrary will of the House of Commons. On the other hand, the House felt strongly that their power of expulsion was almost futile, if their judgment could be immediately set aside by the electors; or, as it was put by General Conway, "if a gentleman who returns himself for any particular borough, were to stand up and say that he would, in opposition to the powers of the House, insist upon being a a member of Parliament."[4]

His election declared void.

Again, with still increasing popularity, Wilkes was reelected without opposition; and again a new writ was issued. In order to prevent a repetition of these fruitless proceedings, an alternative, — already pointed out by Mr. Grenville, — was now adopted. Colonel Luttrell, a member, vacated his seat, and offered himself as a candidate. Wilkes was, of course, returned by a large majority. He received one thousand one hundred and forty-three votes; Colonel Luttrell only two hundred and ninety-six. There were also

Again re-elected, and election declared void.

Opposed by Colonel Luttrell.

[1] So stated by a member who was present; Parl. Hist. xvi. 580.
[2] Feb. 17th, 1769; Cavendish Deb. i. 345.
[3] See May's Law of Parliament (4th Ed.), 59; Townsend's Mem. ii. 100.
[4] Cavendish Deb. i. 352.

two other candidates, Mr. Sergeant Whitaker and Mr. Roache, the former of whom had five votes, and the latter none. The Commons immediately pronounced the return of Wilkes to be null and void; and, having called for the poll-books, proceeded to vote, — though not without a strenuous opposition, — that Henry Lawes Luttrell ought to have been returned.[1] To declare a candidate, supported by so small a number of votes, the legal representative of Middlesex, was a startling step in the progress of this painful contest; but the ultimate seating of another candidate, notwithstanding Wilkes's majorities, was the inevitable result of the decision which affirmed his incapacity.

Again returned; but Colonel Luttrell seated.

Leave was given to petition the House against Colonel Luttrell's election, within fourteen days. Of this permission the electors soon availed themselves; and, on the 8th May, they were heard by counsel, at the bar of the House. Their arguments were chiefly founded upon the original illegality of the vote, by which Wilkes's incapacity had been declared; and were ably supported in debate, particularly by Mr. Wedderburn, Mr. Burke, and Mr. George Grenville;[2] but the election of Colonel Luttrell was confirmed by a majority of sixty-nine.

Wilkes was now effectually excluded from Parliament; but his popularity had been increased, while the House, and all concerned in his oppression, were the objects of popular indignation. As some compensation for his exclusion from the House of Commons, Wilkes was elected an alderman of the city of London. A liberal subscription was also raised, for the payment of his debts.

Popularity of Wilkes.

So dangerous a precedent was not suffered to rest unquestioned. Not only the partisans of Wilkes, but the statesmen and lawyers opposed to the government, continued to protest against it, until it was condemned.

Efforts to reverse the proceedings against him.

1 April 14th, 1769; Cavendish Deb. i. 360–386. Ayes 197, Noes 143 — Majority 54.

2 Cavendish Deb. i. 406.

On the 9th January, 1770, Lord Chatham, — reappearing in the House of Lords after his long prostration, — moved an amendment to the address, denouncing the late proceedings in the House of Commons, as "refusing, by a resolution of one branch of the legislature, to the subject his common right, and depriving the electors of Middlesex of their free choice of a representative." [1] Lord Camden, the Chancellor, now astonished the Lords by a statement "that for some time he had beheld with silent indignation, the arbitrary measures which were pursuing by the ministry;" and, "that as to the incapacitating vote, he considered it as a direct attack upon the first principles of the constitution." [2] Lord Mansfield, while he said that his opinion upon the legality of the proceedings of the House of Commons was "locked up in his own breast, and should die with him," (though for what reason it is not easy to explain,) argued that in matters of election the Commons had a complete jurisdiction, without appeal; that their decisions could only be reversed by themselves, or by Act of Parliament; and that except in discussing a bill, the Lords could not inquire into the question, without violating the privileges of the other House.

By Lord Chatham, Jan., 1770.

Lord Chatham replied in his finest manner. Lord Mansfield's remarks on the invasion of the privileges of the other House, called forth this comment: "What is this mysterious power, — undefined by law, unknown to the subject, which we must not approach without awe, nor speak of without reverence, — which no man may question, and to which all men must submit? My Lords, I thought the slavish doctrine of passive obedience had long since been exploded; and when our kings were obliged to confess that their title to the crown, and the rule of their government, had no other foundation than the known laws of the land, I never expected to hear a divine right, or a divine infallibility at-

1 Parl. Hist. xvi. 653.

2 This speech is not reported in the Parl. Hist., but is printed from the Gentleman's Mag. of Jan., 1770, in a note; Parl. Hist. xvi. 644, *n.*

tributed to any other branch of the legislature." He then proceeded to affirm that the Commons "have betrayed their constituents, and violated the constitution. Under pretence of declaring the law, they have made a law, and united in the same persons, the office of legislator and of judge."[1] His amendment was negatived; but the stirring eloquence and constitutional reasoning of so eminent a statesman, added weight to Wilkes's cause.

Proceedings in the Commons, 1770.

In the Commons also, very strong opinions were expressed on the injustice of Wilkes's exclusion. Sir George Savile especially distinguished himself by the warmth of his language; and accused the House of having betrayed the rights of its constituents. Being threatened with the Tower, he twice repeated his opinion; and, — declining the friendly intervention of Colonel Conway and Lord North, who attributed his language to the heat of debate, — he assured the House that if he was in a rage, "he had been so ever since the fatal vote was passed, and should be so till it is rescinded."[2] Mr. Sergeant Glynn thought "his declaration not only innocent, but laudable." A formidable opposition showed itself throughout the debate; and while in the Lords, the Chancellor had pronounced his opinion against the incapacitating vote, — in the Commons, the Solicitor-General, Mr. Dunning, also spoke and voted against the government. The question had thus assumed a formidable aspect, and led to changes, which speedily ended in the breaking up of the Duke of Grafton's administration.

Mr. Dowdeswell's resolutions

On the 25th January, 1770, Mr. Dowdeswell moved a resolution in a committee of the whole House, "That this House in its judicature in matters of election, is bound to judge according to the law of the land, and the known and established law and custom of Parliament, which is part thereof." This premise could neither be denied nor assented to by the government without

[1] Parl. Hist. xvi. 647.

[2] *Ibid.* 699.

embarrassment; but Lord North adroitly followed it out by a conclusion "that the judgment of this House was agreeable to the said law of the land, and fully authorized by the law and custom of Parliament."[1] On the 31st January, Mr. Dowdeswell repeated his attack in another form, but with no better success.[2]

Lord Rockingham's motion, 2d Feb., 1770.

The matter was now again taken up in the House of Lords. On the 2d February, in committee on the state of the nation, Lord Rockingham moved a resolution similar to that of Mr. Dowdeswell.[3] Though unsuccessful, it called forth another powerful speech from Lord Chatham, and a protest signed by forty-two peers. The rejection of this motion was immediately followed, — without notice, and after twelve o'clock at night, — by a motion of Lord Marchmont, that to impeach a judgment of the House of Commons would be a breach of the constitutional right of that House. Lord Camden, being accused by Lord Sandwich of duplicity, in having concealed his opinion as to the illegality of the incapacitating vote, while a member of the cabinet, asserted that he had frequently declared it to be both illegal and imprudent. On the other hand, the Duke of Grafton and Lord Weymouth complained that he had always withdrawn from the Council Board to avoid giving his opinion, — a circumstance explained by Lord Camden on the ground that as his advice had been already rejected, and the cabinet had resolved upon its measures, he declined giving any further opinion.[4] In either case, it seems, there could have been no doubt of his disapproval of the course adopted by ministers.

The next effort made in Parliament, in reference to Wilkes's case, was a motion by Mr. Herbert for a bill to regulate the consequences of the expulsion of members. But as this bill did not reverse, or directly condemn the proceedings in the case of Wilkes, it was not very warmly

1 Parl. Hist. xvi. 797.
2 *Ibid.* 800.
3 *Ibid.* 814.
4 *Ibid.* 823.

supported by the Opposition; and numerous amendments having been made by the supporters of government, by which its character became wholly changed, the bill was withdrawn.[1]

The city address to the king, 1770.

The scene of this protracted contest was now varied for a time. Appeals to Parliament had been made in vain; and the city of London resolved to carry up their complaints to the throne. A petition had been presented to the king in the previous year, to which no answer had been returned. And now the Lord Mayor, aldermen, and livery, in Common Hall assembled, agreed to an "address, remonstrance, and petition" to the king, which, whatever the force of its statements, was conceived in a tone of unexampled boldness. "The majority of the House of Commons," they said, "have deprived your people of their dearest rights. They have done a deed more ruinous in its consequences than the levying of ship-money by Charles I., or the dispensing power assumed by James II." They concluded by praying the king "to restore the constitutional government and quiet of his people, by dissolving the Parliament and removing his evil ministers forever from his councils."[2]

In his answer, his Majesty expressed his concern that any of his subjects "should have been so far misled as to offer him an address and remonstrance, the contents of which he could not but consider as disrespectful to himself, injurious to Parliament, and irreconcilable to the principles of the constitution."[3]

Joint address of both Houses to the king.

The Commons, whose acts had been assailed by the remonstrance, were prompt in rebuking the city, and pressing forward in support of the king. They declared the conduct of the city "highly

[1] Parl. Hist. xvi. 830–833; Cavendish Deb. i. 435.

[2] The address is printed at length; Cavendish Deb. i. 576.

[3] Having returned this answer, the king is said to have turned round to his courtiers, and burst out laughing. —*Public Advertiser*, cited in Lord Rockingham's Mem. ii. 174.

unwarrantable," and tending "to disturb the peace of the kingdom;" and having obtained the concurrence of the Lords, a joint address of both Houses, conveying this opinion, was presented to the king. In their zeal, they had overlooked the unseemliness of lowering both Houses of Parliament to a level with the corporation of the city of London, and of wrangling with that body, at the foot of the throne. The city was ready with a rejoinder, in the form of a further address and remonstrance to the king.

Lord Chatham condemns the king's answer.

Lord Chatham, meanwhile, and many of the leaders of the Whig party, saw, in the king's answer, consequences dangerous to the right of petitioning. Writing to Lord Rockingham, April 29th, Lord Chatham said: "A more unconstitutional piece never came from the throne, nor any more dangerous, if left unnoticed."[1] And on the 4th of May, not deterred by the joint address already agreed to by both Houses, he moved a resolution in the House of Lords, that the advice inducing his Majesty to give that answer "is of the most dangerous tendency," as "the exercise of the clearest rights of the subject to petition the king for redress of grievances, had been checked by reprimand." He maintained the constitutional right of the subject to petition for redress of all grievances; and the justice of the complaints which the city of London had laid at the foot of the throne. But the motion provoked little discussion, and was rejected.[2] And again, on the 14th May, Lord Chatham moved an address for a dissolution of Parliament. But all strangers, except peers' sons and members of the House of Commons, having been excluded from this debate, no record of it has been preserved. The question was called for at nine o'clock, and negatived.[3]

On the 1st of May, Lord Chatham presented a bill for reversing the several adjudications of the House of Commons,

1 Rockingham Mem. ii. 177; Woodfall's Junius, ii. 104.

2 Parl. Hist. xvi. 966.

3 *Ibid.* 979.

in Wilkes's case. The bill, after reciting all these resolutions, declared them to be "arbitrary and illegal;" and they were "reversed, annulled, and made void." Lord Camden said, "The judgment passed upon the Middlesex election, has given the constitution a more dangerous wound than any which were given during the twelve years' absence of Parliament in the reign of Charles I.;" and he trusted that its reversal would be demanded, session after session, until the people had obtained redress. Lord Mansfield deprecated any interference with the privileges of the Commons, and the bill was rejected by a large majority.[1]

Lord Chatham's bill to reverse the judgment of the Commons, 1770.

The next session witnessed a renewal of discussions upon this popular question. On the 5th December, Lord Chatham moved another resolution; which met the same fate as his previous motions on the subject.[2] On the 30th April, the Duke of Richmond moved to expunge from the journals of the House the resolution of the 2d of February, 1770, in which they had deprecated any interference with the jurisdiction of the Commons, as unconstitutional. He contended that if such a resolution were suffered to remain on record, the Commons might alter the whole law of elections, and change the franchise by an arbitrary declaration; and yet the Lords would be precluded from remonstrance. Lord Chatham repeated his opinion, that the Commons "had daringly violated the laws of the land;" and declared that it became not the Lords to remain "tame spectators of such a deed, if they would not be deemed accessory to their guilt, and branded with treason to their country." The ministers made no reply, and the question was negatived.[3]

Lord Chatham's resolution, 5th Dec., 1770.

Duke of Richmond's motion, April 1771.

A few days afterwards, Lord Chatham moved an address for a dissolution, on the ground of the violations of law by

[1] Parl. Hist. xvi. 955; Walpole's Mem. iv. 121; Rockingham Mem. ii. 177.

[2] Parl. Hist. xvi. 1302. It was superseded by adjournment.

[3] *Ibid.* xvii. 214.

the Commons in the Middlesex election, and the contest which had lately arisen between them and the city magistracy;[1] but found no more than twenty-three supporters.[2]

The concluding incidents of the Middlesex election may now be briefly told, before we advert to a still more important conflict which was raging at this time, with the privileges of the Commons; and the new embarrassments which Wilkes had raised.

Sir George Savile's motion, 1772.

In the next session, Sir George Savile, in order to renew the annual protest against the Middlesex election, moved for a bill to secure the rights of electors, with respect to the eligibility of persons to serve in Parliament. Lord North here declared, that the proceedings of the Commons had "been highly consistent with justice, and the law of the land; and that to his dying day he should continue to approve of them." The motion was defeated by a majority of forty-six.[3]

Mr. Wilkes complains of the Deputy-Clerk of the Crown.

In 1773, Mr. Wilkes brought his case before the House, in the shape of a frivolous complaint against the Deputy-Clerk of the Crown, who had refused to give him a certificate, as one of the members for Middlesex. Sir G. Savile, also, renewed his motion for a bill to secure the rights of electors, and found one hundred and fifty supporters.[4] Mr. Burke took this occasion to predict that, "there would come a time when those now in office would be reduced to their penitentials, for having turned a deaf ear to the voice of the people." In 1774, Sir G. Savile renewed his motion for a bill to secure the rights of electors, with the usual result.[5]

Wilkes elected in the new Parliament, 1774.

The Parliament, which had been in continual conflict with Wilkes for five years, was now dissolved; and Wilkes was again returned for Middlesex. According to the resolution of the Commons, his in-

[1] See *infra*, p. 389.
[2] May 1st, 1771; Parl. Hist. xvii. 224.
[3] Feb. 27th, 1772; *Ibid.* 318.
[4] Parl. Hist. xvii. 838.
[5] *Ibid.* 1057.

capacity had been limited to the late Parliament; and he now took his seat without further molestation. Before the meeting of Parliament, Wilkes had also attained the highest civic honor, — being elected Lord Mayor of London.

Moves to expunge the resolution.

He did not fail to take advantage of his new privileges; and on the 22d February, 1775, he moved that the resolution which had declared his incapacity, be expunged from the journals, "as subversive of the rights of the whole body of electors." He said, "the people had made his cause their own, for they saw the powers of government exerted against the constitution, which was wounded through his sides." He recapitulated the circumstances of his case; referred very cleverly to the various authorities and precedents; and showed the dangerous consequences of allowing a resolution to remain upon the journals, which was a violation of the law. He was ably supported by Mr. Sergeant Glynn, Sir George Savile, and Mr. Wedderburn; and in the division secured one hundred and seventy-one votes.[1]

Resolution expunged, 1782.

He renewed this motion in 1776,[2] in 1777,[3] in 1779,[4] and in 1781.[5] At length, on the 3d of May, 1782, he proposed it for the last time, and with signal success. The Rockingham ministry was in office, and had resolved to condemn the proceedings of the Commons, which its leading members had always disapproved. Mr. Fox was now the only statesman of any eminence, by whom Wilkes's motion was opposed. He had always maintained that the Commons had not exceeded their powers; and he still consistently supported that opinion, in opposition to the premier and the leaders of his party. Wilkes's motion was now carried by a triumphant majority of sixty-eight; and by order of the House, all the declarations, orders, and resolutions, respecting the Middlesex election, were expunged

[1] 171 to 239; Parl. Hist. xviii. 358.
[2] *Ibid.* 1336.
[3] *Ibid.* xix. 193.
[4] *Ibid.* xx. 144.
[5] *Ibid.* xxii. 99.

from the journals, as being subversive of the rights of the whole body of electors in this kingdom.[1]

Thus at length, this weary contest was brought to a close. A former House of Commons, too eager in its vengeance, had exceeded its powers; and now a succeeding Parliament reversed its judgment. This decision of 1782, stands out as a warning to both Houses, to act within the limits of their jurisdiction, and in strict conformity with the laws. An abuse of privilege is even more dangerous than an abuse of prerogative. In the one case, the wrong is done by an irresponsible body: in the other the ministers who advised it, are open to censure and punishment. The judgment of offences especially, should be guided by the severest principles of law. Mr. Burke applied to the judicature of privilege, in such cases, Lord Bacon's description of the Star Chamber, — "a court of criminal equity:" saying, "a large and liberal construction in ascertaining offences, and a discretionary power in punishing them, is the idea of criminal equity, which is in truth a monster in jurisprudence."[2] The vindictive exercise of privilege, — once as frequent as it was lawless, — was now discredited and condemned.

Abuses of privilege; their danger.

But before Wilkes had obtained this crowning triumph over the Commons, he had contrived to raise another storm against their privileges, which produced consequences of greater constitutional importance; and again this bold and artful demagogue became the instrument, by which popular liberties were extended.

Exclusion of strangers from debates.

Among the privileges of Parliament, none had been more frequently exercised by both Houses, than the exclusion of strangers from their deliberations; and restraints upon the publication of debates. The first of these privileges is very ancient; and probably originated in convenience, rather than in any theory of secrecy in their proceedings. The mem-

[1] Ayes 15; Noes 47; Parl. Hist. xxii. 1407.
[2] Present Discontents, Works, ii. 297.

bers met not so much for debate, as for deliberation: they were summoned for some particular business, which was soon disposed of; and as none but those summoned, were expected to attend, the chambers in which they assembled, were simply adapted for their own accommodation. Hence the occasional intrusion of a stranger was an inconvenience, and a disturbance to the House. He was in the midst of the members, — standing with them in the gangway, — or taking his place, where none but members had the privilege of sitting. Such intrusion resembled that of a man who, in the present day, should force his way into Brookes's or the Carlton, and mingle with the members of the club. Some strangers even entered the House, pretending to be members.[1] Precautions were necessary to prevent confusion; for even so late as 1771 a stranger was counted in a division.[2] Hence, from early times, the intrusion of a stranger was generally punished by his immediate commitment, or reprimand.[3] The custom afterwards served as an auxiliary to the most valuable of all privileges, — the freedom of speech. What a member said in his place, might indeed be reported to the king, or given in evidence against him in the Court of King's Bench, or the Stannary Court, by another member of the House; but strangers might be there, for the very purpose of noting his words, for future condemnation. So long, therefore, as the Commons were obliged to protect themselves against the rough hand of prerogative, they strictly enforced the exclusion of strangers.

Relaxation of the privilege.

Long after that danger had passed away, the privilege was maintained as a matter of custom, rather than of policy. At length apprehensions arose from another quarter; and the privilege was asserted as a protection to Parliament, against the clamors and intimidation of the people. But the enforcement of this privilege was grad-

[1] Mr. Perne, March 5th, 1557; Mr. Bukeley, May 14th, 1614.

[2] Com. Journ. xxxiii. 212.

[3] *Ibid.* i. 105, 118, 417, 484; *Ibid.* ii. 74, 433.

ually relaxed. When the debates in Parliament began to excite the interest of the public, and to attract an eager audience, the presence of strangers was connived at. They could be dismissed in a moment, at the instance of any member; but the Speaker was not often called upon to enforce the orders of the House.

Towards the middle of last century, attendance upon the debates of both Houses of Parliament, had become a fashionable amusement. On the 9th of December, 1761, the interest excited by a debate in the Commons, on the renewal of the Prussian Treaties was so great, that Lord Royston, writing to Lord Hardwicke, said: "The House was hot and crowded, — as full of ladies as the House of Lords when the King goes to make a speech. The members were standing above half way up the floor." It became necessary on this occasion, to enforce the standing order for the exclusion of strangers.[1] And in this way, for several years the presence of strangers, with rare exceptions, was freely admitted. But the same Parliament which had persecuted Wilkes, was destined to bring to an issue other great questions, affecting the relations of Parliament to the people. It is not surprising that the worst of Parliaments should have been the most resolute in enforcing the rule for excluding strangers.[2] It was at war with the public liberties; and its evil deeds were best performed in secret. The exclusion of strangers was generally more strict than had been customary; and whenever a popular member of Opposition en-

Exclusion of strangers, 1770.

[1] Rockingham Mem. i. 71.

[2] This Parliament, assembled May 10th, 1768, and dissolved June 22d, 1774, was commonly called the unreported Parliament, in consequence of the strict enforcement of the standing order for the exclusion of strangers. Pref. to Cavendish's Deb. Sir Henry Cavendish has supplied a great *hiatus* in the debates of this period, and it is much to be regretted that the publication of his valuable work has never been completed. They consist of forty-nine small 4to volumes, amongst the Egerton MSS. at the British Museum, of which less than half were edited by Mr. Wright, and published in two volumes.

deavored to make himself heard by the people, the ready expedient was adopted of closing the doors. Burke, describing the position of an opposition member at this period, wrote, "In the House he votes forever in a dispirited minority; if he speaks, the doors are locked."[1] Could any abuse of privilege be more monstrous than this? Was any misrepresentation of reporters half so mischievous?

Proceedings in the Lords.

Lord Chatham's repeated motions impugning the proceedings of the Commons upon the Middlesex election, were naturally distasteful to ministers, and to the majority of the House of Lords; who, being unable to repress his impetuous eloquence, determined that, at least, it should not be heard beyond their walls. Accordingly on the 14th May, 1770, on his motion for a dissolution of Parliament, the Lords ordered the exclusion of all but members of the House of Commons, and the sons of peers; and no reports of the debate reached the public.

Lord Gower desires the House to be cleared.

In the next session, the same tactics were resumed. On the 10th December, the Duke of Manchester rose, to make a motion relative to preparations for the war with Spain, then believed to be impending; when he was interrupted by Lord Gower, who desired that the House might be cleared. He urged as reasons for excluding strangers, that the motion had been brought on without notice; that matters might be stated which ought not to be divulged; that, from the crowded state of the House, emissaries from Spain might be present; and lastly, that notes were taken of their debates. The Duke of Richmond attempted to arrest the execution of the order; but his voice was drowned in clamor. Lord Chatham rose to order, but failed to obtain a hearing. The Lord Chancellor attempted to address the House and restore order; but even his voice could not be heard. Lord Chatham, and eighteen other peers, — indignant at the disorderly uproar, by which every effort to address the House

[1] Present Discontents; Works, ii. 301.

had been put down, — withdrew from their places. The messengers were already proceeding to clear the House, when several members of the House of Commons, who had been waiting at the bar to bring up a bill, desired to stay for that purpose; but were turned out with the crowd, — several peers having gone down to the bar, to hasten their withdrawal. They were presently called in again; but the moment they had delivered their message, — and before time had been allowed them to withdraw from the bar, — an outcry arose, and they were literally hooted out of the House.[1]

Members of the Commons excluded from the Lords.

Furious at this indecent treatment, the members hastened back to their own House. The first result of their anger was sufficiently ridiculous. Mr. George Onslow desired the House to be cleared, "peers and all." The only peers below the bar were the very lords who had in vain resisted the exclusion of strangers from their own House, which they had just left in indignation; and now the resentment of the Commons, — provoked by others, — was first expended upon them.

Misunderstanding between the two Houses.

In debate, the insult to the Commons was warmly resented. Various motions were made: — for inspecting the Lords' journals; for demanding a conference upon the subject; for sending messages by the eldest sons of peers and masters in Chancery, who alone, it was said, would not be insulted; and for restraining members from going to the Lords without leave. But none of them were accepted.[2] The only retaliation that could be agreed upon, was the exclusion of peers, which involved a consequence by no means desired, — the continued exclusion of the public.

In the Lords, sixteen peers signed a strong protest against the riotous proceedings of their House, and deprecating the

[1] Parl. Hist. xvi. 1318–1320; Walpole's Mem. iv. 217; Chatham Corresp. iv. 51.

[2] Dec. 10th and 13th, 1770; Parl. Hist. xvi. 1322; Cavendish Deb. ii. 149, 160; Walpole's Mem. iv. 228.

exclusion of strangers. An order, however, was made that none but persons having a right to be present, should be admitted during the sitting of the House; and instructions were given to the officers, that members of the House of Commons should not be allowed to come to the bar, except when announced as bringing messages; and should then immediately withdraw.[1] To this rule the Lords continued strictly to adhere for the remainder of the session; and none of their debates were reported, unless notes were communicated by the peers themselves. The Commons were less tenacious, or their officers less strict; and strangers gradually crept back to the gallery. Lord Chatham happily expressed his contempt for a senate debating with closed doors. Writing to Colonel Barré on the 22d January, 1771, he says: "I take it for granted that the same declaration will be laid before the tapestry on Friday, which will be offered to the live figures in St. Stephen's;"[2] and again on the 25th he writes to Lady Chatham, "Just returned from the tapestry."[3] The mutual exclusion of the members of the two Houses, continued to be enforced, in a spirit of vindictive retaliation, for several years.[4]

Contest with the printers, 1771.

In the Commons, however, this system of exclusion took a new turn; and, having commenced in a quarrel with the Peers, it ended in a collision with the press. Colonel George Onslow complained of the debates which still appeared in the newspapers; and insinuating that they must have been supplied by members themselves, insisted upon testing this view, by excluding all but members.[5] The reports continued; and now he fell upon the printers.

But before this new contest is entered upon, it will be

1 Parl. Hist. xvi. 1319–1321.
2 Chatham Corresp. iv. 73.
3 *Ibid.* 86.
4 Debate in the Commons, Dec. 12th, 1774; Parl. Hist. xviii. 52; Burke's Speeches, i. 250.
5 Feb. 7th, 1771; Parl. Hist. xvi. 1355, *n.*; Cavendish Deb. ii. 244.

necessary to review the position which the press occupied at this time, in its relation to the debates of Parliament. The prohibition to print and publish the debates, naturally dates from a later period than the exclusion of strangers. It was not until the press had made great advances, that such a privilege was declared. Parliament, in order to protect its freedom of speech, had guarded its proceedings by a strong fence of privilege; but the printing of its debates was an event beyond its prevision.

Publication of debates.

In 1641, the Long Parliament permitted the publication of its proceedings, which appeared under the title of "Diurnal Occurrences in Parliament." The printing of speeches, however, without leave of the House, was, for the first time, prohibited.[1] In particular cases, indeed, where a speech was acceptable to the Parliament, it was ordered to be printed; but if any speech was published obnoxious to the dominant party, the vengeance of the House was speedily provoked. Sir E. Dering was expelled and imprisoned in the Tower, for printing a collection of his speeches; and the book was ordered to be burned by the common hangman.[2]

Progress of reporting.

The prohibition to print debates was continued after the Restoration; but, in order to prevent inaccurate accounts of the business transacted, the House of Commons, in 1680, directed its "votes and proceedings," without any reference to debates, to be printed under the direction of the Speaker.[3] Debates were also frequently published, notwithstanding the prohibition. When it served the purpose of men like Lord Shaftesbury, that any debate should be circulated, it made its appearance in the form of a letter or pamphlet.[4] An-

[1] July 13th and 22d; Com. Journ. ii. 209, 220.

[2] Feb. 2d, 1641; Com. Journ. ii. 411.

[3] *Ibid.* ix. 74; Grey's Deb. viii. 292.

[4] "Letter from a Person of Quality to a Friend in the Country," 1675, by Locke. "Letter from a Parliament-man to his Friend, concerning the Proceedings of the House of Commons, 1675."

drew Marvell reported the proceedings of the Commons, to his constituents at Hull, from 1660 to 1678;[1] and Grey, for thirty years member for Derby, took notes of the debates from 1667 to 1694, which are a valuable contribution to the history of that time.[2]

After the Revolution, Parliament was more jealous than ever of the publication of its proceedings, or of any allusion to its debates. By frequent resolutions,[3] and by the punishment of offenders, both Houses endeavored to restrain "news-letter writers" from "intermeddling with their debates or other proceedings," or "giving any account or minute of the debates." But privilege could not prevail against the press, nor against the taste for political news, which is natural to a free country.

Towards the close of the reign of Anne, regular but imperfect accounts of all the principal debates, were published by Boyer.[4] From that time, reports continued to appear in Boyer's "Political State of Great Britain," the "London Magazine," and the "Gentleman's Magazine," the authors of which were frequently assisted with notes from members of Parliament. In the latter, Dr. Johnson wrote the Parliamentary reports, from the 19th of Nov., 1740, till the 23d of Feb., 1743, from the notes of Cave and his assistants. The names of the speakers, however, were omitted.[5] Until 1738, it had been the practice to give their initials only, and, in order to escape the censure of Parliament, to withhold the publication of the debates, until after the session. In that year, the Commons prohibited the publication of debates, or proceedings, "as well during the recess, as the sitting of Parliament;" and resolved to "proceed with the utmost severity against offenders."[6] After this period, the re-

1 Letters to the Corporation of Hull; Marvell's Works, i. 1–400.

2 They were published in ten volumes 8vo, 1769.

3 Commons, Dec. 22d, 1694. Feb. 11th, 1695, Jan. 18th, 1697, &c.; Lords, Feb. 27th, 1698.

4 Boyer's Political State of Great Britain, was commenced in 1711.

5 Prefaces to Cobbett's Parl. Hist. vols. ix.–xiii.

6 April 13th, 1738. Parl. Hist. x. 800.

porters, being in fear of parliamentary privilege, were still more careful in their disguises. In the "Gentleman's Magazine," the debates were assigned to the "Senate of Great Lilliput;" and in the "London Magazine" to the Political Club, where the speeches were attributed to Mark Anthony, Brutus, and other Roman worthies. This caution was not superfluous; for both Houses were quick to punish the publication of their proceedings, in any form; and printers and publishers became familiar with the Black Rod, the Sergeant-at-Arms, and Newgate.[1] At length, in 1771, at the instigation of Wilkes,[2] notes of the speeches, with the names of the speakers, were published in several journals.[3]

Misrepresentations of reporters.

These papers had rarely attempted to give a correct and impartial account of the debates; but had misrepresented them to suit the views of different parties. Dr. Johnson is said to have confessed that "he took care that the Whig dogs should not have the best of it;" and, in the same spirit, the arguments of all parties were in turn perverted or suppressed. Galling as was this practice, it had been less offensive while the names of the speakers were withheld; but when these were added, members were personally affronted by the misconstruction of their opinions and arguments, and by the ludicrous form in which they were often presented. The chief complaints against reporting had arisen from the misrepresentations, to which it was made subservient. In the debate upon this subject in 1738, nearly all the speakers, including Sir W. Wyndham, Sir W. Yonge, and Mr. Winnington, agreed in these complaints, and rested their objections to reporting, on

1 Woodfall, Baldwin, Jay, Miller, Oxlade, Randall, Egglesham, Owen, and Knight, are amongst the names of publishers committed or censured for publishing debates or proceedings in Parliament. Such was the extravagance with which the Lords enforced their privilege, that in 1729, a part of their Journal having been printed in Rymer's Fœdera, they ordered it to be taken out and destroyed. — *Lords' Journ.* xxiii. 422.

2 Walpole's Mem. iv. 278.

3 The London Evening Post, the St. James's Chronicle, the Gazetteer, and others.

that ground. The case was well and humorously stated, by Sir R. Walpole. "I have read some debates of this House, in which I have been made to speak the very reverse of what I meant. I have read others, wherein all the wit, the learning, and the argument has been thrown into one side, and on the other, nothing but what was low, mean, and ridiculous; and yet, when it comes to the question, the division has gone against the side which, upon the face of the debate, had reason and justice to support it. So that, had I been a stranger to the proceedings, and to the nature of the arguments themselves, I must have thought this to have been one of the most contemptible assemblies on the face of the earth." In this debate, Mr. Pulteney was the only speaker who distinctly objected to the publication of the speeches of members, on the ground "that it looks very like making them accountable without doors, for what they say within." [1]

Offensive adjuncts to reporting.

Indeed, it is probable that the early jealousies of Parliament would soon have been overcome, if the reports had been impartial. The development of the liberty of the press was checked by its own excesses; and the publication of debates was retarded by the unfairness of reporters. Nor were the complaints of members confined to mere misrepresentation. The reports were frequently given in the form of narratives, in which the speakers were distinguished by nicknames, and described in opprobrious terms. Thus, Colonel George Onslow was called "little *cocking* George," [2] "the little scoundrel," [3] and "that little paltry, insignificant insect." [4] The Colonel and his cousin were also spoken of in scurrilous comments, as being like "the constellations of the two bears in the heavens, one being called the *great*, and the other the *little* scoundrel." [5]

1 Parl. Hist. x. 300.
2 Cavendish Deb. ii. 257.
3 *Ibid.* 258.
4 *Ibid.* 377, *n.*
5 *Ibid.* 379.

To report the debates in such a spirit, was at once to violate the orders of the House, and to publish libellous insults upon its members. Parliament had erred in persisting in the prohibition of reporting, long after its occasion had passed away; and the reporters had sacrificed a great public privilege, to the base uses of a scurrilous press. The events of the first ten years of this reign, had increased the violence of public writers, and imbittered the temper of the people. The "North Briton" and "Junius," had assailed the highest personages, and the most august assemblies, with unexampled license and audacity. Wilkes had defied the House of Commons, and the ministers. The city had bearded the king upon his throne. Yet this was the time chosen by an unpopular House of Commons, to insist too rigorously upon its privileges, and to seek a contest with the press.

Complaints against Thompson and Wheble, 1771.

On the 8th February, 1771, Colonel George Onslow made a complaint of "The Gazetteer and New Daily Advertiser," printed for R. Thompson, and of the "Middlesex Journal," printed by R. Wheble, "as misrepresenting the speeches, and reflecting on several of the members of this House." The printers were ordered to attend, — but not without serious warnings and remonstrances from those who foresaw the entanglements, into which the House was likely to be drawn.[1] They kept out of the way, and were ordered to be taken into custody. The Sergeant proceeded to execute the order, and was laughed at by their servants.[2] Thus thwarted, the House addressed the king to issue a proclamation, offering a reward for their apprehension.

Complaints against other printers.

Meanwhile, the offences for which the House was pursuing Thompson and Wheble, were practised by several other printers; and on the 12th March, Colonel Onslow made a complaint against the printers of six other newspapers. The House had not yet succeeded in apprehending the first offenders, and now another host was

[1] Cavendish Deb. ii. 257. [2] *Ibid.* 324.

arraigned before them. In some of these papers, the old disguises were retained. In the "St. James's Chronicle" the speeches were entitled "Debates of the representatives of Utopia;"[1] Mr. Dyson was described as "Jeremiah Weymouth, Esq., the d——n of this country," and Mr. Constantine Phipps as "Mr. Constantine Lincoln."[2] None of the errors of Parliament have been committed, without the warnings and protests of some of its enlightened members; and this further onslaught upon the printers was vigorously resisted. The minority availed themselves of motions for adjournment, amendments, and other parliamentary forms, well adapted for delay, until past four in the morning. During this discussion there were no less than twenty-three divisions, — an unprecedented number.[3] Burke afterwards said of these proceedings: "Posterity will bless the pertinaciousness of that day."[4]

All the six printers were ordered to attend at the bar; and on the day appointed, four of the number appeared, and a fifth, — Mr. Woodfall, — being already in the custody of the Black Rod, by order of the Lords, was prevented from attending. Two of them, Baldwin and Wright, were reprimanded on their knees and discharged; and Bladon, having made a very humble submission, was discharged without a reprimand. Evans, who had also attended the order of the House, went home before he was called in, in consequence, it was said, of an accident to his wife. He was ordered to attend on another day; but wrote a letter to the Speaker, in which he questioned the authority of the House, and declined to obey its order. Lastly, Miller did not attend, and was ordered into custody for his offence.[5]

On the 14th March, Wheble, who was still at large, addressed a letter to the Speaker, inclosing the opinion of

[1] Cavendish Deb. ii. 383.

[2] One represented Weymouth, and the other Lincoln.

[3] Cavendish Deb. ii. 377.

[4] *Ibid.* 395.

[5] Parl. Hist. xvii. 90, *n.*; Com. Journ. xxxiii. 250–259.

counsel on his case, and declaring his determination "to yield no obedience but to the laws of the land." The next day, he was collusively apprehended by Carpenter, a printer, — by virtue of the proclamation, — and taken before Alderman Wilkes! This dexterous and cunning agitator had encouraged the printers to resist the authority of the House, and had concerted measures for defying its jurisdiction, and insulting its officers. He immediately discharged the prisoner, and bound him over to prosecute Carpenter, for an assault and false imprisonment. He further wrote a letter to Lord Halifax, the Secretary of State, acquainting him that Wheble had been apprehended by a person who "was neither a constable nor peace-officer of the city," and for no legal offence, but merely in consequence of the proclamation, — "in direct violation of the rights of an Englishman, and of the chartered privileges of a citizen of this metropolis," — and that he had discharged him.[1]

Wheble taken before Alderman Wilkes.

On the same day, Thompson was apprehended by another printer, and carried before Alderman Oliver at the Mansion House; but "not being accused of having committed any crime," was discharged. In both cases, the captors applied for a certificate that they had apprehended the prisoners, in order to obtain the rewards offered by the proclamation; but the collusion was too obvious, and the Treasury refused to pay them.

And Thompson before Alderman Oliver.

On the following day, a graver business arose. Hitherto the legality of apprehending persons under the proclamation, had alone been questioned; but now the authority of the House was directly contemned. In obedience to the Speaker's warrant for taking Miller into custody, Whittam, a messenger of the House, succeeded in apprehending him, in his shop. But Miller, instead of submitting, sent for a constable, — accused the messenger of having assaulted him in his own house, — and gave him into

Commitment of the messenger.

[1] Parl. Hist. xvii. 95.

custody. They were both taken to the Mansion House, and appeared before the Lord Mayor, Mr. Alderman Oliver, and Mr. Alderman Wilkes. Miller charged the messenger with an assault and false imprisonment. The messenger justified himself by the production of the Speaker's warrant; and the Deputy Sergeant-at-Arms claimed both the messenger and his prisoner. But the Lord Mayor inquired if the messenger was a peace-officer or constable, and if the warrant was backed by a city magistrate; and being answered in the negative, discharged Miller out of custody. The charge of the latter against the messenger was then proved; and Whittam, by direction of the Sergeant, having declined to give bail, was committed under a warrant, signed by the three magistrates. After his commitment, he was admitted to bail on his own application.

The artful contrivances of Wilkes were completely successful. The contumacious printers were still at large; and he had brought the city into open conflict with the House of Commons. The House was in a ferment. Many members who had resisted the prosecution of the printers, admitted that the privileges of the House had now been violated; but they were anxious to avert any further collision between the House, — already too much discredited by recent proceedings, — and the popular magistracy of the city. The Lord Mayor, Mr. Brass Crosby, being a member of the House, was first ordered to attend in his place, on the following day; [1] and afterwards Mr. Oliver, also a member, was ordered to attend in his place, and Mr. Wilkes at the bar, on other days.

The Lord Mayor (Brass Crosby) attends the House.

At the appointed time, the Lord Mayor, though he had been confined for several days by the gout, obeyed the order of the House. His carriage was escorted by a prodigious crowd, — whose attendance had been invited by a handbill; and he was received with such acclamations in the lobby, that the Speaker desired it to be cleared of strangers.[2] The Lord Mayor, — who was

[1] March 19th; Parl. Hist. xvii. 98; Cavendish Deb. ii. 400.
[2] Cavendish Deb. ii. 422.

so ill as to be obliged to speak sitting, — justified himself by his oath of office, which bound him to protect the citizens in their rights and franchises. He stated that by the charters of the city, confirmed by Act of Parliament, no warrant, process, or attachment could be executed within the city but by its own magistrates, and that he should have been guilty of perjury, if he had not discharged the prisoner. He then desired to be heard by counsel, in support of the jurisdiction of the city. The Speaker intimated that the House could not hear counsel against its privileges; and while this matter was under discussion, the Lord Mayor, being too ill to remain in the House, was allowed to go home. It was at length decided to hear counsel on such points as did not controvert the privileges of the House;[1] and the same right was afterwards conceded to Alderman Oliver.[2] The scene was enlivened by Mr. Wilkes, who having been ordered to attend at the bar, wrote to the Speaker, with his usual effrontery, claiming to attend in his place, as member for Middlesex.[3]

Record of recognizances erased.

So far the House had stood upon its unassailable privilege of commitment; but now it proceeded to a violation of the law, at once arbitrary and ridiculous. The clerk to the Lord Mayor had been ordered to attend with the book containing the recognizance of Whittam the messenger; and on its production by that officer, he was ordered to expunge the entry at the table, which he accordingly did.[4] While this scene was being enacted, most of the Opposition members left the House, in order to mark their reprobation of an act, by which a record was effaced, — over which the House had no authority, — and the course of justice violently stayed.[5] According to Lord Chatham, it was the "act of a mob, and not of a Parliament."[6]

1 Cavendish Deb. ii. 436.
2 *Ibid.* 442; Parl. Hist. xvii. 119.
3 Parl. Hist. xvii. 113, *n.*
4 Cavendish Deb. ii. 438; Parl. Hist. xvii. 117; Com. Journ. xxxiii. 275.
5 Ann. Reg. 1771, p. 66; Walpole's Mem. iv. 294.
6 May 1st, 1771; Parl. Hist. xvii. 221.

The House then ordered that no prosecution should be commenced against the messenger, for his pretended assault. He was nevertheless indicted; and a true bill being found against him, he was only saved by the Attorney-General, who entered a *nolle prosequi*.

Messenger saved from prosecution.

Some delay ensued in the proceedings, in consequence of the continued indisposition of the Lord Mayor; but on the 25th March, he and Mr. Alderman Oliver attended in their places. They were accompanied to the House by immense crowds, who cheered them on their way. Before their case was proceeded with, the order for the attendance on that day of Alderman Wilkes, — the prime mover of all this mischief, — was discharged; the court and the ministers being fairly afraid of another contest with so dangerous an antagonist. The Lord Mayor now declined being heard by counsel; and after the reading of the city charters, and oaths of office, he briefly urged that he had acted in obedience to the laws and constitution, and appealed to the justice of the House. An endeavor was made to evade any further proceedings, by the previous question; but after an exciting debate, — interrupted by the shouts and uproar of the crowd, by which the House was surrounded,[1] — resolutions were agreed to, declaring that the privileges of the House had been violated.[2] The Lord Mayor had been allowed to go home early in the evening; when the crowd took the horses from his carriage, and bore him triumphantly to the Mansion House. Alderman Oliver being still in the House, was now called upon for his defence. In a few words he said that he gloried in what he had done; that he was unconcerned at the punishment intended for him, and which nothing he could say would avert; "and as he expected little from their justice, he defied their power."[3] Motions were immediately made that he had been guilty of a breach

The Lord Mayor and Alderman Oliver heard in their places.

Alderman Oliver committed to the Tower.

1 Parl. Hist. xvii. 125; Cavendish Deb. ii. 452, 454.

2 Cavendish Deb. ii. 461.

3 Parl. Hist. xvii. 125.

of privilege, and should be committed to the Tower; and after a debate, protracted, — by earnest protests and remonstrances against this proceeding, — till half-past three in the morning, an order for his commitment was agreed to.[1]

The Lord Mayor committed to the Tower.

At the next sitting of the House, the Lord Mayor attended in his place. Again he was accompanied by a crowd, larger and more tumultuous than before. The members with difficulty made their way through Palace Yard and Westminster Hall. Lord North's carriage was broken to pieces, and he himself escaped, — not without injury, — with the assistance of Sir W. Meredith. Mr. Charles Fox, — a violent champion of privilege, — and his brother Stephen, had their carriages injured; and several members were insulted and pelted with stones and mud. For some time, the House was unable to proceed to business. The magistrates tried in vain to disperse or tranquillize the mob; but the Sheriffs, — who both happened to be members, — being sent by the Speaker, at length succeeded in restoring order. In consideration of the Lord Mayor's state of health, it was at first proposed merely to commit him to the custody of the Sergeant-at-Arms; but as he boldly declined to accept this favor from the House, and desired to bear his friend Oliver company, he was committed to the Tower.[2] Meanwhile Wilkes, the chief offender, was still at large. He had been again ordered to attend on the 8th April; but ministers discreetly moved the adjournment for the Easter Holidays until the 9th; and thus the dreaded culprit was eluded. This subterfuge may have been prudent: but it was not magnanimous.

Ovation of the prisoners.

The authority of the House of Commons had clearly been defied; and however ill-advised the proceedings which had led to the contest with the city magistrates, the House could scarcely have flinched

[1] He was allowed to sleep at his house that night, and early the next morning the Sergeant took him to the Tower. (Gentleman's Mag., cited in Parl. Hist. xvii. 155, *n.*)

[2] March 27th; Parl. Hist. xvii. 157.

from the vindication of its privileges.[1] But Parliament has no means of punishing a popular offender. The Lord Mayor, on leaving the House, accompanied by the Sergeant-at-Arms, was surrounded by the crowd, who took the horses from his carriage, and bore him to Temple Bar. Here they shut the city gates, and would have rescued him from custody, but for the adroitness of the Lord Mayor, who assured them he was going home, accompanied by his friends. He slept that night at the Mansion House, and early the following morning reached the Tower, without observation. Here the prisoners received every mark of public attention and sympathy. Visited by the most distinguished leaders of the Opposition, — attended by deputations, — flattered in addresses, — complimented by the freedom of many cities, — and overloaded with presents, — their imprisonment, instead of being a punishment, was a long-continued ovation. They failed to obtain their release under writs of *habeas corpus*, as the legality of their commitment could not be impeached; but on the 8th May, after six weeks' confinement, the prorogation of Parliament set them at liberty. Attended by a triumphal procession, they proceeded from the Tower to the Mansion House; and the people exulted at the liberation of their popular magistrates.[2]

1 Lord Chatham condemned all the parties to this contest. "Nothing appears to me more distinct than declaring their right to jurisdiction, with regard to printers of their proceedings, and debates, and punishing their member, and in him his constituents, for what he has done in discharge of his oath and conscience as a magistrate." Lord Chatham to Colonel Barré, March 26th, 1771. — *Chatham Corresp.* iv. 136.

Lord Chatham, writing to Earl Temple, April 17th, 1771, said, "Great is the absurdity of the city in putting the quarrel on the exercise of the most tenable privilege the House is possessed of, — a right to summon before them printers printing their debates during the session. Incomparable is the wrong-headedness and folly of the Court, ignorant how to be twenty-four hours on good ground; for they have most ingeniously contrived to be guilty of the rankest tyranny, in every step taken to assert the right." — *Grenville Papers*, iv. 533. See also Junius, Letter xliv.

2 Memoirs of Brass Crosby, 1829; Almon's Life of Wilkes; Ann. Reg., 1771, 59 *et seq.*; Adolphus Hist. chap. xix.

Thus ended this painful and embarrassing conflict. Its results were decisive. The publication of debates was still asserted to be a breach of privilege; but the offence was committed with impunity. Another contest with the press, supported by a powerful opposition and popular sympathies, was out of the question; and henceforth the proceedings of both Houses were freely reported. Parliament as well as the public has since profited by every facility which has been afforded to reporting. The suppression of the names of the speakers, and the adoption of fictitious designations, had encouraged reporters to introduce other fictions into their narratives; and to impute arguments and language, which had never been used, to characters of their own creation.

Reporting henceforth permitted.

But reporters were still beset with too many difficulties, to be able to collect accurate accounts of the debates. Prohibited from taking notes, they were obliged to write mainly from memory. If notes were taken at all, they were written surreptitiously, and in fear of the Sergeant-at-Arms. Nor was this the only impediment to reporting. The accommodation for strangers was very limited; and as no places were reserved for reporters, they were obliged to wait upon the stairs, — sometimes for hours, — before the doors were opened, in order to secure admission. Under such restraints, imperfections in the reports were to be expected. However faithfully the substance of the debates may have been rendered, it is not conceivable that the language of the speakers could have been preserved; and it was probably no vain boast of Dr. Johnson, when, to a company lost in admiration at one of Mr. Pitt's most eloquent speeches, he exclaimed, "That speech *I* wrote in a garret, in Exeter Street."[1]

Its difficulties.

[1] Sir J. Hawkins's Life of Dr. Johnson. The editor of Cobbett's Parliamentary History bears testimony to the general accuracy of Dr. Johnson's reports, and discredits the statements of Sir John Hawkins and others, who had regarded them as the works of his own imagination. — *Prefs.* to vols. xi. and xii.

Nor were any further facilities conceded to reporters, after the struggle of 1771. Lord Malmesbury, speaking of Mr. Pitt's speech, 23d May, 1803, on the renewal of hostilities with France, said: "By a new arrangement of the Speaker's, strangers were excluded till so late an hour, that the newspaper printers could not get in, and of course, no part of Pitt's speech can be printed."[1] A sketch of this speech, however, has been preserved; but the whole debate was very imperfectly reported.[2] Even so late as 1807, it was noticed in the House of Lords, that a person was taking notes in the gallery.[3]

Reports interrupted by exclusion of strangers.

Another interruption to which reporting was still exposed, was the frequent and capricious exclusion of strangers, at the desire of a single member. On the 29th January, 1778, seven years after the contest with the printers, Colonel Luttrell complained of misrepresentation in a newspaper; and said he should move the exclusion of strangers, in order to prevent the recurrence of such a practice; upon which Mr. Fox made this remarkable observation: "He was convinced the true and only method of preventing misrepresentation was by throwing open the gallery, and making the debates and decisions of the House as public as possible. There was less danger of misrepresentation in a full company than a thin one, as there would be a greater number of persons to give evidence against the misrepresentation."[4]

[1] Corresp. and Diary, iv. 262.

[2] Parl. Hist. xxxvi. 1386.

[3] Court and Cabinets of George III. iv. 150; not mentioned in the Parl. Debates.

[4] Parl. Hist. xix. 647. A few days afterwards strangers were ordered to withdraw. This order was enforced against the gentlemen; but the ladies, who were present in unusual numbers, were permitted to remain. Governor Johnstone, however, remonstrated upon the indulgence shown to them, and they were also directed to withdraw. But they showed no disposition to obey this ungracious order, and business was interrupted for nearly two hours, before their exclusion was accomplished. Among the number were the Duchess of Devonshire, and Lady Norton. The contumacy of the ladies

On the 14th June, 1798, the debate on Mr. Sheridan's motion for a committee on the state of Ireland, was lost to the public, by the exclusion of strangers.[1] In 1810, Mr. Yorke enforced the exclusion of strangers during the inquiries, at the bar, into the expedition to the Scheldt; when Mr. Sheridan vainly attempted to obtain a modification of the rule, which vested in a single member, the power of excluding the public.[2] And on some later occasions, the reports of the debates in both Houses have been interrupted from the same cause.[3]

But when the fear of punishment was abated, the reports became more systematic; and were improved in character and copiousness. There were still delays, and other shortcomings: but mainly by the enterprise and ability of Almon, Woodfall, and Perry, the system of reporting and printing the debates gradually attained its present marvellous rapidity and completeness. And what a revolution has it accomplished!

Political results of reporting.

The entire people are now present, as it were, and assist in the deliberations of Parliament. An orator addresses not only the assembly of which he is a member; but, through them, the civilized world. Publicity has become one of the most important instruments of parliamentary government. The people are taken into counsel by Parliament, and concur in approving or condemning the laws, which are there proposed; and thus the doctrine of Hooker is verified to the very letter: "Laws they

on this occasion unhappily led to the withdrawal of the privilege, which they had long enjoyed, of being present at the debates of the House of Commons.

Feb. 2d, 1778. London Chronicle, cited in note to Parl. Hist. vol. xix. p. 673. Hatsell, Prec. ii. 181, *n.* See also Grey's Deb. iii. 222. Parl. Hist. xix. 674, *n.*

[1] Parl. Hist. xxxiii. 1487.

[2] Hansard's Deb. xv. 325.

[3] Even so late as 1849 the doors of the House of Commons were closed against strangers for nearly two hours; and no report of the debate during that time was published.

are not, which public approbation hath not made so." While publicity secures the ready acceptance of good laws by the people, the passing of bad laws, of which the people disapprove, is beyond the power of any minister. Long before a measure can be adopted by the legislature, it has been approved or condemned by the public voice; and living and acting in public, Parliament, under a free representation, has become as sensitive to public opinion, as a barometer to atmospheric pressure. Such being the direct influence of the people over the deliberations of Parliament, they must share, with that body, the responsibility of legislation. They have permitted laws to be passed, — they have accepted and approved them; and they will not afterwards allow them to be disturbed. Hence the remarkable permanence of every legislative settlement. There has been no retrogression in our laws or policy. The people, — if slow to perceive the value of new principles, — hold fast to them when once acknowledged, as to a national faith.[1] No circumstance in the history of our country, — not even parliamentary reform, — has done more for freedom and good government, than the unfettered liberty of reporting. And of all the services which the press has rendered to free institutions, none has been greater than its bold defiance of parliamentary privilege, while laboring for the interests of the people.

Reporting still a breach of privilege.

Reporting, instead of being resented by Parliament, is now encouraged as one of the main sources of its influence; while the people justly esteem it, as the surest safeguard of liberty. Yet such is the tenacity with which ancient customs are observed, — long after their uses have ceased to be recognized, — that the privilege itself has never been relinquished. Its maintenance, how-

[1] Though equal publicity prevails in the United States, their legislation is more sudden and impulsive, and remarkable, therefore, for its instability. — *De Tocqueville, Démocratie en Amérique*, i. 242 (13th ed.). See also an interesting essay of Sismondi, "De la Délibération Nationale:" *Études sur les Constitutions des Peuples Libres*, 131.

ever, is little more than a harmless anomaly. Though it is still a breach of privilege to publish the debates, parliamentary censure is reserved for wilful misrepresentation; and even this offence is now scarcely known. The extraordinary ability, candor, and good faith of the modern school of reporters, have left nothing for Parliament or the public to desire.

Galleries for the accommodation of reporters.

The fire which destroyed both Houses of Parliament in 1834, introduced a new era in reporting. Though for many years past, the reporters of the daily press had enjoyed facilities unknown to their predecessors, they still carried on their difficult labors, in the strangers' gallery. In the temporary Houses, separate galleries, for the accommodation of reporters, were first introduced; and this significant change has been perpetuated in the present buildings.

Presence of strangers recognized.

In 1845 the presence of strangers in the galleries and other parts of the House, not appropriated to members, was for the first time recognized by the orders of the House of Commons; yet this tardy recognition of their presence, did not supersede the ancient rule by which they could be excluded on the word of a single member.

Publication of division lists.

A further change was still wanting to complete the publicity of parliamentary proceedings, and the responsibility of members. The conduct of members who took part in the debates, — until recently a very small number, — was now known; but the conduct of the great majority who were silent, was still a secret. Who were present, — how they voted, — and what members composed the majority, — and therefore the ruling body, — could not be ascertained. On questions of unusual interest, it was customary for the minority to secure the publication of their own names; but it was on very rare occasions indeed, that a list of the majority could also be obtained.[1] In either case

[1] In 1696, the Commons declared the printing the names of the minority,

the publication was due to the exertions of individual members. The House itself took no cognizance of names; but concerned itself merely with the numbers. The grave constitutional objections to this form of voting, had not escaped the notice of parliamentary reformers. Lord John Russell, in his speech on parliamentary reform in 1819, said: — "We are often told that the publication of the debates is a corrective for any defect in the composition of this House. But to these men, such an argument can by no means apply; the only part they take in the affairs of this House, is to vote in the majority; and it is well known that the names of the majority are scarcely ever published. Such members are unlimited kings, — bound by no rule in the exercise of their power, — fearing nothing from public censure, in the pursuit of selfish objects, — not even influenced by the love of praise and historical fame, which affects the most despotic sovereigns; but making laws, voting money, imposing taxes, sanctioning wars, with all the plenitude of power, and all the protection of obscurity; having nothing to deter them but the reproach of conscience, and everything to tempt the indulgence of avarice and ambition."[1]

It was not, however, until 1836, — four years after the passing of the reform act, — that the House of Commons adopted the wise and popular plan of recording the votes of every member; and publishing them, day by day, as part of the proceedings of the House. So stringent a test had never been applied to the conduct of members; and if free constituencies have since failed in their duty of sending able and conscientious representatives, the fault has been entirely their own.

The Commons have since extended the principle of pub-

a breach of privilege, as "destructive of the freedom and liberties of Parliament." — *Com. Journ.* xi. 572. In 1782, the Opposition published division lists, the ministerial members appearing in red letters, and the minority in black. — *Wraxall Mem.* ii. 591.

[1] Hansard's Deb., 3d Ser., xli. 1097.

licity still further. The admission of strangers to debates had been highly prized; but the necessity of excluding them during a division, had never been doubted.[1] Yet in 1853 it was shown by Mr. Muntz [2] that they might be permitted to remain in the galleries, without any embarrassment to the tellers; and they have since looked down upon the busy scene, and shared in the excitement of the declaration of the numbers.

Strangers present at divisions.

In these important changes, the Commons have also been followed by the Lords. Since 1857, their Lordships have published their division lists daily; and during a division, strangers are permitted to remain in the galleries and in the space within the rails of the throne.[3]

Divisions in the Lords.

In a minor, yet not unimportant change, the personal responsibility of members, as well to the House as to the public, has been extended. In the Commons, since 1839, the name of every member addressing questions to witnesses before select committees, has been published with the minutes of evidence; and in 1852 the same practice was adopted by the Lords. It displays the intelligence, the knowledge, and the candor of the questioners; or their obtuseness, ignorance, and prejudice. It exhibits them seeking for truth, or obstinately persisting in error. Their presence at each sitting of the committee, and their votes upon every question, are also recorded and published in the minutes of proceedings.

Names of members on committees.

One other concession to the principle of unrestricted publicity, must not be overlooked. One of the results of increasing activity and vigilance in the Legislature, has been the collection of information, from all sources, on which to found its laws. Financial and statistical accounts, — reports and papers upon every question of foreign and domestic policy, — have been multiplied in so

Publication of parliamentary reports and papers.

[1] In 1849 a committee reported that their exclusion was necessary.

[2] Report of Select Committee on Divisions, 1853.

[3] Resolutions, March 10th, 1857.

remarkable a manner, since the union with Ireland, that it excites surprise how Parliament affected to legislate, in earlier times, without such information. These documents were distributed to all members of the Legislature ; and, by their favor, were also accessible to the public. In 1835 the Commons took a further step in the encouragement of publicity, by directing all their papers to be freely sold, at a cheap rate.[1] The public have since had the same means of information, upon all legislative questions, as the House itself. Community of knowledge, as well as community of discussion, has been established. If comments are justly made upon the extravagance of parliamentary printing, — if voluminous "blue books" are too often a fair object of ridicule, — yet the information they afford is for the public; and the extent and variety of the documents printed, attest at once the activity of members, and the keen interest taken by the people, in the business of legislation.

Freedom of comments upon Parliament.

While the utmost publicity has thus been gradually extended to all parliamentary proceedings, a greater freedom has been permitted to the press, in criticizing the conduct of Parliament. Relying upon the candor of public opinion for a justification of its conduct, Parliament has been superior to the irritable sensitiveness, which formerly resented a free discussion of its proceedings. Rarely has either House thought fit, of late years, to restrain by punishment, even the severest censures upon its own debates and proceedings. When gross libels have been published upon the House itself, or any of its members, the House has occasionally thought it necessary to vindicate its honor, by the commitment of the offenders to custody. But it has rightly distinguished between libels upon character and motives, — and comments, however severe, upon political conduct. In 1810, Mr. Gale Jones was committed to Newgate, for publishing an offensive placard announcing for discussion in a debating society the conduct of two members,

[1] Reports on Printed Papers, 1835.

Mr. G. Yorke and Mr. Windham. Sir Francis Burdett was sent to the Tower, for publishing an address to his constituents, denouncing this act of the House, and denying its right of commitment. Twenty years later, both these offences would probably have been disregarded, or visited with censure only. Again, in 1819, Mr. Hobhouse was committed to Newgate for violent, if not seditious, language in a pamphlet. A few years afterwards, such an offence, if noticed at all, would have been remitted to the Attorney-General, and the Court of Queen's Bench. In 1838, Mr. O'Connell, for a much grosser libel than any of these, was only reprimanded in his place, by the Speaker. The forbearance of both Houses has maintained their dignity, and commanded public respect. Nor has it been without other good results; for, however free the commentaries of newspapers, — they have rarely been disgraced by the vulgar scurrilities which marked the age of Wilkes and Junius, when Parliament was still wielding the rod of privilege over the press. Universal freedom of discussion has become the law of our political system; and the familiar use of the privilege, has gradually corrected its abuses.

Early petitions to Parliament.

The relations of Parliament with the people have also been drawn closer, by the extended use of the popular right of petitioning for redress of grievances. Though this right has existed from the earliest times, it had been, practically, restricted for many centuries, to petitions for the redress of personal and local grievances; and the remedies sought by petitioners, were such as Courts of Equity, and private Acts of Parliament have since been accustomed to provide. The civil war of Charles I. encouraged a more active exercise of the right of petitioning. Numerous petitions of a political character, and signed by large bodies of people, were addressed to the Long Parliament.[1] Freedom of opinion, however,

[1] Clarendon, Rebell. (Oxford Ed., 1826), i. 357; ii. 166, 206, 207, 222; v. 460; vi. 406.

was little tolerated by that assembly. The supporters of their cause, were thanked and encouraged: its incautious opponents, if they ventured to petition, were punished as delinquents.[1] Still it was during this period of revolution, that the practice of addressing Parliament upon general political questions had its rise. After the Restoration, petitions were again discouraged. For long periods, indeed, during the reign of Charles II., the discontinuance of Parliaments effectually suppressed them; and the collecting of signatures to petitions and addresses to the king, or either House of Parliament, for alteration of matters established by law, in church or state, was restrained by Act of Parliament.[2]

Rarely political.

Nor does the Revolution appear to have extended the free use of petitions. In the next ten years, petitions in some numbers were presented, — chiefly from persons interested, — relative to the African Company, — the scarcity and depreciation of the coinage, — the duties on leather, — and the woollen trade; but very few of a general political character. Freedom of opinion was not tolerated. In 1690, a petition from the city of London, hinting at a repeal of the Test Act, so far as it affected Protestant Dissenters, could hardly obtain a reading;[3] and in 1701, the Commons imprisoned five of the Kentish petitioners, until the end of the session, for praying that the loyal addresses of the House might be turned into bills of supply.[4] During the reigns of Queen Anne, and the first two Georges, petitions continued to pray for special relief; but rarely interposed in questions of general legislation. Even the ten first turbulent years of George III.'s reign, failed to develop the agency of petitions, among other devices of agitation. So little indulgence did Parliament then

[1] *Ibid.* ii. 221, 348; Com. Journ. v. 354, 367, 368; Rushworth Coll. v. 462, 487.

[2] 13 Chas. II. c. 5. Petitions to the King for the assembling of Parliament were discountenanced in 1679 by proclamation (Dec. 12th).

[3] Parl. Hist. v. 359.

[4] Somers's Tracts, xi. 242; Parl. Hist. v. 1255; *Ibid.* App. xvii. xviii.

show to petitions, that if they expressed opinions of which the majority disapproved, the right of the subject did not protect them from summary rejection. In 1772, a most temperate petition, praying for relief from subscription to the Thirty-nine Articles, was rejected by the Commons, by a large majority.[1]

Commencement of the modern system of petitioning.

It was not until 1779, that an extensive organization to promote measures of economical and parliamentary reform, called into activity a general system of petitioning, — commencing with the freeholders of Yorkshire, and extending to many of the most important counties and cities in the kingdom.[2] This may be regarded as the origin of the modern system of petitioning, by which public measures, and matters of general policy, have been pressed upon the attention of Parliament. Corresponding committees being established in various parts of the country, were associated for the purpose of effecting a common object, by means of petitions, to be followed by concerted motions made in Parliament. An organization which has since been so often used with success, was now first introduced into our political system.[3] But as yet the number of petitions was comparatively small; and bore little proportion to the vast accumulations of later times. Notwithstanding the elaborate system of association and correspondence established, there do not appear to have been more than forty petitions;[4] but many of these were very numerously signed. The Yorkshire petition was sub-

1 By 217 to 71.

2 Adolphus, iii. 94, 113; Remembrancer, vol. ix.; Wyvil's Political Papers, i. 1–296; Wraxall's Mem. 292.

3 Mr. Hallam, in a valuable note to his Constitutional History, vol. iii. p. 264, to which I am much indebted, says that "the great multiplication of petitions wholly unconnected with particular interests cannot, I believe, be traced higher than those for the abolition of the slave-trade in 1787; though a few were presented for reform about the end of the American War, which would undoubtedly have been rejected with indignation at any earlier stage of our constitution." I have assigned the somewhat earlier period of 1779, as the origin of the modern system of petitioning.

4 Parl. Hist. xxi. 339; Ann. Reg. 1780, p. 165.

scribed by upwards of eight thousand freeholders;[1] the Westminster petition, by five thousand electors.[2] The meetings at which they were agreed to, awakened the public interest in questions of reform, to an extraordinary degree, which was still further increased by the debates in Parliament, on their presentation. At the same time, Lord George Gordon and his fanatical associates were engaged in preparing petitions against the Roman Catholics. To one of these, no less than one hundred and twenty thousand signatures were annexed.[3] But not satisfied with the influence of petitions so numerously signed, the dangerous fanatic who had collected them, sought to intimidate Parliament by the personal attendance of the petitioners; and his ill-advised conduct resulted in riots, conflagrations, and bloodshed, which nearly cost their mischievous originator his head.

Its development.

In 1782, there were about fifty petitions praying for reform in the representation of the Commons in Parliament; and also a considerable number in subsequent years. The great movement for the abolition of the slave-trade soon followed. The first petition against that infamous traffic, was presented from the Quakers in 1782;[4] and was not supported by other petitions for some years. But in the mean time, an extensive association had instructed the people in the enormities of the slave-trade, and aroused the popular sympathies in favor of the African negro. In 1787 and 1788, a greater number of petitions were presented for this benevolent object, than had ever been addressed to Parliament, upon any other political question. There were upwards of a hundred petitions, numerously signed, and from influential places.[5] Never yet had the direct influence of petitions upon the deliberations of

1 Speech of Sir George Savile; Parl. Hist. xx. 1374.
2 Speech of Mr. Fox; *Ibid.* xxi. 287.
3 Ann. Reg. 1780, p. 259.
4 June 17th, 1782; Com. Journ. xxxix. 487; Adolphus, Hist. iv. 301.
5 Com. Journ. xliii. 159 *et seq.*; Adolphus, Hist. iv. 306.

Parliament, been so remarkably exemplified. The question of the slave-trade was immediately considered by the government, by the Privy Council, and by Parliament; and remedial measures were passed, which ultimately led to its prohibition. This consummation was indeed postponed for several years, and was not accomplished without many struggles; but the influence of petitions, and of the organization by which they were produced, was marked throughout the contest.[1] The king and Mr. Pitt appear, from the first, to have regarded with disfavor this agitation for the abolition of the slave-trade, by means of addresses and petitions, as being likely to establish a precedent for forcing the adoption of other measures, less unobjectionable.[2]

Notwithstanding this recognition of the constitutional right of addressing Parliament upon public questions, the growth of petitions was not yet materially advanced. Throughout the reign of George III. their numbers, upon the most interesting questions, were still reckoned by hundreds only.[3] As yet, it was sought to express the sentiments of influential classes only; and a few select petitions from the principal counties and cities, — drawn with great ability, and signed by leading men, — characterized this period of the history of petitions. Even in 1816 there were little more than four hundred petitions against the continuance of the Property Tax, notwithstanding the strong public feeling against it.

It was not until the latter part of the succeeding reign, that petitioning attained that development, by which it has

[1] Mr. Fox, writing to Dr. Wakefield, April 28th, 1801, said: "With regard to the slave-trade, I conceive the great numbers which have voted with us, sometimes amounting to a majority, have been principally owing to petitions." — *Memorials of Fox*, iv. 429.

[2] Malmesbury Corresp. ii. 430.

[3] In 1813, there were 200 in favor of Roman Catholic claims, and about 700 for promulgating the Christian religion in India: in 1814, about 150 on the corn laws, and nearly 1000 for the abolition of the slave-trade: in 1817 and 1818, upwards of 500 petitions for reform in Parliament.

since been distinguished. From that period it has been the custom to influence the judgment of Parliament, not so much by the weight and political consideration of the petitioners, as by their numbers. Religious bodies, — especially of Dissenting communions, — had already contributed the greatest number of petitions; and they have since been foremost in availing themselves of the rights of petitioners. In 1824 an agitation was commenced, mainly by means of petitions, for the abolition of slavery; and from that period until 1833, when the Emancipation Act was passed, little less than twenty thousand petitions were presented: in 1833 alone, nearly seven thousand were laid before the House of Commons. Upon many other subjects, petitions were now numbered by thousands, instead of hundreds. In 1827 and 1828, the repeal of the Corporation and Test Acts was urged by upwards of five thousand petitions. Between 1825 and 1829, there were above six thousand petitions in favor of the Roman Catholic claims, and nearly nine thousand against them. Other questions affecting the Church and Dissenters, — the Maynooth grant, church rates, and the observance of the Sabbath, have since called them forth, in still greater numbers.[1] On a single day, in 1860, nearly four thousand petitions were presented, on the question of church rates.[2]

Petitions from religious bodies.

[1] In 1834 there were upwards of 2,000 petitions in support of the Church Establishment, and 2,400 for relief of Dissenters. In 1837 there were about 10,000 petitions relating to church rates. Between 1833 and 1837, 5,000 petitions were presented for the better observance of the Lord's Day. In 1845, 10,253 petitions, with 1,288,742 signatures, were presented against the grant to Maynooth College. In 1850, 4,475 petitions, with 656,919 signatures, were presented against Sunday labor in the Post-office. In 1851, 4,144 petitions, with 1,016,657 signatures, were presented for repelling encroachments of the Church of Rome; and 2,151 petitions, with 948,081 signatures, against the Ecclesiastical Titles Bill. In 1856, 4,999 petitions, with 629,926 signatures, were presented against opening the British Museum on Sundays; and in 1860, there were 5,575 petitions, with 197,687 signatures, against the abolition of church rates; and 5,538 petitions, with 610,877 signatures, in favor of their abolition.

[2] March 28th, 1860.

Extraordinary increase of petitions.

The people have also expressed their opinions upon all the great political measures of the last thirty years, by prodigious numbers of petitions;[1] and these petitions have been freely received, however distasteful their opinions, — however strong their language. Disrespect and menace have not been suffered; but the wise and tolerant spirit of the age, has recognized unbounded liberty of opinion.

Abuses of petitioning.

This general use of petitions had been originally developed by associations; and in its progress, active organization has ever since been resorted to, for bringing its great influence to bear upon Parliament. Sometimes, indeed, the manner in which petitioning has been systematized, has discredited the right on which it is founded, and the questions it has sought to advance. Petitions in thousands — using the same language, — inscribed in the same handwriting, and on the same description of paper, — and signed by fabulous numbers, — have marked the activity of agents, rather than the unanimity of petitioners; and, instead of being received as the expression of public opinion, have been reprobated as an abuse of a popular privilege. In some cases the unscrupulous zeal of agents has even led them to resort to forgery and other frauds, for the multiplication of signatures.[2]

[1] In 1846 there were 1,958 petitions, with 145,855 signatures, against the repeal of the corn laws; and 467 petitions, with 1,414,303 signatures, in favor of repeal. In 1848 there were 577 petitions, with 2,018,080 signatures, praying for universal suffrage. In the five years ending 1843, 94,000 petitions were received by the House of Commons; in the five years ending 1848, 66,501; in the five years ending 1853, 54,908; and in the five years ending 1858, 47,669. In 1860, 24,279 petitions were received, being a greater number than in any previous year except 1843.

[2] Such practices appear to have been coeval with agitation by means of petitions. Lord Clarendon states that in 1640, "when a multitude of hands was procured, the petition itself was cut off, and a new one framed suitable to the design in hand, and annexed to the long list of names, which were subscribed to the former. By this means many men found their hands subscribed to petitions of which they before had never heard." — *Hist. of Rebellion*, ii. 357.

While the number of petitions was thus increasing, their influence was further extended, by the discussions to which their presentation gave rise. The arguments of the petitioners, were repeated and enforced in debate. Whatever the business appointed for consideration, the claims of petitioners to a prior hearing, were paramount. Again and again, were the same questions thus forced upon the attention of Parliament. A popular question absorbed all others: it was forever under discussion. This free access of petitioners to the inner deliberations of Parliament, was a great privilege. It had long been enjoyed and appreciated; but when it was too often claimed, its continuance became incompatible with good government. After the reform act, the debating of petitions threatened to become the sole business of the House of Commons. For a time, expedients were tried to obtain partial relief from this serious embarrassment; but at length, in 1839, the House was forced to take the bold but necessary step, of prohibiting all debate upon the presentation of petitions.[1] The reformed Parliament could venture upon so startling an invasion of the right of petitioning; and its fearless decision was not misconstrued by the people. Nor has the just influence of petitions been diminished by this change; for while the House restrained desultory and intrusive discussion, it devised other means for giving publicity, and extended circulation to the opinions of petitioners.[2] Their voice is still heard and respected in the consideration of every public measure; but it is no longer suffered to impede the toilsome work of legislation.

Debates on presenting petitions restrained.

To these various modes of subjecting Parliament to the direct control of public opinion, must be added the modern custom of exacting pledges from candidates at elections. The general election of 1774 appears to

Pledges of members.

[1] Com. Journ. xciv. 16; Hansard's Debates, 3d Ser., xlv. 156, 197.

[2] About a thousand petitions are annually printed *in extenso;* and all petitions are classified so as to exhibit the number of petitions, with the signatures, relating to every subject.

have been the first occasion, on which it prevailed so far as to attract public notice.[1] Many popular questions, especially our differences with America, were then under discussion; and in many places, tests were proposed to candidates, by which they were required to support or oppose the leading measures of the time. Wilkes was forward in encouraging a practice so consonant with his own political principles; and volunteered a test for himself and his colleague, Sergeant Glynn, at the Middlesex election. Many candidates indignantly refused the proposed test, even when they were favorable to the views, to which it was sought to pledge them. At this period, Mr. Burke explained to the electors of Bristol, — with that philosophy and breadth of constitutional principle, which distinguished him, — the relations of a representative to his constituents. "His unbiased opinion, his mature judgment, his enlightened conscience, he ought not to sacrifice to you, to any man, or to any set of men living. . . Your representative owes you, not his industry only, but his judgment; and he betrays, instead of serving you, if he sacrifices it to your opinion. . . Government and legislation are matters of reason and judgment, and not of inclination; and what sort of reason is that in which the determination precedes the discussion, — in which one set of men deliberate, and another decide? . . Parliament is not a congress of ambassadors from different and hostile interests; . . but Parliament is a deliberative assembly of one nation, with one interest, — that of the whole; where not local purposes, not local prejudices, ought to guide, but the general good, resulting from the general reason of the whole." [2]

Since that time, however, the relations between representatives and their constituents have become more intimate; and the constitutional theory of pledges has been somewhat modified. According to the true principles of representation, the constituents elect a man in whose character and general

1 Adolphus, Hist. ii. 143.

2 Burke's Works, iii. 18–20.

political views they have confidence; and their representative enters the Legislature a free agent, to assist in its deliberations, and to form his own independent judgment upon all public measures. If the contrary were universally the rule, representatives would become delegates; and government by the entire body of the people, would be substituted for representative institutions.[1] But the political conditions of our own time have brought occasional pledges more into harmony with the spirit of the constitution. The political education of the people, — the publicity of all parliamentary proceedings, — and the free discussions of the press, have combined to force upon constituencies, the estimation of measures as well as men. Hence candidates have sought to recommend themselves by the advocacy of popular measures; and constituents have expected explicit declarations of the political faith of candidates. And how can it be contended that upon such measures as catholic emancipation, parliamentary reform, and the repeal of the corn laws, constituencies were not entitled to know the opinions of their members? Unless the electors are to be deprived of their voice in legislation, such occasions as these were surely fit for their peculiar vigilance At a dissolution, the Crown has often appealed directly to the sense of the people, on the policy of great public measures; and how could they respond to that appeal without satisfying themselves regarding the opinions and intentions of the can-

[1] There is force, but at the same time exaggeration, in the opinions of an able reviewer upon this subject. "For a long time past we have, unconsciously, been burning the candle of the constitution at both ends; our electors have been usurping the functions of the House of Commons, while the House of Commons has been monopolizing those of the Parliament." — *Ed. Rev.*, Oct. 1852, No. 196, p. 469. Again, p. 470: "In place of selecting men, constituencies pronounce upon measures; in place of choosing representatives to discuss questions and decide on proposals in one of three coördinate and coequal bodies, the aggregate of which decree what shall be enacted or done, electors consider and decree what shall be done themselves. It is a reaction towards the old Athenian plan of direct government by the people, practised before the principle of representation was discovered."

didates? Their response was found in the majority returned to the new Parliament, directly or indirectly pledged to support their decision.[1]

But while the right of electors to be assured of the political opinions of candidates has been generally admitted, the first principles of representative government are ever to be kept in view. A member, once elected, is free to act upon his own convictions and conscience. As a man of honor, he will violate no engagement which he may have thought it becoming to accept; but if he has a due respect for his own character, and for the dignity of his office, he will not yield himself to the petty meddling and dictation of busy knots of his constituents, who may assume to sway his judgment.

Servants' privilege discontinued.

Such being the multiplied relations of Parliament to the people, let us inquire how, since its early excesses in the reign of George III., it has deferred to the law, and respected other jurisdictions besides its own. The period signalized by the ill-advised attempts of the House of Commons to enlarge its powers, and assert too tenaciously its own privileges, — was yet marked by the abandonment of some of its ancient customs and immunities. From the earliest times, the members of both Houses had enjoyed the privilege of freedom from arrest in all civil suits; and this immunity, — useful and necessary as regarded themselves, — had also extended to their servants. The abuses of this privilege had long been notorious; and repeated attempts had already been made to discontinue it. For that purpose bills were several times passed by the Lords, but miscarried in the Commons.[2] At length, in 1770, a bill was agreed to by the Commons,[3] and sent up to the House of

1 Speeches from the throne, 24th March, 1784; 27th April, 1807; 22d April, 1831; 21st March, 1857.

2 Lord Mansfield's speech, May 9th, 1770; Parl. Hist. xvi. 974.

3 Walpole says: "The bill passed easily through the Commons, many of the members who were inclined to oppose it, trusting it would be rejected in the other House." — *Mem.* iv. 147. But this is scarcely to be reconciled with the fact that similar bills had previously been passed by the Lords.

Lords. There it encountered unexpected opposition from several peers; but was carried by the powerful advocacy of Lord Mansfield.[1] Nor was this the only privilege restrained by this useful Act. Members and their servants had formerly enjoyed immunity from the distress of their goods, and from all civil suits, during the periods of privilege. Such monstrous privileges had been flagitiously abused; and few passages in parliamentary history are more discreditable than the frivolous pretexts under which protections were claimed by members of both Houses, and their servants. These abuses had already been partially restrained by several statutes;[2] but it was reserved for this Act, to leave the course of justice entirely free, and to afford no protection to members, but that of their persons from arrest.

Prisoners kneeling at the bar.

This same period witnessed the renunciation of an offensive custom, by which prisoners appeared before either House to receive judgment, kneeling at the bar. Submission so abject, while it degraded the prisoner, exhibited privilege as odious, rather than awful, in the eyes of a free people. In the late reign, the proud spirit of Mr. Murray had revolted against this indignity; and his contumacy had been punished by close confinement in Newgate.[3] But in 1772, when privilege was most unpopular, the Commons formally renounced this opprobrious usage, by standing order.[4] The Lords, less candid in their proceedings, silently discontinued the practice; but, by fictitious entries in their journal, still affected to maintain it.

Privilege and the Courts.

Parliament, having relinquished every invidious privilege, has not been without embarrassments in exercising the powers necessary for maintaining its own au-

1 10 Geo. III. c. 50.

2 12 & 13 Will. III. c. 3; 2 & 3 Anne, c. 18; 11 Geo. II. c. 24.

3 Parl. Hist. xiv. 894; Walpole's Mem. of Geo. II. i. 15. In 1647, David Jenkins, a Royalist Welsh judge, had refused to kneel before the Commons; and Sir John Maynard, Sir John Gayre, and others, before the Lords. — Com. Journ. v. 469; Parl. Hist. iii. 844, 880.

4 March 16th, 1772; Com. Journ. xxvi. 48.

thority and independence, and which, — if rightly used, — are no restraint upon public liberty. Each House has exercised a large jurisdiction, in declaring and enforcing its own privileges. It administers the law of Parliament: the courts administer the law of the land; and where subjects have considered themselves aggrieved by one jurisdiction, they have appealed to the other.[1] In such cases the appeal has been to inferior courts, — to courts whose judgments may again be reviewed by the High Court of Parliament. The courts, — without assuming the right to limit the privileges of Parliament, — have yet firmly maintained their own unfettered jurisdiction, to try all causes legally brought before them; and to adjudge them according to the law, whether their judgment may conflict with privilege, as declared elsewhere, or not. A court of equity or common law can stay actions, by injunction or prohibition: but neither House is able to interdict a suit, by any legal process. Hence embarrassing contests have arisen between Parliament and the courts.

Case of Sir Francis Burdett.

The right of both Houses to imprison for contempt, had been so often recognized by the courts, on writs of *habeas corpus*, that it appeared scarcely open to further question. Yet, in 1810, Sir Francis Burdett denied the authority of the Commons, in his place in Parliament. He enforced his denial in a letter to his constituents; and having himself been adjudged guilty of contempt, he determined to defy and resist their power. By direction of the House, the Speaker issued his warrant for the commitment of Sir Francis to the Tower. He disputed its legality, and resisted and turned out the Sergeant, who came to execute it: he barred up his house; and appealed for protection to the Sheriffs of Middlesex. The mob took his part, and being riotous, were dispersed in the streets, by the military. For three days he defended himself in his house,

[1] All the principles and authorities upon this matter are collected in Chap. VI. of the author's Treatise on the Law and Usage of Parliament.

while the authorities were consulting as to the legality of breaking into it, by force. It was held that the Sergeant, in executing the Speaker's warrant, would be armed with all the powers of the law; and accordingly, on the third day, that officer having obtained the aid of a sufficient number of constables, and a military force, broke into the beleaguered house, and conveyed his prisoner to the Tower.[1] The commitment of a popular opponent of privilege was followed by its usual consequences. The martyred prisoner was an object of sympathy and adulation, — the Commons were denounced as tyrants and oppressors.

Overcome by force, Sir Francis brought actions against the Speaker and the Sergeant, in the Court of King's Bench, for redress. The House would have been justified by precedents and ancient usage, in resisting the prosecution of these actions, as a contempt of its authority; but instead of standing upon its privilege, it directed its officers to plead, and the Attorney-General to defend them. The authority of the House was fully vindicated by the court; but Sir Francis prosecuted an appeal to the Exchequer Chamber, and to the House of Lords. The judgment of the court below being affirmed, all conflict between law and privilege was averted. The authority of the House had indeed been questioned; but the courts declared it to have been exercised in conformity with the law.

Where the courts uphold the authority of the House, all is well: but what if they deny and repudiate it? Since the memorable cases of Ashby and White, and the electors of Aylesbury in 1704, no such case had arisen until 1837: when the cause of dispute was characteristic of the times. In the last century, we have seen the Commons contending for the inviolable secrecy of all their proceedings: now they are found declaring their inherent right of publishing all their own papers, for the information of the public.

The circumstances of this case may be briefly told. In

[1] Ann. Reg. 1810, p. 344; Hansard's Deb. xvi. 257, 454, &c.

1836, Messrs. Hansard, the printers of the House of Commons, had printed, by order of that House, the reports of the Inspectors of Prisons, — in one of which a book published by Stockdale, and found among the prisoners in Newgate, was described as obscene and indecent. After the session, Stockdale brought an action against the printers, for libel. The character of the book being proved, a verdict was given against him, upon a plea of justification: but Lord Chief Justice Denman, who tried the cause, took occasion to say that "the fact of the House of Commons having directed Messrs. Hansard to publish all their parliamentary reports, is no justification for them, or for any bookseller who publishes a parliamentary report, containing a libel against any man." The assertion of such a doctrine, was naturally startling to the House of Commons; and at the next meeting of Parliament, after an inquiry by a committee, the House declared "That the power of publishing such of its reports, votes, and proceedings as it shall deem necessary, or conducive to the public interests, is an essential incident to the constitutional functions of Parliament, more especially of this House, as the representative portion of it." It was further resolved, that for any person to institute a suit in order to call its privileges in question, or for any court to decide upon matters of privilege, inconsistent with the determination of either House, was a breach of privilege.[1]

Right of Commons to publish papers affecting character.

Stockdale, however, immediately brought another action, to which the House, — instead of acting upon its own recent resolutions, — directed Messrs. Hansard to plead. The case was tried upon this single issue, — whether the printers were justified by the privilege and order of the House; and the Court of Queen's Bench unanimously decided against them.

Case of Stockdale.

The position of the Commons was surrounded with diffi-

[1] Com. Journ. xcii. 418; May's Law and Usage of Parliament, 4th ed. 170, *et seq.*

culties. Believing the judgment of the court to be erroneous, they might have sought its reversal by a writ of error. But such a course was not compatible with their dignity. It was not the conduct of their officer that was impugned; but their own authority, which they had solemnly asserted. In pursuing a writ of error, they might be obliged, in the last resort, to seek justice from the House of Lords, — a tribunal of equal, but not superior, authority in matters of privilege; and having already pronounced their own judgment, such an appeal would be derogatory to their proper position in the state. They were equally unwilling to precipitate a conflict with the courts. Their resolutions had been set at defiance; yet the damages and costs were directed to be paid! Their forbearance was not without humiliation. It was resolved, however, that in case of any future action, Messrs. Hansard should not plead at all; and that the authority of the House should be vindicated, by the exercise of its privileges.

During the recess of 1839, another action was brought; and judgment having gone against Messrs. Hansard by default, the damages were assessed in the Sheriff's Court at 600*l.*, and levied by the Sheriffs. On the meeting of Parliament in 1840, the Sheriffs had not yet paid over the money to the plaintiff. The House now proceeded with the rigor which it had previously threatened, — but had forborne to exercise. Stockdale was immediately committed to the custody of the Sergeant-at-Arms, while Mr. Howard, his solicitor, escaped with a reprimand. The Sheriffs were directed to restore the money, which they had levied upon Messrs. Hansard. Being bound by their duty to the Court of Queen's Bench, they refused to obey this order; and were also committed to the custody of the Sergeant. In the hope of some settlement of the difficulty, they retained possession of the money, until compelled by an attachment from the Court of Queen's Bench, to pay it over to Stockdale. Much sympathy was justly excited by the imprisonment of these gentlemen, — who, acting in strict obedience to the law and the judgment of the court, had nevertheless endeavored to avoid a contempt of the House of Commons, which, in the execution of their duty, they were constrained to commit. Punished with reluctance, — and without the least feeling of resentment, — they were the innocent victims of conflicting jurisdictions.

In an earlier age the Commons, relying upon their own paramount authority, might even have proceeded to commit the Judges of the Court of Queen's Bench, — for which a precedent was not wanting; [1] but happily, the wise moderation of this age revolted from so violent and unseemly an exercise of power. Confident in the justice and legality of their own proceedings, — defied by a low plaintiff in an unworthy cause, — and their deliberate judgment overruled by an inferior court, — they yet acted with as much temper and forbearance, as the inextricable difficulties of their position would allow.

Stockdale, while in custody, repeated his offence by bringing another action. He and his attorney were committed to Newgate; and Messrs. Hansard were again ordered not to plead. Judgment was once more entered up against them, and another writ of inquiry issued; when Mr. France, the Under-Sheriff, anxious to avoid offence to the House, obtained leave to show cause before the court, why the writ should not be executed. Meanwhile, the indefatigable Stockdale solaced his imprisonment, by bringing another action; for which his attorney's son, and his clerk, Mr. Pearce, were committed.

Actions stayed by statute.

At length these vexatious proceedings were brought to a close, by the passing of an Act, providing that all such actions should be stayed on the production of a certificate or affidavit, that any paper, the subject of an action, was printed by order of either House of Parliament.[2]

[1] Jay *v.* Topham, 1689; Com. Journ. x. 227.

[2] 3 & 4 Vict. c. 9. Papers reflecting upon private character are sometimes printed for the use of members only.

Such an intervention of the supreme authority of Parliament, two years before, would have averted differences between concurrent jurisdictions, which no other power was competent to reconcile. No course was open to the Commons — befitting their high jurisdiction and dignity — by which the obedience of courts and plaintiffs could be insured: their power of commitment was at once impotent and oppressive: yet they could not suffer their authority to be wholly defied and contemned. Hence their proceedings were inevitably marked by hesitation and inconsistency. In a case, for which the constitution has made no provision, — even the wisdom of Sir Robert Peel, and the solid learning of Mr. Sergeant Wilde were unequal to devise expedients, less open to objection.[1]

Case of Howard *v.* Gosset.

Another occasion immediately arose for further forbearance. Howard commenced an action of trespass against the officers of the House, who had taken him into custody. As it was possible that, in executing the Speaker's warrant, they might have exceeded their authority, the action was suffered to take its course. On the trial, it appeared that they had remained some time in the plaintiff's house, after they had ascertained that he was from home; and on that ground, a verdict was obtained against them for 100*l.* Howard brought a second action against Sir W. Gosset, the Sergeant-at-Arms, in which he was also successful, on the ground of the informality of the Speaker's warrant. The Judges, however, took pains to show that their decision in no way impugned the authority of the House itself. The House, while it regarded this judgment as erroneous, could not but feel that its authority had been trifled with, in a spirit of narrow technicality, by an inferior court. Still moderation prevailed in its counsels; and, as the act of an officer, and not the authority of the House itself, was questioned, it was determined not to resist the ex-

1 Proceedings printed by the Commons, 1839, (283); Report of Precedents, 1837; Hansard's Deb. 1847–1849.

ecution of the judgment; but to test its legality by a writ of error. The judgment was reversed by the unanimous decision of the Court of Exchequer Chamber. As this last judgment was founded upon broader principles of law, than those adopted by the court below, it is probable that, in Stockdale's case, a Court of Error would have shown greater respect to the privileges of the Commons, than the Court of Queen's Bench had thought fit to pay; and it is to be regretted that the circumstances were not such as to justify an appeal to a higher jurisdiction.

Increased power of the Commons.

The increased power of the House of Commons, under an improved representation, has been patent and indisputable. Responsible to the people, it has, at the same time, wielded the people's strength. No longer subservient to the Crown, the ministers, and the peerage, it has become the predominant authority in the state. But it is characteristic of the British constitution, and a proof of its freedom from the spirit of democracy, that the more dominant the power of the House of Commons, — the greater has been its respect for the law, and the more carefully have its acts been restrained within the proper limits of its own jurisdiction. While its authority was uncertain and ill-defined, — while it was struggling against the Crown, — jealous of the House of Lords, — distrustful of the press, — and irresponsible to the people, — it was tempted to exceed its constitutional powers; but since its political position has been established, it has been less provoked to strain its jurisdiction; and deference to public opinion, and the experience of past errors, have taught it wisdom and moderation.

Their moderation since the increase of their power.

Conduct of the Commons in regard to Baron Rothschild, 1850.

The proceedings of the House in regard to Wilkes, present an instructive contrast to its recent conduct in forwarding the admission of Jews to Parliament. In the former case, its own privileges were strained or abandoned at pleasure, and the laws of the land outraged, in order to exclude and persecute an obnoxious member.[1] How did this same powerful body act in the case of Baron de Rothschild and Mr. Salomons? Here the House, — faithful to the principles of religious liberty, which it had long upheld, — was earnest in its desire to admit these members to their place in the legislature. They had been lawfully chosen: they labored under no legal disability; and they claimed the privileges of members. A few words in the oath of abjuration, alone prevented them from taking their seats. A large majority of the House was favorable to their claims: the law was doubtful; and the precedent of Mr. Pease, a Quaker, — who had been allowed to omit these words, — was urged by considerable authorities, as a valid ground for their admission. Yet the House, dealing with the seats of its own members, — over which it has always had exclusive jurisdiction, — and with every inducement to accept a broad and liberal interpretation of the law, — nevertheless administered it strictly, and to the very letter.[2] For several years, the House had endeavored to solve the difficulty by legislation. Its failures, however, did not tempt it to usurp legislative power, under the semblance of judicial interpretation. But it persevered in passing bills, in various forms, until it ultimately forced upon the other House an amendment of the law.

Control of either House over the executive.

The limits within which Parliament, or either House, may constitutionally exercise a control over the executive government, have been defined by usage, upon principles consistent with a true distribution of powers, in a free state and limited monarchy. Parliament has no direct control over any single department of the State. It may order the production of papers, for its information:[3] it may investigate the conduct of public officers; and may pronounce its opinion upon the manner in which every

[1] See *supra*, p. 364, &c.

[2] Hansard's Deb. July 29th and 30th, and Aug. 5th, 1850; July 18th and 21st, 1851. See also Chap. XII. on Civil and Religious Liberty.

[3] Many papers, however, can only be obtained by address to the Crown.

function of the government has been, or ought to be, discharged. But it cannot convey its orders or directions to the meanest executive officer, in relation to the performance of his duty. Its power over the executive is exercised indirectly, — but not the less effectively, — through the responsible ministers of the Crown. These ministers regulate the duties of every department of the state; and are responsible for their proper performance, to Parliament, as well as to the Crown. If Parliament disapprove of any act, or policy of the government, — ministers must conform to its opinion, or forfeit its confidence. In this manner, the House of Commons, having become the dominant body in the legislature, has been able to direct the conduct of the government, and control its executive administration of public affairs, without exceeding its constitutional powers. It has a right to advise the Crown, — even as to the exercise of the prerogative itself; and should its advice be disregarded, it wields the power of impeachment, and holds the purse-strings of the state.

It has controlled the exercise of prerogative.

Questions of peace and war.

History abounds with examples, in which the exercise of prerogative has been controlled by Parliament. Even questions of peace and war, which are peculiarly within the province of prerogative, have been resolved, again and again, by the interposition of Parliament. From the reign of Edward III., Parliament has been consulted by the Crown; and has freely offered its advice on questions of peace and war.[1] The exercise of this right, — so far from being a modern invasion of the royal prerogative, — is an ancient constitutional usage. It was not, however, until the power of Parliament had prevailed over prerogative, that it had the means of enforcing its advice.

At a time when the influence of the Crown had attained its highest point under George III., the House of Commons was able to bring to a close the disastrous American War,

[1] *E. g.* Edw. III., Parl. Hist. i. 122; Henry VII., *ibid.* 452; James I., *ibid.* 1293; Queen Anne, *ibid.* vi. 609.

against the personal will of the king himself. Having presented an address against the further prosecution of offensive war, — to which they had received an evasive answer, — the House proceeded to declare, that it would "consider as enemies to his Majesty and this country all who should advise, or by any means attempt the further prosecution of offensive war on the continent of America, for the purpose of reducing the revolted colonies to obedience by force."[1] Nor did the House rest until it had driven Lord North, the king's war minister, from power.

During the long war with France, the government was pressed with repeated motions, in both Houses, for opening negotiations for peace.[2] Ministers were strong enough to resist them; but, — at a period remarkable for assertions of prerogative, — objections to such motions, on constitutional grounds, were rarely heard. Indeed the Crown, by communicating to Parliament the breaking out of hostilities,[3] or the commencement of negotiations for peace,[4] has invited its advice and assistance. That advice may be unfavorable to the policy of ministers; and the indispensable assistance of Parliament may be withheld. If the Crown be dissatisfied with the judgment of Parliament, an appeal may still be made to the final decision of the people. In 1857, the House of Commons condemned the policy of the war with China; but ministers, instead of submitting to its censure, appealed to the country, and obtained its approval.

War with China, 1857.

Upon the same principles, Parliament has assumed the right of advising the Crown, in regard to the exercise of the prerogative of dissolution. In 1675, an address was moved in the House of Lords,

Advice of Parliament concerning dissolution.

1 Feb. 27th and March 4th, 1782; Parl. Hist. xxii. 1064, 1086, 1087.

2 Lord Stanhope, the Marquess of Lansdowne, &c.; Dec. 15th, 1792; June 17th, 1793, &c.; Mr. Grey, Feb. 21st, 1794, &c.; Mr. Whitbread, March 6th, 1794; Mr. Wilberforce, May 27th, 1795; Mr. Sheridan, Dec. 8th, 1795.

3 Feb. 11th, 1793; May 22d, 1815; March 27th, 1854, &c.

4 Dec. 8th, 1795; Oct. 29th, 1801; Jan. 31st, 1856.

praying Charles II. to dissolve the Parliament; and on the rejection of the motion, several Lords entered their protest.[1] Lord Chatham's repeated attempts to induce the House of Lords to address the Crown to dissolve the Parliament which had declared the incapacity of Wilkes, have been lately noticed.[2] The address of the Commons, after the dismissal of the Coalition Ministry, praying the King not to dissolve Parliament, has been described elsewhere.[3] Lord Wharncliffe's vain effort to arrest the dissolution of Parliament in 1831, has also been adverted to.[4]

But though the right of Parliament to address the Crown, on such occasions is unquestionable, — its exercise has been restrained by considerations of policy, and party tactics. The leaders of parties, — profiting by the experience of Mr. Fox and Lord North, — have since been too wise to risk the forfeiture of public esteem, by factiously opposing the right of ministers to appeal from the House of Commons to the people. Unless that right has been already exercised, the alternatives of resigning office or dissolving Parliament have been left, — by general consent, — to the judgment of ministers who cannot command the confidence of the House of Commons. In the exercise of their discretion, ministers have been met with remonstrances; but sullen acquiescence on the part of their opponents, has given place to violent addresses, and measures for stopping the supplies.

Popular addresses concerning prerogative.

As Parliament may tender its advice to the Crown, regarding its own dissolution, so the people, in their turn, have claimed the right of praying the Crown to exercise its prerogative, in order to give them the means of condemning the conduct of Parliament. In 1701, during a fierce contest between the Whig and Tory parties, numerous petitions and addresses were presented to

[1] Lords' Journ. xiii. 33; Lord Rockingham's Mem. ii. 139.

[2] *Supra*, p. 380, 381.

[3] *Supra*, p. 70.

[4] *Supra*, p. 122.

William III. at the instance of the Whigs, praying for the dissolution of the Parliament, which was soon afterwards dissolved.[1] The constitutional character of these addresses having been questioned, was upheld by a vote of the House of Commons, which affirmed "that it is the undoubted right of the people of England to petition or address the King, for the calling, sitting, and dissolving Parliaments, and for the redressing of grievances."[2] In 1710, similar tactics were resorted to by the Tories, when addresses were presented to Queen Anne, praying for a dissolution, and assuring her Majesty that the people would choose none but such as were faithful to the Crown, and zealous for the Church.[3]

In 1769, Lord Chatham sought public support of the same kind, in his efforts to obtain a dissolution of Parliament. Lord Rockingham and some of the leading Whigs, who doubted at first, were convinced of the constitutional propriety of such a course; and Lord Camden expressed a decisive opinion, affirming the right of the subject.[4] The people were justly dissatisfied with the recent proceedings of the House of Commons; and were encouraged by the Opposition to lay their complaints at the foot of the throne, and to pray for a dissolution.

The contest between Mr. Pitt and the Coalition was characterized by similar proceedings. While the Commons were protesting against a dissolution, the supporters of Mr. Pitt were actively engaged in obtaining addresses to his Majesty, to assure him of the support of the people, in the constitutional exercise of his prerogative.[5]

The House of Commons in the first instance, — and the

1 Burnet's Own Time, iv. 543. Rockingham Mem. ii. 105.

2 Parl. Hist. v. 1339; Grenville Papers, iv. 446.

3 Somerville's Reign of Queen Anne, 409; Smollett's Hist. ii. 191; Grenville Papers, iv. 453.

4 "His answer was full and manly, that the right is absolute, and unquestionable for the exercise." Lord Chatham to Lord Temple, Nov. 8th, 1769; Grenville Papers, iv. 479.

5 See Address of the City, Ann. Reg., 1784, p. 4, &c.

people in the last resort, — have become arbiters of the fate of the ministers of the Crown. Ministers may have the entire confidence of their Sovereign, and be all-powerful in the House of Lords; but without a majority of the House of Commons, they are unable to administer the affairs of the country. The fall of ministries has more often been the result of their failure to carry measures which they have proposed, or of adverse votes on general questions of public policy; but frequently it has been due, — particularly in modern times, — to express representations to the Crown, that its ministers have not the confidence of the House of Commons. Where such votes have been agreed to by an old Parliament, — as in 1784, — ministers have still had before them the alternative of a dissolution; but when they have already appealed to the country for support, — as in 1841, and again in 1859, — a vote affirming that they have not the confidence of the House of Commons, has been conclusive.

Votes of want of confidence.

The disapprobation of ministers by the House of Commons being decisive, the expression of its confidence has, at other times, arrested their impending fall. Thus in 1831, Lord Grey's ministry, embarrassed by an adverse vote of the other House, on the second reform bill,[1] was supported by a declaration of the continued confidence of the House of Commons.

Votes of confidence.

And at other times, the House has interposed its advice to the Crown, on the formation of administrations, with a view to favor or obstruct political arrangements, then in progress. Thus, in 1784, when negotiations had been commenced for a fusion of parties, resolutions were laid before his Majesty expressing the opinion of the House of Commons, that the situation of public affairs required a "firm, efficient, extended, and united administration, entitled to the confidence of the people, and such as may have a tendency to put an end to the divisions and distractions of the coun-

[1] *Supra*, p. 122.

try."[1] Similar advice was tendered to the Prince Regent in 1812, after the death of Mr. Perceval; and to William IV., in 1832, on the resignation of Earl Grey.[2]

Impeachments.

But this constant responsibility of ministers, while it has made their position dependent upon the pleasure of Parliament, has protected fallen ministers from its vengeance. When the acts and policy of statesmen had been dictated by their duty to the Crown alone, without regard to the approval of Parliament, they were in danger of being crushed by vindictive impeachments and attainders. Strafford had died on the scaffold; Clarendon had been driven into exile;[3] Danby had suffered a long imprisonment in the Tower;[4] Oxford, Bolingbroke, and Ormond had been disgraced and ruined,[5] at the suit of the Commons. But Parliamentary responsibility has prevented the commission of those political crimes, which had provoked the indignation of the Commons; and when the conduct or policy of ministers has been condemned, loss of power has been their only punishment. Hence the rarity of impeachments in later times. The last hundred years present but two cases of impeachment, — the one against Mr. Warren Hastings, on charges of misgovernment in India, — the other against Lord Melville, for alleged malversation in his office. The former was not a minister of the Crown, and he was accused of offences committed beyond the reach of Parliamentary control; and the offences charged against the latter, had no relation to his political duties as a responsible minister.

The case of Mr. Warren Hastings finally established the

[1] Parl. Hist. xxiv. 450; Ann. Reg. 1784, p. 265.

[2] *Supra*, p. 110, 338; Hansard's Deb., 1st Ser., xxiii. 249.

[3] Having gone abroad pending his impeachment, an Act of banishment and incapacity was passed by Parliament.

[4] Not being brought to trial, he was admitted to bail by the Court of King's Bench, after an imprisonment of five years. St. Tr. xi., 871.

[5] Oxford was imprisoned for two years in the Tower. Bolingbroke and Ormond, having escaped, were attainted.

constitutional doctrine, that an impeachment by the Commons is not terminated by any prorogation or dissolution of Parliament. It had been affirmed by the Lords in 1678, after an examination of precedents:[1] when Lord Stafford fell a victim to its assertion; and six years afterwards, it had been denied, in order to secure the escape of the "popish lords," then under impeachment.[2] Lord Danby's lingering impeachment had been continued by the first decision, and annulled by the last. The same question having arisen after the lapse of a century, Parliament was called upon to review the precedents of former impeachments, and to pass its judgment upon the contradictory decisions of the Lords. Many of the precedents were so obscure as to furnish arguments on both sides of the question; conflicting opinions were to be found amongst text-writers; and the most eminent lawyers of the day were not agreed.[3] But the masterly and conclusive speech of Mr. Pitt was alone sufficient to settle the controversy, even on the grounds of law and precedent. On broad constitutional principles, the first statesmen of all parties concurred in upholding the inviolable right of the Commons to pursue an impeachment, without interruption from any act of the Crown. It could not be suffered that offenders should be snatched from punishment, by ministers who might be themselves concerned in their guilt. Nor was it just to the accused, that one impeachment should be arrested before a judgment had been obtained; and another preferred, — on the same or different grounds, — perhaps after his defence had suggested new evidence to condemn him. Had not the law already provided for the continuance of impeachments, it would have been necessary to declare

Impeachments not abated by a dissolution, 1791.

[1] March 18th, 19th, 1678. Lords' Journ. xiii. 464, 466.

[2] May 22d, 1685. Lords' Journ. xiv. 11.

[3] Lord Thurlow, Lord Kenyon, Sir Richard Arden, Sir Archibald Macdonald, Sir John Scott, Mr. Mitford, and Mr. Erskine contended for the abatement: Lord Mansfield, Lord Camden, Lord Loughborough, and Sir William Grant, maintained its continuance.

it. But it was agreed in both Houses, by large majorities, that by the law and custom of Parliament, an impeachment pending in the House of Lords continued *in statu quo*, from one Session and from one Parliament to another, until a judgment had been given.[1]

Improved relations of the Crown with the Commons.

As parliamentary responsibility has spared ministers the extreme penalties of impeachments, — so it has protected the Crown from those dangerous and harassing contests with the Commons, with which the earlier history of this country abounds. What the Crown has lost in power, it has gained in security and peace. Until the Commons had fully established their constitutional rights, they had been provoked to assert them with violence, and to press them to extreme conclusions; but they have exercised them, when acknowledged, with moderation and forbearance.

Strong and weak governments.

At the same time, ministers of the Crown have encountered greater difficulties, from the increased power and independence of the Commons, and the more direct action of public opinion upon measures of legislation and policy. They are no longer able to fall back upon the Crown for support: their patronage is reduced, and their influence diminished. They are left to secure a majority, not so much by party connections, as by good measures and popular principles. Any error of judgment, — any failure in policy or administration, is liable to be visited with instant censure. Defeated in the Commons, they have no resource but an appeal to the country, unaided by those means of influence, upon which ministers formerly relied.

Their responsibility is great and perilous; but it has at least protected them from other embarrassments, of nearly equal danger. When the Crown was more powerful, what

[1] Com. Deb.; Parl. Hist. xxviii. 1018, *et seq.;* Lords' Deb.; *ibid.* xxix. 514; Report of Precedents; Lords' Journ. xxxix. 125; Tomline's Life of Pitt, iii. 161.

was the fate of ministries? The first ten years of the reign of George III. witnessed the fall of five feeble administrations; and their instability was mainly due to the restless energies of the king. Until Mr. Pitt came into power, there had not been one strong administration during this reign. It was the king himself who overthrew the Coalition Ministry, the absolute government of Mr. Pitt, and the administration of "All the Talents."

For more than ten years after Mr. Pitt's fall, there was again a succession of weak administrations, of short duration. If the king could uphold a ministry, — he could also weaken or destroy it. From this danger, governments under the new parliamentary system, have been comparatively free. More responsible to Parliament, they have become less dependent upon the Crown. The confidence of the one has guarded them from the displeasure of the other.

No cause of ministerial weakness has been more frequent than disunion. It is the common lot of men acting together; and is not peculiar to any time, or political conditions. Yet when ministers looked to the Crown for support, and relied upon the great territorial lords for a parliamentary majority, — what causes were so fruitful of jealousies and dissensions, as the intrigues of the court, and the rivalries of the proprietors of boroughs? Here, again, governments deriving their strength and union from Parliament and the people, have been less exposed to danger in this form. Governments have, indeed, been weakened, as in former times, by divisions among their own party; but they have been, in some measure, protected from faction, by the greater responsibility of all parties to public opinion. This protection will be more assured, when the old system of government, by influence and patronage, shall give place to the recognition of national interests, as the sole basis of party.

The responsibility of ministers has been further simplified, by the dominant power of the Commons. The Lords may sometimes thwart a ministry, reject or mutilate its measures, and even condemn its policy; but they are powerless to overthrow a ministry supported by the Commons, or to uphold a ministry which the Commons have condemned. Instead of many masters, a government has only one. Nor can it be justly said, that this master has been severe, exacting, or capricious.

It can neither be affirmed that strong governments were characteristic of the parliamentary system, subverted by the reform act; nor that weak governments have been characteristic of the new system, and the result of it. In both periods, the stability of administrations has been due to other causes. If in the latter period, ministers have been overthrown, who, at another time might have been upheld by the influence of the Crown; there have yet been governments supported by a parliamentary majority and public approbation, stronger in moral force, — and more capable of overpowering interests adverse to the national welfare, — than any ministries deriving their power from less popular sources.

After the reform act, Lord Grey's ministry was all-powerful, until it was dissolved by disunion in the cabinet. No government was ever stronger than that of Sir Robert Peel, until it was broken up by the repeal of the corn-laws. Lord Aberdeen's cabinet was scarcely less strong, until it fell by disunion and military failures. What government was more powerful than Lord Palmerston's first administration, until it split upon the sunken rock of the Orsini conspiracy?

On the other hand, the ministry of Lord Melbourne was enfeebled by the disunion of the Liberal party. The first ministry of Sir Robert Peel, and both the ministries of Lord Derby were inevitably weak, — being formed upon a hopeless minority in the House of Commons. Such causes would have produced weakness at any time; and are not chargeable upon the caprices, or ungovernable temper, of a reformed Parliament. And throughout this period, all administrations, — whether strong or weak, and of whatever political party, — relying mainly upon public confidence, have labored successfully in the cause of good government; and have secured to the people more sound laws, prosperity, and contentment, than have been enjoyed at any previous epoch, in the history of this country.

Control of the Commons over supplies and taxes.

One of the most ancient and valued rights of the Commons, is that of voting money and granting taxes to the Crown, for the public service. From the earliest times, they have made this right the means of extorting concessions from the Crown, and advancing the liberties of the people. They upheld it with a bold spirit against the most arbitrary kings; and the Bill of Rights crowned their final triumph over prerogative. They upheld it with equal firmness against the Lords. For centuries they had resented any "meddling" of the other House "with matter of supply;" and in the reign of Charles II., they successfully maintained their exclusive right to determine "as to the matter, the measure, and the time" of every tax imposed upon the people.

In the same reign, they began to scrutinize the public expenditure; and introduced the salutary practice of appropriating their grants to particular purposes. But they had not yet learned the value of a constant control over the revenue and expenditure of the Crown; and their liberality to Charles, and afterwards to James II., enabled those monarchs to violate the public liberties.

Their liberality to the Crown.

The experience of these reigns prevented a repetition of the error; and since the Revolution, the grants of the Commons have been founded on annual estimates, — laid before them on the responsibility of ministers of the Crown, — and strictly appropriated to the service of the year. This constant control over the public expenditure has, more than any other cause, vested in the Commons the supreme power of the state; yet the results have been favorable to the Crown. When the Commons had neither information as to the necessities of the state, nor securities for the proper application of their grants,—they had often failed to respond to the solicitation of the king for subsidies,—or their liberality had fallen short of his demands.[1] But not once since the Revolution, have the demands of the Crown for the public service, been refused. Whatever sums ministers have stated to be necessary, for all the essential services of the state, the Commons have freely granted.[2] Not a soldier has been struck from the rank and file of the army; not a sailor or a ship from the fleet, by any vote of the Commons. So far from opposing the demands of the Crown, they have rather laid themselves open to the charge of too facile an acquiescence in a constantly increasing expenditure. Since they have assumed the control of the finances, the expenditure has increased about fifty-fold; and a stupendous national debt has been created. Doubtless their control has been a check upon ministers. The fear of their remonstrances, has restrained the prodigality of the executive; but parsimony cannot be justly laid to their charge. The people may have some grounds for complaining of their stewardship; but assuredly the Crown and its ministers have none.

Ministers defeated on financial measures.

While voting the estimates, however, the Commons have sometimes dissented from the financial arrangements proposed by ministers. Responding to the pecuniary demands of the Crown, they have

[1] In 1625, the Commons postponed the supplies demanded by Charles I. for carrying on the war with Spain.—*Parl. Hist.* ii. 35. In 1675, they refused a supply to Charles II., to take off the anticipations upon his revenue.—*Ibid.* iv. 757. In 1677, they declined a further supply till his Majesty's alliances were made known.—*Ibid.* 879. And in the next year they refused him an additional revenue.—*Ibid.* 1000. In 1685, James II. required 1,400,000*l.*; the Commons granted one half only.—*Ibid.* 1379.

[2] With a few exceptions, so trifling as to be almost ridiculous, it will be found that the annual estimates have been voted without deduction; *e. g.* in 1858, the only result of the vigilance of Parliament was a disallowance of 300*l.* as the salary of the travelling agent of the National Gallery! In 1859, the salary of the Register of Sasines was refused; but on the recommitment of the resolution, was restored!

disapproved the policy, by which it was sought to meet them. In 1767 Mr. Charles Townshend, the Chancellor of the Exchequer, proposed to continue for one year, the land tax of four shillings in the pound; but on the motion of Mr. Grenville, the tax was reduced to three shillings, by which the budget sustained a loss of half a million. This was the first occasion, since the Revolution, on which a minister had been defeated upon any financial measure.[1]

Throughout the French war, the Commons agreed to every grant of money, and to every new tax and loan, proposed by successive administrations. But on the termination of the war, when the ministers desired to continue one half of the war property tax, amounting to about seven millions and a half, — such was the national repugnance to that tax, that they sustained a signal defeat.[2] Again in 1852, Lord Derby's ministry were out-voted on their proposal for doubling the house tax.[3] But when the Commons have thus differed from the ministry, the questions at issue have involved the form and incidence of taxation, and not the necessities of the state; and their votes have neither diminished the public expenditure, nor reduced the ultimate burdens upon the people.

Stopping the supplies.

Nor have the Commons, by postponing grants, or in other words, by "stopping the supplies," endeavored to coerce the other powers in the state. No more formidable instrument could have been placed in the hands of a popular assembly, for bending the executive to its will. It had been wielded with effect, when the prerogative of kings was high, and the influence of the Commons low; but now the weapon lies rusty in the armory of constitutional warfare. In 1781, Mr. Thomas Pitt proposed to delay the granting of the supplies for a few days, in order to extort

[1] Parl. Hist. xvi. 362.

[2] Ayes 201, Noes 238; Hansard's Deb., 1st Ser., xxxiii. 451; Lord Brougham's Speeches, i. 495; Lord Dudley's Letters, 136; Horner's Mem. ii. 318.

[3] Hansard's Deb., 3d Ser., cxxiii. 1693.

from Lord North a pledge regarding the war in America. It was then admitted that no such proposal had been made since the Revolution; and the House resolved to proceed with the committee of supply, by a large majority.[1] In the same session Lord Rockingham moved, in the House of Lords, to postpone the third reading of a land tax bill, until explanations had been given regarding the causes of Admiral Kempenfeldt's retreat; but did not press it to a division.[2]

The precedent of 1784, is the solitary instance in which the Commons have exercised their power of delaying the supplies. They were provoked to use it, by the unconstitutional exercise of the influence of the Crown; but it failed them at their utmost need,[3] — and the experiment has not been repeated. Their responsibility, indeed, has become too great for so perilous a proceeding. The establishments and public credit of the country are dependent on their votes; and are not to be lightly thrown into disorder. Nor are they driven to this expedient for coercing the executive; as they have other means, not less effectual, for directing the policy of the state.

Restraints upon the liberality of the Commons.

While the Commons have promptly responded to the demands of the Crown, they have endeavored to guard themselves against importunities from other quarters, and from the unwise liberality of their own members. They will not listen to any petition or motion which involves a grant of public money, until it has received the recommendation of the Crown;[4] and they have further protected the public purse, by delays and other forms, against hasty and inconsiderate resolutions.[5] Such precautions have been the more necessary, as there are no checks upon the liberality of the Commons, but such as they impose

1 Nov. 30, 1781; Parl. Hist. xxii. 751; Ayes 172, Noes 77. Mr. T. Pitt had merely opposed the motion for the Speaker to leave the Chair.

2 Nov. 19; Parl. Hist. xxii. 865.

3 See *supra*, p. 72.

4 Standing Order, Dec. 11th, 1706.

5 See May's Law and Usage of Parliament, 4th ed. 512.

upon themselves. The Lords have no voice in questions of expenditure, save that of a formal assent to the Appropriation Acts. They are excluded from it by the spirit, and by the forms of the constitution.

Exclusive rights of the Commons concerning taxation.

Not less exclusive has been the right of the Commons to grant taxes, to meet the public expenditure. These rights are indeed inseparable; and are founded on the same principles. "Taxation," said Lord Chatham, "is no part of the governing, or legislative power. The taxes are a voluntary gift and grant of the Commons alone. In legislation the three estates of the realm are alike concerned; but the concurrence of the peers and the Crown to a tax, is only necessary to clothe it with the form of a law. The gift and grant is of the Commons alone."[1] On these principles, the Commons had declared that a money bill was sacred from amendment. In their gifts and grants, they would brook no meddling. Such a position was not established without hot controversies.[2] Nor was it ever expressly admitted by the Lords;[3] but as they were unable to shake the strong determination of the Commons, they tacitly acquiesced, and submitted. For one hundred and fifty years, there was scarcely a dispute upon this privilege. The Lords, knowing how any amendment affecting a charge upon the people, would be received by the Commons, either abstained from making it, or averted misunderstanding, by not returning the amended bill. And when an amendment was made, to which the Commons could not agree, on the ground of privilege alone, it was their custom

[1] Parl. Hist. xvi. 99.

[2] The Reports of the conferences between the two Houses (1640–1703), containing many able arguments on either side, are collected in the Appendix to the third volume of Hatsell's Precedents, and in the Report of the Committee on Tax Bills, 1860.

[3] To the claim, as very broadly asserted by the Commons in 1700, at a conference upon the Bill for the Sale of Irish Forfeited Estates, the Lords replied: "If the said assertions were exactly true, which their Lordships cannot allow."

to save their privilege, by sending up a new bill, embracing the Lords' amendment.

Power of the Lords to reject a money bill.

But if the Lords might not amend money bills, could they not reject them? This very question was discussed in 1671. The Commons had then denied the right of amendment, on the broadest grounds. In reply, the Lords argued thus: — "If this right should be denied, the Lords have not a negative voice allowed them, in bills of this nature; for if the Lords, who have the power of treating, advising, giving counsel, and applying remedies, cannot amend, abate, or refuse a bill in part, by what consequence of reason, can they enjoy a liberty to reject the whole? When the Commons shall think fit to question it, they may pretend the same grounds for it." The Commons, however, admitted the right of rejection. "Your Lordships," they said, "have a negative to the whole." "The king must deny the whole of every Bill, or pass it; yet this takes not away his negative voice. The Lords and Commons must accept the whole general pardon or deny it; yet this takes not away their negative."[1] And again in 1689, it was stated by a committee of the Commons, that the Lords are "to pass all or reject all, without diminution or alteration."[2] But these admissions cost the Commons nothing, at that time. To reject a money bill, was to withhold supplies from the Crown, — an act of which the Lords were not to be suspected. The Lords themselves were fully alive to this difficulty, and complained that "a hard and ignoble choice was left to them, either to refuse the Crown supplies when they are most necessary, or to consent to ways and proportions of aid, which neither their own judgment or interest, nor the good of the government and people, can admit."[3] In argu-

[1] Hatsell, iii. 405, 422, 423.

[2] *Ibid.* 452. This admission, however, is not of equal authority, as it formed part of the reasons reported from a committee, which were recommitted, and not adopted by the House.

[3] Conference, 1671; Hatsell, iii. 405.

ment, the Commons were content to recognize this barren right; yet so broad were the grounds on which they rested their own claims of privilege, — and so stubborn was their temper in maintaining them, — that it may well be questioned whether they would have submitted to its practical exercise. If the Lords had rejected a bill for granting a tax, — would the Commons have immediately granted another? Would they not rather have sat with folded arms, rejoicing that the people were spared a new impost; while the king's treasury was beggared by the interference of the Lords?

Temporary and permanent taxes.

Taxes were then of a temporary character. They were granted for one year, or for a longer period, according to the exigencies of the occasion. Hearth money was the first permanent tax, imposed in 1663.[1] No other tax of that character appears to have been granted, until after the Revolution; when permanent duties were raised on beer,[2] on salt,[3] on vellum and paper,[4] on houses,[5] and on coffee.[6] These duties were generally granted as a security for loans; and the financial policy of permanent taxes increased with the national debt, and the extension of public credit. This policy somewhat altered the position of the Lords, in relation to tax bills. Taxes were from time to time varied and repealed; and to such alterations of the law, the Lords might have refused their assent, without withholding supplies from the Crown. But such opportunities were not sought by the Lords. They had given up the contest upon privilege; and wisely left to the Commons, the responsibility and the odium, of constantly increasing the public burdens. Taxes and loans were multiplied; but the Lords accepted them, without question. They rarely even discussed financial measures; and when in 1763, they op-

1 13 & 14 Charles II. c. 10.
2 1 Will. and Mary, Sess. 1, c. 24.
3 5 & 6 Will. and Mary, c. 31.
4 9 & 10 Will. III. c. 25.
5 5 Anne, c. 13.
6 7 *Ibid.* c. 7.

posed the third reading of the Wines and Cider Duties Bill, it was observed that this was the first occasion, on which they had been known to divide upon a money bill.[1]

Tax bills rejected by the Lords.

But while they abstained from interference with the supplies and ways and means, granted by the Commons for the public service, they occasionally rejected or postponed other bills, incidentally affecting supply and taxation: bills imposing or repealing protective duties; bills for the regulation of trade; and bills embracing other disputable matters of legislation, irrespective of taxation. Of these, the greater part were measures of legislative policy, rather than measures of revenue; and with the single exception of the Corn Bill of 1827, their fate does not appear to have excited any jealousy in the sensitive minds of the Commons.

Paper Duties Repeal Bill, 1860.

At length, in 1860, the Lords exercised their power, in a novel and startling form. The Commons had resolved, among other financial arrangements for the year, to increase the property tax and stamp duties, and to repeal the duties on paper. The Property Tax and Stamp Duties Bills had already received the royal assent, when the Paper Duties Repeal Bill was received by the Lords. It had encountered strong opposition in the Commons, where its third reading was agreed to, by the small majority of nine. And now the Lords determined, by a majority of eighty-nine, to postpone the second reading for six months. Having assented to the increased taxation of the annual budget, they refused the relief, by which it had been accompanied.

Relative rights of the two Houses.

Never until now, had the Lords rejected a bill for imposing or repealing a tax, raised solely for the purposes of revenue,—and involving the supplies and ways and means, for the service of the year. Never had they assumed the right of reviewing the calculations of the Commons, regarding revenue and expenditure.

[1] March 30th, 1763; Parl. Hist. xv. 1316.

In principle, all previous invasions of the cherished rights of the Commons, had been trifling compared with this. What was a mere amendment in a money bill, compared with its irrevocable rejection? But on the other hand, the legal right of the Lords to reject any bill whatever, could not be disputed. Even their constitutional right to "negative the whole" of a money bill, had been admitted by the Commons themselves. Nor was this strictly, and in technical form, a money bill. It neither granted any tax to the Crown, nor recited that the paper duty was repealed, in consideration of other taxes imposed. It simply repealed the existing law, under which the duty was levied. Technically, no privilege of the Commons, as previously declared, had been infringed. Yet it was contended, with great force, that to undertake the office of revising the balances of supplies and ways and means, — which had never been assumed by the Lords, during two hundred years, — was a breach of constitutional usage, and a violation of the first principles, upon which the privileges of the House are founded. If the letter of the law was with the Lords, its spirit was clearly with the Commons.

Proceedings of the Commons.

Had the position of parties, and the temper of the times been such as to encourage a violent collision between the two Houses, — there had rarely been an occasion more likely to provoke it. But this embarrassment the government were anxious to avert; and many causes concurred to favor moderate counsels. A committee was therefore appointed in the Commons, to search for precedents. The search was long and intricate: the report copious and elaborate; but no opinion was given upon the grave question at issue. The lapse of six weeks had already moderated the heat and excitement of the controversy; when on the 5th July, Lord Palmerston, on the part of the government, explained the course which he counselled the House to adopt. Having stated what were the acknowledged privileges of the House, and referred to the precedents collected by the committee, he expressed his opinion that the Lords, in rejecting the Paper Duties Bill, had no desire to invade the constitutional rights of the Commons; but had been actuated, as on former occasions, by motives of public policy. He could not believe that they were commencing a deliberate course of interference with the peculiar functions of the Commons. But should that appear to be their intention, the latter would know how to vindicate their privileges, if invaded, and would be supported by the people. He deprecated a collision between the two Houses. Any one who should provoke it, would incur a grave responsibility. With these views, he proposed three resolutions. The first asserted generally, "that the right of granting aids and supplies to the Crown, is in the Commons alone." The second affirmed, that although the Lords had sometimes exercised the power of rejecting bills of several descriptions, relating to taxation, yet the exercise of that power was "justly regarded by this House with peculiar jealousy, as affecting the right of the Commons to grant the supplies, and to provide the ways and means for the service of the year." The third stated, "that to guard for the future, against an undue exercise of that power by the Lords, and to secure to the Commons their rightful control over taxation and supply, this House has in its own hands, the power so to impose and remit taxes, and to frame bills of supply, that the right of the Commons as to the matter, manner, measure, and time, may be maintained inviolate."

The aim of these resolutions was briefly this: — to assert broadly the constitutional rights of the Commons: to qualify former admissions, by declaring their jealousy of the power exercised by the Lords, of rejecting bills relating to taxation; and to convey a warning that the Commons had the means of resisting that power, if unduly exercised, and were prepared to use them. They were a protest against future encroachments: not a remonstrance on the past. The resolutions, though exposed to severe criticism, as not sufficiently vindicating the privileges of the House, or condemning the recent conduct of the Lords, were yet accepted, — it may be said, unanimously.[1] The soundest friends of the House of Lords, and of constitutional government, hoped that a course so temperate and conciliatory, might prevent future differences of the same kind. Should their hope be falsified, the Commons, having shown an example of forbearance, — which might have been vainly sought, in an assembly less conscious of its strength, — may be provoked to exercise their unquestionable powers. Having gained moral force, by their previous moderation, they would not appeal in vain for popular support, — and who can doubt the result?

Parliamentary oratory.

One of the proud results of our free constitution has been the development of Parliamentary oratory, — an honor and ornament to our history, — a source of public enlightenment, — and an effective instrument of popular government. Its excellence has varied, like our literature, with the genius of the men, and the events of the periods, which have called it forth; but from the accession of George III. may be dated the Augustan era of Parliamentary eloquence.

The great struggles of the Parliament with Charles I. had stirred the eloquence of Pym, Hampden, Wentworth, and Falkland: the Revolution had developed the oratory of Somers; and the Parliaments of Anne, and the two first Georges, had given scope to the various talents of Bolingbroke, Pulteney, Wyndham, and Walpole. The reputation of these men has reached posterity; but their speeches, — if they survived the memory of their own generations, — have come down to us in fragments, — as much the composition of the historian or reporter, as of the orators, to whom they are assigned.[2] Happily the very period distinguished

[1] Debates, July 5th and 6th, 1860; Hansard's Deb., 3d Ser., clix. 1383; Report of Committee on Tax Bills, June 29th, 1860.

[2] Of the speeches of Somers and Bolingbroke there are no remains whatever. Mr. Pitt said he would rather recover a speech of Bolingbroke than the lost books of Livy, or other writings of antiquity.

by our most eloquent statesmen was that in which they had the privilege of addressing posterity, as well as their own contemporaries. The expansion of their audience gave a new impulse to their eloquence, which was worthy of being preserved for all ages.

Lord Chatham.

Lord Chatham had attained the first place among statesmen in the late reign, but his fame as an orator mainly rests upon his later speeches, — in the reign of George III. Lofty and impassioned in his style, and dramatic in his manner, his oratory abounded in grand ideas and noble sentiments, expressed in language simple, bold, and vigorous. The finest examples of his eloquence stand alone, and unrivalled ; but he flourished too early, to enjoy the privilege of transmitting the full fruits of his genius to posterity.[1]

Mr. Pitt.

He was surrounded and followed by a group of orators, who have made their time the classic age of Parliamentary history. Foremost amongst them was his extraordinary son, William Pitt. Inferior to his father in the highest qualities of an orator, — he surpassed him in argument, in knowledge,— in intellectual force, and mastery. Magniloquent in his style, his oratory sometimes attained the elevation of eloquence ; but rarely rose above the level of debate. His composition was felicitously described by Windham, as a "State paper style." He may be called the founder of the modern school of Parliamentary debaters. His speeches were argumentative, admirably clear in statement, skilfully arranged, vigorous and practical. Always marked by rare ability, they yet lacked the higher inspirations of genius. In sarcasm he had few equals. No one held so absolute a sway over the House of Commons. In voice and manner, he was dignified and commanding. The minister was declared in every word he uttered; and the consciousness of

[1] Some of his earlier speeches were composed by Dr. Johnson from the notes of others; and even his later speeches were delivered when reporting was still very imperfect.

power, while it sustained the dignity of his oratory, increased its effect upon his audience.

Mr. Fox.

The eloquence of his great rival, Mr. Fox, was as different as were his political opinions and position. His success was due to his natural genius, and to the great principles of liberty which he advocated. Familiar with the best classical models, he yet too often disdained the studied art of the orator; and was negligent and unequal in his efforts. But when his genius was aroused within him, he was matchless in demonstrative argument, in force, in wit, in animation, and spontaneous eloquence. More than any orator of his time, he carried with him the feelings and conviction of his audience; and the spirit and reality of the man, charm us scarcely less in his printed speeches. Wanting in discretion, — he was frequently betrayed into intemperance of language and opinion: but his generous ardor in the cause of liberty still appeals to our sympathies; and his broad constitutional principles are lessons of political wisdom.

Mr. Burke.

Mr. Fox had been from his earliest youth, the friend and disciple of Mr. Burke, — and vast was the intellect of his master. In genius, learning, and accomplishments, Mr. Burke had no equal either among the statesmen, or writers of his time; yet he was inferior, as an orator, to the three great men who have been already noticed. His speeches, like his writings, bear witness to his deep philosophy, his inexhaustible stores of knowledge, and redundant imagination. They are more studied, and more often quoted than the speeches of any other statesman. His metaphors and aphorisms are as familiar to our ears, as those of Lord Bacon. But transcendent as were his gifts, they were too often disfigured by extravagance. He knew not how to restrain them within the bounds of time and place; or to adapt them to the taste of a popular assembly, which loves directness and simplicity. His addresses were dissertations rather than speeches. To influence men, an orator must appeal directly to their reason, their feelings, and present temper; but Mr. Burke, while he astonished them with his prodigious faculties, wearied them with refinements and imagery, in which they often lost the thread of his argument.

Mr. Sheridan is entitled to the next place in this group of orators. His brilliancy, and pointed wit, — his spirited declamation and effective delivery, — astonished and delighted his audience. Such was the effect of his celebrated speech on the fourth, or "Begum charge" against Warren Hastings, that the peers and strangers joined with the House in a "tumult of applause;" and could not be restrained from clapping their hands in ecstasy. The House adjourned, in order to recover its self-possession. Mr. Pitt declared that this speech "surpassed all the eloquence of ancient or modern times, and possessed everything that genius or art could furnish, to agitate or control the human mind." Mr. Fox said, "eloquent indeed it was; so much so, that all he had ever heard, — all he had ever read, dwindled into nothing, and vanished like vapor before the sun." Mr. Sheridan afterwards addressed the Lords, in Westminster Hall, on the same charge, for four days; and Mr. Burke said of his address, "that no species of oratory, — no kind of eloquence which had been heard in ancient or modern times; nothing which the acuteness of the bar, the dignity of the senate, or the morality of the pulpit could furnish, was equal to what they had that day heard in Westminster Hall." But while particular efforts of this accomplished speaker met with extraordinary success, he was restrained by want of statesmanship and character, from commanding a position in the House of Commons, equal to his great talents as an orator.[1]

Mr. Sheridan.

[1] Lord Byron said of him: "Whatever Sheridan has done, or chosen to do, has been, *par excellence*, always the best of its kind. He has written the best comedy, the best opera, the best farce (it is only too good for a farce), and the best address (the monologue on Garrick), and to crown all, delivered the very best oration, the famous Begum speech, ever conceived or heard in this country."

The qualities of Mr. Windham were of another class. Superior to the last in education and attainments, and little inferior in wit, he never achieved successes so dazzling; yet he maintained a higher place among the debaters of his age. Though his pretensions to the higher qualities of a statesman were inconsiderable, his numerous talents and virtues graced a long and distinguished public life.

Mr. Windham.

Lord Erskine was not inferior, as an orator, to the greatest of his contemporaries; but the senate was not the scene of his most remarkable triumphs. His speeches at the bar combined the highest characteristics of eloquence, — fire, — force, — courage, — earnestness, — the closest argument, — imagery, — noble sentiments, — great truths finely conceived and applied, — a diction pure and simple, — action the most graceful and dignified. But none of these great qualities were used for display. They were all held, by the severity of his taste, and the mastery of his logic, in due subordination to the single design of persuading and convincing his audience. The natural graces of his person completed the orator. Lord Brougham has finely portrayed "that noble figure, every look of whose countenance is expressive, every motion of whose form graceful; an eye that sparkles and pierces, and almost assures victory, while it 'speaks audience ere the tongue.'"

Lord Erskine.

Had his triumphs been as signal in the senate, he would have been the first orator of his age. In that arena there were men greater than himself; but he was admitted to an eminent place amongst them. He fought for many years, side by side, with Mr. Fox; and his rare gifts were ever exerted in the cause of freedom.

To complete the glittering assemblage of orators who adorned the age of Chatham and of Pitt, many remarkable figures yet stand in the foreground. We are struck with the happy wit and resources of Lord North, — the finished precision of Wedderburn, — the rude

Other great orators.

force of Thurlow, — the refinement and dignity of Lord Mansfield, — the constitutional wisdom of Lord Camden, — the logical subtilty of Dunning, — the severe reason of Sir William Grant, — the impassioned gentleness of Wilberforce, — and the statesmanlike vigor of Lord Grenville.

The succession of orators has still been maintained. Some of Mr. Pitt's contemporaries continued to flourish many years after he had passed from the scene of his glory; and others were but commencing their career, when his own was drawing to its close. He lived to hear the eloquence of Mr. Grattan, which had long been the pride of his own country. It was rich in imagination, in vehemence, in metaphor, and pointed epigram. Though a stranger to the British Parliament, his genius and patriotism at once commanded a position, scarcely less distinguished than that which he had won in the Parliament of Ireland. Englishmen, familiar with the eloquence of their own countrymen, hailed his accession to their ranks, as one of the most auspicious results of the Union.

Mr. Grattan.

Mr. Canning's brilliant talents, which had been matured under Mr. Pitt, shone forth in full splendor, after the death of that statesman. In wit and sarcasm, in elegant scholarship, in lively fancy, and in the graces of a finished composition, he was unrivalled. His imagery, — if less original than that of Chatham, Burke, and Erskine, — was wrought up with consummate skill, and expressed in language of extraordinary beauty. For more than twenty years, he was the most successful and accomplished debater in the House of Commons, — delighting his friends with his dazzling wit, — and confounding his opponents with inexhaustible repartee.

Mr. Canning.

Earl Grey had also risen to distinction in the days of Mr. Pitt; but the memorable achievements of his riper age, associate him with a later generation. In dignity and high purpose, — in earnest gravity of argument and exposition, he was the very model of a statesman. His ora-

Lord Grey.

tory bespoke his inflexible virtues, and consistency. While his proud bearing would have pronounced him the leader of an aristocracy, and the mouthpiece of his order, — he devoted a long life to the service of the people.

Lord Eldon.

Lord Eldon exercised so important an influence upon political affairs, that he cannot be omitted from this group of orators, though his claims to oratory alone, would not have entitled him to a place amongst them. From the time when he had been Mr. Pitt's Solicitor-General, until he left the woolsack, — a period of nearly forty years, — his high offices gave authority to his parliamentary efforts. For twenty years he led captive the judgment of the House of Lords: but assuredly neither by eloquence, nor argument in debate. Tears and appeals to his conscience were his only eloquence, — a dread of innovation his only argument. Even upon legal questions, the legislature obtained little light from his discourses. The main service which posterity can derive from his speeches, is to note how recently prejudice and errors were maintained in high places, and how trivial the reasons urged in their defence.

Lord Plunket.

Lord Plunket, like his great countryman, Mr. Grattan, had gained a high reputation for eloquence in the Parliament of Ireland, which he not only sustained, but advanced in the British House of Commons. He had risen to eminence at the bar of Ireland, where his style of speaking is said to have resembled that of Erskine. In debate, — if displaying less originality and genius than Mr. Grattan, and less brilliancy than Mr. Canning, — he was as powerful in sustained argument, as felicitous in illustration, and as forcible and pointed in language, as any orator of his time.

Sir Robert Peel.

Sir Robert Peel was a striking counterpart of Mr. Pitt. At first his extraordinary abilities in debate had been outshone by the dazzling lustre of Mr. Canning, and subdued by the fiery vehemence of Mr. Brougham; but his great powers, always improving and expanding, could not fail to be acknowledged. His oratory, like that of Mr. Pitt, was the perfection of debate. He rarely aspired to eloquence; but in effective declamation, — in close argument, — in rapid appreciation of the points to be assailed or defended, — in dexterity, — in tact, — and in official and Parliamentary knowledge, he excelled every debater of his time. Even when his talents were exercised in maintaining the political errors of his age and party, it is impossible not to admire the consummate skill with which he defended his untenable positions, against assailants who had truth on their side. Arguments which provoke a smile, when we read them in the words of Lord Eldon, surprise us with their force and semblance of truth, when urged by Sir Robert Peel.

The Duke of Wellington.

The oratory of a man so great as the Duke of Wellington, was the least of all of his claims to renown. First in war, in diplomacy, and in the councils of his sovereign, — his speeches in Parliament were but the natural expression of his experience, opinions and purposes. His mind being clear, — his views practical and sagacious, — and his objects singularly direct, — his speaking was plain, and to the point. Without fluency or art, and without skill in argument, he spoke out what his strong sense and judgment prompted. He addressed an audience, whom there was no need to convince. They hung upon his words, and waited upon his opinions; and followed as he led. The reasons of such a man were often weighty; but they were reasons which had determined his own course, and might justify it to others, rather than arguments to prove it right, or to combat opponents.

Mr. O'Connell.

The House of Commons was not the field for the best examples of Mr. O'Connell's oratory. He stood there at a disadvantage, — with a cause to uphold which all but a small band of followers condemned as false and unpatriotic, — and with strong feelings against him, which his own conduct had provoked; yet even there, the massive powers of the man were not unfrequently displayed.

A perfect master of every form of argument, — potent in ridicule, sarcasm and invective, — rich in imagination and humor, — bold and impassioned, or gentle, persuasive and pathetic, — he combined all the powers of a consummate orator. His language was simple and forcible, as became his thoughts;[1] his voice extraordinary for compass and flexibility. But his great powers were disfigured by coarseness, by violence, by cunning, and audacious license. At the bar, and on the platform, he exhibited the greatest, but the most opposite endowments. When he had thrown open the doors of the legislature to himself and his Roman Catholic brethren, the great work of his life was done; yet he wanted nothing but the moral influence of a good cause, and honest patriotism, to have taken one of the highest places in the senate.

Mr. Sheil.

His countryman, Mr. Sheil, displayed powers singularly unlike those of his great master. He was an orator of extraordinary brilliancy, — imaginative, witty, and epigrammatic. Many parts of his speeches were exquisite compositions, — clothing his fancy in the artistic language of the poet. Such passages may be compared with many similar examples, in the speeches of Mr. Canning. He was equally happy in antithesis, and epigram. He excelled, indeed, in the art and graces of oratorical composition. But his thoughts were wanting in depth and reality: his manner was extravagant in its vehemence: his action melodramatic; and his voice, always shrill, was raised in his impassioned efforts, to a harsh and discordant shriek.

Other contemporary orators.

This second group of contemporary orators would be incomplete, without some other striking characters who played their part amongst them. We would point to the classical elegance of Lord Wellesley, — the readiness and dexterity of Perceval, — the high bearing and courage of Lord Castlereagh, — the practical vigor

[1] It was happily said of him by Mr. Sheil, "He brings forth a brood of lusty thoughts, without a rag to cover them."

of Tierney, — the severe virtues, and high intellect of Romilly, — the learned philosophy of Francis Horner, — the didactic fulness of Mackintosh, — the fruitful science of Huskisson, — the lucid argument of Follet, and the brilliant declamation of Macaulay.

Living orators.

All these have passed away; but there are orators still living, who have contended in the same debates, and have won an equal fame. Their portraiture will adorn future histories; but who is there that will not at once fill up this picture of the past, with the transparent clearness, and masterly force of Lord Lyndhurst, and the matchless powers and accomplishments of Lord Brougham?

Improved knowledge and taste in debate.

Progressive excellence in so divine an art as oratary, is no more to be achieved than in poetry or painting, — in sculpture or architecture. Genius is of all ages. But if orators of our own time have been unable to excel their great models, a candid criticism will scarcely assign them an inferior place. Their style has changed, — as the conditions under which they speak, are altered. They address themselves more to the reason, and less to the imagination, the feelings and the passions of their audience, than the orators of a former age. They confront, not only the members of their own body, but the whole people, — who are rather to be convinced by argument, than persuaded by the fascination of the orator. In their language, there is less of study and artistic finish, than in the oratory of an earlier period. Their perorations are not composed, after frequent recitals of Demosthenes;[1] but give direct and forcible expression to their own opinions and sentiments. Their speaking is suited to the subjects of debate, — to the stir and pressure of public affairs, — and to the taste and temper of their audience. The first principles of

[1] "I composed the peroration of my speech for the Queen, in the Lords, after reading and repeating Demosthenes for three or four weeks, and I composed it twenty times over at least, and it certainly succeeded in a very extraordinary degree, and far above any merits of its own." — Lord Brougham to Zachary Macaulay, as advice to his celebrated son, March 10th, 1823.

government are no longer in dispute: the liberties of the people are safe: the oppression of the law is unknown. Accordingly, the councils of the state encourage elevated reason, rather than impassioned oratory. Every age has its own type of excellence; and if the Nestors of our own time insist upon the degeneracy of living orators, perhaps a more cultivated taste may now condemn as rant, some passages from the speeches of Burke and Chatham, which their contemporaries accepted as eloquence.

But whatever may be the claims of different generations, to the highest examples of oratory, the men of our own age have advanced in political knowledge, and statesmanship; and their deliberations have produced results more beneficial to the people. They have also improved in temper and moderation. In the earlier years of George III., party spirit and personal animosities, — not yet restrained by the courtesies of private society, or refined by good taste, — too often gave rise to scenes discreditable to the British senate. The debates were as coarse and scurrilous as the press.

Coarse personalities of former times.

In these excesses, Lord Chatham was both sinned against, and sinning. In the debate upon the Indemnity Bill in 1766, the Duke of Richmond "hoped the nobility would not be browbeaten by an insolent minister"[1] — a speech which Horace Walpole alleges to have driven the Earl from the House of Lords, during the remainder of his unfortunate administration.[2] Some years later, we find Lord Chatham himself using language repugnant to order, and decency of debate. On the 1st February, 1775, he thus addressed the ministers: — "Who can wonder that you should put a negative upon any measure which must annihilate your power, deprive you of your emoluments, and at once reduce you to that state of insignificance, for which God and nature designed you."[3] A few days later, the House of Lords became the scene of personalities still more disorderly. Lord Shelburne having in-

[1] Dec. 10th, 1766.

[2] Walpole's Mem. ii. 410, 411.

[3] Parl. Hist. xviii. 211.

sinuated that Lord Mansfield had been concerned in drawing up the bills of the previous session relating to America, Lord Mansfield rising in a passion, "charged the last noble Lord with uttering the most gross falsehoods," and said that "the charge was as unjust, as it was maliciously and indecently urged." In the same debate Lord Lyttelton imputed to Lord Camden "professional subtlety and low cunning."[1] Again on the 5th December, 1777, we find Lord Chatham accusing Earl Gower of "petulance and malignant misrepresentation."[2]

No man so often outraged propriety and good taste as Edmund Burke. His excessive love of imagery and illustration, often displayed itself in the grossest forms. Who is not familiar with his coarse portrait of Lord North, "extending his right leg a full yard before his left, rolling his flaming eyes, and moving his ponderous frame?" or with the offensive indecency, with which he likened Lord North's ministry to a party of courtesans?[3]

We find Colonel Barré denouncing the conduct of Lord North as "most indecent and scandalous;" and Lord North complaining of this language as "extremely uncivil, brutal, and insolent," until he was called to order, and obliged to apologize.[4] We find Mr. Fox threatening that Lord North's ministry should expiate their crimes on the scaffold, and insinuating that they were in the pay of France.[5] Nay, transgressing the bounds of political discussion, and assailing private character, he went so far as to declare that he should consider it unsafe to be alone with Lord North, in a room;[6] and would not believe his word.[7] Even of the king, he spoke with indecorous violence.[8]

1 Feb. 7th, 1775; Parl. Hist. xviii. 276, 282.
2 *Ibid.* xix. 507.
3 Feb. 5th, 1770; Cavendish Deb. i. 441.
4 Feb. 22d, 1852; Parl. Hist. xxii. 1050.
5 Nov. 27th, 1781.
6 Lord Brougham's Life of Lord North; Works, iii. 56.
7 20th March, 1782; Parl. Hist. xxii. 1216.
8 Wraxall's Mem. ii. 255–258, 517.

There have since been altercations of equal bitterness. The deepest wounds which sarcasm and invective could inflict, have been unsparingly dealt to political opponents. Combatants "have sharpened their tongues like a serpent; adder's poison is under their lips." But good taste and a stricter order in debate, have restrained the grosser outrages to decency. The weapons of debate have been as keen and trenchant as ever; but they have been wielded according to the laws of a more civilized warfare. The first years of the Reformed Parliament threatened the revival of scenes as violent and disorderly as any in the last century;[1] but as the host of new members became disciplined by experience, and the fierce passions of that period subsided, the accustomed decorum of the House of Commons was restored.

Rarer outrages of decorum in recent times.

Indeed, as the Commons have advanced in power and freedom, they have shown greater self-restraint, and a more ready obedience to the authority of the Speaker. They have always been more orderly in their proceedings than the Lords; and the contrast which the scenes of the first twenty years of George III. present to those of later times, can scarcely fail to strike an attentive student of Parliamentary history.

Increased authority of the Chair.

What would now be thought of such scenes as those enacted in the time of Sir John Cust, Sir Fletcher Norton, and Mr. Cornwall, — of rebukes and interruptions,[2] — of unseemly altercations with the Chair, — of the words of the Speaker himself being taken down, — and of a motion that

[1] Mr. Sheil and Lord Althorp, 5th Feb. 1834. — *Hansard's Deb.*, 3d Ser., xxi. 146. Mr. Rigby Wason and Lord Sandon, 12th March, 1834. — *Ibid.* xxii. 116. Mr. Romayne and Mr. O'Connell, 6th May, 1834. — *Ibid.* xxiii. 24. Mr. Hume and Mr. Charlton, 3d June, 1835. — *Ibid.* xxvii. 485. 22d July, 1835. — *Ibid.* 879.

[2] Scenes between Mr. Rigby and the Speaker, Sir John Cust, in 1762. — *Cavendish Deb.* i. 342. And between Sir J. Cavendish and the same Speaker, March 9th, 1769. — *Ibid.* 567. Mr. Burke and the same, April 15th, 1769. — *Ibid.* 878. Scenes with Sir Fletcher Norton, Dec. 14th, 1770. — *Ibid.* ii. 168. March 12th and 27th, 1771. — *Ibid.* ii. 390, 476.

they were disorderly and dangerous to the freedom of debate?[1]

General standard of debate.

In concluding this sketch of Parliamentary oratory, a few words may be added concerning the general standard of debate in the House of Commons. If that standard be measured by the excellence of the best speakers at different periods, we have no cause to be ashamed of the age in which our living orators and statesmen have flourished. But judged by another test, this age has been exposed to disparaging criticisms. When few save the ablest men contended in debate, and the rank and file were content to cheer and vote, a certain elevation of thought and language was, perhaps, more generally sustained. But, of late years, independent members, — active, informed, and business-like, — representing large interests, — more responsible to constituents, and less devoted to party chiefs, — living in the public eye, and ambitious of distinction, — have eagerly pressed forward, and claimed a hearing. Excellence in debate has suffered from the multiplied demands of public affairs. Yet in speeches without pretensions to oratory, are found strong common sense, practical knowledge, and an honesty of purpose that was wanting in the silent legions of former times. The debates mark the activity, and earnest spirit of a representative assembly. At all times there have been some speakers of a lower grade, — without instruction, taste, or elevation. Formerly their commonplace effusions were not reported: now they are freely read, and scornfully criticised. They are put to shame by the writers of the daily press, who discuss the same subjects with superior knowledge and ability. Falling below the educated mind of the country, they bring discredit upon the House of Commons, while they impair its legislative efficiency. But worse evils than these have been overcome; and we may hope to see this abuse of free discussion eventually corrected, by a less tolerant endurance on the part of the House, and by public reprobation and contempt.

[1] Feb. 16th, 1770; Parl. Hist. xvi. 807.

INDEX TO VOL. I.

ABERCORN, Earl of, his rights as peer of Great Britain and of Scotland, 234.
Abercromby, Mr., his motion on Scotch representation, 286.
Aberdeen, Earl of, the Reform Bill of his ministry, 357.
A, Court, Colonel, deprived of command for votes in parliament, 36.
Addington, Mr., mediates between Geo. III. and Pitt on the Catholic question, 86–88; forms an administration, 88; official difficulties caused by the King's illness at this juncture, 163–165; his relations with the King, 89; resigns office, 91; leads the "King's friends," 90; takes office under Pitt, 91; made a peer, *ib.*; his declaration as to the King's competency for business, 167; permits debate on notice of motion, 319, *n.* *See* Sidmouth, Viscount.
Addresses to the crown, from parliament, respecting peace and war, or the dissolution of parliament, 430, 431; from the people, for a dissolution, 432; Lord Camden's opinion, 433; this right affirmed by vote of the Commons, 434.
Admiralty Court, judge of, disqualified from parliament, 299.
Althorp, Lord, the Melbourne ministry dismissed, on his removal from the Commons, 125.
American colonies, the war with, stopped by the Commons, 58, 430.
Anne, Queen, land revenues at her accession, 189; their alienation restrained, 190; her civil list and debts, 192; increase of peerage during her reign, 224; created twelve peers in one day, *ib.*; holders of offices disqualified by Act of Settlement, 295; popular addresses to, praying a dissolution, 433.
Appellate jurisdiction of the House of Lords' bill, 242.
Appropriation of grants by parliament, resolution against issue of unappropriated money, 72; commencement of the system, 440; misappropriation of grants by Chas. II., 191.
Arcot, Nabob of, represented in parliament by several members, 315.
Army and Navy Service Bill opposed by Geo. III., 93; withdrawn, 95.
Assizes, commission for holding, issued during Geo. III.'s incapacity, 157.

BAKER, Mr., his motion against Geo. III.'s secret counsellors, 67.
Ballot, vote by, motions for adoption of, 330, 352.
Baronetage, past and present numbers of, 260.
Barré, Colonel, deprived of command for votes in parliament, 36; resigns his commission, 51; passed over in a brevet, *ib.*
"Bedchamber Question, the," 31.
Bedford, Duke of, remonstrates against Lord Bute's influence, 40.
Berkeley, Mr. H., his motions for the ballot, 354.
Bishops, their number in the House, 242; attempts to exclude them, 243; their present position, 245; their votes upon the Reform Bill, 250, 251; Irish representative bishops, 229.

Blandford, Marquess of, his schemes of reform, 326.
Bolingbroke, Lord, his theory of "a patriot king," 23.
Boroughs, different rights of election in, 266, 283; nomination boroughs. 265, 267, 283, 288, 289; numbers of voters in, 267, 283, 289; seats for, bought or rented, 270, 276; advertised for sale, 270; prices of, 271, 272, 275, 276, 292; law passed against the sale of boroughs, 276; government boroughs, 277.
"Borough-brokers," 272.
Boyer, reports debates in parliament, 391.
Brand, Mr., his motion against the pledge required of the Grenville ministry, 96.
Bribery at elections, prior to parliamentary reform, 267; commenced in reign of Charles II., 268; supported by George III., 274, 276; acts to restrain, 264, 270, 274, 277; bribery since the Reform Act, 341; later bribery acts, 344, 347; proof of agency, 344; inquiry by commission, 345; gross cases, 346; travelling expenses, 347; policy of legislation, 348.
Bribery of members of parliament. *See* Members of the House of Commons.
Brougham, Lord, his motion against influence of the crown, 117; opinion on life peerages, 238; advises, as chancellor, the creation of new peers, 251; his motion for reform, 332; on the duration of parliament, 349.
Buckingham, Marquess of, refuses to transmit the Irish address to the Prince of Wales, 162.
Burdett, Sir F., his schemes of reform, 322, 323; committed for contempt, 409; resists the warrant, 422; apprehended by force, *ib.*; brings actions for redress, 423.
Burgage tenure, franchise, 266.
Burke, Mr., his scheme of economic reform, 54, 197, 211; drew up the prince's reply to Pitt's scheme of a regency, 154; his proposal for sale of crown lands, 208; for reduction of pension list, 211; opposes parliamentary reform, 320; his ideal of representation, 362; opposes Wilkes's expulsion, 372; his remarks on pledges to constituents, 418; character of his oratory, 452, 461.
Bute, county, absurd case of election for, 285.
Bute, Earl of, his unconstitutional instructions to George III., 22; aids his personal interference in government, 28; his rapid rise, 30; becomes premier, 31; arbitrary conduct, *ib.* 32; and parliamentary bribery, 301, 304; his fall, 34; secret influence over the King, 34, 38–40; retires from court, 35.

Cabinet, the, admission of a judge to seat in, 93; all the offices in, held by the Duke of Wellington, 126; the interior cabinet of George III., 24.
Calcraft, Mr., deprived of office for opposition to court policy, 36.
Camden, Lord, disapproves the Middlesex election proceedings, 376, 381; defends his conduct in the cabinet, 378; opinion on popular addresses to the crown, 433.
Campbell, Lord, his opinion on life peerages, 239.
Canning, Mr., his conduct regarding the Catholic question, 87, 98, 118; in office under Mr. Perceval, 98; overtures to, from the court, 109; declines to support George IV. against his Queen, 113, 116, *n.*; character of his oratory, 455.
Carlton House, the cost of, 206.
Carmarthen, Marquess of, proscribed for opposition to court policy, 56.
Caroline, Queen (of George IV.), proceedings against, 113–116; the Divorce Bill, 114; withdrawn, 115.
Catholic Emancipation, opposition to, by George III., 85, 95; by George IV., 118; measure carried, 119; a plea for parliamentary reform, 326.
Cavendish, Lord J., his motion on the American war, 58.
Cavendish, Sir H., reports the Commons' debates (1768–1774), 386, *n.*
Chancellor, Lord. *See* Great Seal, the.
Charles I., alienates the crown lands, 188.
Charles II., crown revenues recovered at accession of, 188; subsequent waste, *ib.*; appropriates

army grants, 191; bribery at elections, and of members, commenced under, 267, 270, 299.

Charlotte, Princess, question as to guardianship over, 222.

Charlotte, Queen (of George III.), accepts the resolutions for a regency, 155, 177.

Chatham, Earl of, in office at accession of George III., 24; retires and accepts peerage, 29; refuses to resume office, 35, 38; his demeanor as a courtier, 45; forms an administration, *ib.*; endeavors to break up parties, 46; ill health, 47; retires, 48; statement as to the King's influence, 49; receives overtures from Lord North, 51; approves the Grenville Act, 292; advocates parliamentary reform, 313; favors triennial parliaments, 349; his opposition to the proceedings against Wilkes, 366, 376; by bill, 380; by resolution, 381; and by addresses to dissolve parliament, 380, 381, 431; condemns the King's answer to the city address, 380; strangers excluded from his speeches, 380, 387; supports popular addresses to the crown, 433; his opinion on the exclusive rights of the Commons over taxation, 444; position as an orator, 451, 460.

Chippenham election petition, Walpole displaced from office by vote upon, 291.

Civil list of the crown, 191; settlement of, on accession of George III., 193; charges and pensions thereon, 194, 210–214; debts incurred upon, 192, 199; charges removed from, 200, 201; Civil List Acts, 1782, 199; 1816, 201; regulation of the civil list, 201, 203; Commons committee on, 202; no debts upon, during the last three reigns, 203. *See* also Pensions from the Crown.

Clerke, Sir P. J., his Contractors' Bill, 322.

Coalition Ministry, the formation of, 63; its policy, 64; overthrown, 68.

Cockburn, Lord, his description of Scotch elections, 285.

Coke, Lady Mary, admired by the Duke of York, 216.

Coke, Lord, an authority for life peerages, 238.

Coke, Mr., moves a resolution hostile to the Pitt ministry, 74.

Commission, for opening parliament during incapacity of George III., questions arising thereupon, 156, 159, 177; form of such commission, 177; his inability to sign commissions for prorogation, 172; the commission for holding assizes, 157.

Commissions to inquire into bribery at elections, 345.

Commons, House of, unconstitutional influence of the crown over the, by undue influence and intimidation, 16, 32, 36, 42, 49, 72, 94; by influence at elections, 277; by places, pensions, and bribes, 293–309; debates thereon, 54–57, 67, 68, 117; their contest with Pitt's first ministry, 70–78; resolutions against a dissolution, 70–72, 432; against the issue of money unappropriated by parliament, 72; against the recent changes in the ministry, 73; resolutions to be laid before Geo. III., 74; resolution against interference by the Lords, 75; comments on this contest, 78–80; debates on the pledge required of the Grenville ministry, 96–98; action of the Commons as regards a regency, 144–185; doubts respecting the issue of new writs during George III.'s incapacity, 148; elect a speaker during King's incapacity, 154; vote authorizing use of great seal, 156, 157, 177; address on King's recovery, 158; regulation of crown revenues and civil list, 191–203; relations between the two houses, 248; as to reform, 249; as to taxation, 443; composition of the house since the revolution, 263; its dependence and corruption, *ib.*; defects in the representation, 264; ill-defined rights of election, 266; nomination boroughs, 265–267, 284, 288; influence of peers in the house, 267, 289; bribery at elections, 267; since reform, 341; at the general elections (1761), 269; (1768), 271; sale of boroughs, 270–277; gross cases of bribery, 272; bribery supported by Geo.

III., 274, 276; government influence over boroughs, 278; revenue officers disfranchised, *ib.*; majority of members nominated, 287; trial of election petitions, 289; by committee of privileges, 290; at the bar of the house, *ib.*; the Grenville Act, 292; corruption of members, 294–309; by places and pensions, 294; measures to disqualify placemen and pensioners, 295; number of, in parliament, 297; judges disqualified, 298; bribes to members, 299–304; under Lord Bute, 301; the shop at the pay-office, *ib.*; apology for refusing a bribe, 303; bribes by loans and lotteries, 305–307; by contracts, 307; parliamentary corruption considered, 309–312; proceedings in Commons regarding reform, 313–355; efforts to repeal Septennial Act, 348; vote by ballot, 352; qualification Acts, 353; proceedings at elections, 355; later measures of reform, *ib.*; relation of the Commons to Crown, law, and people, 364–450; contests on questions of privilege, 364; proceedings against Wilkes, 365; deny him his privilege, *ib.*; expel him, 368; repel his accusation of Lord Mansfield, 370; expel him for libel on Lord Weymouth, 371; his reëlections declared void, 374; Luttrell seated by the house, 375; motions upon Middlesex election proceedings, 376, 382; address to the King condemning the city address, 379; the resolution against Wilkes expunged, 383; exclusion of strangers from debates, 384, 402; the exclusion of ladies, 403, *n.*; the lords excluded from the Commons, 387; contest with the printers, 389; prohibit the publication of debates, 390; increased severity in 1771, 394; proceed against the city authorities for resisting the speaker's warrant, 397–400; erase the messenger's recognizance, 398; report of debates permitted, 402; reporters' galleries, 406; strangers' galleries, *ib.*; publication of division lists, *ib.*; presence of strangers at divisions, 407; publicity given to committee proceedings, 408; to parliamentary papers, *ib.*; early practice regarding petitions, 410; house influenced by the presentation of petitions, 412; debates on, restrained, 417; pledges by members, *ib.*; discontinuance of privileges, 420; to servants, *ib.*; of prisoners kneeling, 421; privilege and the courts of law, 421–426; case of Sir F. Burdett, 422; Stockdale and Howard's actions, 424; commit Stockdale and his agents, 425; commit the sheriffs, *ib.*; right of Commons to publish papers affecting character, 426; increased power of the Commons, 428; conduct of, regarding Jewish disability, *ib.*; control of the Commons over the government, 429; over peace and war, and over dissolutions of parliament, 70, 430, 431; votes of want of confidence, 59, 73, 77, 434; and of confidence, 122, 336, 434; impeachments, 435; relations between the Commons and ministers since the Reform Act, 130, 436; their control over national expenditure, 190, 439; liberality to the crown, 440; stopping the supplies, 442; supplies delayed, 72, 76, 443; restraints upon the liberality of the house, 443; exclusive rights over taxation, 444; power of the lords to reject a money bill, 445–450; sketch of parliamentary oratory, 450; conduct of the house in debate, 459; increased authority of the chair, 462. *See* also Lords, House of; Parliament; Petitions.

Commonwealth, destruction of crown revenues at, 188.

Contracts with Government a means of bribing members, 307; contractors disqualified from parliament, 308.

Conway, General, proscribed for votes in parliament, 36, 37; takes office under Lord Rockingham, 40; disclaims the influence of the "King's friends," 41; his motion on the American war, 58.

Cornwall, Duchy of, revenues of inheritance of Prince of Wales, 204; present amount, *ib.*

Cornwall, Mr. Speaker, death of, during Geo. III.'s incapacity, 153.

County elections, territorial influence over, 282; expenses of contest at, 283.

Courts of law and parliamentary privilege, 421–428; decisions in Burdett's case, 423; in the Stockdale cases, 424, 427.

Crawford, Mr. S., his motion as to duration of parliament, 350.

Crewe, Mr., his Revenue Officers' Bill, 78.

Cricklade, bribery at, 273; disfranchised, *ib.*

Crosby, Brass, Lord Mayor, proceeded against for committing the messenger of the house, 397–400.

Crown, the, constitutional position of, since the revolution, 15; paramount authority of, 16; sources of its influence, 16–19; by government boroughs, 277; by places, peerages, and pensions, 195, 294; by bribes, 299; by loans and lotteries, 304; by contracts, 307; restrictions upon its personal influence over parliament, 19, 20, 131, 247, 437; measures for its diminution, by disqualification of placemen, &c., 61, 278. 295, 298, 308; by the powers of the commons over the civil list expenditure, 189, 211; and over supplies, 439; constitutional relations between crown and ministers, 25, 95, 125, 131, 135, 436; influence of the crown over the government during Lord Bute's ministry, 31; Mr. Grenville's, 36; Lord Rockingham's, 40, 61; Lord North's, 49; Lord Shelburne's, 62; "the coalition," 64; Mr. Pitt's, 81, 84; Addington's, 89; Lord Grenville's, 92; Mr. Perceval's, 103, 108; influence of the crown during reigns of William IV. and her Majesty, 119–140; debates upon the unconstitutional influence of the crown over parliament, 44, 53–57, 67, 73, 117; violation of parliamentary privileges by the crown, 33, 36, 43, 49, 56, 72; bribery at elections, and of members supported by the crown, 274, 276, 303; influence of the crown exerted against its ministers, 43, 65, 83, 94, 118; the attitude of parties a proof of the paramount influence of the crown, 84, 108; its influence exerted in favor of reform, 119, 123; wise exertion of influence of crown in the present reign, 138; its general influence increased, 139; parliament kept in harmony by influence of the crown, 248; the prerogatives of the crown in abeyance, 141–185; the Regency Bills of George III., 142–177; of William IV., 182; of Queen Victoria, 185; powers of the crown exercised by parliament, 152, 155, 177, 178; the Royal Sign-Manual Bill, 179; questions as to accession of an infant king, 181; as to the rights of a posthumous child, 184; ancient revenues of the crown, 186; constitutional results of its improvidence, 189; parliamentary settlement of crown revenues, 190; the civil list, 191–203; private property of the crown, 205; provision for royal family, *ib.*; land revenues, 207; the pension list, 210; rights of crown over the Royal Family, 214; over grandchildren, 216, 222; over royal marriages, 216; Royal Marriage Act, *ib.*; question submitted to the judges, 218; opinion of law officers on marriage of Duke of Sussex, 221; attempt to limit the rights of crown in creation of peers, 225; numerous applications for peerages, 230; the crown receives the advice of parliament as to peace and war, concerning a dissolution, and the conduct of ministers, 430–434; appeals to the people, if dissatisfied with the judgment of parliament, 431; addressed by the people on the subject of a dissolution, 432; improved relations between the crown and commons, 437, 440; the refusal of supplies, 72, 76, 442; its recommendation required to motions for grant of public money, 443.

Crown lands. *See* Revenues of the Crown.

Cumberland, Duke of, conducts ministerial negotiations for the King, 39, 40; protests against resolutions for a regency bill, 155; his name omitted from the commission to open parliament, 157; marries Mrs. Horton, 215.

Curwen, Mr., his Act to restrain the sale of boroughs, 276.

Cust, Sir John, chosen speaker, 28; altercations with, 462.
Customs and excise officers disfranchised, 278; numbers of, 279.

DANBY, Earl, his case cited with reference to ministerial responsibility, 101.
Debates in parliament, publication of, prohibited, 389, 390; sanctioned by the Long Parliament, 390; early publications of debates, 391; abuses of reporting, 392, 393; contest with the printers, 394; reporting permitted, 402; late instance of complaints against persons taking notes, 403; reporting interrupted by the exclusion of strangers, *ib.*; progress of the system, 404; a breach of privilege, 405; galleries for reporters, 406; freedom of comment on debates, 409; improved taste in debate, 459, 461; personalities of former times, 460.
Denman, Lord, his decision in Stockdale *v.* Hansard, 424.
Dering, Sir E., expelled for publishing his speeches, 390.
Derby, Earl of, the reform bill of his ministry, 358; bill lost, 360; ministry defeated on the house tax, 442.
D'Este, Sir A., his claim to dukedom of Sussex, 221.
Devonshire, Duke of, disgraced for opposition to the treaty with France, 32; resigns his lord-lieutenancy, *ib.*
Disraeli, Mr., brings in a reform bill, 358.
Dissolutions of parliament. *See* Addresses to the Crown; Parliament.
Divisions, lists of, published, in the Commons, 406; in the Lords, 408; presence of strangers at, *ib.*
Dowdeswell, Mr., opposes the expulsion of Wilkes, 372, 377.
"Droit le Roi," burnt by order of the Lords, 369.
Droits of the Crown and Admiralty, the, vested in the crown till accession of William IV., 193, 201.
Dundas, Mr., his amendment to Mr. Dunning's resolutions, 55.
Dunning, Mr., his resolutions against influence of the crown, 55; denies the right to incapacitate Wilkes, 377.
Dyson, Mr., his sobriquet, 394.

EAST RETFORD, disfranchisement bill of, 328.
Ebrington, Lord, his motions in support of reform ministry, 336, 338.
Economic reform, Mr. Burke's, 54, 197, 212.
Edinburgh, defective representation of, 284; bill to amend it, 286.
Edward II., revenues of his crown, 187.
Edward VI., his sign-manual affixed by a stamp, 181.
Effingham, Earl of, his motion condemning the Commons's opposition to Mr. Pitt, 74.
Eldon, Lord, Geo. III.'s suspected adviser against the Grenville ministry, 98; disliked by the Regent, 107; condoles with George IV. on the Catholic emancipation, 119; scandalized when the crown supports reform, 121; chancellor to the Addington ministry, 165; his declaration as to Geo. III.'s competency to transact business, 168; obtains the royal assent to bills, *ib.*; his interview with the King, *ib.*; negotiates Pitt's return to office, 169; his conduct impugned, 170; motions to omit his name from Council of Regency, *ib.*, 171; his opinion as to accession of infant king, 182; his position as statesman, 456.
Election petitions, trial of, prior to the Grenville Act, 288; under that Act, 291, 292; later election petition Acts, 294.
Elections, expensive contests at, 267, 272, 283; vexatious contests, 280; Acts to amend election proceedings, 355; writs for, addressed to returning officers, 356. *See* also Reform of Parliament.
Ellenborough, Lord, his admission to the cabinet, when Lord Chief Justice, 93.
Erskine, Lord, his motions against a dissolution, 68, 71; his speech on the pledge required from the Grenville ministry, 99; his support of reform, 319, 321, 323; character of his oratory, 454.
Establishment Bill, brought in by Burke, 198.
Exchequer chamber, court of, re-

verse decision in Howard *v.* Gosset, 428.

FAMILIES, great, state influence of, 20, 283; opposed by George III., 23, 46; influence of, at the present day, 139.
Fitzherbert, Mr., proscribed for opposition to court policy, 37.
Fitzherbert, Mrs., married the Prince of Wales, 220.
Flood, Mr., his reform bill, 318.
Four and a half per cent. duties, the casual sources of revenue of the crown, 193, 202; charged with pensions, 210, 213; surrendered by William IV., 214.
Fox, Mr. C. J., his remarks on George III.'s system of government, 52, 53, 57, 61; coalesces with Lord North, 63; the coalition ministry, 64; brings in the India Bill, 66; dismissed, 68; opposition to Pitt, 70–78; proscribed from office by the King, 90; admitted to office, 93; dismissed, 96; his death alienates the Regent from the Whigs, 106; his conduct regarding the Regency Bill, 149, 152; comments thereon, 161; disapproved of the Royal Marriage Act, 218; the Westminster election, 280; cost of the scrutiny, 281; unfair treatment from Mr. Pitt, 282; denounces parliamentary corruption by loans, 306; supports the proceedings against Wilkes, 383; remarks on unrestrained reporting, 403; carriage broken by mob, 400; position as orator, 452.
Fox, Mr. Henry, Sir R. Walpole's agent in bribery, 301.
France, treaty of peace with, proscription of the Whigs for disapproval of, 32; members bribed to support, 302.
Franchise, the, of England, 266, 282; of Scotland, 284; of Ireland, 288; under the Reform Act, 338–340; proposed alterations in, 355; fancy franchises, 357, 359. *See* Reform in Parliament.
"Friends of the People," society, statements by, as to composition of House of Commons, 266, 289.
Fuller, Mr. R., bribed by pension from the crown, 295.

GASCOYNE, General, his anti-reform motion, 335.
Gatton, number of voters in, prior to reform, 266; price of, 292.
Gazetteer, the, complained against for publishing debates, 394.
Gentleman's Magazine, the, one of the first to report parliamentary debates, 391.
George I., his civil list, 192; powers he claimed over his grandchildren, 216; consents to Peerage Bill, 225.
George II., his Regency Act, 142; his civil list, 192; the great seal affixed to two commissions during his illness, 156; his savings, 194.
George III., accession of, 21; education, 22; determination to govern, 21–28; secret counsellors, 24; his jealousy of the Whig families, 23–29; his arbitrary conduct and violation of parliamentary privileges during Lord Bute's ministry, 32, 33; during Mr. Grenville's ministry, 36; his differences with that ministry, 35, 38, 40; his active interference in the government, 38; pledge not to be influenced by Lord Bute, 39; consents to dismiss Mr. S. Mackenzie, 40; the conditions of the Rockingham ministry, 40; exerts his influence against them, 43, 44; attempts, with Chatham, to destroy parties, 45; his influence during Chatham's ministry, 47, 48; tries to retain him in office, 48; his ascendency in Lord North's time, 49, 52, 60; irritation at opposition, 49, 52; exerts his will in favor of the Royal Marriage Bill, 49; takes notice of proceedings in parliament, *ib.*; proscribes officers in opposition, 51; his overtures to the Whigs, 52, 53; his personal interference in parliament protested against, 53–57, 67; seeks to intimidate opposition peers, 56; defeat of his American policy, 58, 59; approval of Lord North's conduct, *ib.*; results of the King's policy, 60; the Rockingham ministry, 61; measures to repress his influence, 61–65, 278, 295, 298; he reasserts it with Lord Shelburne, 62; resists the "coalition," 63–68; negotiates with Pitt, 63, 64; use of his name

against the India Bill, 66; supports Pitt against the commons, 75–77; his position during this contest, 77–79; its effect upon his policy, 80; his relations with Pitt, 81; his general influence augmented, 82; prepared to use it against Pitt, 83; dismisses him, 85; opposition to the Catholic question, 85–88; illness from agitation on this subject, 89; his relations with Addington, *ib.*, 163; refuses to admit Fox to office, 90; Pitt reinstated, 91; admits Lord Grenville to office, 93; opposes changes in army administration, 94, and the Army and Navy Service Bill, *ib.*; unconstitutional use of his influence, *ib.*; pledge he required of his ministers, 96; his anti-Catholic appeal on the dissolution (1807), 102; his influence prior to his last illness, 103; his character compared to that of the Prince Regent, *ib.*; the King's illnesses, 141–178; the first illness, 141; his scheme for a regency, 142; modified by ministers, 143; speech, and addresses on this subject, 144; consents to the withdrawal of his mother's name from Regency Bill, 146; second illness, 147; recovery, 159; anxious to provide for a regency, 163; third illness, in the interval between the Pitt and Addington ministries, 163, 164; recovery, 165; fourth illness, 166; questions arising as to his competency to transact business, 167–171; gives assent to bills, 168; anecdote of his reading the bills, *ib.*; Pitt's return to office, 169; their interview, 170; his last illness, 172; the passing the Regency Bill, 173–177; his inability to sign commissions for prorogation, 172; difficulties as to issue of public money, 178; his civil list, 192; other sources of revenue, 194; purchases Buckingham House, 195; domestic economy, *ib.*; debts on civil list, 195–199; Sir F. Norton's address, 197; profusion in the household, 198; his message on public expenditure, *ib.*; his pension list, 211; his annoyance at his brothers' marriages, 215; his attachment to Lady S. Lennox, 216; the Royal Marriage Act, *ib.*, 217; claims guardianship of Princess Charlotte, 222; profuse in creation of peers, 226–228; supports bribery at elections, and of members, 274, 276, 303; his opposition to reform, 83, 316; his answer to the city address on the proceedings against Wilkes, 379; objects to political agitation by petitions, 414.

George IV., ascendency of the Tory party under, 112; the proceedings against his Queen, 113; his aversion to Lord Grey and the Whigs, 116; his popularity, 117; his opposition to Catholic claims, 118; yields, and exerts his influence against his ministers, 119; authorized to affix his sign-manual by a stamp, 178; his civil list and other revenues, 200.

Germaine, Lord G., his statement respecting Geo. III.'s personal influence, 52.

Glasgow, defective representation of, 283.

Gloucester, bribery at, 346.

Gloucester, Duke of, marries Lady Waldegrave, 215.

Gordon, Lord G., presents petitions to parliament, 413.

Gosset, Sir W., sued by Howard for trespass, 427.

Government, executive, control of parliament over, 429; strong and weak governments since the Reform Act, 437. *See* also Ministers of the Crown.

Gower, Earl of, his amendment to resolutions for a regency, 176.

Grafton, Duke of, dismissed from lord-lieutenancy for opposing the court policy, 32; accepts office under Lord Chatham, 45; complains of the bad results of Chatham's ill-health, 47; consequent weakness of the ministry, 48; resigns, *ib.*; his ministry broken up by debates upon Wilkes, 377.

Grampound disfranchisement bills, 323, 324.

Grattan, Mr., character of his oratory, 455.

Great seal, the, use of, under authority of parliament, during Geo. III.'s illness, 156–158, 176; questions arising thereupon, 159; affixed by Lord Hardwicke to two commissions during illness of George II., 156.

Grenville Act, trial of election petitions under, 291; made perpetual, 292.

Grenville, Lord, in office with Pitt, 90; forms an administration on his death, 92; differs from the King on army administration, 93; the Army Service Bill, 94; cabinet minute reserving liberty of action on the Catholic question, 95; pledge required by the King on that subject, 96; dismissed, *ib.*; his advice neglected by the Regent, 107; attempted reconciliation, 108; failure of negotiations on the "Household Question," 110; his difficulty in issuing public money during George III.'s incapacity, 178.

Grenville, Mr. George, succeeds Lord Bute as premier, 34; does not defer to George III., 35; remonstrates against Lord Bute's influence, *ib.*, 38; supports the King's arbitrary measures, 35; differences between them, 37; his election petition act, 291; statement of amount of secret service money, 301; the bribery under his ministry, 302; opposes Wilkes's expulsion, 372; motion for reduction of land tax, 442.

Grey, Earl, his advice neglected by the Regent, 107; out of court favor, 112; declines office on the "Household Question," 110; advocates reform, and leads the reform ministry, 121–124, 249, 319, 320, 332; loses the confidence of William IV., 124; accuses Lord Eldon of using George III.'s name without due authority, 168, 171; regulation of the civil list by his ministry, 201; advises the creation of new peers, 250, 253, 337; favored a shorter duration of parliament, 349; character of his oratory, 455.

Grey, Mr., (1667,) reports the debates, 390.

Grosvenor, General, his hostile motion against Mr. Pitt's ministry, 74.

Grote, Mr., advocates vote by ballot, 353.

HALIFAX, Lord, obtains consent of Geo. III. to exclude his mother from the Regency, 145.

Hamilton, Duke of, a Scottish Peer, not allowed the rights of an English peer, 232.

Hamilton, Lord A., advocates reform in Scotch representation, 286.

Hanover, house of, character of the first two kings of, favorable to constitutional government, 20.

Hanover, kingdom of, revenues attached to the crown till her Majesty's accession, 194, 203.

Hansard, Messrs., sued by Stockdale for libel, 423.

Harcourt, Lord, supports the influence of the crown over parliament, 44.

Hardwicke, Lord, affixed great seal to commissions during illness of George II., 156.

Harrowby, Earl of, supports George IV. on the Catholic question, 100.

Hastings, Mr. Warren, impeachments not abated by dissolution established in his case, 436.

Hastings, sale of borough seat, 277.

Hawkesbury, Lord, supposed adviser of Geo. III. against the Grenville ministry, 98; his declaration as to King's competency to transact business, 168.

Heberden, Dr., his evidence regarding the King's illnesses, 170.

Henley, Mr., secedes from the Derby ministry on question of reform, 360.

Henry III., V., VI., and VII., revenues of their crowns, 187, 188.

Henry VIII., his sign-manual affixed by a stamp, 180; his crown revenues, 188.

Herbert, Mr., his bill as to the expulsion of members, 378.

Heron, Sir R., bill for shortening duration of parliament, 349.

Hindon, bribery at, 273.

Hobhouse, Mr., committed for contempt, 409.

Holdernesse, Lord, retires from office in favor of Lord Bute, 29.

Holland, Lord, amendment for an address to Prince of Wales, 175.

Horner, Mr. F., his speech against a regency bill, 174.

Household, the. *See* Royal Household.

House tax, Lord Derby's ministry defeated on, 442.

Howard, Messrs., reprimanded for conducting Stockdale's action, 425; committed, 426; sue the sergeant-at-arms, 427.

Howick, Lord, denounces secret advice to crown, 98, 99. *See* Grey, Earl.

Huskisson, Mr., his prophecy of reform in parliament, 329.

IMPEACHMENT of ministers by parliament, 435; rare in later times, *ib.*; not abated by a dissolution, 436.

India Bill, the, 1783, thrown out by influence of the crown, 68.

Ireland, position of Church, causes alarm to William IV., 124; number of archbishops and bishops of, 229, representative bishops of, *ib.* —— civil list of, 194, 201; pensions on crown revenues of, 210, 212; consolidated with English pension list, 214. —— parliament of, their proceedings on the regency, 162; address the Prince, *ib.*; office-holders disqualified in, 297. —— the representative peers of, 228; restriction upon number of the Irish peerage, *ib.*; absorption of, into peerage of United Kingdom, 235; Irish peers sit in the commons, 229. —— representation of, prior to Reform Bill, 286, 288; nomination boroughs abolished at the Union, 287; Irish judges disqualified, 298. —— Reform Act of, 340; amended (1850), *ib.*

Irnham, Lord, his daughter married to Duke of Cumberland, 215.

JAMES I., amount of his crown revenues, 188.

Jews, admission of, to parliament, 428.

Johnson, Dr., the compiler of parliamentary reports, 391, 392, 403, 451, *n.*

Jones, Mr. Gale, committed for libel on the House, 409.

Judges, introduction of a judge into the cabinet, 93; disqualified from parliament, 298; except the Master of the Rolls, 299.

KENT, Duchess of, appointed Regent (1830), 185.

Kentish petitioners imprisoned by the commons, 411.

Kenyon, Lord, opinion on the coronation oath, 85.

King, Lord, moves to omit Lord Eldon's name from the council of regency, 171.

King, questions as to accession of an infant king, 182; as to the rights of a king's posthumous child, 184; rights of a king over the royal family, 214. *See* also Crown, the; George III.; Regency; &c.

"King's Friends, the," the party so called, 24; their influence, 41; led by Addington, 90, 92, 94; their activity on the Catholic question, 87; against the Army Service Bill, 94; the "nabobs" rank themselves among, 270.

Knighthood, the orders of, 260.

LADIES attending debates in the commons, 386; their exclusion, 404, *n.*

Lambton, Mr., his motion for reform, 288, 324.

Lancaster, Duchy of, revenues of, attached to crown, 188, 194, 204; present amount, 204.

Land revenues of the crown. *See* Revenues of the Crown.

Land tax, the, allowed twice over to crown tenantry, 208; reduced by vote of the commons, 442; third reading of a land tax bill delayed, 70, 443.

Lansdowne, Marquess of, his amendment to resolutions for a regency, 176.

Lauderdale, Earl of, condemns the king's conduct to the Grenville ministry, 100, 101; his rights as peer both of Great Britain and Scotland, 234.

Leicester, case of bribery from corporate funds, 327.

Lennox, Lady S., admired by George III., 216.

Life peerages, 237; to women, *ib.*; the Wensleydale peerage case, 239.

Liverpool, Earl of, his ministry, 112; conduct the proceedings against Queen Caroline, 114, 116.

Loans to government, members bribed by shares in, 304; cessation of the system, 307.

London, city of, address George III. condemning the proceedings against Wilkes, 378.

London Magazine, the, one of the first to report parliamentary debates, 391.

Lords, House of, relations of, with the crown, 16, 17; influence of the crown exerted over the lords, 56, 66, 123, 252; debates on the influence of the crown, 54–57; reject the India Bill, 67; condemn the commons' opposition to Mr. Pitt, 74; proceedings on the reform bills, 122–124, 249, 336; proposed creation of peers, 123, 250, 336; proceedings on the regency bills of George III., 143–178; position of the house of lords in the state, 223, 245; increase of its numbers, 224–228; enlargement a source of strength, 244; number of peers, from Henry VII. to George III., 224, 226; twelve peers created in one day by Queen Anne, 224; representative peers of Scotland and Ireland, *ib.*, 229; sixteen peers created by William IV., 250; proposed restrictions upon the power of the crown, and the regent, in creation of peers, 225, 227; profuse creations by George III., 226; composition of the house in 1860, 229, *n.*; its representative character, 231; rights of peers of Scotland, 232–234; appellate jurisdiction of the lords, 236; bill to improve it, 242; life peerage question, 237; Lords spiritual, 242; past and present number, 243; attempt to exclude them, 244; political position of the house, 245, 263; influence of parties, 247; collisions between the two houses, 248; the danger increased, 249; creation of new peers equivalent to a dissolution, 254; position of the house since reform, 255; their independence, *ib.*; proceedings indicating their power, 256; scanty attendance in the house, 258, 259; smallness of the quorum, 258; deference to leaders, 259; influence of peers over the commons through nomination boroughs, 266; and through territorial influence, 283, 288; refusal of the lords to indemnify the witnesses against Walpole, 301; proceedings against Wilkes, 368, 370; "Droit le Roi" burnt, 367; address to condemn the city address on the Middlesex election proceedings, 379; debates on those proceedings, 375, 380; strangers and members excluded from debates, 386, 403; scene on one occasion, 386; reports of debates permitted, 402, 405; presence of strangers at divisions, 407; publicity given to committee proceedings, 408; to parliamentary papers, *ib.*; privilege to servants discontinued, 420; prisoners kneeling at the bar, 421; control of the lords over the executive government, 429; advise the crown on questions of peace and war, and of a dissolution, 430; rejection of a money bill, 445; sketch of parliamentary oratory, 450.

Lords spiritual. *See* Bishops.

Lottery tickets (government), members bribed by, 305.

Ludgershall, price of seat, 272.

Lushington, Dr., a life peerage offered to, 239; disqualified from parliament, 298.

Luttrell, Colonel, his sister married to the Duke of Cumberland, 215; opposes Wilkes for Middlesex, 374; enforces the exclusion of strangers, 403.

Lyndhurst, Lord, his motion on the life peerage case, 239.

Lyttelton, Lord, his address respecting the regency, 145; his complaint against "Droit le Roi," 369.

Lyttleton, Mr., his motion on the dismissal of the Grenville ministry, 102.

Macclesfield, Lord, decided in favor of rights of crown over grandchildren, 217.

Mackenzie, Mr. S., dismissed from office, 40, 41.

Manchester, Duke of, strangers excluded on his motion relative to war with Spain, 387.

Mansfield, Lord, exhorts George III. to exert his influence over parliament, 44; precedent of his admission to the cabinet cited, 93; his opinion on the right of the commons to incapacitate Wilkes, 376, 381; accused by Wilkes of altering a record, 370.

Marchmont, Lord, his motion on the Middlesex election proceedings, 377.

Martin, Mr., his duel with Wilkes, 368.

Marvell, A., reported proceedings in the commons, 391.

Mary (Queen of England), her sign-manual affixed by a stamp, 101.

Melbourne, Viscount, in office, 125; his sudden dismissal, *ib.*; reinstated, 130; in office at accession of her Majesty, 131; organizes her household, *ib.*; kept in office by the "Bedchamber Question," 132; resigns office, 134.

Melville, Lord, his impeachment, 436.

Members of the House of Commons, number of nominee members, 287; bribed by pensions, 295; bribery under Charles II., 299; under William III., 300; George II., 301; George III., 301–304; bribed by loans and lotteries, 304–307; by contracts, 307; wages to, provided for in Lord Blandford's reform bill, 326; abolition of qualifications, 354; excluded from debates in the Lords, 388; system of pledges to constituents considered, 418; certain privileges of, discontinued, 420. *See* Commons, House of.

Middlesex Journal, the, complaint against, for misrepresenting debates, 394.

Middlesex, sheriffs of, committed by the House in the Stockdale actions, 425.

Military officers, deprived of command for opposition to the policy of Geo. III., 36, 51; practice condemned under the Rockingham ministry, 40.

Miller, proceeded against for publishing debates, 396; the city authorities interpose, 397.

Ministers, of the crown, responsibility of, 19, 95; regarded with jealousy by George III., 21; constitutional relations between crown and ministers, 25–28, 95, 125, 131, 135, 436; influence of the crown exerted against its ministers, 43, 65, 83, 94, 119; the pledge exacted by George III. of his ministers, 95; supported by the crown and the commons in reform, 120, 250, 335; influence of great families over ministries, 139; numerous applications to, for peerages, 241; votes of want of confidence, 59, 74, 77, 434; and of confidence, 122, 336, 434; ministers impeached by the commons, 435; the stability of recent ministries considered, 437; their financial arrangements dissented from, 441.

Minorities, proposed representation of, at elections, in reform bill (1854), 358.

Moira, Earl, his mission to the Whig leaders, 110; the "Household Question," 110.

Morton, Mr., moves insertion of Princess of Wales's name into Regency Bill, 147.

Murray, Lady A., married to the Duke of Sussex, 221.

Murray, Mr., refused to kneel at the bar of the commons, 421.

Mutiny bill, the passing of, postponed, 77.

"NABOBS," the, their bribery at elections, 269, 272; rank themselves among the "King's friends," 270.

Newcastle, Duke of, in office at accession of George III., 11; resigns, 30; dismissed from lord lieutenancy, 32.

Newenham, Mr., motion for address on debts of Prince of Wales, 206.

New Shoreham, bribery at, 272; disfranchised, 273.

Nomination boroughs. *See* Boroughs.

North, Lord, his relations, as premier, with Geo. III., 48; complete submission, 49, 51, 60; his overtures to Chatham, 51; to the Whigs, 52; his ministry overthrown, 57, 58; his conduct approved by the King, 59; joins the "coalition ministry," 63, 64; dismissed from office, 69; liberal in creation of peers, 226; in the bribery of members, 303; with money sent by George III., *ib.*; by shares in a loan, 306; his second loan, 307; approved the Middlesex election proceedings, 382; carriage broken by mob, 400; his personalities in debate, 461.

Northampton borough, cost of electoral contest (1768), 272; case of bribery from corporate funds, 327.

North Briton (No. 45), the publication of, 365; riot at the burning of, 367.

Northumberland, Duke of, supported in bribery at elections by George III., 274.

Norton, Sir F. (the speaker), supports Dunning's resolutions, 55; his speech to George III. touching the civil list, 197; altercations with, 463.

O'Connell, Mr., advocates universal suffrage, &c., 327, 330; reprimanded for libelling the house, 410; his position as an orator, 457.

Officers under the crown, disqualified from parliament, 278, 294–299; number of, in parliament, 118, 296, 298.

Oldfield, Dr., his statistics of parliamentary patronages, 288.

Oliver, Mr. Alderman, proceeded against by the commons for committing their messenger, 398, 399.

Onslow, Mr. G., orders the house to be cleared, 389; complains of publication of debates, 390, 394; his sobriquet, 393.

Orators and oratory. *See* Parliamentary Oratory.

Oxford, seat for, sold by corporation, 271.

Pains and penalties, bill of, against Queen Caroline, 114, 115.

Palmerston, Viscount, his removal from office, 1851, 136; reform bill of his ministry, 360; his resolutions on the Lords' rejection of the paper duties bill, 448.

Paper duties repeal bill (1860), rejected by the Lords, 257, 447.

Parke, Sir J. *See* Wensleydale, Baron.

Parliament, government by, established at the Revolution, 15; subservient to the crown, 16; constitutional position of, at the accession of George III., 27; violation of parliamentary privileges by the crown, 32, 36, 43, 49, 56, 72; the reform of parliament, 120, 248, 312; the dissolution of 1807, 102; of 1830, 830; of 1831, 121, 335; of 1834, 128; of 1841, 134; influence of families over parliament, 139; meeting of parliament during George III.'s illnesses, 147, 172; commissions for opening, 156, 157, 177; second opening after King's recovery (1789), 159; adjournments caused by King's inability to sign commission for prorogation, 147–172; parliament and the revenues of the crown and the civil list, 189–207; duration of parliament, 348; motions for triennial parliaments, 349; time between summons and meeting of, shortened, 355; relations of parliament to crown, law, and people, 364–450; the unreported parliament, 387, *n.*; publication of debates, 390, 407; petitions, 410; publicity given to parliamentary papers, 408; relinquishment of parliamentary privileges, 420; privilege and the courts of law, 422; publication of papers affecting character, 426; control of parliament over the executive government, 427; sketch of parliamentary oratory, 450; group of parliamentary orators of the age of Chatham and Pitt, 451; of later times, 455; character of modern oratory, 459; personalities of former times, 460. *See* Commons, House of; Lords, House of.

Pease, Mr., his case cited regarding Jewish disability, 429.

Peel, Sir R., obtains consent of George IV. to Catholic emancipation, 118; his first administration, 126; his absence abroad, 127; ministerial efforts, 128–130; advises a dissolution, 129; resignation, 130; called to office, 132; declines on the "Bedchamber Question," *ib.*; his second administration, 134; his anti-reform declaration, 330; character of his oratory, 457.

Peerage, number of, 224; of the United Kingdom, 230 and *n.*; antiquity of, *ib.*; claims to, 231;

changes in its composition, *ib.*; the representative character, 232; fusion of peerages of the three kingdoms, 235; life peerages, 237; to women, *ib.*; peerages with remainders over, 238; authorities favoring life peerages, *ib.*; offer of a life peerage to Dr. Lushington, 239; the Wensleydale peerage, *ib.* *See* also Lords, House of; Ireland, peerage of; Scotland, peerage of.

Peerage Bill (1720), rejected by the commons, 225.

Peers, scanty attendance of, at the House, affecting their political weight, 257; social relations of, 259–262; their influence at county elections, 283; excluded from debates in the House of Commons, 388. *See* also Lords, House of.

Pelham, Mr., bribery to members, a system under, 301.

Pembroke, Earl of, proscribed for opposition to court policy, 56.

Penryn, the disfranchisement bill, 327; proposal to transfer the franchise to Manchester, 328.

Pensions from the crown charged on civil list, 210–212; on crown revenues, 210; restrained by parliament, *ib.*, 212; consolidation of pension lists, 214; regulation of (1837), *ib.*; bribery by pensions, 294; holders of, disqualified from parliament, 295.

Perceval, Mr., forms an administration, 96; denies secret advice to George III., 97; dissolution during his ministry, 102; his relations with the King, 103; his position at commencement of regency, 106; obnoxious to the Regent as adviser of Princess Caroline, 107; ministerial negotiations at his death, 109.

Petitions to parliament, commencement of the practice, 410; of political petitions, 411; forbidden under Charles II., *ib.*; commencement of the modern system, 412; petitions rejected, *ib.*; objected to by George III., 414; progress of the system, *ib.*; the numbers presented of late years, 416, *n.*; abuses of petitioning, 417; debates on presentation of, restrained, *ib.*; for grant of public money to be recommended by the crown, 443.

Pitt, Mr. *See* Chatham, Earl of.

Pitt, Mr. William, Chancellor of the Exchequer under Lord Shelburne, 63; refusals to take office, 64, 65; is premier, 69; opposed in the commons, 70–78; his attitude respecting a dissolution, 72; final triumph, 78; reflections on this contest, 71–78; his relations with George III., 63, 82; furthers his views, 82; in opposition to the King on reform, 83; quits office on the Catholic question, 85; refusal to abandon that question, 87, 88; his mismanagement of it, 88; his pledge to the King not to revive it, 89; again in office, 90; with Addington, 91; evades the Catholic question, *ib.*; his opinion on the rights of Prince of Wales as Regent, 149–152; his letter to him respecting the regency, 151; moves resolutions for a bill, *ib.*, 155; proposition as to use of the great seal, 152, 156; introduces the bill, 158; his conduct in these proceedings considered, 161; confirms the King's confidence in him, 162; embarrassment caused by the King's illness on his leaving office, 163, 165; brought forward budget after resignation, 164; his doubts as to the King's sanity, on his return to office, 170; profuse in the creation of peers, 226, 227; his unfair conduct as to the Westminster scrutiny, 281; abolished some of the Irish nomination boroughs, 288; discontinued bribes to members, 304; by loans and lotteries, 307; advocates reform, 315, 316; his reform bill, 316; opposes reform, 319; his position as an orator, 451.

Pitt, Mr. Thomas, moves to delay the grant of supplies, 443.

Placemen. *See* Officers under the Crown.

Pledges by members to constituents considered, 418.

Plunket, Lord, his oratory, 457.

Poole, corruption at, 271.

Portland, Duke of (1696), enormous grant to, by William III., 189.

Portland, Duke of, heads the "coalition," 64; assists George III. in opposing the Army Service Bill, 94.

Potwallers, electoral rights of, 266.

Prince Regent. *See* Wales, Prince of.

Printers, contest of the Commons with, 389, 394. *See* also Debates in Parliament.

Privileges and elections committee, trial of election petitions before, 291.

Privileges of parliament. *See* Parliament; Crown, the.

Public money, difficulties in the issue of, caused by George III.'s incapacity, 178; motions for, to be recommended by the crown, 443.

Public Works Commission separated from Woods and Forests, 210.

QUALIFICATION Acts, 354; repealed, 355.

Queen's Bench, Court of, decide in favor of Stockdale, 424, 426; compel the sheriffs to pay over the damages, 426.

Queensberry, Duke of, his rights as a peer of Great Britain and of Scotland, 233.

RAWDON, Lord, moves address to the Prince to assume the regency, 152.

Reform in parliament, arguments for, 312; advocated by Chatham, 313; Wilkes, *ib.*; the Duke of Richmond, *ib.*; the Gordon riots unfavorable to, 314; Pitt's motions, 315; discouraging effect of the French Revolution, 319; Earl Grey's reform scheme, 320; Burdett's, 322, 323; Lord John Russell's, 323–329; Mr. Lambton's, 324; Lord Blandford's, 326; later cases of corruption, 327; O'Connell's motion for universal suffrage, 330; the dissolution of 1830, *ib.*; impulse given by French Revolution, 331; storm raised by Duke of Wellington's declaration, *ib.*; Brougham's motion, 332; Lord Grey's reform ministry, 333; the first reform bill, 334; ministers defeated by the commons, 121, 335; supported by the crown, *ib.*; the dissolution of 1831, *ib.*; second reform bill, 122, 336; sixteen peers created by William IV., 250; bill thrown out by the Lords, 122, 250, 336; proposed creation of peers, 123, 251, 337; resignation of reform ministry, 123, 252, 338; supported by the commons and recalled to office, 123, 252, 338; the third bill passed, 124, 252, 338; the act considered, 338; Scotch and Irish acts, 340, 341; Irish franchise extended, 341; political results of reform, 130, 341, 437; bribery and bribery acts since reform, 341–347; triennial parliaments, 348; vote by ballot, 352; reform, later measures for, 355–362.

Regency Act (1751), 142; the Act of 1765, 144–146; Princess of Wales excluded by Lords, and included by Commons in the Act, 145; resolutions for Regency Bill (1788–9), 151–155; protest against, 155; proposed restrictions over the Regent's power to create peers, 227; resolutions accepted by Prince of Wales, 155; bill brought in, 158; progress interrupted by Geo. III.'s recovery, 158; comments on these proceedings, 159; comparison of them to the proceedings at the Revolution, 160; the Regency Act of 1810, arguments against, 173–175, 178; resolutions for a bill agreed to, 175–177; laid before the Prince, 177; bill passed, *ib.*; Regency Act (1830), provides for accession of an infant king, 182; for case of a posthumous child, 184; the Regency Acts of Her Majesty, 185.

Regent, question as to origin and intent of the word, 153 and *n.* *See* also Wales, Prince of.

Reporters. *See* Debates in Parliament.

Representation in Parliament, defects in, 264. *See* also Reform in Parliament.

Revenues of the crown, its ancient possessions, 186; forfeitures, *ib.*; grants and alienations, 187; increase of revenues by Henry VII. and VIII., 188; destruction of revenues at Commonwealth, *ib.*; recovery and subsequent waste,

188, 189; restraints on alienation of crown property, 189; constitutional result of improvidence of kings, 190; settlement of crown revenues by parliament, *ib.*; revenues prior to Revolution, *ib.*; the civil list from William III. to George III., 191–193; settlement of Civil List at accession of George III., 193; charges thereon, 194–199; means of crown influence, 195; surplus revenues, 199; regulation of civil list, 200, 204; other crown revenues, 194, 200; loss of Hanover revenues, 204; Duchies of Lancaster and Cornwall, *ib.*; private property of crown, 205; provision for royal family, *ib.*; mismanagement of land revenues, 207; proposal for sale of crown lands, 208; appropriation of proceeds, 209; pensions charged on lands and revenues, 211–214.

Revenue commissioners, the, first office-holders disqualified from parliament, 295; — Officers' Disfranchisement Bill carried by the Rockingham ministry, 62, 278.

Revolution, The, parliamentary government established at, 15; position of the crown since the Revolution, 16; revenues of the crown prior to, 190; commencement of permanent taxation at, 446.

Revolutions in France, effects on the cause of reform, 319, 331.

Rialton, Lady, case of, cited on the "Bedchamber Question," 133.

Richard II., revenues of his crown, 187.

Richmond, Duke of, his motion respecting the regency, 145; for reduction of civil list, 197; statement as to the nominee members, 288; advocates parliamentary reform, 313; his motion on the Middlesex election proceedings, 381.

Roache, Mr., opposes Mr. Wilkes for Middlesex, 375.

Rockingham, Marquess, dismissed from lord-lieutenancy for opposing the crown, 32; made premier, 40; his ministerial conditions, 41; influence of the crown in parliament exerted in opposition, 44, 45; dismissed from office, 46; statements respecting the influence of the crown, 55, 57; his second administration, 61; carries the contractors', the civil list, and the revenue officers' bills, 62, 199, 211, 278, 297, 309; and the reversal of the Middlesex election proceedings, 383; denounces parliamentary corruption by loans, 306; his motion condemning the resolution against Wilkes, 378; moves to delay the third reading of a land-tax bill, 443.

Rolls, Master of, sole judge not disqualified from parliament, 299.

Roman Catholic emancipation. *See* Catholic Emancipation.

Romilly, Sir S., his opinion on the pledge required from the Grenville ministry, 97; his justification of the purchase of seats, 275, 276.

Ross, General, complains of court intimidation, 72.

Rothschild, Baron, admission of, to parliament, 428.

Rous, Sir J., his hostile motion against Lord North's ministry, 59.

Royal family, provision for, 205, 207; power of the crown over, 214–222; exempted from Lord Hardwicke's Marriage Act, 216.

Royal household, the, a question between the Whig leaders and the Regent, 110; profusion in George III.'s, 197; proposed reduction of William IV.'s household, 203.

Royal Marriage Act (1772), 49, 217; its arbitrary principles, 218.

Royal Sign-Manual Bill, authorizing George IV. to sign documents by a stamp, 179–181.

Russell, Lord John, his first motions for reform, 323–329; his disfranchisement bills, 324–328; advocates the enfranchisement of Leeds, Birmingham, and Manchester, 329; moves the first reform bill, 330; his later reform measures, 356, 360.

St. Albans disfranchised, 343.

Salomons, Mr., admission of, to Parliament, 429.

Sandwich, Earl of, denounces Wilkes for the "Essay on Woman," 368; "Jemmy Twitcher," 369, *n.*

Savile, Sir G., his motion condemning the resolution against Wilkes,

377; his bills to secure the rights of electors, 382.
Sawbridge, Mr., his motion for reform, 317; for shortening duration of parliament, 349.
Say and Sele, Lord, his apology to Mr. Grenville for refusing a bribe, 303.
Scot and lot, a franchise, 266.
Scotland, defective representation of, prior to reform bill, 283, 288. —— hereditary crown revenues of, 194, 201; pensions charged upon, 210, 213; consolidation of Scotch and English civil lists, 214. —— peerage of, the representative peers of, 224; Scottish peers created peers of England, 232; alleged disability, 233; rights of representative peers, *ib.*, 234; probable absorption of Scottish peerage into that of the United Kingdom, 235. —— Scottish judges disqualified, 298. —— Reform Act of, 339.
Scott, Sir John, the ministerial adviser during the regency proceedings, 160.
Secret service money, issue of, restrained, 199; statement of amount of, 302.
Selkirk, Earl of, supports the King on the Catholic question, 100.
Septennial Act, efforts to repeal, 348; arguments against, 349; in favor, 350.
Shaftesbury, bribery at, 273.
Shaftesbury, Lord, publishes a debate as a pamphlet, 390.
Sheil, Mr., character of his oratory, 458.
Shelburne, Earl of, dismissed from command for opposition to the crown, 36; his motion on the public expenditure, 55; on the intimidation of peers, 56; his administration, 62; supports the royal influence, *ib.*
Sheridan, Mr., character of his oratory, 453.
Shrewsbury, Duke of, his precedent cited as to the temporary concentration of offices in the Duke of Wellington, 127.
Sidmouth, Viscount, withdrew from Pitt's administration, 91; takes office under Lord Grenville, 92; joins George III. in opposing the Army Service Bill, 94; resigns of-

fice, *ib.*; supports the King, *ib.*, 100. *See* also Addington, Mr.
Slave Trade, abolition of, advocated by petitions to parliament, 413.
Smith, Mr. W., his anecdote as to bribery of members by Lord North, 304, *n.*
Speaker of the House of Commons, elected during George III.'s incapacity, 154; altercations with, 462; increased authority of the chair, *ib.*
Spencer, Earl, election expenses of, 272.
Stafford, Marquess of, his motion on the pledge exacted from the Grenville ministry, 99.
Stamp Act (American), influence of the crown exerted against repeal of, 43.
Steele, Sir R., opposes Peerage Bill, 226.
Stockdale, Mr., his actions against Hansard for libel, 424–428; committed for contempt, 427.
Strangers, exclusion of, from debates in parliament, 384; commencement of their attendance, 386; attendance of ladies, *ib.*; their exclusion, *ib.*, *n.*; presence of strangers permitted, 406.
Sudbury, seat for, offered for sale, 270; disfranchised, 343.
Sunderland, Lady, case of, cited on the "Bedchamber Question," 133.
Supplies to the crown delayed, 73, 76, 443; refused, 440; granted, 441.
Surrey, Earl of, his motion on the dismissal of the "coalition," 73.
Sussex, Duke of, votes against a Regency Bill, 175; his marriages, 221.

TAXATION and expenditure, control of the commons over, 191, 439, 444; temporary and permanent taxation, 446.
Taylor, Sir H., his circular letter, by command of William IV., to opposition peers, 124.
Temple, Earl, proscribed for intimacy with Wilkes, 36; agent in the exertion of the crown influence against India Bill, 66, 67; employed to dismiss the "coalition," 69; accepts and resigns office, *ib.*

Tennyson, Mr., motions to shorten duration of parliament, 349.
Thompson, proceeded against for publishing debates, 394; interposition of the city authorities, 396.
Thurlow, Lord, negotiates for George III. with the Whigs, 53; his advice to the King on proposed retreat to Hanover, 64; coöperates in his opposition to the India Bill, 66, 67; is made Lord Chancellor, 70; supports the resolutions for a Regency, 153; affixes the great seal to commissions under authority of parliament, 155–157; announces the King's recovery, 158; resists the Cricklade Disfranchisement Act, 273.
Tory party supplies the greater number of the "King's friends," 24; ascendency of, under George IV., 112; ascendency of, in the House of Lords, 248.
Townshend, Mr., his manœuvre to secure a share in a loan, 305; his proposed land tax reduced by the commons, 442.
Treasury warrants, for issue of public money during George III.'s incapacity, 178.

UNDERWOOD, Lady C., married the Duke of Sussex, 221.
Universal suffrage, motions for, 314, 323, 330.

VICTORIA, Queen, her Majesty, her accession, 131; the ministry then in office, *ib.*; her household, *ib.*; the "Bedchamber Question," 132, 134; her memorandum concerning acts of government, 135; judicious exercise of her authority, 138; the Regency Acts of her reign, 185; her civil list, 203; her pension list, 214.

WAKEFIELD, bribery at (1860), 346.
Waldegrave, Dowager Countess of, married to the Duke of Gloucester, 215.
Waldegrave, Earl of, his opinion on the education of George III., 22.
Wales, Prince of (George IV.), united with the opposition, 84; his character, 105; subject to court influence, *ib.*; indifferent to politics and political friends, 106, 108; his separation from the Whigs, 108, 111; raises and disappoints their hopes, 107; proposals for their union with the Tories, 108, 199; the "household" question between him and the Whigs, 110; debates as to his rights as Regent (1788), 149–152; disclaims his rights, 151; his reply to the Regency scheme, 154; accepts the resolutions, 155; name omitted from commission to open parliament, 157; the address from the Irish parliament, 162; accepts resolutions for Regency Bill (1810), 176; his civil list, 201; his debts, 205; his marriage with Mrs. Fitzherbert, 220; the guardianship over Princess Charlotte, 222.
Wales, Prince of, Duchy of Cornwall his inheritance, 204.
Wales, Princess Dowager of, her influence over George III., 22; advocates the exercise of his personal authority, 33; the insertion of her name into the Regency Bill, 145.
Walpole, Horace, cited in proof of parliamentary corruption, 269, *n.*, 301, 305; the appointment offered to his nephew, 297.
Walpole, Mr., secedes from Lord Derby's ministry on question of reform, 360.
Walpole, Sir R., opposes Peerage Bill, 225; displaced from office by vote on election petition, 291; bribery of members a system under, 300; the charges of bribery not proved, 301; his remark on misrepresentations by reporters, 393.
Warburton, Bishop, his name affixed to notes in the "Essay on Woman," 368.
Ward, Mr., advocates vote by ballot, 354.
Wellesley, Marquess, commissioned to form a ministry, 109.
Wellington, Duke of, obtains consent of George IV. to Catholic emancipation, 119; anti-reform character of his ministry, 329; his anti-reform declaration, 331; fails to form an anti-reform ministry, 123, 252; forms a ministry

with Peel, 125, 126; his assumption of different cabinet offices during Peel's absence, 127; his opinion on proposed creation of new peers, 253; his position as an orator, 457.
Wensleydale, Baron, the life peerage case (1856), 239–242.
West India duties, the, vested in the crown till accession of William IV., 202.
Westminster election (1784), Fox's vexatious contest at, 280; scrutiny, and writ withheld, 281; act passed in consequence, 282.
Westmoreland county, expense of a contested election for, 283.
Weymouth, Lord, overtures to, from Geo. III., 52; libelled by Wilkes, 370.
Wharncliffe, Lord, his motion against the dissolution (1831), 122, 432.
Wheble proceeded against for publishing debates, 394; discharged from custody by Wilkes, 396.
Whig party, the, period of ascendency of, 20; regarded with jealousy by George III., 23, 26, 45; proscription of, under Lord Bute, 32; position at time of regency, 106, 107; separation between them and Prince Regent, 106, 108, 111; decline office on the "Household Question," 110; unsuccessful against the ministry, 112; espouse the Queen's cause, 116; lose the confidence of William IV., 124; ascendency in House of Lords, 248.
Whitaker, Mr., opposes Wilkes for Middlesex, 375.
Whitbread, Mr., his remarks on the Perceval ministry, 98; moves to omit Lord Eldon's name from the council of regency, 171.
Whittam, a messenger of the house, committed by the Lord Mayor for apprehending a printer, 397; his recognizance erased, 398; saved from prosecution, 399.
Wilkes, Mr., advocates parliamentary reform, 313; denied his parliamentary privilege, 365; proceeded against for libel in the "North Briton," 366, 368; absconds, and is expelled, 368; returned for Middlesex, 370; committed, *ib.*; accusations against Lord Mansfield, *ib.*; question he raised at the bar of the house, *ib.*; expelled for libel on Lord Weymouth, 371; reëlected, 374; again elected, but Luttrell seated by the house, 375; elected alderman, *ib.*; complaint against deputy-clerk of the crown, 382; takes his seat, *ib.*; lord mayor, 383; the resolution against him expunged, 61, 383; instigates the publication of debates, 392; interposes to protect the printers, 395; proceeded against by the commons, 397; advocates pledges to candidates by members, 418.
William III., his personal share in the government, 19; his sign-manual affixed by a stamp, 181; revenues of his crown, 189; grants to his followers, *ib.*; his civil list, 191; tries to influence parliament by the multiplication of offices, 294; bribes to members during reign of, 300; popular addresses to, praying dissolution of parliament, 432.
William IV. supports parliamentary reform, 120; dissolves parliament (1831), 121, 335; created sixteen peers in favor of reform, 250; further creation of peers proposed, 123, 251, 337; exerts his influence over the peers, 123, 252, 338; withdraws his confidence from the reform ministry, 124; suddenly dismisses the Melbourne ministry, 125; the Wellington and Peel ministry, 126; the Melbourne ministry reinstated, 130, 131; regency question on his accession, 182; as to rights of a king's posthumous child, 184; his civil list, 202; proposed reduction of the household, 203; surrenders the four and a half per cent. duties, 214.
Williams, Sir Hugh, passed over in a brevet for opposition to court policy, 51.
Windham, Mr., his position as an orator, 454.
Wines and Cider Duties Bill (1763), first money bill divided upon by the Lords, 447.
"Woman, Essay on," Wilkes prosecuted for publishing, 368.
Woods, Forests, and Land Reve-

nues Commission, 209; separated from Public Works, 210.
Wortley, Mr. S., his motion for address to Regent to form an efficient ministry, 110.
Wray, Sir C., opposed Fox at the Westminster election, 281.
Writs for new members, doubt respecting issue of, during King's illness, 149; writs of summons for elections, addressed to returning officers, 356.
YARMOUTH, freemen of, disfranchised, 343.
York, Duke of, opposes a regency bill, 155, 175; his name omitted from commission to open parliament, 157, 177; attached to Lady Mary Coke, 216.
Yorke, Mr., enforces the exclusion of strangers from debates, 404.
Yorkshire petition, the, for parliamentary reform, 315, 412.

END OF VOL. I.

CAMBRIDGE: PRINTED BY H. O. HOUGHTON.

www.ingramcontent.com/pod-product-compliance
Lightning Source LLC
LaVergne TN
LVHW020924110826
845150LV00004B/761
* 9 7 8 1 4 2 5 5 5 4 1 6 3 *